Lecture Notes in Computer Science   9817

Commenced Publication in 1973
Founding and Former Series Editors:
Gerhard Goos, Juris Hartmanis, and Jan van Leeuwen

More information about this series at http://www.springer.com/series/7409

Francesco Buccafurri · Andreas Holzinger
Peter Kieseberg · A Min Tjoa
Edgar Weippl (Eds.)

Availability, Reliability, and Security in Information Systems

IFIP WG 8.4, 8.9, TC 5 International
Cross-Domain Conference, CD-ARES 2016
and Workshop on Privacy Aware Machine Learning
for Health Data Science, PAML 2016
Salzburg, Austria, August 31 – September 2, 2016
Proceedings

 Springer

Editors
Francesco Buccafurri
University Mediterranea of Reggio Calabria
Reggio Calabria
Italy

Andreas Holzinger
Medical University Graz
Graz
Austria

Peter Kieseberg
SBA Research
Vienna
Austria

A Min Tjoa
Vienna University of Technology
Vienna
Austria

Edgar Weippl
SBA Research
Vienna
Austria

ISSN 0302-9743   ISSN 1611-3349 (electronic)
Lecture Notes in Computer Science
ISBN 978-3-319-45506-8   ISBN 978-3-319-45507-5 (eBook)
DOI 10.1007/978-3-319-45507-5

Library of Congress Control Number: 2016949120

LNCS Sublibrary: SL3 – Information Systems and Applications, incl. Internet/Web, and HCI

Printed on acid-free paper

This Springer imprint is published by Springer Nature
The registered company is Springer International Publishing AG Switzerland

Preface

The Cross-Domain Conference and Workshop CD-ARES is focused on the holistic and scientific view of applications in the domain of information systems.

The idea of organizing cross-domain scientific events originated from a concept presented by IFIP president Leon Strous at the IFIP 2010 World Computer Congress in Brisbane, which was seconded by many IFIP delegates in further discussions. Therefore CD-ARES concentrates on the multitudinous aspects of information systems, in bridging the gap between the research results in computer science and the many application fields.

This effort leads us to the consideration of the various important issues of massive information sharing and data integration, which will (in our opinion) dominate scientific work and discussions in the area of information systems in the second decade of this century.

The organizers of this event, who are engaged within IFIP in the area of Enterprise Information Systems (WG 8.9), Business Information Systems (WG 8.4), and Information Technology Applications (TC 5), very much welcome the typical cross-domain aspect of this event.

To guarantee a high-quality event, we assembled a program for CD-ARES 2016 consisting of 12 selected papers. CD-ARES 2016 provided a good mix of topics ranging from knowledge management and software security to mobile and social computing.

Machine learning is the fastest growing field in computer science, and health informatics is among the greatest challenges, where privacy, data protection, safety, information security, and fair use of data is of utmost importance. Experts of work area 1 (data science), 2 (machine learning), and 7 (privacy) of the international expert network HCI-KDD carefully selected five papers for the PAML (Privacy Aware Machine Learning) session.

The papers presented at this conference were selected after extensive reviews by the Program Committee with the essential help of associated reviewers.

We would like to thank all PC members and the reviewers who made great efforts contributing their time, knowledge, expertise and foremost the authors for their contributions.

August 2016

Francesco Buccafurri
Andreas Holzinger
Peter Kieseberg
A Min Tjoa
Edgar Weippl

Organization

The International Cross-Domain Conference and Workshop (CD-ARES 2016)

General Chairperson

Edgar Weippl   SBA Research, Austria (IFIP WG 8.4 Chair)
A Min Tjoa   TU Vienna, Austria (IFIP WG 8.9. Chair, Honorary
            Secretary IFIP)

Program Committee Chairpersons

Francesco Buccafurri   University of Reggio Calabria, Italy
Andreas Holzinger   Graz University of Technology, Austria

Program Committee

Sibel Adali   Rensselaer Polytechnic Institute, USA
Andrea Bondavalli   University of Florence, Italy
Andrea Calì   University of London, Birkbeck College, UK
Francisco Chiclana   De Montfort University, UK
Juan Manuel Corchado University of Salamanca, Spain
 Rodríguez
Josep Domingo-Ferrer Rovira i Virgili University, Spain
Anna Fensel   University of Innsbruck, Austria
Eduardo Fernandez   Florida Atlantic University, USA
Mariagrazia Fugini   Politecnico di Milano, Italy
Abdelkader Hameurlain Paul Sabatier University of Toulouse, France
Carlos A. Iglesias   Technical University of Madrid, Spain
Janusz Kacprzyk   Polish Academy of Sciences, Poland
Dominique Laurent   Cergy-Pontoise University, France
Gianluca Lax   University of Reggio Calabria, Italy
Apostolos Malatras   European Commission, Joint Research Centre,
           Belgium
Paolo Mori   National Research Council – CNR, Italy
Marek Ogiela   AGH University of Science and Technology, Poland
Witold Pedrycz   University of Alberta, Canada
Christophe Rosenberg University of Caen, France
Gustavo Rossi   National University of La Plata, Argentina

Alex Thomo	University of Victoria, Canada
Vicenç Torra	University of Skovde, Sweden
Rakesh Verma	University of Houston, USA
Sherali Zeadally	University of Kentucky, USA

Special Session on Privacy Aware Machine Learning for Health Data Science (PAML 2016)

General Chairpersons

Andreas Holzinger	Graz University of Technology, Austria
Peter Kieseberg	SBA Research, Austria
Edgar Weippl	SBA Research, Austria
A Min Tjoa	TU Vienna, Austria

International Scientific Committee

Elisa Bertino	Purdue University, USA
Michele Bezzi	SAP Labs France, France
Igor Bilogrevic	Google Research Zurich, Switzerland
Rainer Böhme	Innsbruck University, Austria
Malin Bradley	Vanderbilt University, USA
Srdjan Capkun	ETH Zürich, Switzerland
Kamalika Chaudhuri	University of California, USA
Krzysztof J. Cios	Virginia Commonwealth University, USA
Chris Clifton	Purdue University, USA
Josep Domingo-Ferrer	Universitat Rovira i Virgili, Spain
Kuda Dube	Massey University New Zealand, New Zealand
Isao Echizen	National Institute of Informatics, Japan
Aristides Gionis	Aalto University, Finland
Jihun Hamm	Ohio State University, USA
Zhisheng Huang	Vrije University of Amsterdam, The Netherlands
Prateek Jain	Microsoft Research Lab Bangalore, India
Nathalie Japkowicz	University of Ottawa, Canada
Xiaoqian Jiang	University of California San Diego, USA
Murat Kantarcioglu	University of Texas at Dallas, USA
Patrick Gage Kelley	University of New Mexico, USA
Haibin Ling	Temple University, USA
Sjouke Mauw	University of Luxembourg, Luxembourg
Kazuhiro Minami	Institute of Statistical Mathematics, Japan
Prateek Mittal	Princeton University, USA
Roberto Perdisci	University of Georgia, USA
Konrad Rieck	TU Braunschweig, Germany
Lior Rokach	Ben-Gurion University of the Negev, Israel

Pierangela Samarati	University of Milan, Italy
Bracha Shapira	Ben-Gurion University of the Negev, Israel
Jessica Staddon	NC State University, USA
Joaquin Vanschoren	Eindhoven University of Technology, The Netherlands
Qian Wang	Wuhan University, China
Shuang Wang	University of California San Diego, USA
Marcel Winandy	Huawei European Research Center, Germany
Elena Zheleva	University of Maryland, USA

Contents

Visualization and Risk Management

**Special Session on Privacy Aware Machine Learning for Health Data
Science (PAML 2016)**

The International Cross Domain Conference (CD-ARES 2016)

Algebra of RDF Graphs for Querying Large-Scale Distributed Triple-Store

Iztok Savnik[1]([⊠]) and Kiyoshi Nitta[2]

[1] Jožef Stefan Institute, University of Primorska, Koper, Slovenia
`iztok.savnik@upr.si`
[2] Yahoo JAPAN Research, Tokyo, Japan
`knitta@yahoo-corp.jp`

Abstract. Large-scale RDF graph databases stored in shared-nothing clusters require query processing engine that can effectively exploit highly parallel computation environment. We propose algebra of RDF graphs and its physical counterpart, physical algebra of RDF graphs, designed to implement queries as distributed dataflow programs that run on cluster of servers. Operations of algebra reflect the characteristic features of RDF graph data model while they are tied to the technology provided by relational query execution systems. Algebra of RDF graphs allows for the expression of pipelined and partitioned parallelism. Preliminary experimental results show that proposed algebra and architecture of query execution system scale well with large clusters of data servers.

1 Introduction

Recent development of graph-based semantic web shows the enormous interest of society to construct a detailed knowledge base (graph) including properties of categories from all popular areas of human activities. Knowledge bases such as Knowledge Graph, Wikidata, YAGO and Knowledge Vault currently include from 1000 up to 350.000 categories, up to 570 Mega instances of categories, up to 35.000 relationship types, and, up to 18 Giga relation instances [8]. However, from many aspects existent knowledge graphs are in their infant stage—more systematic use of intelligent tools for extracting the knowledge from various data sources has just begun.

The need for triple-store systems capable to store and manage from Tera (10^{12}) towards Peta triples is obvious. The scalability of storage system and query processing system to this amount of data is currently possible by using large-scale distribution of data into shared-nothing clusters. Query execution system in such environment must be able to employ various types of parallelism to allow simultaneous execution of huge amount of queries and provide reasonable response time.

Distributed triple-store big3store is based on dataflow architecture of query processing. Each query is a tree of algebra operations that is dynamically mapped to the tree composed of processes interconnected by streams of graphs, i.e., sets

© IFIP International Federation for Information Processing 2016
Published by Springer International Publishing Switzerland 2016. All Rights Reserved
F. Buccafurri et al. (Eds.): CD-ARES 2016, LNCS 9817, pp. 3–18, 2016.
DOI: 10.1007/978-3-319-45507-5_1

of triples. The scheduler that maps query trees to set of processes balances the computation load among the servers of cluster.

Triple-store of big3store is distributed into columns that store replicas of partitions into rows—cluster data servers. Data distribution is achieved by means of semantic distribution function [14] that splits the triples on the basis of the relation of each particular triple to the taxonomy of RDF classes and properties.

Algebra of RDF graphs is an abstract model used for the implementation of query execution system. Algebra is defined using set semantics—inputs and outputs of operations are sets of graphs. We present the denotational semantics of algebra and its implementation in the form of physical algebra that is further mapped to sets of processes implementing algebra operations. The architecture of query execution system based on algebra allows for the use of pipelined and partitioned parallelism [7].

Programming environment of parallel programming language Erlang [2] is used for the implementation of big3store. Erlang, together with database management system Mnesia that is tightly integrated with Erlang, may represent alternative data processing system for big data to Hadoop [17]. Indeed, it provides simple and robust parallel programming environment allowing processes to be effectively used in cluster of servers, it incorporates mechanisms that allow for the implementation of reasonable level of fault-tolerance, and, it integrates low-level database system appropriate for telecommunication applications that includes key-value indexes comparable to those of Hadoop storage system.

The contributions of this paper are the following. The architecture of distributed query execution system for processing large-scale RDF graphs based on algebra of RDF graphs is proposed. Query processor uses left-deep query trees to implement pipelined parallelism of algebra operations. Furthermore, it employs semantic triple distribution function [14] to achieve highly flexible partitioned parallelism. Access methods for tripe-patterns that address large partitions of triple-base are distributed to larger number of data servers, while the queries that address small partitions are executed on a single server. Query processor uses affinity scheduling, i.e., two level scheduling that persists to allocate the same data servers for execution of algebra operations for particular user. Finally, it uses key-value indexes in a similar manner to Hadoop to access data triples and to implement index-based nested-loop join operations.

The rest of the paper is organized as follows. The following Sect. 2 presents algebras of RDF graphs closely related to big3store algebra. Section 3 gives formal definition of algebra of RDF graphs and describes its physical counterpart, physical algebra of RDF graphs. The architecture of big3store query execution system together with detailed description of algebra implementation, is presented in Sect. 4. Preliminary experimental results are described in Sect. 5. Finally, Sect. 6 gives some conclusions and presents further work.

2 Related Work

Algebra of RDF graphs implemented in distributed triple-store big3store is based on relational algebra and technology of relational database management systems [10,11]. Database algebras are by nature functional languages where inputs and outputs of algebra operations can be treated as input and output flows of database objects. Operations of database algebra can be combined to form graph structure where operations (nodes) are interconnected by flows of objects [7].

The design of big3store algebra of graphs follows the leading ideas of relational algebra [5] while we identified and incorporated in it the salient features of triple-store data model. Firstly, instead of access methods scanning relational tables we use triple-pattern based access method to triple-store that can use all possible indexes on SPO attributes. Secondly, the results of algebra operations are not relations—sets of tuples—but sets of graphs. Consequently, operations *select*, *project* and *join* are adapted for graphs. Selection is based on expressions defined by means of graph nodes. Similarly, operation *project* eliminates graph edges. Finally, operation *join* is defined on graphs by introducing graph matching as join predicate.

Similar approach to definition of algebra for querying triple-stores are proposed by Angles and Gutierrez in [1]. Their formalization of SPARQL operations is based on mappings that follow semantics of *triples*. While their definition is tuned for studying expressive power of the language, our work is focused more on the implementation of algebra of graphs in shared-nothing cluster. They have shown in the paper that SPARQL have equivalent expressive power to non-recursive Datalog with negation that has, in turn, equivalent expressive to classical relational algebra.

Schmidt et.al. have proposed SPARQL algebra [15] to be used as foundations for SPARQL query optimization. They have defined set-based semantics for SPARQL by introducing SPARQL set algebra including similar operations to our algebra of graphs. They have identified fragments of SPARQL together with their complexity classes. For instance, they have shown that OPTIONAL-free fragments of SPARQL are either NP-complete or in PTIME. Furthermore, they have introduced algebraic equivalence rules that can be used for SPARQL query optimization, and, extensions of classical chase algorithm for optimization of AND queries.

Cyganiak proposed in [6] the use of relational algebra for SPARQL query processing. He presents the transformation from SPARQL into abstract relational algebra and shows differences between semantics of SPARQL and relational model. This approach allows for direct use of relational query optimization and query evaluation techniques for processing SPARQL queries. The transformation from relational algebra to SQL is defined. In comparison to Cyganiak's proposal, our approach focuses on distributed implementation of algebra of graphs while, in the similar manner, we use knowledge and technology gathered in area of relational systems for the implementation of triple-store database system.

3   Algebra of RDF Graphs

Algebra of RDF graphs is a functional language defined on sets of RDF graphs. Inputs and outputs of algebra operations are sets of RDF graphs that are linked to other operations forming in this way a tree. As we will show later, algebra expressions i.e. trees of algebra operations are converted to trees of Erlang processes that can be located on different data servers.

Let us first define the basic terminology used in presentation. Let I be the set of URI-s, B the set of blanks and L be the set of literals. Let us also define sets $S = I \cup B$, $P = I$, and $O = I \cup B \cup L$.

RDF triple is a triple $(s, p, o) \in S \times P \times O$. *RDF graph* $g \subseteq S \times P \times O$ is a set of triples. Set of all graphs will be denoted as G. We suppose the existence of a set of variables V and the set of *terms* $T = O \cup V$. Term $t \in T$ is ground if $t \in O$.

We say that RDF graph g_1 is *sub-graph* of g_2, denoted $g_1 \sqsubseteq g_2$, if all triples in g_1 are also triples from g_2.

3.1   Ground Graphs and Graph Patterns

Triple pattern $(s, p, o) \in (S \cup V) \times (P \cup V) \times (O \cup V)$ is a triple that can include variables as components. *Graph pattern* $gp \subseteq (S \cup V) \times (P \cup V) \times (O \cup V)$ is a set of triple patterns, i.e., graph defined as set of triples that can include variables as components. The set of all graph patterns is in the sequel denoted as G_P.

We will separate between ground and abstract entities. Ground triples are triples that include ground terms. Abstract triples, that can include variables, are triple patterns. Similarly, ground graphs are graphs that include triples composed of ground values, and, graph patterns represent abstract graphs that stand for a set of graphs from a given triple-store.

To be able to determine set of variables included in graph pattern gp we define function $vars : G_P \rightarrow \mathcal{P}(V)$.

Matching of Graphs. Let us now define relationship "match", denoted as $\sim$, between graphs including graph patterns. Graphs g_1 and g_2 match, denoted $g_1 \sim g_2$, iff the following conditions hold.

1. Two terms $t_1, t_2 \in T$ match, written $t_1 \sim t_2$, if either t_1 and t_2 are ground and $t_1 = t_2$, or, one of values is variable and the other is ground value.
2. Matching between two triples r_1 and r_2 exists, written $r_1 \sim r_2$, if all components of r_1 and r_2 match.
3. Graph g_1 matches graph g_2, written $g_1 \sim g_2$, when there exists bijection $alpha : g_1 \rightarrow g_2$ so that each triple $t_1 \in g_1$ matches $alpha(t_1) = t_2 \in g_2$.

Let gp be graph pattern. Function $val : V \times G_P \times G \rightarrow O$ maps variables $v \in vars(gp)$, graph patterns $gp \in G_p$ and ground graphs $g \in G$ that match gp to values $o \in O$. Let $t_1 \in gp$ be triple that includes variable v, then $val(v, gp, g) = o$ is component of triple $alpha(t_1) = t_2 \in g$ that corresponds to v in gp.

Interpretation of Graph Pattern. Interpretation of graph pattern gp in database of triples storing graph db is a set of all sub-graphs g of db that match gp.

$$[\![gp]\!]_{db} = \{g \mid g \sqsubseteq db \wedge g \sim gp\}$$

Special case of graph pattern is triple pattern tp where complete graph is one single triple that can include variables possibly in all three positions. Interpretation of tp is a set of all triples from db that match tp.

Triple patterns represent graph counterpart of relational access methods [4]. They are always the leafs of query tree. Implementation of query node for a given triple pattern can use SPO indexes to access ground triples.

3.2 Definition of Algebra

Let us now present algebra of RDF graphs. We denote graph query as Q, triple pattern as TP, selection condition as C, condition operations as OP, sets of variables as SV, and, variables as V. Syntax of algebra is defined as follows.

$$
\begin{aligned}
Q \quad &::= TP \mid select(Q,C) \mid project(Q,SV) \mid join(Q,Q) \mid union(Q,Q) \mid \\
&\quad\ intsc(Q,Q) \mid diff(Q,Q) \mid leftjoin(Q,Q) \\
TP \quad &::= (S \mid V, P \mid V, O \mid V) \\
C \quad &::= V\ OP\ V \mid V\ OP\ O \mid C \wedge C \mid C \vee C \mid \neg\ C \\
OP \quad &::= = \mid\ \neq\ \mid\ >\ \mid\ \geq\ \mid\ <\ \mid \leq \\
SV \quad &::= \{V+\} \\
S \quad &::= \text{URI} \mid \text{Blank-Node} \\
P \quad &::= \text{URI} \\
O \quad &::= \text{URI} \mid \text{Blank-Node} \mid \text{Literal} \\
V \quad &::= ?a\ ..\ ?z
\end{aligned}
$$

We extend previously defined function $vars$ to queries. Let (Q) be the set of all queries. The function $vars : \mathcal{Q} \to \mathcal{P}(V)$ maps each query to the set of variables that are included in the query. Let us now present the denotational semantics of RDF algebra by defining the interpretation of each particular operation.

Access paths to database of triples storing graph db are defined using *triple patterns* (t_1, t_2, t_3) where $t_1 \in (S \cup V)$, $t_2 \in (P \cup V)$ and $t_3 \in (O \cup V)$.

$$[\![(t_1, t_2, t_3)]\!]_{db} = \{\ (s, p, o) \mid (s, p, o) \sqsubseteq db \wedge (s, p, o) \sim (t_1, t_2, t_3)\ \}$$

SPARQL operation FILTER is represented by means of operation $select(q, C)$ where q is query and C is condition expression.

$$[\![select(q, C)]\!]_{db} = \{\ g \mid g \in [\![q]\!]_{db} \wedge C(g) = true\ \}$$

The evaluation of condition C on graph g is defined by the following rules. Value of $C(g)$ is presented by cases of C structure.

– $C = ?a\ OP\ o$, where $?a \in V$ and $o \in O$: if $val(?a, q, g)\ OP\ o = true$ then $C(g) = true$, else $false$.

- $C = ?a\ OP\ ?b$, where $?a, ?b \in V$: if $val(?a, q, g)\ OP\ val(?b, q, g) = true$ then $C(g) = true$, else $false$.
- $C = C_1 \wedge C_2$: if $C_1(g) = true$ and $C_2(g) = true$ then $C(g) = true$, else $false$.
- $C = C_1 \vee C_2$: if $C_1(g) = true$ or $C_2(g) = true$ then $C(g) = true$, else $false$.
- $C = \neg C_1$: if $C_1(g) = false$ then $C(g) = true$, else $false$.

Operation $project(q, s)$ projects graphs $g \in [\![q]\!]_{db}$ to graphs composed of triples that include values of variables from set s. Let $tr\text{-}vars : db \times G_P \rightarrow \mathcal{P}(V)$ denote function that maps triples $t \in [\![q]\!]_{db}$ and query q to set of variables $vs \in \mathcal{P}(V)$ such that for each $var \in vs$ value of variable var is a component of t.

$$[\![project(q, s)]\!]_{db} = \{\ g_1 \mid g \in [\![q]\!]_{db} \wedge \forall t \in g(tr\text{-}vars(t, q) \subseteq s \Longrightarrow t \in g_1)\ \}$$

Operation $join(q_1, q_2)$ joins two sets of graphs that are interpretations of queries q_1 and q_2. Let vs be a set of variables $vars(q_1) \cap vars(q_2)$. The result of $join$ includes union of graphs $g_1 \in [\![q_1]\!]_{db}$ and $g_2 \in [\![q_2]\!]_{db}$ such that they agree in the values of all common variables from vs. Observe also that joining two graphs is obtained by making union of graph triples from both graphs. Semantics of operation $join$ can be defined as follows.

$$[\![join(q_1, q_2)]\!]_{db} = \{\ g_1 \cup g_2 \mid g_1 \in [\![q_1]\!]_{db} \wedge g_2 \in [\![q_2]\!]_{db} \wedge$$
$$\forall v \in vs : val(v, q_1, g_1) = val(v, q_2, g_2)\ \}$$

Set operations are defined in a usual way except that argument sets can include graphs that have heterogeneous structure. Union, intersection and difference of q_1 and q_2 is defined as union, intersection and difference of their interpretations $[\![q_1]\!]_{db}$ and $[\![q_2]\!]_{db}$. Set operations of RDF algebra are defined as follows.

$$[\![union(q_1, q_2)]\!]_{db} = \{\ g \mid g \in [\![q_1]\!]_{db} \vee g \in [\![q_2]\!]_{db})\ \}$$
$$[\![intsc(q_1, q_2)]\!]_{db} = \{\ g \mid g \in [\![q_1]\!]_{db} \wedge [\![q_2]\!]_{db})\ \}$$
$$[\![diff(q_1, q_2)]\!]_{db} = \{\ g \mid g \in [\![q_1]\!]_{db} \wedge g \notin [\![q_2]\!]_{db}\ \}$$

Finally, to implement SPARQL operation OPTION we define operation $leftjoin(q_1, q_2)$, that is, left outer join of two sets of graphs which are elements of the interpretations of queries q_1 and q_2. For each pair $g_1 \in [\![q_1]\!]_{db}$ and $g_2 \in [\![q_2]\!]_{db}$ the result of $leftjoin(q_1, q_2)$ includes either $g_1 \cup g_2$ in the case that g_1 can be joined with g_2, or g_1 if g_1 can not be joined with g_2. Let vs be a set of variables $vars(q_1) \cap vars(q_2)$. Operation $leftjoin(q_1, q_2)$ can be defined as follows.

$$[\![leftjoin(q_1, q_2)]\!]_{db} = \{\ g \mid g_1 \in [\![q_1]\!]_{db} \wedge g_2 \in [\![q_2]\!]_{db} \wedge$$
$$((is\text{-}join(g_1, g_2) \wedge g = g_1 \cup g_2) \vee (\neg is\text{-}join(g_1, g_2) \wedge g = g_1))\ \},$$

where $is\text{-}join(g_1, g_2)$ is defined as

$$is\text{-}join(g_1, g_2) = \forall v \in vs : val(v, q_1, g_1) = val(v, q_2, g_2)$$

3.3   Physical Algebra of RDF Graphs

The design of physical algebra of RDF graphs follows the ideas used for implementation of relational algebra in the frame of relational database management systems [10,11]. Previously presented operations of RDF algebra are converted into three physical operations: physical access method (AM) AM, physical join denoted join, and, physical set operations union, diff and intsc.

All physical operations now include besides the functionality of their logical counterparts also the functionality of operations *select* and *project* operations. Each physical operation therefore includes also *select list* and *project list*. There are more reasons for folding more logical operations into single physical operation.

Firstly, it makes sense to perform selection of triples immediately after data needed for selection is available. For instance, immediately after obtaining triples by means of a given triple-pattern access method, they are filtered using selection conditions.

For similar reason operation *project* is performed as soon as possible. Immediately after some triple in a result RDF graph is not useful, it is dropped. For instance, after using particular triple for performing *join* operation, it can be omitted from result graph, if of course it is not needed as the result of query, or, for some other operation higher in the query.

The above two rules resemble "pushing" selections and projections down towards the leafs of query tree in relational database systems.

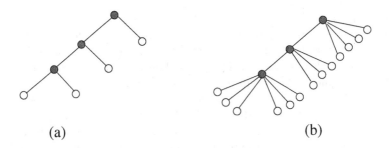

(a)   (b)

Fig. 1. (a) Left-deep query tree (b) Left-deep query tree with multiple AM operations

Secondly, the reasons for folding selections and projection into AM and join are: (1) the possibility to use join reordering algorithm for query optimization, and, (2) the possibility to implement *left-deep* as well as *bushy query trees* [10]—both of them have operations AM as leafs and operations join as the inner nodes of query trees.

big3store is currently using left-deep query trees. An example of left-deep query tree with 3 join operations and 4 AM operations is given in Fig. 1(a). The most important advantage of using left-deep trees is the *pipeline* that is formed by physical join operations. The results of retrieving graphs from outer query node of `join` operation is used for index-based access to the inner query node. The graph that is constructed as the result of `join` operation is then sent to the parent query node i.e. `join` query node. Consequently, there is no need to store intermediate results during query evaluation.

Triples related to some class with very large number of instances are, by using of semantic distribution algorithm, distributed to more data servers. Therefore, physical operation `AM`, defined using some triple-pattern, may be executed on number of data servers. Indeed, it is desirable that triple-pattern based operations `AM`, that tackle large number of triples, are distributed to more servers. The number of servers depends on the size of targeted set of triples. Left-deep query trees can therefore have multiple `AM` query nodes as presented in Fig. 1(b).

4   Distributed Query Execution System

Storing and querying huge volumes of data efficiently is currently possible by using shared-nothing cluster architecture [16]. Efficient data servers with huge amount of RAM and disk storage are available as inexpensive commodity hardware. This allows heavy distribution and replication of data as well as massive distribution of query processing on servers forming very large clusters.

Big3store is a *data-flow system* [3] where triple-store is composed of an array of data servers arranged into columns and rows. The complete triple-store is partitioned and distributed into *columns* based on semantic information attached to triples via triple-store schema. Each column stores a partition of triple store that is replicated to the column *rows*. Rows of the column therefore contain replicas of triple-store partitions assigned to columns.

While triple store partitioning affects significantly the performance of query executions, it is not the focus of this paper. Detailed presentation of big3store partitioning algorithm is given in [14]. Let us here present only some important ideas that have guided the design of triple-store (graph) partitioning.

Hash-based partitioning can not be employed for storing huge triple datasets that are expected to grow significantly in the following decade. Splitting data into a large number of partitions based on hashing can increase significantly the communication traffic among the data servers, especially, when large number of transactions is executed in parallel.

Big3store uses *semantic distribution algorithms* to partition triple-store into chunks that are suitable for distribution and that are related to a set of schema entities which serve as the key for distribution. Since distribution is based on rich taxonomy of classes spanning more then ten hierarchical levels we can achieve *well-defined distribution* in the sense that triples defined for classes including large number of instances are split into larger number of chunks. Triples defined for a class that has small number of instances is stored in one chunk. Query distribution must follow data distribution: larger the class of triples addressed by query, larger the number of columns where query will be executed.

Figure 2 shows a cluster composed of two types of servers: *front servers* represented as the nodes of plane A, and *data servers* represented as the nodes

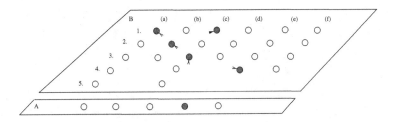

Fig. 2. Configuration of servers for a particular query

of plane B. Data servers are configured into *columns* labeled from (a) to (f). A complete database is distributed to columns such that each column stores a portion of the complete database.

The portion of the database stored in a column is replicated into rows labeled from 1 to 5. The number of rows for a particular column is determined dynamically based on the query workload for each particular column. The heavier the load on a given column, larger the number of row data servers chosen for replication. The particular row used for executing a query is selected dynamically based on the current load of servers in a column.

4.1   Architecture of Query Execution System

Erlang programming environment [2] is used for the implementation of big3store as an alternative to Hadoop-like systems [17]. It provides remarkably simple and effective parallel programming model based on lightweight processes. Erlang processes use "shared nothing" philosophy where the communication among processes is realized solely by means of synchronous and asynchronous messages.

Query execution system of big3store is composed of modules presented in Fig. 3. Each module includes the implementation of particular type of process.

State modules b3s_state and node_state are used for efficient sharing of big3store configuration data structures as well as for storing and querying current state of system, such as for instance number of processes running at each particular data server.

Each data server runs one instance of Erlang Mnesia database system that serves as *local triple-store*. Triple-store is realized by means of a single table triple_store that is accompanied with 6 indexes for all combination of SPO attributes. Mnesia provides transaction-based access to local triple-store through module db_interface. However, since db_interface provides only very simple cursor based access to a single table, local triple-store can be easily replaced by other database engine, and, even file-based access to RDF triples.

Module triple_distributor implements various schema-based algorithms for the distribution of triple-store into a set of cluster columns [14].

Session processes are implemented in module session. They serve as user-interface for interaction with users, initiate creation of query-tree processes,

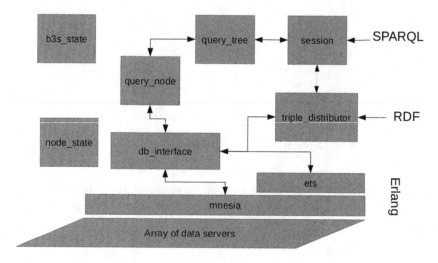

Fig. 3. Architecture of big3store query executor

control the execution of query tree, and collect the results of query execution. One session can spawn many query trees in parallel.

Module `query-tree` implements query tree processes that run on front-servers. The main task of query-tree process is to prepare, schedule and initiate the execution of query in the form of query tree composed of query-node processes interconnected by means of streams. Therefore, each query-tree process controls one or more query node processes that constitute query. This is presented in more detail in Subsect. 4.2.

Physical algebra operations `AM`, `join`, `union`, `intsc` and `diff` are implemented in `query-node` modules. Each physical algebra operation is realized as independent Erlang query-node process that runs on one of data servers. All operations are implemented as state machines executing particular protocol: access method to local triple-store, indexed nested-loop join algorithm, or, particular set operation. Subsects 4.4 and 4.5 give more detailed description of operations `AM` and `join`.

4.2   Query-Tree Process

Query-tree module implements processes that serve as front-end of query tree represented as tree of inter-connected processes running on array of servers. Query is received from session process in the form of a list of triple-patterns augmented with projections and selections as presented in previous section.

Query of type `qt_query()` presented to query tree process as parameter of message `start` is converted into tree data structure stored as process dictionary entry. First element of list representing `qt_query()` is triple-pattern of the lower leftmost query node. Last element of list is triple-pattern of the upper rightmost query node. All other triple-patterns are placed as inner query nodes in order between lower leftmost and upper rightmost.

Query-tree process analyzes the query, computes all components of query node processes to be started, determines cluster columns associated to each query node, and, schedules the rows of columns to be employed for running each particular query node of query tree.

Query-tree process determines the location of each query node in terms of column and row in array (cluster) of servers. Each query node is executed on location determined by query tree process. Firstly, the column of query node is computed by using *distribution function* that translates triple-patterns to columns in array of servers. Secondly, rows in given columns are scheduled dynamically based on current load of servers in columns.

We use two types of scheduling of column rows to query nodes. First type of scheduling is random assignment of rows to query nodes. The second method used for scheduling is bookkeeping the execution of each particular query node on particular server. Bookkeeping is realized by means of local `node_state` process. Besides bookkeeping `node_state` provides a function that selects row server with least load.

Both types of scheduling resemble *affinity scheduling* where we tend to select the same servers for the same session. The benefits of assigning the same servers (rows) in columns for same session is primarily in utilizing cache of local database management system Mnesia. Experiments are currently under way to present the benefits of affinity scheduling in terms of execution speed.

4.3   Triple-Pattern Query Node

Triple-pattern (abbr. TP) query node is implemented as Erlang `gen-process`. It realizes access method at local triple-store implemented as Mnesia table. Access method is defined by means of triple-pattern, and, it can use index based access to triple-store.

TP query node is implemented as state machine. Input and output messages trigger coroutines that comprise protocol. The states of TP query node are: `active`, `db_access`, `eos`, and `inactive`. Message `start` initializes TP query node process and moves state to `active`. Message `eval` starts with evaluation and moves state to `read_db`.

After obtaining triples from local Mnesia database, TP query node process checks them against *selection list*. The selected triples are sent to parent of query node by using `data` messages. Protocol requires that each `data` message is sent to parent process only after receiving `empty` message from parent process. Therefore, protocol can control the number of `data/empty` messages that comprise stream. Subsequent messages `empty` retain state `read_db`.

After `end_of_stream` is obtained from function accessing triple-store, state moves to `eos`. Message `eval` can be received multiple times if in state `active` or `eos`. Finally, `stop` message puts TP query node to state `inactive`.

4.4 Join Query Node Process

Join query node is implemented as independent Erlang `gen-process`. Join query node is a state-machine realizing protocol that has incoming and outcoming messages. Each message is implemented as coroutine.

Join query node state-machine has the following states: `active`, `wait_next_outer`, `wait_next_inner`, `eos` and `inactive`. Message `start` initializes the main data structures of join query node and sets state of protocol to `active`. Message `eval` start the evaluation of join query node by sending message `eval` to all children, and, moves state to `wait_next_outer`. After this, state alternates between `wait_next_outer` and `wait_next_inner`. State moves to `eos` after end of outer streams is detected.

Join query node implements join method which is a variant of indexed nested-loop join algorithm. However, it can have multiple outer query nodes as well as multiple inner query nodes. Since we suppose that every local triple-store indexes triple table on all possible subsets of SPO, all join variables are supported by indexes.

Algorithm of join method is defined as follows. Each graph obtained from outer query nodes causes initialization of inner query nodes by means of message `eval`. Initialization of inner query nodes uses the values of join variables obtained from outer graph. Only those graphs are retrieved from inner query nodes that match previously obtained outer graph. Each outer and inner graphs are merged into one graph which is tested against *selection list* and projected using *project list* of given query node. If selected then resulting graph is sent to parent query node.

4.5 Fault Tolerance

Erlang programming environment provides the tools for the construction of fail-safe process hierarchies by means of Erlang supervision processes [2]. Important process state data structures are circulating among supervision and supervised processes. The mechanism is integrated into message sending/receiving protocol. Each message received by process A includes the current state of A that was stored by its supervision process. After completing the task, process A returns its new state as a function result. In this way, a supervision process always has up-to-date state of all processes that it manages. In the case that process failure is detected by supervision process it can be restarted using the last state. Furthermore, supervised processes can form various types of structures with specific behavior.

5 Experimental Results

As a preliminary study, the execution time of benchmark queries in big3store are compared with the execution time obtained with Virtuoso [9].

Benchmark environment comprises six server machines. All of them have the same physical specifications. Each server has two 2.9 GHz Xeon E5-2960 CPU and 256 GB of RAM. One Erlang interpreter process was invoked on each server. Benchmark configuration uses one server as *front server* and the other five servers as *data servers*.

Virtuoso was installed on one of the servers that were used to execute big3store.

```
SELECT * WHERE {
  ?sbj <startedOnDate> ?obj.
}

Query Q1

SELECT * WHERE {
  ?sbj <startedOnDate> ?obj1.
  ?sbj <endedOnDate>   ?obj2.
}

Query Q2

SELECT * WHERE {
  <Slovenia> ?prd ?obj1.
  <Japan>    ?prd ?obj2.
}

Query Q5

SELECT * WHERE {
  ?a1 <actedIn>     ?movie.
  ?a2 <actedIn>     ?movie.
  ?a1 <livesIn>     ?c1.
  ?c1 <isLocatedIn> <England>.
  ?a2 <livesIn>     ?c2.
  ?c2 <isLocatedIn> <England>.
}

Query Q6

SELECT * WHERE {
  ?p1 <isMarriedTo> ?p2.
  ?p1 <wasBornIn> ?city.
  ?p2 <wasBornIn> ?city.
}

Query Q8
```

```
SELECT * WHERE {
  ?p rdf:type
  <wikicategory_Japanese_computer_scientists> .
  ?p <created> ?o .
  ?o rdf:type <wordnet_programming_language> .
}

Query Q3

SELECT * WHERE {
  <Ericsson> <created> ?pl.
  ?pl rdf:type <wordnet_language>.
  ?pl <wasCreatedOnDate> ?dt.
}

Query Q4

SELECT * WHERE {
  ?p <hasGivenName>  ?gn.
  ?p <hasFamilyName> ?gn.
  ?p rdf:type <wordnet_scientist>.
  ?p <wasBornIn>     ?c1.
  ?c1 <isLocatedIn> <Switzerland>.
  ?p <hasAcademicAdvisor> ?a.
  ?a <wasBornIn>     ?c2.
  ?c2 <isLocatedIn> <Germany>.
}

Query Q7

SELECT * WHERE {
  <Tim_Burton> <directed> ?movie1.
  <Johnny_Depp> <actedIn> ?movie1.
  ?p1 <directed> ?movie1.
  ?p2 <influences> ?p1.
  ?p3 <actedIn> ?movie1.
  ?p3 <actedIn> ?movie1.
  ?p4 ?prd1 ?p3.
  ?p4 <actedIn> ?movie2.
  ?p1 ?prd1 ?p4.
}

Query 9
```

Fig. 4. Benchmark queries

Let us first describe benchmark queries presented in Fig. 4. The first group of queries are simple queries that produce small number of intermediate and final results. Query Q1 finds all triples having property `<startedOnDate>`. It returns 9 triples from *YAGO2s*. Query Q2 finds all sets (graphs) of triples sharing the same subject that has `<startedOnDate>` and `<endedOnDate>` properties in the graph. It returns 1 triple. Query Q3 finds graphs that describe Japanese computer scientists that have created a programming language. Query Q4 returns the

Table 1. Benchmark results (in seconds)

Query	big3store	Virtuoso
Q1	0.015	0.149
Q2	0.086	0.133
Q3	0.033	0.159
Q4	0.009	0.608
Q5	95.594	0.054
Q6	3.652	0.262
Q7	7.549	0.279
Q8	23.512	0.182
Q9	104.364	0.558

creation dates of all things classified as wordnet_language that were created by Ericsson.

Query Q5 compares <Slovenia> and <Japan> by using the same predicate in triple patterns. While it is similar to query Q2, query Q3 returns 241,596 graphs. Query causes large number of intermediate results that are transferred as messages among data servers.

Queries Q6, Q7, and Q8 correspond to YAGO queries B1, A1, and B2 from [13], respectively. Because YAGO and YAGO2s [12] have different schema structures, queries were rewritten to have similar meaning.

Query Q6 returns pairs of actors that were playing in the same film and live in the same city in England. Query Q7 returns graphs describing scientists that were born in a city in Switzerland, and have academic advisor who was born in a city in Germany. Query Q8 returns all married couples that were born in the same city.

Query Q9 was constructed to test circular queries. While current version of query Q9 is specific and executes fast, a circular query can be constructed by removing the first two triple patterns of <Tim_Burton> and <Johnny_Depp>.

Let us now give some comments on comparison presented in Table 1. System big3store executed queries Q1, Q2, Q3 and Q4 faster than Virtuoso. One reason for this is that Mnesia copies complete database in main memory, if it is possible.

It is also apparent that queries that do not produce a lot of traffic execute in big3store much faster that queries that produce a lot of traffic among the servers. There are more reasons for this. Firstly, we currently do not use any data compression, so data is stored in raw form. Secondly, streams are implemented by sending one message for one graph.

The improved version of big3store will map IRIs to integers to optimize storage and transfer speed. Furthermore, the speed of stream transfer will be improved by packing more graphs into bundles that will serve as unit of transfer.

Another reason for slow performance of some queries is in the implementation of cursors in Mnesia. Index-based access to table always returns all results in one package. Consequently, there is almost no parallelism in the execution of queries. The improved version of big3store will replace Mnesia with BerkeleyDB.

6   Conclusions

Algebra of RDF graphs and its implementation on shared-nothing clusters is presented. Algebra is described by first defining denotational semantics of abstract algebra. Physical algebra corresponding to its abstract counterpart is based on technology of relational and parallel database systems. The architecture of distributed query processing system based on the presented algebra is described. Finally, some preliminary experimental results are discussed.

We have a list of tasks that remain to be completed. Among the most important are: distributed implementation of mapping from strings (URIs) to integers and its inverse mapping, more deep study of the effects of structure and distribution of query trees to the execution speed, experimental study that will give more insight into interrelations between data and query distribution, and, improving the communication speed among cluster servers by packing triples into bundles.

Acknowledgments. We thank Andreas Schmidt for valuable suggestions on draft version of this paper. This work was supported by the Slovenian Research Agency and the ICT Programme of the EC under PlanetData (ICT-NoE-257641).

References

1. Angles, R., Gutierrez, C.: The expressive power of SPARQL. In: Sheth, A.P., Staab, S., Dean, M., Paolucci, M., Maynard, D., Finin, T., Thirunarayan, K. (eds.) ISWC 2008. LNCS, vol. 5318, pp. 114–129. Springer, Heidelberg (2008)
2. Armstrong, J.: Programming Erlang: Software for a Concurrent World. Pragmatic Bookshelf, Raleigh (2013)
3. Babu, S., Herodotou, H.: Massively parallel databases and mapreduce systems. Found. Trendsin Databases **5**(1), 1–104 (2012)
4. Carey, M.J., DeWitt, D.J., Richardson, J.E., Shekita, E.J.: Storage management for objects in exodus. In: Kim, W., Lochovsky, F. (eds.) Object-Oriented Concepts, Applications, and Databases. Addison-Wesley Publishing Co. (1988)
5. Codd, E.F.: A relational model of data for large shared data banks. Commun. ACM **13**(6), 377–387 (1970)
6. Cyganiak, R.: A relational algebra for SPARQL (2005)
7. DeWitt, D., Gray, J.: Parallel database systems: the future of high performance database processing. Commun. ACM **36**(6), 85–98 (1992)
8. Dong, X.L., Gabrilovich, E., Heitz, G., Horn, W., Lao, N., Murphy, K., Strohmann, T., Sun, S., Zhang, W.: Knowledge vault: a web-scale approach to probabilistic knowledge fusion. In: KDD2014, ACM (2014)
9. Erling, O., Mikhailov, I.: RDF support in the virtuoso DBMS. In: Pellegrini, T., Auer, S., Tochtermann, K., Schaffert, S. (eds.) Networked Knowledge - Networked Media. SCI, vol. 221, pp. 7–24. Springer, Heidelberg (2009)

10. Graefe, G.: Query evaluation techniques for large databases. ACM Comput. Surv. **25**(2), 73–169 (1993)
11. Graefe, G.: Dynamic query evaluation plans: some course corrections? IEEE Data Eng. Bull. **23**(2), 3–6 (2000)
12. Hoffart, J., Suchanek, F.M., Berberich, K., Weikum, G.: Yago2: a spatially and temporally enhanced knowledge base from wikipedia. Artif. Intell. **194**, 28–61 (2013). Artificial Intelligence, Wikipedia and Semi-Structured Resources
13. Neumann, T., Weikum, G.: RDF-3X: a risc-style engine for RDF. Proc. VLDB Endow. **1**(1), 647–659 (2008)
14. Savnik, I., Nitta, K.: Semantic partitioning method for very large rdf graphs. University of Primorska, Technical report (In preparation), FAMNIT (2014)
15. Schmidt, M., Meier, M., Lausen, G.: Foundations of SPARQL query optimization. In: Proceedings of the 13th International Conference on Database Theory, ICDT 2010, pp. 4–33. ACM, New York (2010)
16. Stonebraker, M.: The case for shared nothing. Database Eng. Bull. **9**(1), 4–9 (1986)
17. White, T.: Hadoop: The Definitive Guide. O'Reilly Media Inc., Firenze (2009)

Your Paper has been Accepted, Rejected, or Whatever: Automatic Generation of Scientific Paper Reviews

Alberto Bartoli, Andrea De Lorenzo, Eric Medvet$^{(\boxtimes)}$, and Fabiano Tarlao

Department of Engineering and Architecture, University of Trieste, Trieste, Italy
emedvet@units.it

Abstract. Peer review is widely viewed as an essential step for ensuring scientific quality of a work and is a cornerstone of scholarly publishing. On the other hand, the actors involved in the publishing process are often driven by incentives which may, and increasingly do, undermine the quality of published work, especially in the presence of unethical conduits. In this work we investigate the feasibility of a tool capable of generating fake reviews for a given scientific paper automatically. While a tool of this kind cannot possibly deceive any rigorous editorial procedure, it could nevertheless find a role in several questionable scenarios and magnify the scale of scholarly frauds.

A key feature of our tool is that it is built upon a small knowledge base, which is very important in our context due to the difficulty of finding large amounts of scientific reviews. We experimentally assessed our method 16 human subjects. We presented to these subjects a mix of genuine and machine generated reviews and we measured the ability of our proposal to actually deceive subjects judgment. The results highlight the ability of our method to produce reviews that often look credible and may subvert the decision.

1 Introduction

Peer review, i.e., the process of subjecting a work to the scrutiny of experts in order to determine whether the work deserves publication, is a keystone in scholarly publishing. The review process should ensure that a published paper is of high scientific quality, which in its turn preserves the reputation of the corresponding publishing venue and improves the prestige of its author. On the other hand, peer review is just a piece of broader process involving several entities whose incentives may or may not actually drive the overall process toward those ideal goals. Authors are increasingly subject to strong pressures in the form of research evaluation procedures in which the indicators that play a key role are often mostly numerical [1]. Reviewers tend to be overworked and often receive little credit for their hard work [2], while at the same time being interested in increasing some counter of program committees or editorial boards in which they are involved. Commercial publishers may find in scholarly publishing excellent

© IFIP International Federation for Information Processing 2016
Published by Springer International Publishing Switzerland 2016. All Rights Reserved
F. Buccafurri et al. (Eds.): CD-ARES 2016, LNCS 9817, pp. 19–28, 2016.
DOI: 10.1007/978-3-319-45507-5_2

opportunities for profit [3], even in the form of journals with little or no scrutiny: a periodically updated list of *predatory publishers* has grown by 50 times in the last 5 years, including 923 publishers in its latest release [4].

While there is no doubt that most published research follows a rigorous and honest path, it is evident that actors involved in research may now find ways to maximize their personal benefits disregarding the ideal objective of the scientific environment as a whole, by following practices that are questionable or simply fraudulent [5,6]. Unfortunately, this claim is not a mere theoretical possibility. Questionable operators have emerged that run bogus journals and conferences which have no other purpose than generating profit while uttering worthless scientific literature [7]. Supposedly peer-reviewed journals accept for publication papers that have been randomly generated [8] or publish papers which clearly have not been proof-read by anyone [9]. Misbehaving researchers attempt to inflate their records by ghostwriting papers on nonexistent research [10]. Not surprisingly, the critical reviewing step has been exploited as well. Computer intrusions on the editorial system of a major commercial publisher have forced the publisher to retract several published papers [11]. In the last few years, hundreds of published papers have been retracted by several commercial publishers in many independent events [12–14], due to the discovery of reviews fabricated by the authors themselves which provided journals with suggested reviewers along with fake contact information which actually routed communication to the authors or their colleagues.

In this work, we investigate the feasibility of more fraud opportunities in the form of a procedure for *automatic generation of fake reviews*. We propose a method for generating automatically text which (a) looks like the typical scientific paper review, (b) is tailored to the specific paper being reviewed, and (c) conveys a recommendation specified as input. A tool that is capable of generating fake reviews systematically and at *no cost* may be misused in several ways. Busy people which want to be involved in as many reviewing committees as possible might choose a recommendation and then generate reviews very quickly, perhaps without even reading the paper or after just a superficial look. Predatory publishers might attempt to improve their credibility by sending many reviews to authors. Of course, reviews generated by our tool will certainly be detected as being fake by any decent editorial process. On the other hand, as pointed out above, perverse incentives and unethical conducts might find a role for a tool of this kind, which may potentially magnify the scale of frauds in the reviewing process in several ways. In this respect, it is important to keep in mind that a few years ago Springer and IEEE retracted more than 120 published papers which were computer-generated nonsense [15]. Our proposed tool could find more constructive applications, though. For example, the steering committee of a conference could inject fake reviews in the discussion phase without informing the program committee and then observe the outcome.

Our proposed method constructs a review tailored to a specific paper, with a specified recommendation, based solely on the paper text and a corpus of reviews written by humans for other papers. A key aspect of our proposal is that it builds upon a relatively small knowledge base (some tens of reviews) while commonly used methods for text generation, such as Artificial Neural Networks (ANN), typically require a very large amount of data in order to build an effective generative model. Applying those methods in the context of scientific review generation is difficult because of the difficulty in finding a large amount of samples of scientific reviews, in particular, of negative reviews.

An important contribution of our work is the experimental campaign performed involving human subjects. We performed an *intrinsic* evaluation aimed at assessing the ability of our method to generate reviews which look like as being written by a real human reviewer. Moreover, we performed an *extrinsic* evaluation aimed at assessing the impact on the decision about accepting or rejecting a paper under review. Although our experimental campaign is not a replica of a real editorial process and thus may provide only a preliminary assessment, our results do provide interesting insights.

2   Related Work

To the best of our knowledge, no method for the automatic generation of reviews of scientific papers has been proposed before. From a broader point of view, our proposal is a form of Natural Language Generation (NLG), which is widely used in many different fields such as spoken dialogue systems [16], machine translation [17], and as a mean for creating editorial content by turning structured data into prose [18].

A notable use of NLG for scientific purpose, which is particularly relevant to our work, is the software SCIgen[1]. This tool generates pdf files consisting of syntactically correct random text which is formatted like a scientific publication, including randomly generated figures, plots, and code fragments. Later and independently from its creators, SCIgen has been used in order to test the submissions standard of conferences and to prove that nonsense papers may actually be published, even by respected publishers [15]. This phenomenon has been investigated also in [19], which studies the spread of fakes and duplicates through notable publishers. The fact that a tool which was born as a "toy" for Computer Science researchers led to actual malicious behaviors suggests that other types of cheating may arise, including the creation of false reviews: this consideration is indeed the main motivation of our work.

Our work proposes a *corpus-based* NLG method. Corpus-based methods aim at training text generation rules automatically from text examples of the desired text generator output. An example of corpus-based method applied to text generation in dialogue is the work in [20]. The cited work proposes a class-based n-gram language model (LM) that improves over template-based and rule-based text generation systems. Belz [21] proposes a corpus-based probabilistic generation methodology and apply it to the automatic generation of weather forecast texts. The work in [22] assesses a new model for NLG in dialogue systems by maximizing the expected reward using reinforcement learning.

---

[1] http://pdos.csail.mit.edu/scigen/.

A different approach to NLG is based on Artificial Neural Networks (ANN). Kukich [23] implemented a stock reporter system where text generation is done at phrase level using an ANN-based approach. A recent work demonstrated the effectiveness of Recurrent Neural Networks (RNN) for natural language generation at character level [24]. A variant of RNN, Long Short-Term Memory (LSTM) [25], proved its ability to generate characters sequences with long-range structure [26]. The authors of [27] showed the ability of a LSTM framework to automatically generate rap lyrics tailored to the style of a given rapper. Zhang and Lapta [28] proposed an RNN-based work for generating Chinese poetry. Beyond unbounded text generation, LSTM for NLG has also been used in the generation of image descriptions [29–31] and in the generation of descriptive captions for video sequences [32].

All the generative methods based on neural networks require a huge amount of learning data, usually orders of magnitude more than the amount of data that we could find in our scenario (i.e., scientific reviews). Methods for *data augmentation* capable of decreasing the amount of learning data required for training a neural network effectively certainly deserve investigation in our context [33].

3   Our Approach

The problem consists in generating, given a paper a and an overall recommendation $o \in \{\text{accept}, \text{neutral}, \text{reject}\}$, a review r which (i) appears as generated by a human (ii) for the paper a and (iii) which expresses a recommendation o for a. In our work, we assume that the paper a is a plain text which consists of the concatenation of the paper title, abstract and main content.

Our method requires a set R of real paper reviews, i.e., each review $r \in R$ has been written by humans. We pre-process each review in R as follows: (i) we split the document in a sequence $\{t_1, t_2, \dots\}$ of tokens according to the Penn-Treebank procedure; (ii) we execute a *Named-entity Recognition* (NER)[2] [34] on the token sequence; and (iii) we execute a *Part-of-Speech* (POS) annotation[3] [35] on the token sequence; finally (iv) we classify each token in $\{t_1, t_2, \dots\}$ as being or not being a specific term, according to an heuristic procedure (see below).

When generating a review for a paper a with a specified recommendation o, our method performs 3 steps, described below in full detail: (i) it builds a set S of sentences from reviews in R and replaces each specific term in each sentence with a specific term of a; (ii) it removes from S the sentences which express a sentiment which is not consistent with o; (iii) it reorders and concatenates the sentences in S obtaining a review for a.

Specific terms identification. With this procedure, we aim at identify the *specific terms* of a document d—i.e., those terms which are relevant to d. To this end, we defined a simple heuristic. Let $\{t_1, t_2, \dots\}$ the sequence of tokens for d, where each token has been annotated with NER and POS taggers. A token

---

[2] http://nlp.stanford.edu/software/CRF-NER.shtml.
[3] http://nlp.stanford.edu/software/tagger.shtml.

$t \in \{t_1, t_2, \dots\}$ is a specific term if it meets all the following criteria: (i) t has been annotated as a noun (NN) or as an adjective (JJ); (ii) the length in characters of t is at least 2; (iii) t contains at least one letter.

Specific terms replacement. In this step, we aim at constructing a set S of review sentences tailored to a. To this end, we proceed as follows, starting with $S = \emptyset$. For each review $r \in R$, we split the review in a set S_r of sentences. We obtain (according to the procedure described above) the set W'_a of specific terms of a, retrieve the set W'_r of specific terms of r, and set $W_a = W'_a \setminus W'_r$ and $W_r = W'_r \setminus W'_a$. Then, for each sentence $s_r \in S_r$, we generate a random mapping from items in the set W^s_r of specific terms of W_r which occur in s_r to items in W_a such that: (a) each item in W^s_r is mapped to exactly one item in W_a, (b) no items in W^s_r exist such that they are mapped to the same item in W_a, and (c) for each item w^s_r mapped to an item w_a, the POS and NER annotations of w^s_r are the same of respective annotations of w_a. If such mapping is possible, we replace each occurrence of a term of W^s_r in s_r with the mapped term in W_a and add the modified sentence to S; otherwise, we proceed to the next sentence.

In other words, after this procedure, S contains all the suitable sentences generated by iterating the term replacement procedure for all the reviews in R.

Sentiment analysis. In this step, we aim at selecting the sentences of S which express a sentiment consistent with the specified overall recommendation o. To this end, we apply a pre-trained Naive Bayes sentiment classifier[4] [36] to each sentence $s \in S$, basing on the assumption that a positive sentiment can be associated with an accept recommendation, a negative sentiment with a reject recommendation, and a neutral sentiment with a neutral recommendation.

After the application of the sentiment classifier, we retain in S only the sentences for which the outcome is consistent with o.

Sentences reordering. In this step, we aim at generating the final output of our method (the automatically generated review) by selecting, reordering, and concatenating a subset of sentences of S. The rationale for the selection and reordering is to obtain a review (a) whose length is realistic, w.r.t. a typical review, and (b) which has an overall structure which resembles a typical review— e.g., an opening sentence, some considerations, a conclusive remark.

Concerning the reordering, we based on the assumption that sentences may be classified as suitable for opening part, central content, and closing part. Accordingly, we built a classifier which takes as input a single sentence and outputs a label in {opening, central, closing}. We took the general purpose text classifier based on maximum entropy[5] described in [37] and trained it using all the sentences of the reviews in R, which we automatically labeled as follows: if the sentence was the first sentence in its review, we associated it with the label opening; otherwise, if it was the last sentence, we associated it with closing; otherwise, we associated it with central.

---

[4] http://sentiment.vivekn.com.

[5] http://nlp.stanford.edu/software/classifier.shtml.

When generating a review, we apply the classifier to each sentence in S and then randomly select 1 opening sentence, 3 central sentences, and 1 closing sentence. Finally, we concatenate those 5 sentences and obtain the review for a.

4   Experimental Evaluation

We performed two experimental evaluations involving human subjects for assessing our proposed method ability to generate reviews which (a) look like as they have been written by real human reviewers for the specified paper, and (b) can affect the decision about accepting or rejecting the specified paper. That is, we performed an intrinsic evaluation and an extrinsic evaluation, respectively.

We built a dataset composed of 48 papers and 168 reviews, which we obtained from the F1000Research, Elifescience, Openreview and PeerJ web sites—which publish reviews of accepted papers along with corresponding full texts—and from our lab publication records; we used the reviews of the dataset as the set R while running our method. Moreover, for the purpose of performing our evaluations, we associated an overall recommendation (i.e., a label in {accept, neutral, reject} with each review in the dataset. Since the sources we considered vary in the way, if any, they classify reviews according to overall recommendation, we proceeded as follows. If a review was explicitly associated with an overall recommendation by its author, we associated it with the suitable label—e.g., positive recommendations to accept, negative recommendations to reject, and all the other recommendations to neutral. Otherwise, if a review was not explicitly associated with an overall recommendation, we considered the outcome of the publishing process which, for published papers, was always acceptance.

In order to provide a comparison baseline for our review generation method, we designed and built a simple baseline generation method based on Markov chains. To this end, we trained a second order Markov chain, operating on tokens, on all the reviews in the dataset: before the training, we added a special token t_{end} at the end of each review. When generating a review with the baseline method, the specified paper a and the overall recommendation o are not considered and the following steps are performed. First, a review in the dataset is randomly chosen and its first two tokens are fed into the Markov chain generative model. Then, the generative model is run until the token t_{end} is obtained. Finally, the output is obtained by concatenating all the generated tokens.

In our experimentation, we involved a number of human subjects, who were asked to examine the generated reviews and then to answer some questions. In order to gain more insights about our method effectiveness, we grouped the subjects according to their presumed familiarity with scholarly publishing, resulting in 3 classes. The experienced class is composed of professors, PhD student, and postdocs; the intermediate class is composed of undergraduate students; the novice class is composed of all the remaining subjects (who were anyway sufficiently proficient with English).

4.1   Intrinsic Evaluation

In the intrinsic evaluation, we built a number of forms, each showing the title of a paper a randomly chosen from our dataset and a set of 10 reviews randomly sampled for the following sets: (a) the real reviews in the dataset actually related to a, (b) the real reviews in the dataset not related to a, (c) a set of reviews generated using the baseline method, and (d) a set of reviews generated using our method with a and a random overall recommendation o as input. Since the size in characters of the real reviews can widely vary, we limited the number of sentences presented to the subject to 5, as for our generated reviews, randomly sampled from the corresponding reviews while maintaining the original ordering. We asked the subject to say, for each review in the form, if "it appeared as a genuine review written by a human reviewer for the paper with the shown title". We gathered results from 16 subjects—5 novice, 3 intermediate, and 8 experienced.

Figure 1 shows the key findings of the intrinsic evaluation: the figure plots the percentage of positive answers (on the y axis) to the form questions for each kind of review (bar group) and for each class of subjects (bar fill pattern). It can be seen that our method generates reviews that are considered as written by a human in almost one case on three—the figure being greater for novice subjects an smaller for experienced subjects. Moreover, the deceiving ability is larger than the baseline: approximately 30 % vs. 10 %. Concerning the real reviews, Fig. 1 shows that, as expected, they are properly recognized ≈85 % of the times: this finding suggests that the truncation of real reviews does not severely affect their appearance.

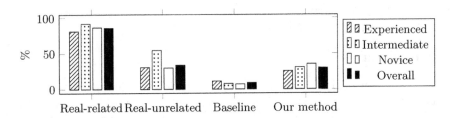

Fig. 1. Percentage of reviews considered as written by a human for the specified paper.

4.2   Extrinsic Evaluation

In the extrinsic evaluation, we built a number of forms, each showing the title of a paper a randomly chosen from our dataset and a set of 3 reviews randomly sampled for the sets described at points a, b, and d in the previous section. Real reviews were possibly limited in length as in the intrinsic evaluation. The form also showed, next to each review, the corresponding overall recommendation. We asked the subject to answer the following two questions: 1. "basing on these 3 reviews, would you recommend to accept or reject the paper?"; 2. "while taking

your decision, in which order the 3 reviews influenced you?" We gathered results
from 13 subjects—3 novice, 3 intermediate, and 7 experienced.

Table 1 summarizes the key findings of the extrinsic evaluation. In the left
portion the table shows, for each subject class and for all the subjects, the number of forms in which at least a real and a generated reviews were discordant
w.r.t. the recommendation (Discordant column), the number of discordant forms
for which the subject took a decision in line with the generated reviews (and
hence against the real reviews, Subverted column), and the ratio among Subverted and Discordant. In the right portion it shows the number of forms, for
each kind of reviews, in which a review of the corresponding type were stated
to be the most influencing by the subject; moreover it shows the percentage of
forms in which the generated reviews were stated to be the most influencing.

Table 1. Results of the extrinsic evaluation (see text).

Subject class	Subverted	Discordant	%	Our method	Original	Others	%
Experienced	4	16	25.0	10	21	4	28.6
Intermediate	4	15	26.7	11	18	14	25.6
Novice	5	21	23.8	11	25	9	24.4
Overall	13	52	25.0	32	64	27	26.0

The most interesting, and somewhat surprising, finding is that in the 25 % of
cases the decision of an experienced subject agreed with the generated reviews
and disagreed with the real reviews: from another point of view, through a
generated review we were able to manipulate the outcome of the (simulated)
peer review process. Table 1 also shows that, in 26 % of cases, a generated review
was stated to be the most influencing by the subjects.

5   Conclusions

We proposed a method for the automatic generation of scientific reviews. The
method is able to generate a review of a given research paper with a specified
overall recommendation. To this end, it performs multiple steps aimed at generating reviews which resemble human written reviews and hence might potentially
induce the reader to accept or reject the reviewed paper.

A key contribution of our work is the experimental evaluation, which involved
16 human subjects. The results show that in ≈30 % of cases a generated review is
considered genuine by the human subjects; moreover, in about 1 among 4 cases,
we were able to manipulate the outcome of a (simulated) peer review process
through generated reviews which we mixed with genuine reviews.

Beyond these promising results, our proposal needs further investigation and,
in this respect, we plan to compare it with other NLG methods, such as ANN,
for which, however, a much larger amount of data need to be collected. Finally,
it could be interesting to investigate if and how an ontology can improve the
review generation process.

References

1. Bartoli, A., Medvet, E.: Bibliometric evaluation of researchers in the internet age. Inf. Soc. **30**(5), 349–354 (2014)
2. Csiszar, A.: Peer review: troubled from the start. Nature **532**(7599), 306–308 (2016)
3. HEFC: Identification and dissemination of lessons learned by institutions participating in the research excellence framework (ref) bibliometrics pilot. Technical report, Higher Education Funding Council for England (2009)
4. Beall, J.: List of predatory publishers (2016). https://scholarlyoa.com/2016/01/05/bealls-list-of-predatory-publishers-2016. Accessed 29 April 2016
5. Bowman, J.D.: Predatory publishing, questionable peer review, and fraudulent conferences. Am. J. Pharm. Educ. **78**(10), 6 pages (2014). http://www.ajpe.org/doi/abs/10.5688/ajpe7810176
6. Dadkhah, M., Alharbi, A.M., Al-Khresheh, M.H., Sutikno, T., Maliszewski, T., Jazi, M.D., Shamshirband, S.: Affiliation oriented journals: don't worry about peer review if you have good affiliation. Int. J. Electr. Comput. Eng. **5**(4), 621 (2015)
7. Butler, D., et al.: The dark side of publishing. Nature **495**(7442), 433–435 (2013)
8. Eldredge, N.: Mathgen paper accepted! Technical report, That's Mathematics (2012)
9. Oremus, W.: This is what happens when no one proofreads an academic paper (2016). http://www.slate.com/blogs/future_tense/2014/11/11/_crappy_gabor_paper_overly_honest_citation_slips_into_peer_reviewed_journal.html
10. Qiu, J., Schrope, M., Jones, N., Borrell, B., Tollefson, J., Kaplan, M., Lovett, R.A., Dalton, R., Merali, Z.: News publish or Perish in China. Nature **463**, 142–143 (2010)
11. Reller, T.: Faking peer reviews. Technical report, Elsevier Connect (2012)
12. Fischman, J.: Fake peer reviews, the latest form of scientific fraud, fool journals. Technical report, The Chronicle of Higher Education (2012)
13. Ferguson, C., Marcus, A., Oransky, I.: Publishing: the peer-review scam. Nature **515**(7528), 480–482 (2014)
14. Callaway, E.: Faked peer reviews prompt 64 retractions. Nature, August 2015. http://www.nature.com/news/faked-peer-reviews-prompt-64-retractions-1.18202
15. Noorden, R.V.: Publishers withdraw more than 120 gibberish papers. Nature **24**, February 2014. http://www.nature.com/news/publishers-withdraw-more-than-120-gibberish-papers-1.14763
16. Wen, T.H., Gasic, M., Mrkšić, N., Su, P.H., Vandyke, D., Young, S.: Semantically conditioned LSTM-based natural language generation for spoken dialogue systems, pp. 1711–1721, September 2015
17. Sutskever, I., Vinyals, O., Le, Q.V.: Sequence to sequence learning with neural networks. In: Advances in Neural Information Processing Systems, pp. 3104–3112 (2014)
18. Wright, A.: Algorithmic authors. Commun. ACM **58**(11), 12–14 (2015)
19. Labbé, C., Labbé, D.: Duplicate and fake publications in the scientific literature: how many scigen papers in computer science? Scientometrics **94**(1), 379–396 (2013)
20. Oh, A.H., Rudnicky, A.I.: Stochastic natural language generation for spoken dialog systems. Comput. Speech Lang. **16**(3), 387–407 (2002)
21. Belz, A.: Automatic generation of weather forecast texts using comprehensive probabilistic generation-space models. Nat. Lang. Eng. **14**(4), 431–455 (2008)
22. Rieser, V., Lemon, O.: Natural language generation as planning under uncertainty for spoken dialogue systems. In: Krahmer, E., Theune, M. (eds.) Empirical Methods in NLG. LNCS(LNAI), vol. 5790, pp. 105–120. Springer, Heidelberg (2010)

23. Kukich, K.: Where do phrases come from: Some preliminary experiments in connectionist phrase generation. In: Kempen, G. (ed.) Natural Language Generation. NATO ASI Series, vol. 135, pp. 405–421. Springer, Netherlands (1987)

24. Mikolov, T., Karafiát, M., Burget, L., Černocký, J., Khudanpur, S.: Recurrent neural network based language model. In: INTERSPEECH, vol. 2, p. 3 (2010)

25. Hochreiter, S., Schmidhuber, J.: Long short-term memory. Neural Comput. **9**(8), 1735–1780 (1997)

26. Graves, A.: Generating sequences with recurrent neural networks (2013). arXiv preprint: arXiv:1308.0850

27. Potash, P., Romanov, A., Rumshisky, A.: Ghostwriter: using an LSTM for automatic RAP lyric generation, pp. 1919–1924 (2015)

28. Zhang, X., Lapata, M.: Chinese poetry generation with recurrent neural networks. In: EMNLP, pp. 670–680 (2014)

29. Karpathy, A., Fei-Fei, L.: Deep visual-semantic alignments for generating image descriptions. In: Proceedings of the IEEE Conference on Computer Vision and Pattern Recognition, pp. 3128–3137 (2015)

30. Mao, J., Xu, W., Yang, Y., Wang, J., Huang, Z., Yuille, A.: Deep captioning with multimodal recurrent neural networks (m-RNN) (2014). arXiv preprint: arXiv:1412.6632

31. Vinyals, O., Toshev, A., Bengio, S., Erhan, D.: Show and tell: a neural image caption generator. In: Proceedings of the IEEE Conference on Computer Vision and Pattern Recognition, pp. 3156–3164 (2015)

32. Venugopalan, S., Xu, H., Donahue, J., Rohrbach, M., Mooney, R., Saenko, K.: Translating videos to natural language using deep recurrent neural networks (2014). arXiv preprint: arXiv:1412.4729

33. Chatfield, K., Simonyan, K., Vedaldi, A., Zisserman, A.: Return of the devil in the details: Delving deep into convolutional nets (2014). arXiv preprint: arXiv:1405.3531

34. Finkel, J.R., Grenager, T., Manning, C.: Incorporating non-local information into information extraction systems by gibbs sampling. In: Proceedings of the 43rd Annual Meeting on Association for Computational Linguistics, pp. 363–370. Association for Computational Linguistics (2005)

35. Toutanova, K., Klein, D., Manning, C.D., Singer, Y.: Feature-rich part-of-speech tagging with a cyclic dependency network. In: Proceedings of the 2003 Conference of the North American Chapter of the Association for Computational Linguistics on Human Language Technology, vol. 1, pp. 173–180. Association for Computational Linguistics (2003)

36. Narayanan, V., Arora, I., Bhatia, A.: Fast and accurate sentiment classification using an enhanced Naive Bayes model. In: Yin, H., Tang, K., Gao, Y., Klawonn, F., Lee, M., Weise, T., Li, B., Yao, X. (eds.) IDEAL 2013. LNCS, vol. 8206, pp. 194–201. Springer, Heidelberg (2013)

37. Manning, C., Klein, D.: Optimization, maxent models, and conditional estimation without magic. In: Proceedings of the 2003 Conference of the North American Chapter of the Association for Computational Linguistics on Human Language Technology: Tutorials, vol. 5, p. 8. Association for Computational Linguistics (2003)

Generic UIs for Requesting Complex Products Within Distributed Market Spaces in the Internet of Everything

Michael Hitz[1]([✉]), Mirjana Radonjic-Simic[2], Julian Reichwald[2], and Dennis Pfisterer[3]

[1] Baden-Wuerttemberg Cooperative State University Stuttgart, Stuttgart, Germany
`michael.hitz@dhbw-stuttgart.de`
[2] Baden-Wuerttemberg Cooperative State University Mannheim, Mannheim, Germany
`{mirjana.radonjic-simic,julian.reichwald}@dhbw-mannheim.de`
[3] Institute of Telematics, University of Lübeck, Lübeck, Germany
`pfisterer@itm.uni-luebeck.de`

Abstract. Distributed Market Spaces (DMS), refer to an exchange environment in emerging Internet of Everything, that supports users in making transactions of complex products; a novel type of products made up of different products and/or services that can be customized to better fit the individual context of the user. In order to express their demand for a particular complex product in a way that is interpretable by the DMS, users need flexible User Interfaces (UIs) that allow context-focused data collection related to the complexity of the user's demand. This paper proposes a concept for generic UIs that enables users to compose their own UIs for requesting complex products, by combining existing UI descriptions for different parts of the particular complex product, as well as to share and improve UI descriptions among other users within the markets.

Keywords: Automatic user interface generation · Semantic web · Internet of Everything · User Interface Ontologies · Commercial exchange · Distributed Market Spaces · Complex products

1 Introduction

Emerging Internet of Everything (IoE) is opening up new opportunities for commercial exchange, giving the rise to novel types of products and services. Due to the increased interconnectivity of its participants (companies, institutions, individuals) on one hand and processes, data and things on the other [3], the IoE is enabling exchange environments, where products and services are customized and compound, as they are made up of many components provided by different suppliers [6]. Furthermore, these products and services can be orchestrated in complex products (i.e., an arbitrary combinations of individual products and/or

© IFIP International Federation for Information Processing 2016
Published by Springer International Publishing Switzerland 2016. All Rights Reserved
F. Buccafurri et al. (Eds.): CD-ARES 2016, LNCS 9817, pp. 29–44, 2016.
DOI: 10.1007/978-3-319-45507-5_3

services) and customized in a way to consider the unique conditions determined by the user's context. As such, complex products can better fit the individual needs of the users, thus, create richer consumer experiences that have not been possible before.

Contemporary solutions for commercial exchange are mostly focused on availability of individual products and services within their domain boundaries, or certain pre-defined combination of them traditionally bought together, however, are limited in their ability to support complex products, which need to fulfill particular user-defined criteria, going beyond the existing product/service descriptions. Consider the simple use case of booking a flight, hotel, rental car and guided tour. While already feasible today, it is a complex task to solve in order to fulfill different constraints (e.g., place, time, price, personal preferences). It can get exceptionally complex if many auxiliary conditions or products are involved. To make informed decisions, users need to know where and how to find viable product and/or service offers i.e., to engage search engines, visit diverse online platforms, shops, etc. while confronting with plenty of different user interfaces, search/selection criteria and representations of product/service description. After finding viable offers, users must compare, aggregate and infer all relevant information, considering the particular user context. The complexity of above mentioned activities and related user involvement lead to the adverse selection [2] i.e., choosing good enough, instead of optimal products/services, and increases the transaction costs (i.e., the buyers' costs to acquire information about seller prices and product offerings).

Distributed Market Spaces (DMS) proposed by [18], refers to a IoE exchange environment that supports market participants (i.e., consumers and producers) in making (distributed) transactions for complex products. But, to build a complex product requests on their own, the users need an alternative *to express their demand for a particular complex product, in a way, that is interpretable by the DMS*. Therefore, flexible user interfaces are needed to allow data collection of an arbitrary combination of the products and/or services, fulfilling user-defined criteria and spanning over different product/service domains related to the complexity of the user's demand.

In this paper, we propose a concept for *generic user interfaces (UIs) for requesting complex products within Distributed Market Spaces in the Internet of Everything* – a concept that alleviates the effects of adverse selection by supporting the users crafting complex product requests in a seamless manner; a manner of enabling users to:

- compose a new, customized UI for requesting a complex product in a particular user-defined context, by combining existing UI descriptions for different parts of the complex product, which can be rendered for different platforms / technical contexts (e.g., mobile or webbased apps)
- create a request for complex products interpretable by the DMS and
- share and improve UIs for complex products within markets.

This paper is organized as follows: First, Sect. 2 describes the setting in which our proposed concept is applied and defines the main requirements. Next, Sect. 3

presents the architecture and functional structure of the proposed solution, followed by a demonstrator implementation in Sect. 4. Thereafter, Sect. 5 discusses on related work and Sect. 6 concludes the paper with a summary and outlook.

2   Motivation and Background

In the following, we briefly describe the setting, i.e., the context in which the proposed concept of generic UIs is applied. Afterwards, we define the overall objectives and consider these as the requirements for the demonstrator implementation, as shown later in Sect. 4.

2.1   The Application Context

Distributed Market Spaces (DMS) [18], refers to a model of commercial exchange that supports market participants in making distributed transactions of complex products. Figure 1 illustrates the conceptual structure of the DMS, showing the involved parties, their roles and relationships on the left, and on the right, the DMS functional structure with its components and high-level interfaces, represented through the sets of exchanging messages, required to support the interactions along involved parties.

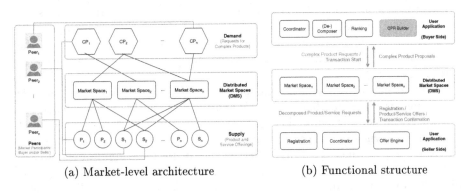

(a) Market-level architecture   (b) Functional structure

Fig. 1. Conceptual structure of the DMS.

As shown in Fig. 1a, the DMS is used by peers, i.e., potential transaction partners defined by their intention; buyers are peers intending to buy complex products while sellers are peers intending to sell products and/or services. Peers connect to one or more independent market spaces (MS) and multiple of these market spaces form the Distributed Market Spaces (DMS). A peer may offer products and services on one or more market spaces (e.g., $Peer_2$ offers product P_1 and service S_2) as well as, request a complex product by sending the request to one or more market spaces (e.g., $Peer_2$ also requests the complex product CP_1).

The peer interface component (user application), as shown in Fig. 1b, is split into two parts: a seller and a buyer side. In this paper, we focus on the user application *buyer side*, which is responsible to: transform a user's intention into a complex product request, distribute these requests to multiple market spaces, receive (partial) complex product offers and re-combine them into multiple complete complex product proposals, rank them according to the buyer's context and requirements, as well as to coordinate the distributed buying transaction. The user application is therefore comprised of the CPR Builder, Coordinator, the (De-) Composer and Ranking component.

The proposed concept of generic UIs is applied in the context of Complex Product Request Builder, CPR Builder component highlighted blue (Fig. 1b).

2.2   Overall Objectives

The main task of the CPR Builder as a component of the user application, is to transform a user's intention into a complex product request, which can be distributed to one/multiple market spaces within the DMS.

For the generic UIs concept to be implemented in context of the CPR Builder, following two basic prerequisites need to be assumed. First, in order to be able to match the incoming requests with the available offerings, the market space needs to understand the semantics of the product/service offerings (i.e., 'supply semantics'). Second, it needs to understand the semantics of the different requests, provided by the user as a complex product request (i.e., 'demand semantics').

As to [18], the DMS supports the 'supply semantics' using a domain-agnostic database, containing the information about registered sellers, as well as the description of available products and services they can potentially offer, encoded in RDF [24].

The challenge at this point, is the possible gap between the product/service descriptions provided by the supply-side and the demand descriptions requested by the demand-side. That is, because the data to describe a complex request is usually different from the data contained in the product/service descriptions. For example, a product description usually contains a *price tag* for one unit – a demand usually contains a *price range*. A more complex example is the generalisation of the demand: a product description could be a specific offering for a Ticket for the musical 'Chicago' – a general demand for a concert could be 'all musicals and rock concerts' that somehow are related to 'Chicago'. Given that, it is not always possible to use the product/service description data as a blueprint for the demand requests. Therefore, the DMS uses dedicated demand descriptions, defining the demand in a way, that can be mapped to the descriptions of the offerings.

As the main purpose of the CPR Builder is to enable users to craft complex product requests in a seamless manner, the potential buyers should be able to combine different product/service requests into a single complex product request, hence to compose a specific UI variant that:

- is tailored to their demand for a particular complex product – i.e., an arbitrary combination of products and/or services, e.g., a flight, hotel, rental car and tickets for the events at the destination,
- supports the context-information defined by the user, i.e., user's preferences and criteria e.g., a ticket for a certain musical vs. more general proposal for events like theater, concert or ship cruise, and
- produces output in the form of a request for complex product interpretable by the DMS.

Composing a specific UI variant includes finding, selecting and combining existing UI descriptions for the different parts of the complex products, while considering the user's preferences in terms of the generalisation (e.g., concert vs. general event planning) or granularity (e.g., less questions vs. detailed specification depending on the user's context). Hence, we can detail this overall objective into following functional requirements:

R_1: *Different UI descriptions for the same demand request* supplying different questions based on the user's preference for more/less specific questions.

R_2: *Different UI descriptions containing demands for multiple products* to allow context-focussed interfaces.

R_3: *Composition of different UI descriptions into a single UI description* for the particular complex product request

Having outlined the main prerequisites and requirements, in following, we use them as the rationale for the conceptualisation of the overall solution.

3 Proposed Solution

As an explanation of the proposed solution, in this section, we first introduce the foundations and core elements, followed by the functional aspects and more detailed description of the inner workings.

3.1 Overview - Generic UIs for Complex Product Requests

The proposed solution extends the DMS concept, outlined in Sect. 2.1, by enabling users to craft complex product requests. It uses the Complex Product Builder to combine individual UIs and generate complex product requests from the collected data. For the automatic generation of the involved UIs, the solution builds on the results of the mimesis project [10] and extensions that map the approach to ontological descriptions [11].

In the proposed solution of generic UIs, we use Semantic Web technologies as they provide the necessary mechanisms to get a rich description of the data involved and incorporate techniques for reasoning on that data. The foundation of the proposed solution is built on ontologies describing different views of the participants (demand-, DMS- and supply-side) and ontological descriptions for the UIs to meet the requirements R_1, R_2 and R_3 (cf. Sect. 2.2).

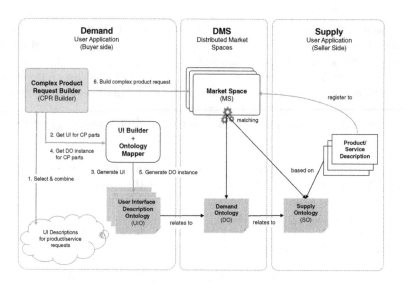

Fig. 2. Core elements of the solution architecture.

Figure 2 shows the core elements of the proposed solution. The central component is the **Complex Product Builder**, that orchestrates the generation of the UI. It allows the selection of UI descriptions, the generation of their concrete UIs, aggregation into a single UI (similar to 'mesh-up' approaches [16], though using generated content) and building of a complex product request based on the data entered by the user.

A **Supply Ontology (SO)** is used by the peers (seller side) to describe product instances on which market spaces within the DMS can operate. To describe the demand for a product/service, a **Demand Ontology (DO)** is used; it defines the possible request data to be specified by the peers (buyer side) and thus, can be interpreted by the market spaces. Finally, **User Interface Description Ontologies (UIO)** describe the UI variants based on the data to be collected. These are used to build the concrete UI and to generate output, that corresponds to the related demand ontologies.

The following Sect. 3.2, outlines the functional structure of the solution needed to fulfil defined requirements (R_1, R_2, R_3), followed by Sect. 3.3, that provides a detailed description of the ontologies, used in this solution – especially focussing the UIO and its mapping to the DO.

3.2   Functional View - Processing Complex Product Demands

The workflow for building a complex product request starts with the buyer aggregating the UI for a specific complex product need. As shown in Fig. 2 (Step 1), the buyer selects suitable, task related UI descriptions provided by a **UI Description Repository** – e.g., a search engine collecting UI descriptions for demands on the Internet, or a repository of community-rated UI descriptions (which usually were manually or semi-automatically crafted based on the related

DOs). The result of this step, is a collection of user-selected, context-related UI descriptions to be presented to the user by the CPR Builder.

The collection of UI descriptions is sent to the **generic UI Builder** component, that generates the final UIs based on that descriptions and returns the results. The components are aggregated by the CPR Builder into a single UI and are presented to the user (Steps 2 and 3). When the user finished entering data, the data for each UI component is mapped to instances of the corresponding DO (Steps 4 and 5). The information on how the data elements relate to DO elements is part of the UIO (cf. Sect. 3.3). The resulting DO instances are aggregated into one complex product request, that is enriched with context data and thus, as shown in Step 6, ready for further processing.

3.3   Information View - Ontologies in Detail

Supply Ontology (SO): The Supply Ontology is the common vocabulary to describe products/services provided by a seller. As in [18], this enables a market space to process product/service data and clearly determines the data and semantics that can be used for a certain product/service instance description. A simple product instance is shown in Listing 1.1 as an example. It describes a ticket offer for the musical 'Chicago' at the 'Alte Oper Frankfurt' [18] using existing ontologies *GoodRelations*[1] and *Ticket* ontology[2].

Listing 1.1. Exemplary description of a offering.

```
PREFIX rdf: <http://www.w3.org/1999/02/22-rdf-syntax-ns#>          1
PREFIX rdfs: <http://www.w3.org/2000/01/rdf-schema#>               2
PREFIX xsd: <http://www.w3.org/2001/XMLSchema#>                    3
PREFIX gr: <http://purl.org/goodrelations/v1#>                     4
PREFIX tio: <http://purl.org/tio/ns#>                              5
PREFIX dms: <http://www.itm.uni-luebeck.de/dms/#>                  6
                                                                   7
dms:ticket1 a tio:TicketPlaceholder ;                              8
    rdfs:label "Ticket_for_Chicago_Musical_at_Alte_Oper_Frankfurt"@en ;  9
    tio:accessTo <http://data.linkedevents.org/event/chicagomusical> .   10
    dms:TRIO Tickets ltd. gr:offers dms:PSO1 .                     11
dms:PSO1 a gr:Offering ;                                           12
    gr:name "Ticket_for_Chicago_Musical"@en ;                      13
    gr:description "The_#1_American_Musical_in_Broadway_History:Chicago_at_Alte   14
        _Oper_Frankfurt"@en ;                                      15
    gr:includes dms:ticket1 ;                                      15
    gr:hasBusinessFunction gr:Sell ;                               16
    gr:hasPriceSpecification                                       17
        [ a gr:UnitPriceSpecification ;                            18
        gr:hasCurrency "USD"@en ;                                  19
        gr:hasCurrencyValue "49.50"^^xsd:float ;                   20
        gr:validThrough "2016-09-26T23:59:59"^^xsd:dateTime ] .    21
```

Demand Ontology (DO): The Demand Ontology is closely related to the Supply Ontology and defines the data that can be used to describe the demand for a certain product (e.g., concert ticket) or product category (e.g., ticketing

---

[1] http://www.heppnetz.de/projects/goodrelations/.

[2] http://www.heppnetz.de/ontologies/tio/ns.

Listing 1.2. Example of a request for a ticket.

```
@prefix : <http://mimesis.solutions/products/concert/individuals#> .        1
@prefix ... owl: rdf: xml: xsd: rdfs:                                        2
@prefix gr: <http://purl.org/goodrelations/v1#>                             3
@prefix tio: <http://purl.org/tio/ns#>                                      4
@prefix tido: <http://demandontologies.org/ticketdemands#>                  5
@base <http://mimesis.solutions/products/concert/individuals> .             6
                                                                            7
### http://mimesis.solutions/products/concert/individuals#_i1462530726859  8
:_i1462530726859 rdf:type owl:NamedIndividual ;                             9
   :concertdata :ticketrequest_i1462530726859 .                            10
                                                                           11
### http://mimesis.solutions/products/concert/individuals#                 12
   ticketrequest_i1462530726859
:ticketrequest_i1462530726859 rdf:type <tido:TicketRequest> ,              13
   owl:NamedIndividual ;                                                    14
   gr:name "Chicago" ;                                                      15
   tido:eventcategory "musical|rockconcert"^^<tido:eventcategorylist> ;     16
   gr:hasPriceSpecification :hasPriceSpecification_i1462530726859 .         17
                                                                           18
### http://mimesis.solutions/products/concert/individuals#                 19
   hasPriceSpecification_i1462530726859
:hasPriceSpecification_i1462530726859 rdf:type <gr:UnitPriceSpecification> , 20
   owl:NamedIndividual ;                                                    21
   gr:hasMaxCurrencyValue "35"^^<xsd:float> .                              22
```

in general). The DO describes the maximum of requestable information, thus, what the market space is *able to understand and handle* regarding the questions related to the corresponding Supply Ontology. Listing 1.2 shows an example of a request following a DO for event tickets. It describes a demand for a ticket for a *musical or rock concert* with a name containing 'Chicago' (could be the musical or the band).

Although, the DO is related to a corresponding SO (here the Ticket Ontology), it extends the elements with request-related extensions (e.g., *tiod:eventcategory*; for a more general demand for event categories, or the use of *gr:hasMaxCurrencyValue* for specifying a maximum price for a ticket.

User Interface Description Ontologies (UIO): A set of User Interface Description Ontologies is used to describe the possible UIs for the buyer side. A UIO describes the UI for a **specific dialog variant** by describing the **data to be collected** in sufficient detail. It contains all necessary information needed to (1) derive a User Interface and (2) to relate the collected data to a demand instance specified by Demand Ontologies.

For **the description of UIs** we apply the approach of the mimesis project introduced in [10] and its application onto ontologies [11]. The basic idea of the approach is to define a model of the data processed/collected by the application and derive UIs for different platforms and user contexts from this model. For this purpose, the basic data model is enriched with information needed to derive UIs: this includes *structural information* (e.g., type restrictions, grouping, sequence of elements) and *behavioural information* (e.g., visibility rules, reactions to the changes, validations to perform). The resulting model is data centric, technology agnostic and can be used to derive UIs for different kinds of platforms and contexts of use (e.g., mobile apps, web based-, rich client- or speech based UIs). Further details of the approach can be found in [10].

The idea of the mimesis approach – to describe the semantics of the data in more detail – additionally allows to add information for each element on **how it is to be mapped to elements defined within a DO**. Using that information an instance (individual) of the UIO containing the user input can be used to generate a corresponding instance of the DO as resulting output.

The approach is suitable to meet the requirements R_1, R_2 and R_3 listed in Sect. 2.2. To achieve that, ontological descriptions of the UI for different product demands are used. These contain:

- a description of the **data with UI specific enhancements**, as defined in mimesis for the derivation of UIs (as proposed in [11]) and
- the information for the **mapping of that data onto DO instances,** needed to produce the demand requests.

Hereby, different UI variants for a demand can be defined, that might contain different questions depending on the user's context (cf. R_1). Since the mapping information contained in the UI description can reference arbitrary ontologies, it is also possible to provide UIs containing questions spanning different DOs (cf. R_3). The approach is also capable to address requirement R_3: the CPR Builder is able to choose a set of different UIOs as building blocks from which an aggregated UI can be presented to the user.

Figure 3a shows a possible variant for a UI relating to the above example DO instance, in Listing 1.2. The UI for a *concert demand* contains two groups of questions (*Details for title or genre* and *Price range*). It illustrates, that the relation to the DO is not one-to-one. For example, the data are grouped differently and there is no currency selectable (which is already set by the CPR Builder from the user's context data). Additionally, there is a value restriction

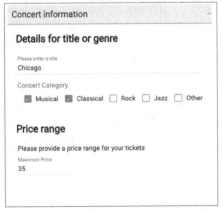

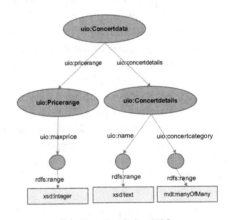

(a) UI Variant for a concert demand.   (b) Graph of the UIO.

Fig. 3. UI and its structure.

Listing 1.3. Basic User Interface Ontology for a concert demand (excerpt).

```
@prefix : <http://mimesis.solutions/products/concert#> .         1
@prefix owl: rdf: xsd: rdfs:                                      2
@prefix mdt: <http://mimesis.solutions/datatypes#>.              3
@prefix man: <http://mimesis.solutions/annotations#>            4
@base <http://mimesis.solutions/products/concert> .              5
<http://mimesis.solutions/products/concert> rdf:type owl:Ontology .  6
                                                                 7
##########    Classes    ##########                              8
:Concertdata rdf:type owl:Class .                                9
:Concertdetails rdf:type owl:Class .                            10
:Pricerange rdf:type owl:Class .                                11
...                                                             12
##########    Object Properties    ##########                   13
:Concertdata.concertdetails rdf:type owl:FunctionalProperty , owl:  14
    ObjectProperty ;
    rdfs:domain :Concertdata ; rdfs:range :Concertdetails .     15
:Concertdata.pricerange rdf:type owl:FunctionalProperty ,owl:ObjectProperty ;  16
    rdfs:domain :Concertdata ; rdfs:range :Pricerange .         17
...                                                             18
##########    Data properties    ##########                     19
:Concertdetails.concertcategory rdf:type owl:DatatypeProperty , ... ;  20
    rdfs:range  mdt:manyOfMany ; rdfs:domain :Concertdetails .  21
:Concertdetails.name rdf:type owl:DatatypeProperty , owl:FunctionalProperty ;  22
    rdfs:range xsd:text ; rdfs:domain :Concertdetails .         23
:Pricerange.maxprice rdf:type owl:DatatypeProperty , owl:FunctionalProperty ;  24
    rdfs:domain :Pricerange ;  rdfs:range xsd:integer .         25
    ...                                                         26
```

for *concert category*, which might be a subset of the possible values defined in the DO.

Figure 3b shows a structural graph of the UIO for the displayed UI. The UI consists of two groups (*Pricerange* and *Concertdetails*). These encompass the data fields and their types (e.g., *name* and *concertcategory*) to be presented to the user. Listing 1.3 shows an excerpt of the UIO in OWL/Turtle notation [23].

The additional information needed for the derivation of a concrete UI and for the mapping to the Demand Ontology is shown in Listing 1.4. As this is meta information, describing the element in more detail, mimesis uses the annotation concept of OWL to specify these details. For each element (data element or group) there exist mimesis-specific entries (e.g., the *sequence* of the questions in line 3, or specific *type information and restrictions* in lines 4 and 5). The mapping onto instances for DO elements is provided using annotations starting with the prefix '*sw:*'. It contains information to which class an entity belongs to (e.g., line 19 maps *Concert.concertdata* to a *tiod:TicketRequest*). It is defined to which property a data element maps, which type it has and to which individual it belongs to (e.g., lines 6–8 map *Concertdetails.concertcategory* to the type *tiod:eventcategorylist* and assigns it to the *ticketrequest* instance using the property name *tiod:eventcategory*). Given that information a demand instance, following the DO as shown in Listing 1.2, can be generated in combination with the instance data gathered by the UI.

4   Demonstrator

As a proof of the concept, we built a demonstrator that implements the proposed approach for aggregating the UIs for a complex product request and matching

Listing 1.4. Additional UI and DO related Data for a concert demand.

```
                                                                       1
########## Annotations  ##########                                     2
:Concertdetails.concertcategory man:sequence "2" ;                     3
    man:type "manyOfMany" ;                                            4
    man:restrictedTo>"musical|classical|rock|jazz|all" ;               5
    man:swForIndividual "ticketrequest" ;                             6
    man:swProperty "tiod:eventcategory" ;                             7
    man:swType "tiod:eventcategorylist" .                             8
:Concertdetails.name man:sequence "1" ;                                9
    man:swProperty "gr:name" ;                                        10
    man:swType "gr:name" ;                                            11
    man:swForIndividual "ticketrequest" .                             12
:Concertdata.pricerange man:sequence "2" ;                            13
    man:swClass "gr:UnitPriceSpecification" ;                         14
    man:swProperty "gr:hasPriceSpecification" ;                       15
    man:swIndividual "hasPriceSpecification" ;                        16
    man:swForIndividual "ticketrequest" .                             17
:Concert.concertdata man:sequence "0" ;                               18
    man:swClass "TicketRequest" ;                                     19
    man:swIndividual "ticketrequest" .                                20
:Pricerange.maxprice man:sequence "1" ;                               21
    man:initialValue "30" ;                                           22
    man:unit "EUR" ;                                                  23
    man:swProperty "gr:hasMaxCurrencyValue" ;                         24
    man:swForIndividual "gr:hasPriceSpecification" ;                  25
    man:type "number" ;                                               26
    man:swType "xmls:float" .                                         27
:Concertdata.concertdetails man:sequence "1" .                        28
...                                                                    29
```

the collected data to a Demand Ontology. As a use case, we chose 'organising a city trip' which includes the planning of events, transportation and overnight stays. The buyer should be able to select the desired components for his trip, and enter the required demand information for each component. As the final step of the demonstrator, the collected data for each component is shown as an instance of the related Demand Ontologies.

The demonstrator implements the solution architecture outlined in Sect. 3.2 and shown in Fig. 2. Its central component, the CPR Builder, is implemented as a web application using HTML/JavaScript as a platform technology, and uses a local repository for the management of available UI descriptions. Additionally, the *UI Builder and Ontology Mapper* components are implemented as separate Web Services, based on the work in [11].

The UI Builder Service is responsible for generating the UIs based on the UI Description Ontologies; it accepts UIOs as input and is able to generate a final UI for different technology platforms (here HTML/Javascript). The Ontology Mapper Service, on the other hand, is responsible for generating a DO instance, based on a certain UIO and corresponding user input submitted in the form of a JSON object.

The demonstrator follows the workflow outlined in Sect. 3.2. First, the buyer searches for product components using a google-like search facility, and selects/-collects the components according to his preferences and requirements as shown in Fig. 2, Step 1. An example of such a search is shown in Fig. 4a, where the user enters 'travel' into the search field, and gets available components matching the search criteria (e.g., 'visit a concert' of 'rent a car'). The user selects viable components, which are collected like products in a *shopping cart* (Fig. 4a). When the

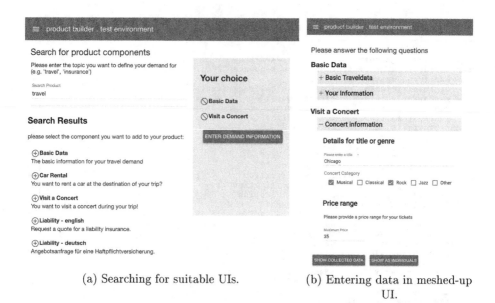

(a) Searching for suitable UIs.

(b) Entering data in meshed-up UI.

(c) Gathered data as Demand Ontology instance.

Fig. 4. Aggregating UI and entering data

user finished the selection, the corresponding UIOs of the selected components are sent to the **UI Builder Service** that generates final UIs (Fig. 2, Steps 2 and 3). These are aggregated by the client application into one UI and presented to the user for input. The aggregation of the UI based on the selected components is shown in Fig. 4b.

After having entered the demand data for each component, the CPR Builder sends the collected data along with the corresponding UIO to the **Ontology Mapper Service**, which is responsible for mapping the collected data to the DO according to the information contained in the UIO, and returns an instance of the DO (Fig. 2, Steps 4 and 5). The results of this step are finally displayed by the demonstrator for each component as shown in Fig. 4c. In a further step (not part of the demonstrator) these DO instances can be aggregated into one complex demand and processed by the CPR Builder, as described in Sect. 2.1.

Summarizing, the demonstrator shows that it is basically possible to dynamically generate UIs for complex products, satisfying the requirements defined in Sect. 2.2. Users can be enabled to choose the UIs they want/need and combine them to build requests for desired complex products. These UIs may span different domains and can be combined to build a unified interface for the users. Moreover, the demonstrator also underlines the advantage of using UIOs as separate descriptions; since a UIO contains all information to generate a UI, as well as the information about how to produce instance data (understandable by the market spaces), the UIOs are actually independent from the target system. Therefore, they can be independently distributed and modified – as long as the output conforms to the specified demand ontologies.

Yet, our demonstrator does not cover all functionality needed to combine different demands in a seamless manner; currently it combines UIs for product components as separate, self relying units – ignoring possible relations between them. For example, it does not implement a context, which components and their UIs may share and react to (e.g., recognizing and omitting questions, that were already asked in other components, or pre-fill values from a global context).

5 Related Work

In this section, we provide an overview of the operational solutions, concepts and approaches relevant to the presented work, and briefly discuss why these are not suitable to meet the defined requirements.

Electronic marketplaces (e-marketplaces), as well-established solutions for commercial exchange, enable only compositions of individual products/services within their domain boundaries, or they offer pre-defined combinations of them, which are traditionally bought together and determined by recommender systems. Even though there exist some advanced solutions, such as, e.g., [8] enabling the composition of individual services considering a wider set of user-defined criteria, these are domain-specific solutions, and as such, are limited in their capabilities to support users requesting complex products spanning over different product/service domains related to the complexity of the user's demand.

The Intention Economy (IE) [22], also called Project Vendor Relationship Management (VRM), refers to an exchange environment that focuses on a buyers' intention to conduct a transaction with potential sellers (i.e., vendors). By using VRM tools, buyers are supported to describe their needs by creating a personal request for proposal (pRFP) and make them visible for the vendors. Even though, the VRM tools support pRFP there is no obvious evidence that they support composing context-focussed UIs.

Web of Needs (WoN) [14], refers to a framework for a distributed and decentralized e-marketplace on top of the Web. WoN aims to standardize the creation of owner proxies, which describe supply or demand, represent the intention to enter a transaction, as well as contain information of the owner needed for conducting the transaction [13]. Generally, WoN supports describing the user's need for complex products, but, if the user wants the system to process the complex product, he can publish a 'complex need', waiting for a matching service capable of interpreting his 'complex need'. Given that, the effects of adverse selection are still retained, and native support for requesting complex products remains insufficient.

Concluding, contemporary solutions of commercial exchange are limited in supporting users requesting complex products; approaches such as IE or WoN, address some of the requirements, but do not represent a comprehensive solution. Either they provide tools that need to be integrated with other solutions to be fully usable, or they address our requirements only partly.

Next, we elaborate on the approaches focusing on automatic generation of UIs and the different aspects of the UI generation that can be applied to our presented work.

User Interface Description Languages (UIDL) focus mainly on the description of concrete UIs in a technology independent way. Examples are JavaFX [7], UIML [1], and XForms [5]. The essential idea is to model dialogs and forms by declarative descriptions of in-/output controls and relations between elements and behavior (e.g., visibility) within a concrete UI.

Task-/conversation based approaches describe applications by dialog flows which are derived from task models - e.g., MARIA [17] or model conversations, like in [19, 20]. They focus on a model of the dialog flows and their variants. To generate an application frontend, the steps in a dialog flow are associated with technology independent UI descriptions displayed to the user.

Existing **ontology based approaches** generally rely on the concepts of the mentioned approaches and use ontologies to represent the information. For instance, in analogy of UIDL approaches, Liu et al. [15] propose an ontology driven framework to describe UIs based on concepts stored in a knowledge base. Khushraj et al. [12] use web service descriptions to derive UI descriptions based on a UI ontology, adding UI related information to the concept descriptions. In analogy with task based approaches, Gaulke et al. [9] use a profiled domain model enriched with UI related data to describe a UI and associate it with an ontology driven task model which models the interaction. ActiveRaUL [21] combines an UIDL with a data-centric approach and thus contributes to the generation of UIs for arbitrary ontologies. They derive a hierarchical presentation of an ontology and map it to an – yet simple – ontology based on the UI description.

In view of our requirements (cf. Sect. 2.2) it can be stated that the aforementioned approaches are restricted mainly to the definition of UIs and dialog flows. They do not contain concepts to associate (map) the collected data to results of arbitrary ontology instances that might have a different structure as in the UI. Additionally, they are restricted to the environments where a reasoner is available at runtime to infer the dynamic behavior of UIs based on already entered data (e.g., showing/hiding UI parts, as in [15]). This is a drawback for environments like web-based, single-page applications, where a reasoner is not available at runtime. Finally, UIs and task models are mostly modeled using a large amount of artifacts, thus, they can hardly be used to generate target-system independent variants that differ in content, depending on the context of use [4].

6   Conclusion and Future Work

In this paper, we proposed a concept for generic UIs that enables users requesting complex products within DMS in the IoE. In order to express their demand for a particular complex product, in a way, that is interpretable by the DMS, users need flexible UIs that allow context-focused data collection related to the complexity of the user's demand.

In order to identify the overall objectives, which need to be supported by the generic UIs concept, we first looked at the prerequisites and objectives derived from the DMS as the application context. Afterwards, we operationalized these objectives into the requirements and used them as the rationale to conceptualize the overall solution as well as to elaborate on existing approaches and initiatives related to the presented work. Thereafter, and in the view of these requirements, we implemented an initial demonstration of the proposed generic UIs concept, using an exemplary use case.

As the demonstrator shows, it is basically possible to dynamically generate UIs for complex products where UIs may span different domains, and can be combined to build a unified interface for the users. It also underlines the advantage of using User Interface Ontologies as separate descriptions, so that they can be independently shared and modified. However, the presented demonstrator does not cover all functionality needed to combine different demands; currently it composes UIs for product/service components as separate, self-relying parts ignoring possible relations between them. Furthermore, it does not consider a wider user-related context that components and their UIs may share and react to.

In our future work, we will concentrate on these two areas of improvements, as well as, on the extensive prototypical implementation to conduct a sophisticated analysis of the strengths and weaknesses of the proposed concept.

References

1. Abrams, M., Phanouriou, C., Batongbacal, A.L., Williams, S.M., Shuster, J.E.: UIML: an appliance-independent XML user interface language. In: WWW 1999 Proceedings of the Eighth International Conference on World Wide Web, pp. 1695–1708 (1999)
2. Akerlof, G.A.: The market for lemons: quality uncertainty and the market mechanism. Q. J. Econ. **84**, 488–500 (1970)
3. Cisco: The internet of everything for cities (2013). http://www.cisco.com/web/about/ac79/docs/ps/motm/IoE-Smart-City_PoV.pdf
4. Coutaz, J.: User interface plasticity: model driven engineering to the limit! In: EICS 2010 Proceedings of the 2nd ACM SIGCHI Symposium on Engineering Interactive Computing Systems, No. Eics, pp. 1–8 (2010)

5. Dubinko, M., Klotz, L., Merrik, R., Raman, T.: XForms 1.0 W3C Recommendation (2003). http://www.w3.org/TR/xforms
6. El Sawy, O.A., Pereira, F.: Business Modelling in the Dynamic Digital Space: An Ecosystem Approach. Springer, Heidelberg (2013)
7. Fedortsova, I., Brown, G.: JavaFX Mastering FXML, Release 8 (2014). http://docs.oracle.com/javase/8/javafx/fxml-tutorial/preface.htm
8. García-Gómez, S., Jimenez-Ganan, M., Taher, Y., Momm, C., Junker, F., Biro, J., Menychtas, A., Andrikopoulos, V., Strauch, S.: Challenges for the comprehensive management of cloud services in a paas framework. Scalable Comput. Pract. Exp. **13**(3), 201–213 (2012)
9. Gaulke, W., Ziegler, J.: Using profiled ontologies to leverage model driven user interface generation. In: Proceedings of the 7th ACM SIGCHI Symposium on Engineering Interactive Computing Systems - EICS 2015, pp. 254–259 (2015)
10. Hitz, M.: mimesis: Ein datenzentrierter Ansatz zur Modellierung von Varianten für Interview-Anwendungen. In: Nissen, V., Stelzer, D., Straßburger, S., Fischer, D. (eds.) Proceedings - Multikonferenz Wirtschaftsinformatik (MKWI) 2016, vol. 4, pp. 1155–1165 (2016)
11. Hitz, M., Kessel, T.: mimesis: a data-centric approach for generating user interfaces for interview applications using ontologies. Unpublished - in consideration (2016)
12. Khushraj, D., Lassila, O.: Ontological approach to generating personalized user interfaces for web services. In: Gil, Y., Motta, E., Benjamins, V.R., Musen, M.A. (eds.) ISWC 2005. LNCS, vol. 3729, pp. 916–927. Springer, Heidelberg (2005)
13. Kleedorfer, F., Busch, C.M.: Beyond data: building a web of needs. In: Proceedings of the WWW 2013 Workshop on Linked Data on the Web (2013)
14. Kleedorfer, F., Busch, C.M., Pichler, C., Huemer, C.: The case for the web of needs. In: 2014 IEEE 16th Conference on Business Informatics (CBI), vol. 1, pp. 94–101. IEEE (2014)
15. Liu, B., Chen, H., He, W.: Deriving user interface from ontologies: a model-based approach. In: Proceedings of the International Conference on Tools with Artificial Intelligence, ICTAI 2005, pp. 254–259 (2005)
16. Pascalau, E.: Mashups: behavior in Context(s). In: Proceedings of 7th Workshop on Knowledge Engineering and Software Engineering (KESE7) (2011)
17. Paterno, F., Santoro, C., Spano, L.D.: Maria: a universal, declarative, multiple abstraction-level language for service-oriented applications in ubiquitous environment. ACM Trans. Comput. Hum. Interact. **16**(4), Article ID 19, 30 pages (2009)
18. Pfisterer, D., Radonjic-Simic, M., Reichwald, J.: Business model design and architecture for the internet of everything. J. Sens. Actuator Netw. **5**(2), 7 (2016)
19. Popp, R., Falb, J., Arnautovic, E., Kaindl, H., Kavaldjian, S., Ertl, D., Horacek, H., Bogdan, C.: Automatic generation of the behavior of a user interface from a high-level discourse model. In: Proceedings of the 42nd Annual Hawaii International Conference on System Sciences, HICSS (2009)
20. Raneburger, D., Kaindl, H., Popp, R., Šajatovi, V., Armbruster, A.: A process for facilitating interaction design through automated GUI generation. In: SAC 2014 Proceedings of the 29th Annual ACM Symposium on Applied Computing, pp. 1324–1330. ACM, New York (2014)
21. Sahar, A., Armin, B., Shepherd, H., Lexing, L.: ActiveRaUL: automatically generated web interfaces for creating RDF data 0, In: Proceedings of 12th International Semantic Web Conference ISWC 2013, Vol. 1035, pp. 117–120 (2013)
22. Searls, D.: The Intention Economy: When Customers Take Charge. Harvard Business Press, Massachusetts (2013)
23. W3C: Rdf 1.1 turtle (2014). http://www.w3.org/TR/turtle/
24. W3C: Resource description framework (rdf) (2015). http://www.w3.org/RDF/

Diagnosis of Complex Active Systems with Uncertain Temporal Observations

Gianfranco Lamperti[1(✉)] and Xiangfu Zhao[2]

[1] Department of Information Engineering, University of Brescia, Brescia, Italy
gianfranco.lamperti@unibs.it
[2] College of Mathematics, Physics and Information Engineering,
Zhejiang Normal University, Jinhua, China

Abstract. Complex active systems have been proposed as a formalism for modeling real dynamic systems that are organized in a hierarchy of behavioral abstractions. As such, they constitute a conceptual evolution of active systems, a class of discrete-event systems introduced into the literature two decades ago. A complex active system is a hierarchy of active systems, each one characterized by its own behavior expressed by the interaction of several communicating automata. The interaction between active systems within the hierarchy is based on special events, which are generated when specific behavioral patterns occur. Recently, the task of diagnosis of complex active systems has been studied, with an efficient diagnosis technique being proposed. However, the observation of the system is assumed to be linear and certain, which turns out to be an over-assumption in real, large, and distributed systems. This paper extends diagnosis of complex active systems to cope with uncertain temporal observations. An uncertain temporal observation is a DAG where nodes are marked by candidate labels (logical uncertainty), whereas arcs denote partial temporal ordering between nodes (temporal uncertainty). By means of indexing techniques, despite the uncertainty of temporal observations, the intrinsic efficiency of the diagnosis task is retained in both time and space.

Keywords: Complex systems · Discrete-event systems · Fault diagnosis · Communicating automata · Uncertainty

1 Introduction

Often, dynamic systems can be modeled as discrete-event systems [4]. Seminal works on diagnosis of discrete-event systems (DES's) maximize offline preprocessing in order to generate an efficient online *diagnoser* [20,21]. However, this requires generating the global DES model, which is bound to be impractical for large and distributed systems.

Other approaches, like diagnosis of active systems (AS's) [1,13,15], avoid generating the global model of the system by reconstructing online only the

F. Buccafurri et al. (Eds.): CD-ARES 2016, LNCS 9817, pp. 45–62, 2016.
DOI: 10.1007/978-3-319-45507-5_4

behavior which is consistent with the observation. Still, in the worst case, the number of behavior states is exponential with the number of components. This is why efficient techniques need to be designed in order to mitigate the explosion of the reconstructed behavior.

This paper deals with diagnosis of a class of DES's called *complex active systems* (*CAS's*), based on a class of observations called *uncertain temporal observations*.

In the literature, the term *complex system* is used to encompass a research approach to problems in a variety of disciplines [2,6–8,10,19,22]. Generally speaking, a complex system is a group or organization which is made up of many interacting components. In a complex system, interactions between components lead to an *emergent behavior*, which is unpredictable from a knowledge of the behavior of the individual components only. Inspired by complex systems in nature and society, complexity has been injected into the modeling and diagnosis of active systems [13], a special class of discrete-event systems [4], which are modeled as networks of interacting components, where the behavior of each component is described by a communicating automaton [3]. To this end, the notion of context-sensitive diagnosis was first introduced in [14] and then extended in [18], for active systems that are organized within abstraction hierarchies, so that candidate diagnoses can be generated at different abstraction levels. Active systems have been equipped with behavior stratification [16,17], where different networks of components are accommodated within a hierarchy. This resembles emergent behavior that arises from the vertical interaction of a network with superior levels based on pattern events. Pattern events occur when a network performs strings of component transitions matching patterns which are specific to the application domain. Complex patterns are also considered in research on cognitive systems [5,23,24].

Recently, diagnosis of complex active systems has been addressed, with an efficient diagnosis technique being proposed [11]. However, the observation of the system is assumed to be linear and certain, which turns out to be an over-assumption in real, large, and distributed systems. This paper extends diagnosis of complex active systems to cope with uncertainty in temporal observations. An uncertain temporal observation is a DAG where nodes are marked by candidate labels, whereas arcs denote partial temporal ordering, as proposed in [12] for diagnosis of (plain) active systems. In virtue of specific indexing techniques, the efficiency of the diagnosis task introduced in [11] is kept in both time and space when uncertain temporal observations come into play.

2   Active Systems

An active system A is a network of components, each one being defined by a *topological model* and a *behavioral model*. The topological model embodies a set of *input terminals* and a set of *output terminals*. The *behavioral model* is a communicating automaton where each state transition is triggered by an event ready at one input terminal. When triggered, the transition may generate

Fig. 1. Component models *sensor* (left) and *breaker* (right)

Fig. 2. Active-system model *Protection* (left) and its instantiation into active system P (right)

events at some output terminals. Since each output terminal of a component c is connected with the input terminal of another component c', a transition in c may cause the triggering of a transition in c'. More generally, since components in A form a network, one single transition in one component may result in a *reaction* of A involving several (possibly all) components in A.

Example 1. Displayed in Fig. 1 are the topological models (top) and behavioral models (bottom) of *sensor* and *breaker*. The connection of output terminal O of *sensor* with input terminal I of *breaker* gives rise to an active-system model, namely *Protection*, outlined on the left-hand side of Fig. 2. An active system P is obtained as an instantiation of *Protection* model, which requires the instantiations of *sensor* and *breaker* component models by relevant components, namely s and b, respectively, as outlined in the right-hand side of Fig. 2. We assume that active system P is designed to protect one side of a power transmission line from short circuits. To this end, sensor s detects variation in voltage, possibly commanding breaker b to either open or close. Transitions in behavioral models are detailed below, where event e at terminal t is written $e(t)$:

- *(Sensor)* s_1 detects low voltage and outputs $op(O)$; s_2 detects normal voltage and outputs $cl(O)$; s_3 detects low voltage, yet outputs $cl(O)$; s_4 detects normal voltage, yet outputs $op(O)$;
- *(Breaker)* b_1 consumes $op(I)$ and opens; b_2 consumes $cl(I)$ and closes; b_3 consumes $op(I)$, yet keeps being closed; b_4 consumes $cl(I)$, yet keeps being closed; b_5 consumes $cl(I)$; b_6 consumes $op(I)$.

An active system (AS) A can be either *quiescent* or *reacting*. If quiescent, no event occurs and, consequently, no transition is performed. A becomes reacting when an external event occurs, which can be consumed by a component in A. When reacting, the occurrence of a component transition moves A to a new state, with each state being a pair $(\mathbb{S}, \mathbb{E})$, where $\mathbb{S} = (s_1, \dots, s_n)$ is the array of the states of components in A, whereas $\mathbb{E} = (e_1, \ldots, e_m)$ is the array of events within links in A.[1] We assume that, sooner or later, A becomes quiescent anew.

The sequence of component transitions moving A from the initial (quiescent) state to the final (quiescent) state is the *trajectory* of A. Given the initial state a_0 of A, the graph embodying all possible trajectories of A, rooted in a_0, is the *behavior space* of A, written $Bsp(A)$. A trajectory $h = [t_1(c_1), t_2(c_2), \ldots, t_q(c_q)]$ in $Bsp(A)$, from initial state a_0 to final state a_q, can be represented as:

$$a_0 \xrightarrow{t_1(c_1)} a_1 \xrightarrow{t_2(c_2)} a_2 \ldots \xrightarrow{t_{q-1}(c_{q-1})} a_{q-1} \xrightarrow{t_q(c_q)} a_q$$

where intermediate states $a_1, a_2, \ldots, a_{q-1}$ of A are indicated.

3   Complex Active Systems

A complex active system $\mathcal{A}$ is a hierarchy of interacting active systems $A_1, \ldots, A_k$. In order to make AS's interact with one another, four actions are required for each AS A:

1. Definition of a set of *input terminals*, each one being connected with an input terminal of a component in A;
2. Definition of a set of *output terminals*;
3. Specification of a set of *patterns*, with each pattern being a pair $(p(\omega), r)$, where p is a *pattern event*, ω an output terminal of A, and r a regular expression whose alphabet is a set of component transitions in A.[2]
4. Connection of each output terminal of A with an input terminal of another AS A'.

Given a pattern $(p(\omega), r)$, pattern event p is generated at output terminal ω of A when a subsequence of the trajectory of A matches regular expression r. Since there is a link from output terminal ω of A to an input terminal of A', which is in its turn connected with an input terminal of a component c' of A', it follows that the occurrence of p is bound to trigger a transition of c'. This way, the behavior of A is doomed to influence (although not completely determine) the behavior of A'.

Like an active system, a complex active system $\mathcal{A}$ can be either quiescent or reacting. $\mathcal{A}$ is quiescent when all AS's in $\mathcal{A}$ are quiescent and all generated pattern events (if any) have been consumed. When reacting, the occurrence of an AS transition moves $\mathcal{A}$ to a new state. Each state of $\mathcal{A}$ is a triple $(\mathbb{A}, \mathbb{E}, \mathbb{P})$, where:

---

[1] We assume that at most one event can be stored in a link. If the link is empty (no stored event), the corresponding value in array $\mathbb{E}$ is denoted ε (*empty* event).

[2] We assume the classical operators for regular expressions, namely concatenation, disjunction, optionality, and repetition. If necessary, additional more specific operators can be involved.

- $\mathbb{A} = (a_1, \ldots, a_n)$ is the array of the states of AS's in $\mathcal{A}$, namely $A_1, \ldots, A_n$;
- $\mathbb{E} = (e_1, \ldots, e_m)$ is the array of pattern events within links between AS's in $\mathcal{A}$;
- $\mathbb{P} = (p_1, \ldots, p_k)$ is the array of states of pattern-event recognizers.[3]

The sequence of AS transitions moving $\mathcal{A}$ from the initial (quiescent) state to the final (quiescent) state is the *trajectory* of $\mathcal{A}$. Given the initial state α_0 of $\mathcal{A}$, the graph embodying all possible trajectories of $\mathcal{A}$, rooted in α_0, is the *behavior space* of $\mathcal{A}$, written $Bsp(\mathcal{A})$. A trajectory $h = [t_1(A_1), t_2(A_2), \ldots, t_q(A_{q-1}), t_q(A_q)]$ in $Bsp(\mathcal{A})$, from initial state α_0 to final state α_q, can be represented as:

$$\alpha_0 \xrightarrow{t_1(A_1)} \alpha_1 \xrightarrow{t_2(A_2)} \alpha_2 \ldots \xrightarrow{t_{q-1}(A_{q-1})} \alpha_{q-1} \xrightarrow{t_q(A_q)} \alpha_q$$

where intermediate states $\alpha_1, \alpha_2, \ldots, \alpha_{q-1}$ of $\mathcal{A}$ are indicated.

Example 2. Displayed in Fig. 3 is a power transmission line. Each side of the line is protected from short circuits by two *breakers*, namely b and r on the left, and b' and r' on the right. Both b and b' (the primary breakers) are connected to a *sensor* of voltage. If a short circuit (for instance, a lightning) strikes the line, then each sensor will detect the lowering of the voltage and command the associated breaker to open. If both breakers open, then the line will be isolated, thereby causing the short circuit to vanish. If so, the two breakers are commanded to close in order to restore the line.

Fig. 3. Protected power transmission line

However, faulty behavior may occur: either the sensor does not command the breaker to open or the breaker does not open. Such misbehavior is detected by a *monitor* (one for each side of the line). For example, similarly to the sensor, the monitor on the left-hand side commands the recovery breaker r to open. In doing so, it also informs the monitor on the right-hand side to perform the same action on recovery breaker r'. For safety reasons, once opened, recovery breakers cannot be closed again, thereby leaving the line isolated.

The protected line can be modeled as the CAS outlined in Fig. 4, called $\mathcal{L}$, which is composed of four AS's, namely: P (the protection hardware on the left, including sensor s and breaker b), P' (the protection hardware on the right, including sensor s' and breaker b'), M (the monitoring apparatus, including monitors m and m', and recovery breakers r and r'), and L (including line l). Arrows within AS's denote links between components. For instance, P includes a link from s to b, meaning that an event generated by s can be consumed by b.

---

[3] As detailed in Sect. 6, the need for pattern matching of (possibly overlapping) pattern events against relevant regular expressions requires the (offline) generation of specific recognizers, these being DFA's named *pattern spaces*.

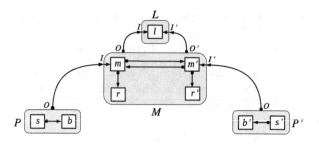

Fig. 4. CAS $\mathcal{L}$ modeling the protected power transmission line displayed in Fig. 3

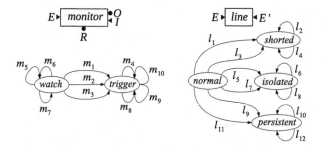

Fig. 5. Component models *monitor* (left) and *line* (right)

For the sake of simplicity, we assume that, when an event is already present in a link, no transition generating a new event on the same link can be triggered. Links between m and m' allow monitors to communicate to one another. Instead, arrows between AS's denote links aimed at conveying pattern events. For instance, the link from P to M makes pattern events (occurring in P) available to m in M.

Models *monitor* and *line* are displayed in Fig. 5. As such, *monitor* involves input terminals E and I, and output terminals O and R. Terminal E is entered by the link exiting the protection hardware (either P or P'), conveying the pattern events occurring in the latter. R is linked with the recovery breaker, while O and I are linked with the other monitor. Displayed under the topological models are the behavioral models. Transitions for *monitor* and *line* are detailed below (where pattern events are in bold).

- (*Monitor*) m_1 consumes $\mathbf{nd}(E)$ and outputs $op(R)$ and $rc(O)$; m_2 consumes $\mathbf{nd}(E)$ and outputs $op(R)$ only; m_3 consumes $rc(I)$ and outputs $op(R)$; m_4 consumes $\mathbf{nd}(E)$; m_5 consumes $\mathbf{di}(E)$; m_6 consumes $\mathbf{co}(E)$; m_7 consumes $\mathbf{nc}(E)$; m_8 consumes $\mathbf{di}(E)$; m_9 consumes $\mathbf{co}(E)$; m_{10} consumes $\mathbf{nc}(E)$.
- (*Line*) l_1, l_2: consume $\mathbf{ni}(E)$; l_3, l_4: consume $\mathbf{ni}'(E')$; l_5, l_6: consume $\mathbf{nr}(E)$; l_7, l_8: consume $\mathbf{nr}'(E')$; l_9, l_{10}: consume $\mathbf{ps}'(E')$; l_{11}, l_{12}: consume $\mathbf{ps}(E')$.

Pattern events have the following meaning. $\mathbf{di}$: the protection hardware disconnects the side of the line; $\mathbf{co}$: the protection hardware connects the side of the line; **nd**: the protection hardware fails to disconnect the side of the line; **nc**: the protection hardware fails to connect the side of the line; **nr, nr'**: the left/right side of the line cannot be reconnected; **ni, ni'**: the left/right side of the line cannot be isolated; **ps', ps**: the short circuit persists on the left/right side of the line.

Patterns for P, P', and L are listed in Table 1. For example, pattern event **nd** occurs either when $s_3(s)$ (the sensor fails to open the breaker) or $s_1(s)\, b_3(b)$ (the sensor commands the breaker to open, yet the breaker fails to open). For each pattern $(p(\omega), r)$ in Table 1, the alphabet of r is defined as follows. For P and P', the alphabet of r is the whole set of transitions of the involved components (breaker and sensor). For M, the alphabet equals the set of transitions involved in r only.

4   Uncertain Temporal Observations

During its trajectory, a CAS $\mathcal{A}$, embodying AS's $A_1, \ldots, A_k$, generates a sequence of observable labels, called the *trace* of the trajectory. Observable labels are generated for observable transitions only. In this respect, the trace is the projection of the trajectory on the labels associated with observable component transitions. Still, what is perceived by the observer, and given in input to the diagnosis engine, is a *relaxation* of the trace called an *uncertain temporal observation*. An uncertain temporal observation is an array $(\mathcal{O}_1, \ldots, \mathcal{O}_k)$, where $\mathcal{O}_i$, $i \in [1 .. k]$, is the uncertain temporal observation of A_i. The relaxation of a trace $\mathcal{T} = [\ell_1, \ldots, \ell_m]$ into $\mathcal{O} = (\mathcal{O}_1, \ldots, \mathcal{O}_k)$ is obtained as follows:

1. $\mathcal{T}$ is relaxed into an array $\mathcal{T}^* = (\mathcal{T}_1, \ldots, \mathcal{T}_k)$ of sequences, with each $\mathcal{T}_i$, $i \in [1 .. k]$, being the subsequence of $\mathcal{T}$ involving the labels of $\mathcal{T}$ which are associated with transitions of components in A_i;
2. Each $\mathcal{T}_i = [\ell_1^i, \ldots, \ell_{m_i}^i]$ in $\mathcal{T}^*$ is relaxed into a sequence $\mathcal{L}_i = [S_1^i, \ldots, S_{m_i}^i]$, where S_j^i, $j \in [1 .. m_i]$, is a set of labels including ℓ_j^i, along with possibly additional *spurious* labels (possibly including the null ε label), thereby obtaining $\mathcal{T}_S^* = [\mathcal{L}_1, \ldots, \mathcal{L}_k]$;
3. Additional *spurious* sets can be inserted into each $\mathcal{L}_i$ in $\mathcal{T}_S^*$, with each spurious set involving at least two labels, one of which is necessarily ε, thereby obtaining $\mathcal{T}_\varepsilon^* = [\mathcal{L}_1', \ldots, \mathcal{L}_k']$;
4. Each $\mathcal{L}_i'$ in $\mathcal{T}_\varepsilon^*$ is relaxed into a DAG $\mathcal{O}_i$, where sets in $\mathcal{L}_i'$ are the nodes of $\mathcal{O}_i$, while an arc $S_p^i \to S_q^i$ is in $\mathcal{O}_i$ only if S_p^i precedes S_q^i in $\mathcal{L}_i'$, thereby obtaining the uncertain temporal observation $\mathcal{O} = (\mathcal{O}_1, \ldots, \mathcal{O}_k)$.

The mode in which a trace is relaxed into an uncertain temporal observation is not under the control of the observer; therefore, the original trace generated by the CAS is, generally speaking, unknown to the observer.

Example 3. Let $\mathcal{T} = [awk, awk', trg, opb', opr]$ be the trace of CAS $\mathcal{L}$ (displayed in Fig. 4). Based on the steps above, a relaxation of $\mathcal{T}$ into $\mathcal{O}$ can be obtained as follows:

Table 1. Specification of patterns by regular expressions

Active system	Pattern event $p(\omega)$	Regular expression
P	$\mathbf{di}(O)$	$b_1(b)$
	$\mathbf{co}(O)$	$b_2(b)$
	$\mathbf{nd}(O)$	$s_3(s) \mid s_1(s)\,b_3(b)$
	$\mathbf{nc}(O)$	$s_4(s) \mid s_2(s)\,b_4(b)$
P'	$\mathbf{di'}(O)$	$b_1(b')$
	$\mathbf{co'}(O)$	$b_2(b')$
	$\mathbf{nd'}(O)$	$s_3(s') \mid s_1(s')\,b_3(b')$
	$\mathbf{nc'}(O)$	$s_4(s') \mid s_2(s')\,b_4(b')$
M	$\mathbf{nr}(O)$	$m_7(m) \mid m_{10}(m) \mid b_1(r)$
	$\mathbf{ni}(O)$	$(m_1(m) \mid m_2(m) \mid m_4(m))\,b_3(r) \mid b_3(r)\,m_4(m)$
	$\mathbf{ps'}(O)$	$m_6(m)\,m_5(m)$
	$\mathbf{nr'}(O')$	$m_7(m') \mid m_{10}(m') \mid b_1(r')$
	$\mathbf{ni'}(O')$	$(m_1(m') \mid m_2(m') \mid m_4(m'))\,b_3(r') \mid b_3(r')\,m_4(m')$
	$\mathbf{ps}(O')$	$m_6(m')\,m_5(m')$

1. $\mathcal{T}^* = (\ [awk]\ ,\ [awk',\ opb']\ ,\ [trg,\ opr]\ ,\ [\,]\ )$;
2. $\mathcal{T}_S^* = ([\{awk,\ alr\}], [\{awk',\varepsilon\}, \{opb'\}], [\{trg,\ opr\}, \{opr\}], [\,])$;
3. $\mathcal{T}_\varepsilon^* = ([\{awk,\ alr\}, \{clb,\varepsilon\}], [\{awk',\varepsilon\}, \{clb',\varepsilon\}, \{opb'\}], [\{trg,\ opr\}, \{opr\}], [\,])$;
4. $\mathcal{O} = (\mathcal{O}_P, \mathcal{O}_{P'}, \mathcal{O}_M, \mathcal{O}_L)$, where the DAG's representing $\mathcal{O}_P$, $\mathcal{O}_{P'}$, and $\mathcal{O}_M$ are outlined on the left-hand side of Fig. 6, whereas $\mathcal{O}_L$ is empty.

Within a DAG $\mathcal{O}_A$ representing the uncertain temporal observation of an AS A, the notion of *precedence* '$\prec$' between two nodes is used. This is defined as the smallest relation satisfying the following two conditions (where n, n', and n'' denote nodes, while $n \to n'$ denotes an arc from n to n'): (1) if $n \to n'$ is an arc then $n \prec n'$; (2) if $n \prec n'$ and $n' \prec n''$ then $n \prec n''$.

The *extension* of a node n in $\mathcal{O}_A$, denoted $\|n\|$, is the set of labels associated with n. A *candidate trace* $\mathcal{T}_c$ of $\mathcal{O}_A$ having set N_A of nodes, is a sequence of labels so defined:

$$\mathcal{T}_c = [\ell \mid \ell \in \|n\|, n \in N_A] \tag{1}$$

where nodes n are chosen based on the partial order defined by arcs, while ε labels are removed. The *extension* of $\mathcal{O}_A$ is the set of candidate traces of $\mathcal{O}_A$, written $\|\mathcal{O}_A\|$.

Likewise, the notion of extension can be defined for an uncertain temporal observation $\mathcal{O} = (\mathcal{O}_1, \ldots, \mathcal{O}_k)$ as follows:

$$\|\mathcal{O}\| = \{\ (\mathcal{T}_1, \ldots, \mathcal{T}_k) \mid \forall i \in [1 .. k], \mathcal{T}_i \in \|\mathcal{O}_i\|\ \}. \tag{2}$$

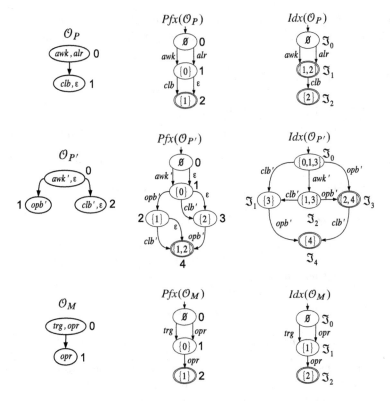

Fig. 6. Uncertain temporal observations (left), prefix spaces (center), and index spaces (right)

It is possible to prove that, for each $\mathcal{T}_i$ in array $\mathcal{T}^*$, $i \in [1 .. k]$, resulting from the first relaxation step of $\mathcal{T}$, we have $\mathcal{T}_i \in \|\mathcal{O}_i\|$. Hence, in virtue of Eq. (2), $\mathcal{T}^* \in \|\mathcal{O}\|$.

Example 4. With reference to Example 3 and the uncertain temporal observations $\mathcal{O}_P$, $\mathcal{O}_{P'}$, and $\mathcal{O}_M$ displayed on the left-hand side of Fig. 6, we have:

- $\|\mathcal{O}_P\| = \{[awk, clb],\ [awk]\ , [alr, clb], [alr]\}$,
- $\|\mathcal{O}_{P'}\| = \{[awk', opb', clb'],\ [awk', opb']\ , [opb', clb'], [opb'], [awk', clb', opb'], [clb', opb']\}$,
- $\|\mathcal{O}_M\| = \{\ [trg, opr]\ , [opr, opr]\}$,

where shadowed candidate traces equal the corresponding traces in $\mathcal{T}^*$.

In order to match the behavior of the CAS reconstructed by the diagnosis engine against the uncertain temporal observation $\mathcal{O} = (\mathcal{O}_1, \ldots, \mathcal{O}_k)$, each $\mathcal{O}_i$, $i \in [1 .. k]$, needs to be somehow indexed. To this end and for efficiency reasons, for each $\mathcal{O}_i$, an *index space* of $\mathcal{O}_i$, namely $Idx(\mathcal{O}_i)$ is generated. This is a deterministic finite automaton (DFA) obtained by determinization of a nondeterministic finite automaton (NFA) called the *prefix space* of $\mathcal{O}_i$, namely $Pfx(\mathcal{O}_i)$.

To define $Pfx(\mathcal{O}_i)$, we need to define a prefix of $\mathcal{O}_i$ and the index of a prefix. A *prefix* of $\mathcal{O}_i$ with set of nodes N_i, is a subset of N_i defined inductively as follows:

1. The empty set $\emptyset$ is a prefix of $\mathcal{O}_i$;
2. If p is a prefix of $\mathcal{O}_i$ and $n' \in N_i - p$ where $\forall n \in N_i$ such that $n \prec n'$ we have $n \in p$, then $p \cup \{n'\}$ is a prefix of $\mathcal{O}_i$.

The *index* of a prefix p, denoted $I(p)$, is the subset of p defined as follows:

$$I(p) = \{ n \mid n \in p, \forall n', n' \prec n \, (n' \in p), \forall n'', n \prec n'' \, (n'' \notin p) \}. \tag{3}$$

Given an index I of p, the set of nodes in p is denoted by I^{-1}. An index I is *final* when $I^{-1} = N_i$.

The *prefix space* of $\mathcal{O}_i$ is the NFA $Pfx(\mathcal{O}_i) = (\Sigma, S, \tau, s_0, S_f)$, where:

- Σ is the alphabet, which is composed of the labels in $\mathcal{O}_i$;
- S is the set of states, with each state being the index of a prefix of $\mathcal{O}_i$;
- $s_0 = \emptyset$ is the initial state;
- S_f is the singleton $\{s_f\}$, where $s_f \in S$, $I^{-1}(s_f) = N_i$;
- $\tau : S \times \Sigma \mapsto 2^S$ is the nondeterministic transition function, where $s \xrightarrow{\ell} s' \in \tau$ iff:

$$s' = I\,(s \cup \{n\})\,, \ell \in \|n\|, n \in N_i - s, \forall\, n' \to n \in \mathcal{O}_i \,(n' \in s)\,. \tag{4}$$

Example 5. Consider the uncertain temporal observations $\mathcal{O}_P$, $\mathcal{O}_{P'}$, and $\mathcal{O}_M$ displayed on the left-hand side of Fig. 6. The corresponding prefix spaces $Pfx(\mathcal{O}_P)$, $Pfx(\mathcal{O}_{P'})$, and $Pfx(\mathcal{O}_M)$ are outlined in the center, with states being renamed by numbers. Index spaces $Idx(\mathcal{O}_P)$, $Idx(\mathcal{O}_{P'})$, and $Idx(\mathcal{O}_M)$ are shown on the right-hand side of the figure, with states being renamed by symbols $\Im_i$, $i \in [0\,..\,4]$.

5   Problem Formulation

Once a real system is modeled as a CAS $\mathcal{A}$ composed of AS's $A_1, \ldots, A_k$, it can be diagnosed based on the uncertain temporal observation $\mathcal{O} = (\mathcal{O}_1, \ldots, \mathcal{O}_k)$. In this paper we focus on a posteriori diagnosis. That is, we assume that $\mathcal{O}$ is relevant to a complete trajectory of $\mathcal{A}$, which moves $\mathcal{A}$ from the known initial (quiescent) state to an unknown final (quiescent) state.

In order to match $\mathcal{O}$ against the behavior of $\mathcal{A}$ it is essential to know which are the observable transitions of components and their associated observable labels. This is specified by a *viewer* of $\mathcal{A}$, namely $\mathcal{V} = (\mathcal{V}_1, \ldots, \mathcal{V}_k)$, which is the array of the *local viewers* of the AS's, with each local viewer $\mathcal{V}_i$, $i \in [1\,..\,k]$, being a set of pairs (t, ℓ), where t is an observable transition of a component in A_i and ℓ an observable label.

The *projection* of a trajectory h of $\mathcal{A}$ on viewer $\mathcal{V} = (\mathcal{V}_1, \ldots, \mathcal{V}_k)$ is the array of AS traces defined as follows:

$$h_{[\mathcal{V}]} = (\mathcal{T}_1, \ldots, \mathcal{T}_k), \forall i \in [1\,..\,k] \, (\mathcal{T}_i = [\ell \mid t(c) \in h, c \in A_i, (t(c), \ell) \in \mathcal{V}_i])\,. \tag{5}$$

We say that trajectory h is *consistent* with $\mathcal{O}$ when $h_{[\mathcal{V}]} \in \|\mathcal{O}\|$. Generally speaking, $\mathcal{O}$ is not sufficient to identify the actual trajectory. Rather, several (possibly an infinite number of) *candidate trajectories* of $\mathcal{A}$ are possibly consistent with $\mathcal{O}$.

Similarly to a local viewer which specifies observable transitions, faulty transitions are specified by a *local ruler*, a set of pairs (t, f), where t is a component *faulty transition* and f a *fault*. The array of all local rulers $\mathcal{R}_i$, one for each A_i in $\mathcal{A}$, gives rise to the *ruler* of $\mathcal{A}$, namely $\mathcal{R} = (\mathcal{R}_1, \ldots, \mathcal{R}_k)$.

For each candidate trajectory h of $\mathcal{A}$, there is a *candidate diagnosis* of $\mathcal{A}$, denoted $h_{[\mathcal{R}]}$, which is the set of faults associated with the faulty transitions within the trajectory:

$$h_{[\mathcal{R}]} = \{f \mid t(c) \in h, c \in A_i, (t(c), f) \in \mathcal{R}_i\}. \tag{6}$$

A *diagnosis problem* for $\mathcal{A}$ is a quadruple:

$$\wp(\mathcal{A}) = (\alpha_0, \mathcal{V}, \mathcal{O}, \mathcal{R}) \tag{7}$$

where α_0 is the initial state of $\mathcal{A}$, $\mathcal{V}$ a viewer of $\mathcal{A}$, $\mathcal{O}$ the uncertain temporal observation of $\mathcal{A}$, and $\mathcal{R}$ a ruler of $\mathcal{A}$.

The *solution* of $\wp(\mathcal{A})$, namely $\Delta(\wp(\mathcal{A}))$, is the set of candidate diagnoses δ associated with the candidate traces of $\mathcal{A}$ that are consistent with $\mathcal{O}$:

$$\Delta(\wp(\mathcal{A})) = \{\delta \mid \delta = h_{[\mathcal{R}]}, h \in Bsp(\mathcal{A}), h_{[\mathcal{V}]} \in \|\mathcal{O}\|\}. \tag{8}$$

However, the diagnosis engine is not expected to generate the solution of a diagnosis problem based on Eq. (8). In fact, Eq. (8) relies on $Bsp(\mathcal{A})$, the behavior space of $\mathcal{A}$, whose generation is, generally speaking, practically infeasible. Still, the set of candidate diagnoses generated by the diagnosis engine shall equal $\Delta(\wp(\mathcal{A}))$. In other words, the diagnosis technique shall be not only efficient but also sound and complete.

Example 6. With reference to Example 2, we define a diagnosis problem for $\mathcal{L}$ as:

$$\wp(\mathcal{L}) = (\lambda_0, \mathcal{V}, \mathcal{O}, \mathcal{R}) \tag{9}$$

where:

- In initial state λ_0, breakers are *closed*, sensors are *idle*, and monitors are *watch* (see component models in Figs. 1 and 5);
- $\mathcal{V} = (\mathcal{V}_P, \mathcal{V}_{P'}, \mathcal{V}_M, \mathcal{V}_L)$, where $\mathcal{V}_P = \{(b_1(b), opb), (b_2(b), clb), (b_5(b), alr), (b_6(b), alr), (s_1(s), awk), (s_2(s), ide), (s_3(s), awk), (s_4(s), ide)\}$, $\mathcal{V}_{P'} = \{(b_1(b'), opb'), (b_2(b'), clb'), (b_5(b'), alr'), (b_6(b'), alr'), (s_1(s'), awk'), (s_2(s'), ide'), (s_3(s'), awk'), (s_4(s'), ide')\}$, $\mathcal{V}_M = \{(m_1(m), trg), (m_2(m), trg), (m_3(m), trg), (b_1(r), opr), (b_2(r), clr), (m_1(m'), trg'), (m_2(m'), trg'), (m_3(m'), trg'), (b_1(r'), opr'), (b_2(r'), clr')\}$, and $\mathcal{V}_L = \emptyset$ (that is, L is unobservable);

- $\mathcal{O} = (\mathcal{O}_P, \mathcal{O}_{P'}, \mathcal{O}_M, \mathcal{O}_L)$, where $\mathcal{O}_P$, $\mathcal{O}_{P'}$, and $\mathcal{O}_M$ are displayed on the left-hand side of Fig. 6, whereas $\mathcal{O}_L$ is empty (necessarily so, being L unobservable);
- $\mathcal{R} = (\mathcal{R}_P, \mathcal{R}_{P'}, \mathcal{R}_M, \mathcal{R}_L)$, where $\mathcal{R}_P = \{(b_3(b), fob), (b_4(b), fcb), (s_3(s), fos), (s_4(s), fcs)\}$, $\mathcal{R}_{P'} = \{(b_3(b'), fob'), (b_4(b'), fcb'), (s_3(s'), fos'), (s_4(s'), fcs')\}$, $\mathcal{R}_M = \{(m_2(m), fm), (m_2(m'), fm'), (b_3(r), for), (b_4(r), fcr), (b_3(r'), for'), (b_4(r'), fcr')\}$, $\mathcal{R}_L = \{(l_1(l), fls), (l_2(l), fls), (l_3(l), fls'), (l_4(l), fls'), (l_5(l), fli), (l_6(l), fli), (l_7(l), fli'), (l_8(l), fli'), (l_9(l), flp), (l_{10}(l), flp), (l_{11}(l), flp'), (l_{12}(l), flp')\}$.

6   Preprocessing

For efficiency reasons, it is convenient to perform some preprocessing on the CAS specification before the diagnosis engine is operating. The extent of such offline preprocessing is varying and depends on the performance requirements of the application domain. In particular, in order to detect pattern events, we need to maintain the recognition states of patterns. Since patterns are described by regular expressions, specific automata-based recognizers are to be generated as follows:

1. For each pattern $(p(\omega), r)$, a *pattern automaton* P equivalent to r is generated, with final states marked by $p(\omega)$;
2. The set **P** of pattern automata is partitioned based on AS and the alphabet of r;
3. For each part $\mathbb{P} = \{P_1, \ldots, P_h\}$ in **P**, four actions are performed:
   (3a) A nondeterministic automaton $\mathcal{N}$ is created by generating its initial state n_0 and one empty transition from n_0 to each initial state of P_i, $i \in [1 .. h]$;
   (3b) In each P_i, $i \in [1 .. h]$, an empty transition from each non-initial state to n_0 is inserted (this allows for pattern-matching of overlapping strings of transitions);
   (3c) $\mathcal{N}$ is determinized into $\mathcal{P}$, where each final state d is marked by the pattern event that is associated with the states in d that are final in the corresponding pattern automaton (in fact, each state d of the deterministic automaton is identified by a subset of the states of the equivalent nondeterministic automaton; besides, we assume that only one pattern event at a time can be generated);
   (3d) $\mathcal{P}$ is minimized into the *pattern space* of part $\mathbb{P}$.

Example 7. Displayed on the left-hand side of Fig. 7 is the nondeterministic automaton $\mathcal{N}$ generated in action (3b) for pattern events $\mathbf{di}(O)$, $\mathbf{co}(O)$, $\mathbf{nd}(O)$, and $\mathbf{nc}(O)$. The tabular representation of the resulting pattern space $\mathcal{P}_P$ is outlined on the right-hand side. Listed in first column are the states (0 is the initial state), with final states being shaded. For each pair state-transition, the next state is specified. Listed in the last column are the pattern events associated with final states. Pattern space $\mathcal{P}_{P'}$ is generated in the same way.

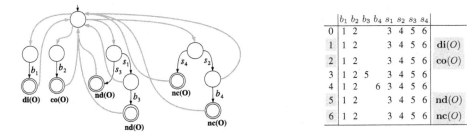

	b_1	b_2	b_3	b_4	s_1	s_2	s_3	s_4	
0	1	2			3	4	5	6	
1	1	2			3	4	5	6	$di(O)$
2	1	2			3	4	5	6	$co(O)$
3	1	2	5		3	4	5	6	
4	1	2		6	3	4	5	6	
5	1	2			3	4	5	6	$nd(O)$
6	1	2			3	4	5	6	$nc(O)$

Fig. 7. Generation of pattern space $\mathcal{P}_P$

Since regular expressions of pattern events for M are defined on different alphabets, six additional pattern spaces are to be generated: $\mathcal{P}_{nr}$, $\mathcal{P}_{ni}$, $\mathcal{P}_{ps'}$, $\mathcal{P}_{nr'}$, $\mathcal{P}_{ni'}$, and $\mathcal{P}_{ps}$.

7 Problem Solving

Behavior reconstruction in diagnosis of CAS's avoids materializing the behavior of the CAS, that is, the automaton whose language equals the set of CAS trajectories. Instead, reconstruction is confined to each single AS based on the local observation *and* the interface constraints on pattern-event occurrences coming from neighboring inferior AS's within the hierarchy of the CAS.

The essential point is that such pattern events come with diagnosis information from inferior AS's, which is eventually combined with the diagnosis information of the superior AS, thereby allowing for the sound and complete solution of the diagnosis problem.

Intuitively, the flow of reconstruction in the hierarchy of the CAS is bottom-up. For an AS A with children $A_1, \ldots, A_k$, the behavior of A, namely $Bhv(A)$, is reconstructed based on the *interfaces* of the children, namely $Int(A_1), \ldots, Int(A_k)$, and the local observation of A, namely $\mathcal{O}_A$. The interface is derived from the behavior. Thus, for any AS A, both $Bhv(A)$ and $Int(A)$ are to be generated (with the exception of the root, for which no interface is generated).

As such, the notions of behavior and interface depend on each other. However, such a circularity does not hold for leaf nodes of the CAS (e.g. P and P' in Fig. 4): given a leaf node A, the behavior $Bhv(A)$ is reconstructed based on $\mathcal{O}_A$ only, as no interface constraints exist for A. On the other hand, the behavior of the root node (e.g. L in Fig. 4) needs to be submitted to further decoration-based processing in order to distill the set of candidate diagnoses.

In short, four sorts of graphs are required in reconstruction: *unconstrained behavior* (for leaf nodes), *interface* (for non-root nodes), *constrained behavior* (for non-leaf nodes), and *decorated behavior* (for root node).

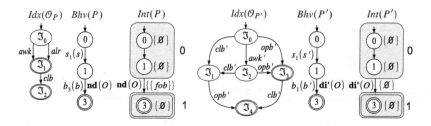

Fig. 8. Index space, unconstrained behavior, and interface for P (left) and P' (right)

Table 2. Details on states for $Bhv(P)$ and $Bhv(P')$ displayed in Fig. 8

| | Behavior $Bhv(P)$ | | | | | | Behavior $Bhv(P')$ | | | | |
State	s	b	$I(b)$	$\mathcal{P}_P$	$Idx(\mathcal{O}_P)$	State	s'	b'	$I(b')$	$\mathcal{P}_{P'}$	$Idx(\mathcal{O}_{P'})$
0	idle	closed		0	$\Im_0$	0	idle	closed		0	$\Im_0$
1	awaken	closed	op	3	$\Im_1$	1	awaken	closed	op	3	$\Im_2$
3	awaken	closed		5	$\Im_1$	3	awaken	open		1	$\Im_3$

Example 8. With reference to CAS $\mathcal{L}$ in Fig. 4 and the diagnosis problem defined in Example 6, namely $\wp(\mathcal{L}) = (\lambda_0, \mathcal{V}, \mathcal{O}, \mathcal{R})$, we first need to generate the unconstrained behavior of AS's P and P' based on local observations $\mathcal{O}_P$ and $\mathcal{O}_{P'}$, respectively.

Displayed in Fig. 8 are the index space, the unconstrained behavior, and the interface relevant to P (left) and P' (right). Consider the generation of $Bhv(P')$. As detailed in the right-hand side of Table 2, each state is identified by five fields: the state of sensor s', the state of breaker b', the event (if any) ready at terminal $I(b')$, the state of pattern space $\mathcal{P}_{P'}$, and the state of the index space $Idx(\mathcal{O}_{P'})$.

The generation of the behavior starts at the initial state 0 and progressively materializes the transition function by applying triggerable transitions to each state created so far. A state is final when all events are consumed and the state of the index space is final. The transition from 1 to 3 is marked by $\mathbf{di'}(O)$ pattern event as the state of $\mathcal{P}_{P'}$ becomes final in 3 (namely, state 1 in the right-hand side of Fig. 7, where $\mathbf{di}(O)$ needs to be replaced by $\mathbf{di'}(O)$).

In what follows, a diagnosis δ is a set of faults. We make use of the *join* operator between two sets of diagnoses, namely Δ_1 and Δ_2, defined as follows:

$$\Delta_1 \bowtie \Delta_2 = \{\, \delta' \mid \delta' = \delta_1 \cup \delta_2, \delta_1 \in \Delta_1, \delta_2 \in \Delta_2 \,\}. \tag{10}$$

Example 9. Shown on the right of each behavior in Fig. 8 are interfaces $Int(P)$ and $Int(P')$, derived from the corresponding behavior as follows.

1. The identifier of a component transition $t(c)$ marking an arc of the behavior and associated with a pattern event is replaced by:
   - The singleton $\{\emptyset\}$, if $t(c)$ is normal;
   - The singleton $\{\{f\}\}$, if $t(c)$ is faulty, with f being the associated fault.

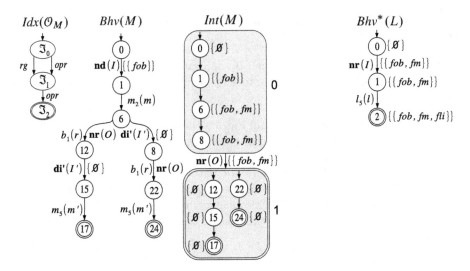

Fig. 9. Index space, constrained behavior, and interface for M (left-hand side), and decorated behavior for L (right-hand side)

2. Interpreting as ε-transitions those transitions which are not associated with pattern events, the obtained nondeterministic automaton (NFA) is determinized so that each state of the resulting deterministic automaton (DFA) contains the ε-closure in all its structure (rather than the subset of NFA states only, as is in the classical determinization algorithm [9]).

3. Within each state d of the DFA, each NFA state n is marked by the diagnosis set generated by all paths starting at the root state in d and ending at n, while identifiers of component transitions are eventually removed.

4. Let p be the pattern event marking a transition t exiting a state d in the DFA, Δ_p the diagnosis set associated with p in step 1, and Δ the diagnosis set associated with the NFA state in d from which t is derived in the determinization process. Δ_p is replaced by $\Delta \bowtie \Delta_p$.

Example 10. Displayed in Fig. 9 is the constrained behavior $Bhv(M)$, which is generated based on index space $Idx(\mathcal{O}_M)$. Each state of $Bhv(M)$ includes two sorts of additional information: the pattern events ready (if any) at input terminals of M, and the pair (i, i') of interfaces states relevant to interfaces $Int(P)$ and $Int(P')$, respectively. A final state needs the additional condition that both states in (i, i') are final in the respective interface. When reconstructing a transition triggered by a pattern event, the latter is required to mark a transition exiting the corresponding state in the interface, otherwise the transition cannot be reconstructed.

Compared with Example 9, the derivation of interface $Int(M)$ shown in Fig. 9 exhibits two peculiarities: step 2 creates a DFA state resulting from two NFA transitions, exiting states 6 and 8 respectively, both marked by pair

$(b_1(r), \mathbf{nr}(O))$, and step 3 shall account for the diagnosis sets associated with pattern events.

Once generated, the behavior shall be decorated by sets of diagnoses associated with states, in a way similar to step 3 in marking NFA states within interface states.

Example 11. Outlined on the right of Fig. 9 is the decorated behavior $Bhv^*(L)$. Starting from the singleton $\{\emptyset\}$ marking state 0, the candidate set associated with state 1 is $\Delta(1) = \{\emptyset\} \bowtie \{\{fob, fm\}\} = \{\{fob, fm\}\}$. Since $l_5(l)$ is faulty (associated with fault fli), eventually we have $\Delta(2) = \Delta(1) \bowtie \{\{fli\}\} = \{\{fob, fm, fli\}\}$. Hence, the solution of the diagnosis problem $\wp(\mathcal{L})$ defined in Example 6 consists of one single diagnosis involving three faults: breaker b fails to open (fob), monitor m fails to communicate with monitor m' (fm), and line l is isolated (fli).

8   Conclusion

As shown in [11], despite their complexity, CAS's can be diagnosed more efficiently than monolithic DES's, whose diagnosis is affected by exponential complexity (in the number of components), either offline when generating the diagnoser [20, 21], or online when reconstructing the system behavior [1, 13]. Specifically, in [11], complexity (in time and space) is shown to be linear with the number of components within the CAS.

The contribution of this paper is to extend diagnosis of CAS's introduced in [11] by means of uncertain temporal observations. Unlike a (certain) temporal observation, which consists of a sequence of totally ordered observable labels, within an uncertain observation, observable labels are both uncertain and partially ordered. Despite this dissimilarity, an uncertain temporal observation can be thought of as a set of candidate temporal observations. The notion of index space allows the diagnosis engine to account for all candidate temporal observations by means of a scalar value, the observation index $\Im$, which is a surrogate of an integer indexing a temporal observation within states of the reconstructed behavior. In other words, when uncertain temporal observations are considered, the integer is replaced by a scalar value $\Im$ identifying a state of the index space. Consequently, neither space nor time complexity is expected to deteriorate when uncertain temporal observations come into play in diagnosis of CAS's.

Despite being introduced based on a simple reference example, diagnosis of CAS's is a general technique which can be applied to any real system that can be conveniently modeled as a CAS, in terms of interconnected AS's and relevant pattern events.

Diagnosis of CAS's is still in its infancy. Further research is expected in several directions. Offline preprocessing can be performed in order to accelerate the online diagnosis engine by generating in a suitable form the behavior space of each AS embedded in the CAS. Also, monitoring-based diagnosis can be envisioned, where the diagnosis engine does not operate a posteriori but, rather, it reacts to each fragment of available observation by providing the diagnosis information relevant to such a fragment only.

Acknowledgment. This work was supported in part by Zhejiang Provincial Natural Science Foundation of China (No. LY16F020004), and National Natural Science Foundation of China (No. 61003101).

References

1. Baroni, P., Lamperti, G., Pogliano, P., Zanella, M.: Diagnosis of large active systems. Artif. Intell. **110**(1), 135–183 (1999)
2. Bossomaier, T., Green, D.: Complex Systems. Cambridge University Press, Cambridge (2007)
3. Brand, D., Zafiropulo, P.: On communicating finite-state machines. J. ACM **30**(2), 323–342 (1983)
4. Cassandras, C., Lafortune, S.: Introduction to Discrete Event Systems. The Kluwer International Series in Discrete Event Dynamic Systems, vol. 11. Kluwer Academic Publishers, Boston (1999)
5. Christensen, H., Kruijff, G., Wyatt, J. (eds.): Cognitive Systems. Springer, Berlin (2010)
6. Chu, D.: Complexity: against systems. Theor. Biosci. **130**(3), 229–245 (2011)
7. Gell-Mann, M.: What is complexity? In: Curzio, A.Q., Fortis, M. (eds.) Complexity and Industrial Clusters, pp. 13–24. Springer, Heidelberg (2002)
8. Goles, E., Martinez, S.: Complex Systems. Springer, Heidelberg (2014)
9. Hopcroft, J., Motwani, R., Ullman, J.: Introduction to Automata Theory, Languages, and Computation, 3rd edn. Addison-Wesley, Reading (2006)
10. Kaneko, K., Tsuda, I.: Complex Systems: Chaos and Beyond: A Constructive Approach with Applications in Life. Springer, Heidelberg (2013)
11. Lamperti, G., Quarenghi, G.: Intelligent monitoring of complex discrete-event systems. In: Czarnowski, I., Caballero, A., Howlett, R., Jain, L. (eds.) Intelligent Decision Technologies 2016. Smart Innovation, Systems and Technologies, vol. 56, pp. 215–229. Springer International Publishing, Switzerland (2016)
12. Lamperti, G., Zanella, M.: Diagnosis of discrete-event systems from uncertain temporal observations. Artif. Intell. **137**(1–2), 91–163 (2002)
13. Lamperti, G., Zanella, M.: Diagnosis of Active Systems - Principles and Techniques. The Springer International Series in Engineering and Computer Science, vol. 741. Springer, Dordrecht (2003)
14. Lamperti, G., Zanella, M.: Context-sensitive diagnosis of discrete-event systems. In: Walsh, T. (ed.) Twenty-Second International Joint Conference on Artificial Intelligence IJCAI 2011, vol. 2, pp. 969–975. AAAI Press, Barcelona (2011)
15. Lamperti, G., Zanella, M.: Monitoring of active systems with stratified uncertain observations. IEEE Trans. Syst. Man Cybern. Part A Syst. Hum. **41**(2), 356–369 (2011)
16. Lamperti, G., Zhao, X.: Diagnosis of higher-order discrete-event systems. In: Cuzzocrea, A., Kittl, C., Simos, D.E., Weippl, E., Xu, L. (eds.) CD-ARES 2013. LNCS, vol. 8127, pp. 162–177. Springer, Heidelberg (2013)
17. Lamperti, G., Zhao, X.: Specification and model-based diagnosis of higher-order discreteevent systems. In: IEEE International Conference on Systems, Man, and Cybernetics – SMC 2013, Manchester, United Kingdom, pp. 2342–2347 (2013)

18. Lamperti, G., Zhao, X.: Diagnosis of active systems by semantic patterns. IEEE Trans. Syst. Man Cybern. Syst. **44**(8), 1028–1043 (2014)
19. Licata, I., Sakaji, A.: Physics of Emergence and Organization. World Scientific, Singapore (2008)
20. Sampath, M., Lafortune, S., Teneketzis, D.: Active diagnosis of discrete-event systems. IEEE Trans. Autom. Control **43**(7), 908–929 (1998)
21. Sampath, M., Sengupta, R., Lafortune, S., Sinnamohideen, K., Teneketzis, D.: Diagnosability of discrete-event systems. IEEE Trans. Autom. Control **40**(9), 1555–1575 (1995)
22. Sibani, P., Jensen, H.: Stochastic Dynamics of Complex Systems, Complexity Science, vol. 2. World Scientific, Singapore (2013)
23. Vernon, D.: Artificial Cognitive Systems: A Primer. MIT Press, Cambridge (2014)
24. Woods, D., Hollnagel, E.: Joint Cognitive Systems: Patterns in Cognitive Systems Engineering. CRC Press, Boca Raton (2006)

A Cloud-Based Prediction Framework
for Analyzing Business Process Performances

Eugenio Cesario, Francesco Folino$^{(\boxtimes)}$, Massimo Guarascio, and Luigi Pontieri

ICAR-CNR, National Research Council of Italy,
Via P. Bucci 41C, 87036 Rende, CS, Italy
{cesario,ffolino,guarascio,pontieri}@icar.cnr.it

Abstract. This paper presents a framework for analyzing and predicting the performances of a business process, based on historical
data gathered during its past enactments. The framework hinges on an
inductive-learning technique for discovering a special kind of predictive
process models, which can support the run-time prediction of some performance measure (e.g., the remaining processing time or a risk indicator)
for an ongoing process instance, based on a modular representation of
the process, where major performance-relevant variants of it are equipped
with different regression models, and discriminated through context variables. The technique is an original combination of different data mining
methods (namely, non-parametric regression methods and a probabilistic trace clustering scheme) and ad hoc data transformation mechanisms,
meant to bring the log traces to suitable level of abstraction. In order
to overcome the severe scalability limitations of current solutions in the
literature, and make our approach really suitable for large logs, both
the computation of the trace clusters and of the clusters' predictors are
implemented in a parallel and distributed manner, on top of a cloud-
based service-oriented infrastructure. Tests on a real-life log confirmed
the validity of the proposed approach, in terms of both effectiveness and
scalability.

Keywords: Data mining · Prediction · BPM · Cloud/grid computing

1 Introduction

In many real-life application contexts, business processes are bound to the
achievement of goals expressed in terms of performance measures (possibly
representing an indicator security/risk or a measurement of quality), which
are monitored continuously at run-time. Historical log data, gathered during
past enactments of a process, are a valuable source of hidden information on
the behavior of the process, which can be extracted with the help of process
mining techniques [1], and exploited to improve the process, and meet such
performance-oriented goals. In particular, it is definitely relevant to this regard
the recent stream of research on the automated discovery of predictive process

© IFIP International Federation for Information Processing 2016
Published by Springer International Publishing Switzerland 2016. All Rights Reserved
F. Buccafurri et al. (Eds.): CD-ARES 2016, LNCS 9817, pp. 63–80, 2016.
DOI: 10.1007/978-3-319-45507-5_5

models (see, e.g., [2,7]), capable to estimate a given performance measure over new instances of a process, as long as they are carried out. Indeed, such performance forecasts can help optimize the process at run time, by possibly developing advanced operational support services, such as task/resource recommendation [11], and the notification of alerts (possibly associated with some form of diagnostics).

Technically, all current approaches to the (log-based) discovery of a performance prediction model rely on abstracting the given log traces into a summarized propositional form, suitable for recognizing patterns that are likely to be correlated to the analyzed performance measure (constituting the target of the prediction task). For example, in [2], an annotated finite-state machine (AFSM) model is induced from a given log, where the states correspond to different abstract representations of all the sequences of process activities appearing in the log. The discovery of such AFSM models was combined in [7] with a context-driven (predictive) clustering approach, so that different execution scenarios can be discovered for the process, and equipped with distinct local predictors. However, choosing the right abstraction level is a delicate task, requiring to reach an optimal balance between the risks of overfitting and of underfitting.

In order to free the analyst from the responsibility of choosing the right level of abstraction for the log's traces, it was proposed in [8] to induce the prediction model of each discovered trace cluster by applying any standard regression method to propositional representation of the traces falling in the cluster. The context-aware prediction models obtained with such a clustering-based learning strategy were empirically proven to improve the accuracy of previous solutions. However, both the approaches in [7,8] require that a number of frequent structural patterns are preliminary extracted from the log traces, in order to map the latter onto a space of performance-oriented target features, in order to guide the clustering phase towards the discovery of groups of traces with similar performance trends. Once such clusters have been discovered, a distinct performance predictor can be induced from each cluster, by either using an AFSM-based learner [7] or standard regression algorithms [8]. Such a pattern-based clustering technique suffers from two main drawbacks: *(i)* the computation of structural patterns is not guaranteed to scale well over large logs, seeing as the number of discovered patterns may be, in general, combinatorial in the number of process activities; *(ii)* the discovered trace clusters are not guaranteed to reach the highest predictive clustering model, due to the loss of information determined when converting the log into a propositional dataset.

Contribution. Still relying on the core idea of [7,8] of combining performance prediction with a clustering technique, we try to overcome the two major limitations mentioned above at two levels. First, we resort to a rougher form of log sketch than [7,8] for clustering the log traces, which can be quickly computed by picking up a fixed number of performance values at predefined positions within the traces, but are yet capable of helping recognize groups of traces exhibiting similar performance over the time—as confirmed by our experimental findings. Moreover, we replace the traditional (hard) clustering of the logics-based predictive clustering framework [3] used in [7,8] with a probabilistic clustering scheme, in order to reduce the risk of obtaining lowly accurate cluster predictors (due to the greedy clustering algorithm and to the underlying approximated representation of the log). In order to overcome the severe scalability limitations of [7,8] and make our approach suitable for large logs, both the computation of (probability-aware) trace clusters and of the clusters' predictors are implemented in a parallel and distributed manner, according to the Grid-services-based conceptual architecture defined in [4] for the specification and execution of *Distributed Data Mining* (DDM) tasks. The underlying grid services were developed according to the WSRF (Web Services Resource Framework) specifications of the WS-Core (a component of the Globus Toolkit 4 (GT4) [9]), and deployed onto a private Cloud-computing platform. By the way, the usage of a Cloud infrastructure to automatically deploy virtual machines hosting a GT4 container is not new (see, e.g., [10,12]), and it widely reckoned as a successful way of providing a high flexible and customizable environment for transparently and efficiently running costly computational tasks.

2 Preliminaries

Log Data. As usually done in the literature, we assume that for each process instance (a.k.a "case") a *trace* is recorded, storing the sequence of *events* happened during its unfolding. Let $\mathcal{T}$ be the universe of all (possibly partial) traces that may appear in any log of the process under analysis. For any trace $\tau \in \mathcal{T}$, $len(\tau)$ is the number of events in τ, while $\tau[i]$ is the i-th event of τ, for $i = 1 \ldots len(\tau)$, with $task(\tau[i])$ and $time(\tau[i])$ denoting the task and timestamp of $\tau[i]$, respectively. We also assume that the first event of each trace is always associated with task A_1, acting as unique entry point for enacting the process. This comes with no loss of generality, seeing as, should the process not have such a such a unique initial task, it could be added artificially at the beginning of each trace, and associated with the starting time of the corresponding process instance.

Let us also assume that, like in [7], for any trace τ, a tuple $context(\tau)$ of data is stored in the log to keep information about the execution context of τ, ranging from internal properties of the process instance to environmental factors pertaining the state of the process enactment system. For ease of notation, let $\mathcal{A}^\mathcal{T}$ denote the set of all the tasks (a.k.a., activities) that may occur in some trace of $\mathcal{T}$, and $context(\mathcal{T})$ be the space of context vectors— i.e., $\mathcal{A}^\mathcal{T} = \cup_{\tau \in \mathcal{T}} tasks(\tau)$, and $context(\mathcal{T}) = \{context(\tau) \mid \tau \in \mathcal{T}\}$.

Further, $\tau(i)$ is the *prefix* (sub-)trace containing the first i events of a trace τ and the same context data (i.e., $context(\tau(i) = context(\tau))$, for $i = 0 .. len(\tau)$.

A *log* L is a finite subset of $\mathcal{T}$, while the *prefix set* of L, denoted by $\mathcal{P}(L)$, is the set of all the prefixes of L's traces, i.e., $\mathcal{P}(L) = \{\tau(i) \mid \tau \in L \text{ and } 1 \leq i \leq len(\tau)\}$.

Let $\hat{\mu} : \mathcal{T} \rightarrow \mathbb{R}$ be an (unknown) function assigning a performance value to any (possibly unfinished) trace. For the sake of concreteness, we will focus next on a particular instance of such a function, where the performance measure corresponds to the *remaining time* (denoted by μ_{RT}), i.e. the time needed to finish the respective process instance. In general, we assume that performance values are known for all prefix traces in $\mathcal{P}(L)$, for any given log L. This is clearly true for the measure mentioned above. Indeed, for each trace τ, the (actual) remaining-time of $\tau(i)$ is $\hat{\mu}_{RT}(\tau(i)) = time(\tau[len(\tau)]) - time(\tau[i])$.

SOA, OGSA and WSRF. The *Service oriented architecture (SOA)* is a model for building flexible, modular, and interoperable software applications. The key aspect of SOA is the concept of *service*, a software block capable of performing a given task or business function. The most popular implementation of SOA is represented by *Web Services*, whose popularity is mainly due to the adoption of widely accepted technologies such as XML, SOAP, and HTTP. Also the Grid provides a SOA framework whereby a great number of services can be dynamically located, balanced, and managed, so that applications are always guaranteed to be securely executed, according to the principles of on demand computing. The Grid community has adopted the *Open Grid Services Architecture (OGSA)* as an implementation of the SOA model within the Grid context. In OGSA every resource is represented as a Web Service that conforms to a set of conventions and supports standard interfaces. OGSA provides a well-defined set of Web Service interfaces for the development of interoperable Grid systems and applications.

WSRF has been defined as an evolution of early OGSA implementations [5]. WSRF defines a family of technical specifications for accessing and managing stateful resources using Web Services, as required by OGSA. In other words, WSRF depicts some specifications to implement OGSA-compliant Web Services. Another way of expressing this relation is that, while OGSA is the architecture, WSRF is the infrastructure on which that architecture is built on [13]. The composition of a Web Service and a stateful resource is termed as *WS-Resource*. The possibility to define a state associated with a service is the most important difference between WSRF–compliant Web Services, and pre-WSRF ones. This is a key feature in designing Grid applications, since WS-Resources provide a way to represent, advertise, and access properties related to both computational resources and applications. In order to implement services in a highly decentralized way, it is commonly used a design pattern that allows a client to be notified when interesting events happen in a server. The *WS-Notification* specification defines a *publish/subscribe* notification model for Web Services, which is exploited to notify interested clients and/or services about changes that occur to the status of a WS-Resource. In other words, a service can publish a set of topics that a generic client can subscribe to; as soon as the topic changes, the client receives a notification of the new status.

Cloud Computing. Cloud computing can be defined as a distributed computing paradigm in which all the resources, dynamically scalable and often virtualized, are provided as services over the Internet. Cloud systems are typically classified on the basis of their service model (*Software-as-a-Service, Platform-as-a-Service, Infrastructure-as-a-Service*) and their deployment model (*public cloud, private cloud, hybrid cloud*). *Software-as-a-Service* (or SaaS) defines a delivery model in which software and data are provided through Internet to customers as ready-to-use services (e.g. Google Docs or MS Office 365). In this case, both software and data are hosted by providers, and customers typically can access them in a easy way (without using any additional hardware or software) on a pay-per-use basis. *Platform-as-a-Service* (or PaaS) provides users with a programming environment and APIs for creating Cloud-based applications exploiting the computational resources of the platform (like e.g. Google App Engine, and Microsoft Azure). Finally, *Infrastructure-as-a-Service* (or IaaS) is a model under which customers ask for physical resources (e.g. CPUs, disks) to support their computational requirements (e.g., Amazon EC2, RackSpace Cloud). Cloud computing services are further classified according to three main deployment models: *public, private*, and *hybrid*. In a public cloud model, providers directly manage their data centers, and publicly delivers services built on top of them through the Internet. In a private cloud schema, operations and functionalities are offered as-a-service and usually hosted in a company intranet or in a remote data center. Finally, a hybrid cloud is obtained by composing two or more (private or public) clouds that, yet linked together, remain different entities.

3 Reference Architecture for Distributed Data Mining

This section is meant to briefly illustrate the service-oriented architecture proposed in [4] for carrying out Distributed Data Mining (*DDM*) tasks over a Grid.

The architecture, shown in Fig. 1, supports the specification and execution on the Grid of DDM algorithms, designed according to a master-worker pattern. Specifically, it features two kinds of Grid Services: the *GlobalMiner-WS* and the *LocalMiner-WS*. The architecture was conceived to follow a typical DDM schema contemplating the presence of an entity acting as coordinator (the *GlobalMiner-WS*) and a certain number of entities acting as miners (*LocalMiner-WS*) on local sites. A resource is associated with each service: the *GlobalModel Resource* with the *GlobalMiner-WS* and the *LocalModel Resource* with the *LocalMiner-WS*. Such resources are used to store the state of the services, in this case represented by the computed models (globally and locally, respectively). Additionally, the resources are published also as *topics*, in order to be considered as "items of interest of subscription" for *notifications*. As it appears clearly in Fig. 1, the two types of nodes are equipped with code libraries that implement the mining algorithms to be executed, which are named *Global Algorithm Library (GAL)* and a *Local Algorithm Library (LAL)*, respectively. In the following we describe all the steps composing the whole process, by pointing out details of the interactions between entities composing the architecture. Let us suppose that a client wants to execute a distributed mining algorithm on a dataset D, which is split in N partitions, $\{D_1, ..., D_N\}$, each one stored on one of the nodes $\{Node_1, ..., Node_N\}$. In order to be processed correctly, any request to perform a mining task needs to follow a three-step scheme.

In the first step, a client wanting to submit a request must invoke the `createResource` operation of the *GlobalMiner-WS* to create a *GlobalModel*

Resource. In turn, the *GlobalMiner-WS* dispatches this operation in a similar way: for each local site with a running *LocalMiner-WS* (assuming the *GlobalMiner-WS* to hold a list of them), it invokes the `createResource` operation (of the *LocalMiner-WS*) to create a *LocalModel Resource*. At this point, the client invokes the `subscribe` method to subscribe a listener (inside the Client) as consumer of notifications on the *GlobalModel* topic. Finally, the *GlobalMiner-WS* invokes the `subscribe` method to subscribe a listener as consumer of notifications on the *LocalModel* topic. As an effect of such subscription steps, as soon as a resource changes, its new value will be delivered to its listener.

The second step constitutes the core of the application, i.e., the execution of the mining process and the result return. The Client invokes the `submitGlobalTask` operation, by passing a *GlobalTaskDescriptor*, i.e. a complete description of the task to be executed (algorithm name, parameters, initialization type, etc.). By interacting with the *Global Algorithm Library*, the *GlobalMiner-WS* runs the code executing the steps to be done. During this phase, suitable data structures are initialized and a suitable set of *LocalTaskDescriptor* are created. It invokes the `submitLocalTask` operation, by passing a LocalTaskDescriptor. At this stage, each ith *LocalMiner-WS* begins the analysis of the local dataset for computing a local model and local statistics. Such a task is executed, with the support of the *LocalAlgorithmLibrary*, concurrently on different Grid sites. While every local task is in progress, the *GlobalMiner-WS* does not need to periodically poll if they are terminated: the notification mechanism, indeed, is able to deliver asynchronous messages warning about the termination of local tasks. As soon as a local computation terminates, the value of the *LocalModel Resource* is set by the value of the computed local model. The changes in this resource are automatically notified to the listener on the *GlobalMiner-WS*; this way, the local model computed at the ith local site is delivered to the global site. As soon as all the local models are delivered to the *GlobalMiner-WS*, the integration of all these local models is performed. According to the logic of the chosen algorithm (provided by the *GlobalAlgorithmLibrary*), the *GlobalMiner-WS* evaluates whether the algorithm is terminated (or not). If it is, the global model computed by the *GlobalMiner-WS* is stored on the *GlobalModel Resource*, which is immediately delivered (via the notification mechanism) to the client. Otherwise, the *GlobalMiner-WS* asks for further processing, by invoking one more time a `submitLocalTask` operation and waiting for the delivering of the result. Such latter actions are executed as many times as the *GlobalMiner-WS* needs, until the computation reaches some convergence condition.

In the final step, as soon as the computation terminates and its results have been notified to the Client, the Client invokes the `destroy` operation of the *GlobalMiner-WS*, which eliminates the resource previously created (*GlobalModel*). Similarly, the *GlobalMiner-WS* asks for the destruction of the *LocalModel*.

From a practical (user-side) point-of-view, any new DDM task can be executed on this architecture provided that it suitably implements the interfaces `globalAlgorithm` and `localAlgorithm`. Specifically, they export the signatures

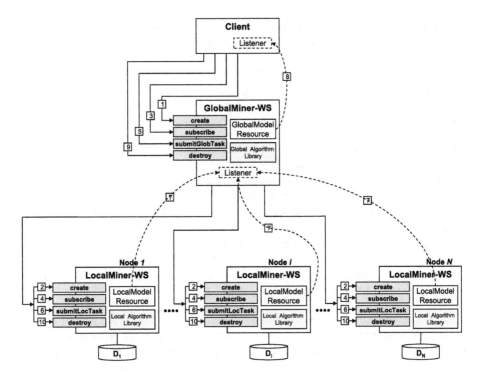

Fig. 1. Architectural model of distributed data mining services.

for those methods each distributed algorithm running on this architecture needs to invoke, i.e. *initialize*, *computeGlobalModel*, *needsMoreIteration* and *finalize* for the `globalAlgorithm`; *initialize*, *computeLocalModel* and *finalize* for the `localAlgorithm`.

4   Formal Framework for Process Performance Prediction

The ultimate goal of this work is to devise a scalable approach to the discovery of a (predictive) *Process Performance Model* (*PPM*), capable to accurately predict the performance outcome of any ongoing process case, based on the information stored in its associated (partial) trace. Such a model can be viewed as a function $\mu : \mathcal{T} \to \mathbb{R}$ that provides an estimate for $\hat{\mu}$ all over the trace universe —including the prefix traces of all possible process instances. Discovering a PPM is an inductive learning task, where the training set takes the form of a log L, and the value $\hat{\mu}(\tau)$ of the target measure is known for each (sub-)trace $\tau \in \mathcal{P}(L)$. Notably, current approaches to this problem [2,7,8] rely on preliminary converting the given process traces in to a propositional form, with the help of some suitable trace abstraction function. The rest of this section provides the reader with a few technical details on the trace abstraction functions considered in our approach, as well as on the specific (clustering-based and probability-aware) kind of PPM that we want to eventually learn from the abstracted traces.

Trace Abstraction. An abstracted (structural) view of a trace summarizes the tasks executed during the corresponding process enactment. Two simple ways to build such a view consist in regarding the trace as a tasks' set or multiset (a.k.a. bag), as follows.

Definition 1 (Structural Trace Abstraction). Let $\mathcal{T}$ be a trace universe and $A_1, \ldots, A_n$ be the tasks in $\mathcal{A}^{\mathcal{T}}$. A *structural (trace-) abstraction function* $struct^{mode} : \mathcal{T} \to \mathcal{R}_{\mathcal{T}}^{mode}$ is a function mapping each trace $\tau \in \mathcal{T}$ to an *abstract representation* $struct^{mode}(\tau)$, taken from an *abstractions' space* $\mathcal{R}_{\mathcal{T}}^{mode}$. Two concrete instantiations of the above function, denoted by $struct^{bag} : \mathcal{T} \to \mathbb{N}^n$ (resp., $struct^{set} : \mathcal{T} \to \{0,1\}^n$), are defined next, which map each trace $\tau \in \mathcal{T}$ to a bag-based (resp., set-based) representation of its structure: *(i)* $struct^{bag}(\tau) = \langle count(A_1, \tau), \ldots, count(A_n, \tau) \rangle$, where $count(A_i, \tau)$ is the number of times that task A_i occurs in τ; and *(ii)* $struct^{set}(\tau) = \langle occ(A_1, \tau), \ldots, occ(A_n, \tau) \rangle$, where $occ(A_i, \tau) = \mathtt{true}$ iff $count(A_i, \tau) > 0$, for $i = 1, \ldots, n$.   □

The two concrete abstraction "modes" (namely, *bag* and *set*) defined above summarize any trace τ into a vector, where each component corresponds to a single process task A_i, and stores either the number of times that A_i appears in the trace τ, or (respectively) a boolean value indicating whether A_i occur in τ or not. Notice that, in principle, we could define abstract trace representations as sets/bags over another property of the events (e.g., the executor, instead of the task executed), or even over a combination of event properties (e.g., the task plus who performed it).

As a matter of fact, the structural abstraction functions in Definition 1 are similar to those used in previous approaches to the discovery of predictive process models [2,7,8].

PPM Discovery as Predictive Clustering: Limitations of Current Solutions. From a conceptual point of view, we rephrase the induction of a PPM, out of a given log, as a predictive clustering [3] task, similarly to [7,8]. Essentially, the core idea underlying predictive clustering approaches is that suitably partitioning the training instances into clusters and inducing a specific predictor from each cluster helps obtain better predictions than using a single predictor (learnt from the whole training set). At run-time, for any new instance, the prediction is built by first assigning the instance to one of the clusters, and then making it undergo the predictor of that cluster. More precisely, these approaches assume that two kinds of features are available for any element z in the reference instance space, say $Z = X \times Y$: *descriptive* features and *target* features (to be predicted), denoted by $descr(z) \in X$ and $targ(z) \in Y$, respectively. Then, a *predictive clustering model* (PCM), for a given training set $L \subseteq Z$, is a function $q : X \to Y$ of the form $q(x) = p(c(x), x)$, where $c : X \to \mathbb{N}$ is a partitioning function that assigns x to a cluster, and $p : \mathbb{N} \times X \to Y$ is a (possibly multi-target) prediction function. Clearly, whenever there are more than one target features, q encodes a multi-regression model.

Following this general scheme, and similarly to [7,8], we adopt a modular kind of PPM that consists of two different types of components: a partitioning function c that maps any trace to a distinguished cluster, and a collection $\mu_1, \ldots, \mu_k$ of PPMs, one per cluster. A propositional encoding $enc(\tau)$ is exploited for any possible trace τ, which mixes up the context data possibly available for τ with an abstracted view of the history of τ, obtained with the help of one of the abstraction function in Definition 1. The features appearing in $enc(\tau)$ play the role of descriptive attributes, while clearly considering the the performance values $\mu(\tau)$ as the target of prediction. Clearly, applying standard predictive clustering solutions to such data would not make sense, since we are not interested in predicting the final performance measure of a complete trace (as are those stored in the above-described training set), but rather in making predictions on all possible prefixes (i.e. partial incremental versions) of any new trace as far as it unfolds, in a step-by-step fashion—as discussed in [7], learning the clustering model based on all partial traces in $\Pr(L)$ is costly and hardly effective. Therefore, both the approaches in [7,8] faced the problem heuristically, by dividing it into two sub-problems: *(1)* induce a predictive clustering model out of a summarized representation (named "log sketch") of the given log, where each (full) trace in the log is used as a single clustering instances, associated with a number of target values that capture the evolution of the μ at several relevant ("pivot") stages of the process *(2)* induce a PPM out of each discovered cluster. In particular, in [7,8], the computation of the target attributes for the traces relied on the preliminary extraction of frequent structural patterns chosen greedily, based on their apparent capability to discriminate among different performance profiles.

However, such a approach suffers from two main drawbacks: *(i)* the computation scheme cannot scale over large logs, mainly due to the fact that the extraction of structural patterns may take a time that is combinatorial in the number of process activities; *(ii)* the discovered clusters of traces are not guaranteed to reach the highest predictive clustering model (due to both the very two-phase optimization scheme, and to the loss of information determined by converting the original log into a propositional dataset).

A New Kind of (Clustering-Based) PPMs: PCB-PPM. We here try to overcome both these limitations at two levels. First, we resort to a rougher form of log sketch than [7,8] for clustering the log traces, which does not require the computation of frequent structural patterns, but simply consists on extracting a fixed number of performance values at predefined positions of the traces. These additional (target-oriented) features, which are formally defined in the next Section (cf. Definition 3), are meant to introduce a bias towards the discovery of groups of traces exhibiting similar performance patterns over the time. On the other hand, we extend the traditional (hard) clustering of standard predictive clustering settings with a probabilistic clustering scheme. This choice is meant to curb the risk of obtaining a poorly accurate PPM as a result of the heuristics clustering strategy adopted in [7,8] (due to both the very greedy clustering method and the usage of an approximated representation of the traces). In particular, as discussed in the following section, such a probabilistic clustering model is computed efficiently through a parallelized distributed version of the well-known *EM* method [6], hence solving the scalability limitations of [7,8].

We are now in a place to formally define the novel, probabilistic-aware clustering-based, type of PPM that our learning approach is meant to extract from a given log.

Definition 2 (Probabilistic Clustering-Based PPM Model (PCB-PPM)).
Let L be a log (over $\mathcal{T}$), with context features $context(\mathcal{T})$, structural abstract representations $struct^{mode}(\mathcal{T})$ (where $mode \in \{set, bag\}$), and $\hat{\mu} : \mathcal{T} \rightarrow \mathbb{R}$ be a performance measure, known for all $\tau \in \mathcal{P}(L)$. Let also $enc(\tau) = context(\tau) \oplus struct^{mode}(\tau)$ be the propositional encoding for each $\tau \in \mathcal{P}(L)$, where $\oplus$ stands for tuple concatenation. Then a *probabilistic clustering-based performance prediction model* (PCB-PPM) for L is a pair $\mathcal{M} = \langle c, \langle \mu_1, \ldots, \mu_k \rangle \rangle$ (where k is the number of clusters found for L) encoding a probabilistic predictive clustering model, where *(i)* $c : enc(\mathcal{T}) \times \{1, \ldots, k\} \rightarrow [0, 1]$ is a probabilistic clustering function that assigns any (possibly partial) new trace τ to each cluster with a certain probability (based on the encoding of τ), and *(ii)* $\mu_i : \mathcal{T} \rightarrow \mathbb{R}$ is a *PPM* associated with the i-th cluster, for $i \in \{1, \ldots, k\}$. Model $\mathcal{M}$ is meant to estimate the unknown performance function $\hat{\mu}$ as follows: for any trace $\tau \in \mathcal{T}$, the corresponding performance value $\hat{\mu}(\tau)$ is computed as $\sum_{j=1}^{k} c(enc(\tau), j) \cdot \mu_j(enc(\tau))$.   □

In such a model, each cluster is equipped with a separate PPM, tailored to capture how $\hat{\mu}$ depends on both the structure and context of any trace that may be assigned to the cluster. The prediction for any new trace τ is computed as a linear combination of the predictions made by the PPMs of all the clusters τ is estimated to possibly belong to, with their respective membership probabilities used as weights. In general, such an articulated kind of PPM can be built by inducing a predictive clustering model and multiple PPMs (as the building blocks implementing c and all μ_i, respectively). In our approach, we face this sub-task by resorting to standard regression methods, defined for propositional data. As observed in [8], indeed, this frees the analyst from the burden of defining a suitable level of details over the representation of the relevant states of the process (as required in the case of the AFSM models used in [2,7]).

5   Solution Approach to the Discovery of a PCB-PPM

Figure 2 illustrates the main steps of our approach to the discovery of a PCB-PPM model, in the form of an algorithm, named PCB-PPM Discovery. Essentially, the problem is approached in three main phases. In the first phase (Step 1), the given log L is transformed into a propositional dataset D_{traces}, containing one distinguished tuple for each trace of the log. As in [7,8], the tuple encoding any trace τ in L stores both the context-oriented attributes of τ and the summarized structural view $struct^{mode}(\tau)$, produced according to the abstraction criterion

Input: A log L over some trace universe $\mathcal{T}$, with associated target performance measure $\hat{\mu}$, an abstraction mode $mode \in \{set, bag\}$, a regression method $REGR$, the number K of desired trace clusters, and the number M of local miners for the clustering.
Output: A PCB-PPM model for L (fully encoding $\hat{\mu}$ all over $\mathcal{T}$).
Method: Perform the following steps:
1 $D_{traces} := \{ context(\tau) \oplus struct^{mode}(\tau) \oplus pProf(\tau) \mid \tau \in L \}$; // see Def. 3.
2 Randomly split D_{traces} into M (nearly) equally sized datasets $D_1, \ldots, D_M$;
3 $C :=$ P-EM$(D_1, \ldots, D_M, K)$; // compute a probabilistic clustering model C via EM.
4 $D_{prefixes} := \{ context(\tau) \oplus struct^{mode}(\tau) \oplus \hat{\mu}(\tau) \mid \tau \in Pr(L) \}$;
5 Let $D'_1, \ldots, D'_K$ be the K clusters of trace prefixes resulting from applying C to $D_{prefixes}$;
   // each $z \in D_{prefixes}$ is assigned to cluster D'_i iff $i = \underset{j \in \{1, \ldots, K\}}{\arg\max} \; C(z, j)$.
6 $\langle r_1, \ldots, r_K \rangle :=$ P-REGR$(D'_1, \ldots, D'_K, REGR)$; // r_i is the regression model obtained by applying the learning method $REGR$ to the tuples in D'_i, while regarding their last field as target variable, and all of the other ones as predictor variables.
7 Encode C into a probabilistic clustering model $\hat{c} : enc(\mathcal{T}) \times \{1, \ldots, K\} \to [0, 1]$, and each r_i into a prediction model $\mu_i : \mathcal{T} \to M$; // where $enc(\mathcal{T}) = context(\mathcal{T}) \times struct^{mode}(\mathcal{T})$.
8 **return** $\langle \hat{c}, \langle \mu_1, \ldots, \mu_K \rangle \rangle$.

Fig. 2. Algorithm PCB-PPM Discovery.

$mode$ (specified as input to the algorithm)—these two kinds of information are here represented as two different sub-tuples, concatenated one with the other. A series of performance-oriented attributes (denoted as $pProf(\tau)$) are stored as well in the propositional representation of τ, in order to bias the clustering phase towards the discovery of groups of traces that exhibit similar performance patterns over the time. These trace attributes are formally defined next.

Definition 3 (Performance profile (for trace clustering)). Let $\mathcal{T}$ be a trace universe, and $\hat{\mu} : \mathcal{T} \to \mathbb{R}$ be a performance measure. Let h be a number in $\mathbb{N}^+$ chosen by the analyst[1]. For any trace τ in $\mathcal{T}$, the *performance profile* of τ (w.r.t. $\hat{\mu}$ and m) is an h-sized (sub-)tuple $pProf(\tau) = \langle pProf(\tau, 1), pProf(\tau, 2), \ldots, pProf(\tau, h) \rangle$, such that, for each $j \in \{1, \ldots, h\}$, it holds:

$$pProf(\tau, j) = \begin{cases} \tau[i_j], & \text{if } i_j < len(\tau) \\ \text{NULL}, & \text{otherwise} \end{cases}$$

where $i_j = (j - 1) \times \left\lfloor \frac{len(\tau)}{h} \right\rfloor + 1$. $\qquad\square$

Notably, computing such a representation of a trace's performance profile simply amounts to picking up a fixed number of performance values at predefined positions of the trace, which can be done in linear time in the size of the input log. By converse, the propositional log sketch used in [7,8] for trace clustering requires the preliminary extraction of frequent structural patterns, which is far

---

[1] In all the tests described here, we simply set h as the 40th percentile of the log's traces length.

more expensive (possibly combinatorial in the number of process activities) in terms of computation time.

In the second phase (Steps 2–3), a probabilistic clustering model is mined out of D_{traces} by exploiting a distributed version of popular algorithm EM [6], implemented by function P-EM according to the data-parallel scheme of Fig. 1. This function, described in details later on, requires the data to be preliminary split into different datasets $\{D_1, \ldots, D_M\}$, based on some partitioning strategy. Specifically, here we simply divided the tuples of D_{traces} into groups of (approximately) the same size (Step 2).

In the third phase (Steps 4–5), a regression model is induced from each of the discovered trace clusters, by applying the learning method $REGR$ specified as input to the algorithm. In order to obtain a predictive model that can be applied to (new) ongoing process instances, the learner is provided with a set of training instances representing partial (prefix) traces, labelled each with the respective performance measurement. To this purpose, all the prefix traces in $Pr(L)$ are preliminary stored into a propositional dataset $D_{prefixes}$), which encodes all the context-oriented and structure-oriented features of each trace (in addition to its target performance value). The discovered clustering model C is then applied to $D_{prefixes}$ in a "hard" way, in order to obtain a partition $D'_1, \ldots, D'_K$ of it, where each tuple $z \in D_{prefixes}$ is assigned to the cluster it appears the most likely to belong to (Step 5). These clusters of prefix traces are then exploited to train a list of regression models, one per cluster. This is accomplished by the distributed function P-REGR (Step 6), following the same distributed paradigm as P-EM— further details on the function too are given later on. Clearly, in such a regression task, for each prefix trace τ, the features in $context(\tau)$ and $struct^{mode}(\tau)$ are considered as input values, while the performance measurement $\hat{\mu}(\tau)$ is the target variable to be predicted.

The rest of the algorithm is simply meant to put the discovered clustering model and regression models in the form of a PCB-PPM, and to eventually return the latter.

Function P-EM *Expectation Maximization* (EM). is a well-known method for inducing a probabilistic clustering model. The method relies on the assumption that the given dataset were generated by a *mixture* of K probability distributions of some given form (e.g., Gaussian), representing each a distinguished cluster. The clustering task then consists in trying to maximize the fit between the dataset and such a probabilistic model, by suitably setting, the membership probabilities of the data instances and the parameters of the overall generative model—indeed, this information is not assumed to be known in advance, and it must be estimated from the given data. Classic EM algorithm needs to be provided with an initial (typically randomly chosen) setting of the mixture model's parameters. Each EM iteration computes new estimates for these parameters that are proven not to decrease the likelihood of the model, denoted hereinafter as $Perf_{EM}$. The process is repeated until the value of $Perf_{EM}$ converges to a local maximum.

Different distributed versions of EM algorithm have been presented in the literature. Our approach essentially exploits the distributed computation scheme defined in [4], in accordance with the DDM framework of Fig. 1.

In a nutshell, function P-EM takes as input different subsets, say $D_1, \ldots, D_N$, of the dataset, and the maximum number of clusters, say K. The clustering process is distributed among N local miners (i.e., nodes equipped with an instance of *LocalMiner-WS*, as explained in Sect. 3), storing each one of the sub-datasets $D_1, \ldots, D_N$, with a further node acting as coordinator (provided with an instance of a *GlobalMiner-WS*).

Specifically, in the initialization phase (method *initialize*), the coordinator randomly initializes, for each of cluster C_k (with $k = 1, \ldots, K$), the center m_k, the covariance matrix Σ_k and the mixing probability $p(m_k)$, and sends a copy of these data to each local node.

The method *computeLocalModel*, implemented by each local miner, consists of three steps that are described next. First, the local miner estimates (for each $x \in D$, for each $k = 1, \ldots, K$) the probability $p(m_k|x)$ that x belongs to cluster C_k—precisely, it computes $p(m_k|x) = \frac{p(x|m_k) \cdot p(m_k)}{\sum_{k=1}^{K} p(x|m_k) \cdot p(m_k)}$, where $p(m_k)$ is the mixing probability and $p(x|m_k)$ is the prior probability, taking the specific form of a Gaussian distribution. Then, it computes a collection $SS^{(i)}$ of local statistics, consisting of the following values: $f^{(i)} = \sum_{x \in D_i} [-\log \sum_{k=1}^{K} p(x|m_k)p(m_k)]$; $s1_k^{(i)} = \sum_{x \in D_i} p(m_k|x)$; $s2_k^{(i)} = \sum_{x \in D_i} p(m_k|x)x$; and $s3_k^{(i)} = \sum_{x \in D_i} p(m_k|x)(x - m_k)^T (x - m_k)$, (with $k = 1, \ldots, K$). As a last step of *computeLocalModel*, these local statistics are sent to the coordinator.

In order to implement method *computeGlobalModel*, the coordinator needs to combine local information stored in the data summaries $SS^{(1)}, \ldots SS^{(N)}$ (received from the local nodes), and update the clustering model. In particular, for each cluster C_k, the updated versions of the center m_k, the covariance matrice Σ_k, the mixing probabilities $p(m_k)$ for $k, k = 1, \ldots, K$ are produced—namely, $m_k = \sum_{i=1}^{N} s2_k^{(i)} / \sum_{i=1}^{N} s1_k^{(i)}$, $\Sigma_k = \sum_{i=1}^{N} s3_k^{(i)} / \sum_{i=1}^{N} s1_k^{(i)}$, and $p(m_k) = \sum_{i=1}^{N} s1_k^{(i)} / |D|$. Moreover, a performance measure $Perf_{EM}$ is computed for the resulting clustering model as follows: $Perf_{EM} = \sum_{i=1}^{N} f^{(i)}$.

At the end of each iteration of this computation scheme, the coordinator must check (through an invocation of method *needsMoreIteration*) if the measure $Perf_{EM}$ has converged to a (local) optimum or the number of iterations has reached a given bound. If one of these conditions holds, the algorithm finishes; otherwise a new iteration of the algorithm starts, where the coordinator sends a copy of the novel clustering parameters (i.e., m_k, Σ_k and $p(m_k)$, for $k = 1, \ldots, K$) to the local miners, and so on.

Function P-REGR. Due to space limitations, we do not describe this function in detail. In fact, rephrasing this function in terms of the framework in Fig. 1 is simple enough for being explained without any precise formalization.

Basically, the method *initialize* of interface `globalAlgorithm` simply consists in assigning the given K datasets to different local miners (i.e. instances of *LocalMiner-WS*). Each local miner is responsible for extracting a single regressor out of one of the datasets by using the selected regression algorithm *REGR* (hence playing as the actual implementation of method *computeLocalModel* in `localAlgorithm`). Once each local regressor has been induced, it is passed to the global miner (i.e. the node implementing an instance of *GlobalMiner-WS*), which does not need to perform any further computation—method *needsMoreIteration* in `globalAlgorithm` is "immaterial" in that it always returns `false`. Finally, the method *computeGlobalModel* of `GlobalModel` only must store all the local regressors received from the remote sites, into a list, ensuring that they follow the same mutual order as the clusters they have been induced from.

6   Experimental Results

In order to test our approach, we implemented both the distributed functions `P-EM` and `P-REGR` (see Sect. 5) as a composition of Grid Services, according to the model of Fig. 1. The services have been developed by using the Java WSRF library provided by the WS-Core, a component of the Globus Toolkit 4 [9]. These GT4-based Grid Services were deployed onto a private Cloud computing infrastructure, by instantiating a pool of virtual machines (one for each grid node). Precisely, we used a physical Grid consisting of 18 nodes, each running a Linux CentOS 7.0 distribution and equipped with 1TB (SATA) hard drive, a dual-core processor Intel Xeon E2 2650 2GHz, and 128GB of RAM. For scalability analyses, different subsets of these nodes, namely, of size $N = 1, 2, 4, \ldots, 16$, were allocated to the execution of the whole `PCB-PPM Discovery`.

The *LocalMiner-WS* services (using either in `P-EM` or in `P-REGR`) were distributed as uniformly as possible over a number of dedicated virtual machines in the Cloud – in practice, M local miners were deployed onto V virtual machines by assigning M/V local miners to each machine. Each virtual machine, instead, is instantiated on a distinct node of the Grid. It is worth noticing that two distinguished nodes were kept reserved for the *GlobalMiner-WS* services of the functions `P-EM` and `P-REGR`, and another one for the main algorithm `PCB-PPM Discovery`—acting as a client of those *GlobalMiner-WS*'s.

The rest of the section discusses a series of experimental activities that we conducted to assess the validity of our approach, in terms of both effectiveness and scalability. To this purpose, we used a collection of 5336 log traces generated by a real transshipment system. Each trace stores a sequence of major logistic activities (4 on the average) that were applied to a distinguished container, passing through the system in the first third of year 2006. Basically, each container is unloaded from a ship, temporarily placed by the dock, and then carried to a yard slot for being stocked. Symmetrically, at boarding time, the container is first placed close to the dock, and then loaded on a cargo. Different kinds of vehicles can be used for moving a container, including, e.g., cranes, "straddle-carriers", and "multi-trailers". This basic life cycle may be extended with further transfers, devoted to make the container approach its final embark point or to leave room for other ones. Several data attributes are available for each container as context data, which include: the origin and final ports, its previous and next calls, various properties of the ship unloading it, physical features (such as, e.g., size, weight), and some information about its contents. As in [7], we also considered several "environmental" context features for each container: the hour (resp., day of the week, month) when it arrived, and the total number of containers that were in the port at that moment.

In all the tests described next, the remaining processing time (for all the prefix traces extracted by this log) was considered as the target performance measure to predict.

Table 1. Average errors made by **PCB-PPM Discovery** (here denoted as **Ours**) and the competitors, for different abstraction modes (namely, *BAG* and *SET*). The best outcomes are in bold.

Metric	BAG					SET				
	Ours (IB-k)	Ours (RepTree)	AA-TP (IB-k)	AA-TP (RepTree)	CA-TP	Ours (IB-k)	Ours (RepTree)	AA-TP (IB-k)	AA-TP (RepTree)	CA-TP
rmse	0.217	0.213	0.205	**0.203**	0.291	0.299	0.294	0.287	0.286	0.750
mae	0.061	**0.059**	0.064	0.073	0.142	0.102	0.098	0.105	0.112	0.447
mape	0.117	**0.111**	0.119	0.189	0.704	0.225	0.189	0.227	0.267	2.816

Effectiveness Results. Since the ultimate goal of our approach is to predict a performance measure (namely, the remaining processing time) over partial log traces, the effectiveness of our approach was evaluated by computing (via 10-fold cross validation) three standard error metrics, quantifying all how much the predicted values differ from the real ones in the average: *root mean squared error (rmse)*, *mean absolute error (mae)*, and *mean absolute percentage error (mape)*. For ease of interpretation, the results have been divided by the average processing time (over all the log's traces).

As a term of comparison we considered two approaches that were defined in the literature for the discovery of a clustering-based PPM: **AA-TP** [8], and **CA-TP** [7]. By the way, it is known from the literature such these techniques were all capable to neatly improve the achievements of non clustering-based predictors. In a sense, the quality of the forecasts that a clustering-based PPM eventually provides can be considered as an indirect indicator of the validity of its underlying clustering model (which has indeed a "predictive clustering" nature, and serves the purpose of supporting the prediction task). Following this line of reasoning, no quality measure is shown here for the discovered clusters, in addition to the very accuracy of the predictions that they allowed to make.

For our empirical effectiveness analysis, we run **PCB-PPM Discovery** by heuristically setting the number K of clusters to $\lceil log_2(|L|) \rceil$, where $|L|$ is the number of traces in the given log, while always keeping $M = 16$.

Tables 1 shows the average errors made by our algorithm, for two different instantiations of the regression method *REGR* (namely, and *IB-k* and *RepTree*)—in both cases we resorted to the implementations available in the popular Weka [14] library. In particular, the first half of the table regards the case when the *bag* mode is used for abstracting traces, whereas the second half concerns the usage of *set* abstractions.

The values shown for AA-TP were computed by averaging the ones obtained with different settings of its parameters, namely $minSupp \in \{0.1, \ldots 0.4\}$, $kTop \in \{4, \infty\}$, and $maxGap \in \{0, 4, 8, \infty\}$. For CA-TP, instead, we report the average of the results that it obtained with different values of the horizon parameter h (precisely, $h = 1, 2, 4, 8, 16$), and the best-performing setting for all the remaining parameters.

In order to correctly interpret the results in Table 1, it is important to notice that the kind of clustering used by AA-TP and CA-TP is more precise than the one adopted in our approach, as discussed in Sect. 4. In spite of this, PCB-PPM still achieves better results in terms of *mae* and *mape* than AA-TP (our *rmse* outcomes, instead, are slightly worse than AA-TP's ones), and more accurate outcomes (over all error metrics) than CA-TP, irrespective of the abstraction function (i.e. *BAG* or *SET*) used. The former behavior can be explained as an effect of the probabilistic clustering scheme that underlies our PCB-PPM's, and makes the prediction of trace performances more robust to the discovery of sub-optimal trace clusters. The lower prediction errors produced by both PCB-PPM and AA-TP, w.r.t. CA-TP, find a justification on their capability to fully exploit the context information available for the log traces in both the clustering and prediction phases—whereas CA-TP uses them during the clustering step only.

Efficiency Results. To test the scalability of our approach, we first generated 4 distinct datasets with different sizes (namely, $DS1$, $DS2$, $DS3$, $DS4$), obtained by replicating every trace in the given log L for 256, 512, 1024, and 2048 times, respectively. We studied the scalability, speedup and efficiency performances when varying the number of grid nodes (from 1 to 16) that were actually used. For space reasons, we next focus on the case where $REGR = RepTree$ and $mode = BAG$—similar trends were obtained, indeed, with the SET abstraction and $IB\text{-}k$. Similarly to what done in the effectiveness tests, the number of desired trace clusters was set to $\lceil log_2(|L|) \rceil$.

Figure 3(a) shows the *execution times* spent against each of the datasets, when using 1 to 16 Grid nodes. We can simply observe that these times strongly decrease for all datasets when increasing the number of available nodes. It is important to observe that the time needed to process the dataset $DS4$ (i.e., the biggest one, with more than 10M traces and 43M of events) is longer than 4 hours when using a single node, while it decreases to only 16.3 min when exploiting 16 nodes. In Fig. 3(b) the execution *speed-up* curves are depicted for each of the datasets. The speed-up is almost linear for all datasets up to the case where 8 Grid nodes are used; an appreciable trend of gain is maintained over higher numbers of nodes. Notably, a speed-up value of 15 is obtained for the extreme case of dataset $DS4$ when using all of the 16 nodes, hence substantiating the scalability of our distributed computation strategy and of the underlying framework. Finally, Fig. 3(c) shows the system *efficiency*, vs the number of nodes and for different datasets. As shown in the figure, a good efficiency trend can be seen as long as the number of nodes increases. As a matter of fact, for the

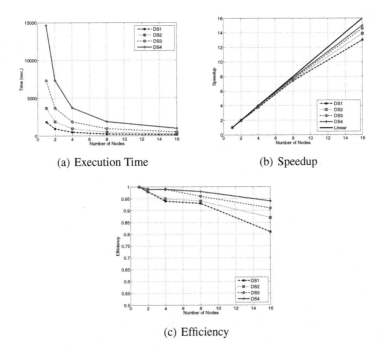

(a) Execution Time   (b) Speedup

(c) Efficiency

Fig. 3. Efficiency results of **PCB-PPM** for different data sizes when *RepTree* is used as regressor.

largest dataset $DS4$, the efficiency on 8 nodes is equal to 0.99, whereas on 16 nodes it is equal to 0.94, i.e. the 99 % and 94 % of the computing power of each used node is exploited, respectively.

7   Conclusions

We have presented a novel context-aware clustering-based approach to the discovery of predictive models for supporting the forecast of process performance measures. The approach overcomes the severe scalability limitations of similar solutions currently available in the literature, and takes advantage of a distributed implementation of its more expensive computational tasks, based on a collection of ad hoc grid services, deployed on top of a cloud-computing platform. It is worth noticing that, despite the approach introduces some approximation in the computation of trace clusters (for the sake of efficiency), the accuracy of the predictions obtained in a real-life application scenario is quite satisfactory. This is likely due to the capability of our probabilistic clustering scheme to compensate such a loss of precision in the clustering phase.

As future work, we plan to integrate more powerful regression methods into our approach, as well as investigate the possibility to exploit sequence-oriented kernel-based methods for both the clustering of the traces and for inducing each cluster's predictor.

References

1. van der Aalst, W.M.P., van Dongen, B.F., Herbst, J., Maruster, L., Schimm, G., Weijters, A.J.M.M.: Workflow mining: a survey of issues and approaches. Data Knowl. Eng. **47**(2), 237–267 (2003)
2. van der Aalst, W.M.P., Schonenberg, M.H., Song, M.: Time prediction based on process mining. Inf. Syst. **36**(2), 450–475 (2011)
3. Blockeel, H., Raedt, L.D.: Top-down induction of first-order logical decision trees. Artif. Intell. **101**(1–2), 285–297 (1998)
4. Cesario, E., Talia, D.: Distributed data mining patterns and services: an architecture and experiments. Concurr. Comput. Pract. Exp. **24**(15), 1751–1774 (2012)
5. Czajkowski, K., et al.: From Open Grid Services Infrastructure To Ws-resource Framework: Refactoring & Evolution (2004)
6. Dempster, A.P., Laird, N.M., Rubin, D.B.: Maximum likelihood from incomplete data via the EM algorithm. J. Roy. Stat. Soc. **39**(1), 1–38 (1977)
7. Folino, F., Guarascio, M., Pontieri, L.: Discovering context-aware models for predicting business process performances. In: Proceedings of the 20th International Conference on Cooperative Information Systems (CoopIS 2012), pp. 287–304 (2012)
8. Folino, F., Guarascio, M., Pontieri, L.: A data-adaptive trace abstraction approach to the prediction of business process performances. In: Proceedings of the 15th International Conference on Enterprise Information Systems (ICEIS 2013), pp. 56–65 (2013)
9. Foster, I.: Globus toolkit version 4: software for service-oriented systems. In: Jin, H., Reed, D., Jiang, W. (eds.) NPC 2005. LNCS, vol. 3779, pp. 2–13. Springer, Heidelberg (2005)
10. Moltó, G., Hernández, V.: On demand replication of wsrf-based grid services via cloud computing. In: Proceedings of the 9th International Meeting on High Performance Computing for Computational Science (VecPar 2010) (2010)
11. Schonenberg, H., Weber, B., van Dongen, B.F., van der Aalst, W.M.P.: Supporting flexible processes through recommendations based on history. In: Dumas, M., Reichert, M., Shan, M.-C. (eds.) BPM 2008. LNCS, vol. 5240, pp. 51–66. Springer, Heidelberg (2008)
12. Sempolinski, P., Thain, D.: A comparison and critique of eucalyptus, opennebula and nimbus. In: Proceedings of the 2nd IEEE International Conference on Cloud Computing Technology and Science (CLOUDCOM 2010), pp. 417–426 (2010)
13. Sotomayor, B., Childers, L.: Globus Toolkit 4: Programming Java Services. Morgan Kaufmann, San Francisco (2006)
14. Witten, I.H., Frank, E.: Data Mining: Practical Machine Learning Tools and Techniques, 2nd edn. Morgan Kaufmann Publishers Inc., San Francisco (2005)

Towards interactive Machine Learning (iML): Applying Ant Colony Algorithms to Solve the Traveling Salesman Problem with the Human-in-the-Loop Approach

Andreas Holzinger[1]([✉]), Markus Plass[1], Katharina Holzinger[1],
Gloria Cerasela Crişan[2], Camelia-M. Pintea[3], and Vasile Palade[4]

[1] Holzinger Group HCI-KDD, Institute for Medical Informatics,
Statistics & Documentation, Medical University Graz, Graz, Austria
{a.holzinger,m.plass,k.holzinger}@hci-kdd.org
[2] Vasile Alecsandri University of Bacău, Bacău, Romania
ceraselacrisan@ub.ro
[3] Technical University of Cluj-Napoca, Cluj-Napoca, Romania
dr.camelia.pintea@ieee.org
[4] Faculty of Engineering, Environment and Computing, Coventry University,
Coventry, UK
vasile.palade@coventry.ac.uk

Abstract. Most Machine Learning (ML) researchers focus on automatic Machine Learning (aML) where great advances have been made, for example, in speech recognition, recommender systems, or autonomous vehicles. Automatic approaches greatly benefit from the availability of "big data". However, sometimes, for example in health informatics, we are confronted not a small number of data sets or rare events, and with *complex* problems where aML-approaches fail or deliver unsatisfactory results. Here, interactive Machine Learning (iML) may be of help and the *"human-in-the-loop"* approach may be beneficial in solving computationally hard problems, where human expertise can help to reduce an exponential search space through heuristics.

In this paper, experiments are discussed which help to evaluate the effectiveness of the iML-"human-in-the-loop" approach, particularly in opening the "black box", thereby enabling a human to directly and indirectly manipulating and interacting with an algorithm. For this purpose, we selected the Ant Colony Optimization (ACO) framework, and use it on the Traveling Salesman Problem (TSP) which is of high importance in solving many practical problems in health informatics, e.g. in the study of proteins.

Keywords: interactive Machine Learning · Human-in-the-loop · Traveling Salesman Problem · Ant Colony Optimization

© IFIP International Federation for Information Processing 2016
Published by Springer International Publishing Switzerland 2016. All Rights Reserved
F. Buccafurri et al. (Eds.): CD-ARES 2016, LNCS 9817, pp. 81–95, 2016.
DOI: 10.1007/978-3-319-45507-5_6

1   Introduction and Motivation for Research

Automatic Machine Learning (aML) is increasingly making big theoretical as well as practical advances in many application domains, for example, in speech recognition [1], recommender systems [2], or autonomous vehicles [3].

The aML-approaches sometimes fail or deliver unsatisfactory results, when being confronted with complex problem. Here interactive Machine Learning (iML) may be of help and a *"human-in-the-loop"* may be beneficial in solving computationally hard problems, where human expertise can help to reduce, through heuristics, an exponential search space.

We define iML-approaches as algorithms that can interact with *both computational agents and human agents* and can optimize their learning behaviour through these interactions [4]. To clearly distinguish the iML-approach from a classic supervised learning approach, the first question is to define the human's role in this loop (see Fig. 1), [5].

Fig. 1. The iML human-in-the-loop approach: The main issue is that humans are not only involved in pre-processing, by selecting data or features, but actually during the learning phase they are directly interacting with the algorithm, thus shifting away the black-box approach to a glass-box; there might also be more than one human agent interacting with the computational agent(s), allowing for crowdsourcing or gamification approaches

There is evidence that humans sometimes still outperform ML-algorithms, e.g. in the instinctive, often almost instantaneous interpretation of complex patterns, for example, in diagnostic radiologic imaging: A promising technique to fill the semantic gap is to adopt an expert-in-the-loop approach, by integrating the physicians high-level expert knowledge into the retrieval process and by acquiring his/her relevance judgments regarding a set of initial retrieval results [6].

Despite these apparent assumption, so far there is little quantitative evidence on effectiveness and efficiency of iML-algorithms. Moreover there is practically no evidence of *how* such interaction may really optimize these algorithms as it is a subject that is still being studied by cognitive scientists for quite a while and even though "natural" intelligent agents are present in large numbers throughout the world [7].

From the theory of human problem solving it is known that for example, medical doctors can often make diagnoses with great reliability - but without being able to explain their rules explicitly. Here iML could help to equip algorithms with such "instinctive" knowledge and learn thereof. The importance of iML becomes also apparent when the use of automated solutions due to the incompleteness of ontologies is difficult [8].

This is important as many problems in machine learning and health informatics are $\mathcal{NP}$-hard, and the theory of $\mathcal{NP}$-completeness has crushed previous hopes that $\mathcal{NP}$-hard problems can be solved within polynomial time [9]. Moreover, in the health domain it is sometimes better to have an approximate solution to a complex problem, than a perfect solution to a simplified problem - and this within a reasonable time, as an average medical doctor has on average less than five minutes to make a decision [10].

Consequently, there is much interest in approximation and heuristic algorithms that can find near optimal solutions within reasonable time. Heuristic algorithms are typically among the best strategies in terms of efficiency and solution quality for problems of realistic size and complexity. Meta-heuristic algorithms are widely recognized as one of the most practical approaches for combinatorial optimization problems. Some of the most useful meta-heuristic algorithms include genetic algorithms, simulated annealing and Ant Colony Optimization (ACO).

In this paper we want to address the question whether and to what extent a human can be beneficial in direct interaction with an algorithm. For this purpose we developed an online-platform in the context of our iML-project [11], to evaluate the effectiveness of the "human-in-the-loop" approach and to discuss some strengths and weaknesses of humans versus computers. Such an integration of a "human-into-the-loop" may have many practical applications, as e.g. in health informatics, the inclusion of a "doctor-into-the-loop" [12,13] can play a significant role in support of solving hard problems, particularly in combination with a large number of human agents (crowdsourcing).

2 Background

2.1 Problem Solving: Human Versus Computer

Many ML-methods perform very badly on extrapolation problems which would be very easy for humans. An interesting experiment was performed by [14]: humans were presented functions drawn from Gaussian Processes (GP) with known kernels in sequence and asked to make extrapolations. The human learners extrapolated on these problems in sequence, so having an opportunity to progressively learn about the underlying kernel in each set. To further test progressive function learning, they repeated the first function at the end of the experiment, for six functions in each set. The authors asked for extrapolation judgements because it provides more information about inductive biases than interpolation and pose difficulties for conventional GP kernels [15].

Research in this area, i.e. at the intersection of cognitive science and computational science is fruitful for further improving aML thus improve performance on a wide range of tasks, including settings which are difficult for humans to process (for example big data and high dimensional problems); on the other hand such experiments may provide insight into brain informatics.

The first question is: When does a human still outperform ML-algorithms? ML algorithms outperform humans for example in high-dimensional data processing, in rule-based environments, or in automatic processing of large quantities of data (e.g. image optimization). However, ML-algorithms have enormous problems when lacking contextual information, e.g. in natural language translation/curation, or in solving $\mathcal{NP}$-*hard* problems. One important issue is in so-called *unstructured problem solving:* Without a pre-set of rules, a machine has trouble solving the problem, because it lacks the *creativity* required for complex problem solving. A good example for the literal competition of the human mind and its supposed artificial counterpart are various games, because they require human players to use their skill in logic, strategic thinking, calculating or creativity. Consequently, it is a good method to experiment on the strength and weaknesses of both brains and algorithms. The field of ML actually started with such efforts: In 1958 the first two programs to put the above question to the test were a checker program by Arthur Samuel and the first full chess program by Alex Bernstein [16]. Whilst Samuel's program managed to beat Robert Nealey, the Connecticut checkers champion at that time, chess proved to be the computers weakness at that time; because on average just one move offers a choice of 30 possibilities, with an average length of 40 moves that leaves 10^{120} possible games. Recently, computers had impressive results in competitions against humans: In 1997, the world chess champion Garry Kasparov lost a six-game match against Deep Blue. A more recent example is the 2016 Google DeepMind Challenge, a five-game match between the world Go champion Lee Sedol and AlphaGo, developed by the Google DeepMind team. Although AlphaGo won the overall game, it should be mentioned that Lee Sedol won one game. These examples just shall demonstrate how much potential a combination of both sides may offer [17].

As test case for our approach we selected the Traveling Salesman Problem, which is a classical hard problem in computer science and studied for a long time, and where Ant Colony Optimization has been used to provide approximate solutions [18].

2.2   Traveling Salesman Problem (TSP)

The TSP appears in a number of practical problems in health informatics, e.g. the native folded three-dimensional conformation of a protein is its lowest free energy state and both a two- and three-dimensional folding processes as a free energy minimization problem belong to a large set of computational problems, assumed to be very hard (conditionally intractable) [19].

The TSP basically is about finding the shortest path through a set of points, returning to the origin. As it is an intransigent mathematical problem, many heuristics have been developed in the past to find approximate solutions [20].

Numerical examples of real-world TSP tours are given in [21]; so, for example in Sweden for 24,978 cities the length is approximative 72,500 km [22] and in Romania: for 2950 cities, the length is approximative 21,683 km) [23]. The World TSP tour, with the length 7,516,353,779 km was obtained by K. Helsgaun using 1,904,711 cities [22].

The Mathematical Background of TSP. The TSP is a important graph-based problem which was firstly claimed to be a mathematical problem in 1930 [24]. Given a list of cities and their pairwise distances: find the shortest possible tour that visits each city exactly once. It is a $\mathcal{NP}$-*hard* problem, meaning that there is no polynomial algorithm for solving it to optimality. For a given number of n cities there are $(n-1)!$ different tours.

In terms of integer linear programming the TSP is formulated as follows [25–27].

The cities, as the nodes, are in the set $\mathcal{N}$ of numbers $1,\ldots,n$; the edges are $\mathcal{L} = \{(i,j) : i,j \in \mathcal{N}, i \neq j\}$

There are considered several variables: x_{ij} as in Eq. (1), the cost between cities i and j denoted with c_{ij}.

$$x_{ij} = \begin{cases} 1, \text{ the path goes from city i to city j} \\ 0 \qquad\qquad\qquad\qquad\qquad \text{otherwise} \end{cases} \tag{1}$$

The Traveling Salesman Problem is formulated to optimize, more precisely to minimize the objective function illustrated in Eq. (2).

$$\min \sum_{i=1}^{n} \sum_{i \neq j, j=1}^{n} c_{ij} x_{ij} \tag{2}$$

The TSP constraints follow.

- The first condition, Eq. (3) is that each node i is visited only once.

$$\sum_{i \in \mathcal{N}, (i,j) \in \mathcal{L}} x_{ij} + \sum_{j \in \mathcal{N}, (i,j) \in \mathcal{L}} x_{ji} = 2 \tag{3}$$

- The second condition, Eq. (4), ensures that no subtours, $\mathcal{S}$ are allowed.

$$\sum_{i,j \in \mathcal{L}, (i,j) \in \mathcal{S}} x_{ij} \leq |\mathcal{S}| - 1, \forall \mathcal{S} \subset \mathcal{N} : 2 \leq |\mathcal{S}| \leq n - 2 \tag{4}$$

For the symmetric TSP the condition $c_{ij} = c_{ji}$ holds. For the metric version the triangle inequality holds: $c_{ik} + c_{kj} \geq c_{ij}, \forall i,j,k$ nodes.

3   Ant Algorithms

There are many variations of the Ant Colony Optimization applied on different classical problems. For example an individual ant composes a candidate solution, beginning with an empty solution and adding solution components iteratively until a final candidate solution has been generated [28]. The ants solutions are not guaranteed to be optimal and hence may be further improved using local search methods. Based on this observation, the best performance is obtained using hybrid algorithms combining probabilistic solution constructed by a colony of ants with local search algorithms as 2-opt, 3-opt, tabu-search etc. In hybrid algorithms, the ants can be seen as guiding the local search by constructing promising initial solutions. Conversely, the local search guides the colony evolution, because ants preferably use solution components which, earlier in the search, have been contained in good locally optimal solutions.

3.1 Ant Behaviour and Pheromone Trails

Ants are (similar as termites, bees, wasps) socially intelligent insects living in organized colonies where each ant can communicate with each other. *Pheromone trails* laid by foraging ants serve as a *positive feedback mechanism* for the sharing of information. This feedback is nonlinear, in that ants do not react in a proportionate manner to the amount of pheromone deposited, instead, strong trails elicit disproportionately stronger responses than weak trails. Such nonlinearity has important implications for how an ant colony distributes its workforce, when confronted with a choice of food sources [29].

This leads to the emergence of shortest paths and when an obstacle breaks the path, ants try to get around the obstacle randomly choosing either way. If the two paths encircling the obstacle have the different length, more ants pass the shorter route on their continuous pendulum motion between the nest points in particular time interval. While each ant keeps marking its way by pheromone the shorter route attracts more pheromone concentrations and consequently more and more ants choose this route. This feedback finally leads to a stage where the entire ant colony uses the shortest path. Each point at which an ant has to decide which solution component to add to its current partial solution is called a choice point.

The ant probabilistically decides where to go by favouring the closer nodes and the nodes connected by edges with higher pheromone trails. After the solution construction is completed, the ants give feedback on the solutions they have constructed by depositing pheromone on solution components which they have used in their solution. Solution components which are part of better solutions or are used by many ants will receive a higher amount of pheromone and, hence, will more likely be used by the ants in future iterations of the algorithm. To avoid the search getting stuck, typically before the pheromone trails get reinforced, all pheromone trails are decreased by a factor [30,31].

Such principles inspired from observations in nature can be very useful for the design of *multi-agent systems* aiming to solve hard problems such as the TSP. Pioneer work in that respect was done by Marco Dorigo, the inventor of the Ant Colony Optimization (ACO) meta-heuristic for combinatorial optimization problems [32].

In summary it can be stated that ACO algorithms are based on simple assumptions:

- Foraging ants construct a path in a graph and some of them (according to updating rules) lay pheromone trail on their paths
- Decisions are based on pheromone deposited on the available edges and on the distance to the available nodes
- Pheromone evaporates over time
- Every ant remembers already visited places
- Foragers prefer to follow the pheromone trails and to choose close nodes
- Local information improve the information content of pheromone trails
- The colony converges to a high quality solution.

Convergence is a core-competence of distributed decision-making by insect colonies; an ant colony operates without central control, regulating its activities through a network of local interactions [33]. The evolution in this case is a probabilistic stepwise construction of a path, making use of pheromones and problem-specific heuristic information to incrementally find a solution [34,35].

ACO Procedure. Ant Colony Optimization (ACO) metaheuristic is a framework for solving combinatorial optimization problems. Depending on the specific problem tackled, there are many successful ACO realizations. One of the oldest and specifically dedicated to TSP is the Ant Colony System (ACS) [36]. In ACS, ants concurrently traverse a complete graph with n nodes, construct solutions and deposit pheromone on their paths. The distances between nodes are stored in the matrix (d_{ij}), and the pheromone on edges are in (τ_{ij}).

The pseudocode of Ant Colony Systems is illustrated in Algorithm 1.

Algorithm 1. Ant Colony System Algorithm

Input : ProblemSize, m, β, ρ, σ, q_0
Output: *Pbest*
Pbest $\leftarrow$ CreateHeuristicSolution(ProblemSize);
$Pbest_{cost} \leftarrow$ Cost(*Pbest*);
$Pheromone_{init} \leftarrow \frac{1.0}{ProblemSize \times Pbest_{cost}}$;
$Pheromone \leftarrow$ InitializePheromone($Pheromone_{init}$);
while $\neg StopCondition()$ **do**
    for $i = 1$ to m **do**
        $S_i \leftarrow$ ConstructSolution(Pheromone, ProblemSize, β, q_0);
        $Si_{cost} \leftarrow$ Cost(S_i);
        if $Si_{cost} \leq Pbest_{cost}$ **then**
            $Pbest_{cost} \leftarrow Si_{cost}$;
            $Pbest \leftarrow S_i$;
        end
        LocalUpdateAndDecayPheromone(Pheromone, S_i, Si_{cost}, ρ);
    end
    GlobalUpdateAndDecayPheromone(Pheromone, *Pbest*, $Pbest_{cost}$, ρ);
end
return *Pbest*;

The characteristics of ACS are:

- the decision rule for an ant staying in node i for choosing the node j is a mix of deterministic and probabilistic processes.
- two rules define the process of pheromone deposit.

The most important ACS parameters are: the number of ants (m), the balance between the effect of the problem data and the effect of the pheromone

(β), the threshold for deterministic decisions (q_0) and the evaporation rate of the pheromone (ρ). These parameters allow the following description of ACS.

At the beginning, a TSP solution is generated, using a heuristic method (for example, the Nearest Neighbor). At this step, this solution is considered the global best. The ants are deployed at random in the nodes and they move to other nodes, until they complete a solution. If an ant stays in the node i, it can move to one of the unvisited nodes. The available nodes form the set J_i.

The next node j is chosen based on the pheromone quantity on the corresponding edge, on the edge's length, and on an uniformly generated random value $q \in [0, 1]$. η is considered the inverse of the distance between two nodes. If $q \leq q_0$, then the Eq. (5) holds. Otherwise, j is randomly selected from the available nodes using a proportional rule, based on the probabilities (Eq. 6).

$$j = argmax_{l \in J_i}(\tau_{il} \cdot [\eta_{il}]^\beta) \tag{5}$$

$$p_{ij} = \frac{\tau_{ij} \cdot [\eta_{ij}]^\beta}{\sum_{l \in J_i} \tau_{il} \cdot [\eta_{il}]^\beta} \tag{6}$$

After all the solutions are constructed, their lengths are computed, and the global best is updated, if a better solution is founded. The local pheromone update is applied. Each ant updates the pheromone on its path using Eq. (7).

$$\tau_{ij}(t+1) = (1 - \rho) \cdot \tau_{ij}(t) + \rho \frac{1}{n \cdot L_{initial}} \tag{7}$$

where $L_{initial}$ is the length of the initial tour. The current iteration of the ACS is ended by applying the global pheromone update rule: Only the current best ant reinforces the pheromone on its path, using Eq. (8).

$$\tau_{ij}(t+1) = (1 - \rho) \cdot \tau_{ij}(t) + \rho \frac{1}{L_{best}} \tag{8}$$

where L_{best} is the length of the best tour. The algorithm is repeated until the stopping conditions are met and exits with the best solution.

3.2   Inner Ant System for TSP

In [37] the *Inner Ant System (IAS)* is introduced, also known as *Inner Update System* in [38] where the "inner" rule was firstly introduced to reinforce the local search during an iteration. The structure of the IAS is similar with the *Ant Colony System*. After the inner rule the Lin-Kernighan 2-opt and 3-opt [39] are used to improve the local solution.

After each transition the trail intensity is updated using the inner correction rule, Eq. (9), from [38].

$$\tau_{ij}(t+1) = (1 - \rho)\tau_{ij}(t) + \rho \frac{1}{n \cdot L^+} \tag{9}$$

where L^+ is the cost of the best tour.

In *Ant Colony Systems* only ants which generate an optimal tour are allowed to *globally* update the pheromone. The global update rule is applied to the edges belonging to the *best tour*. The correction rule is Eq. (8). In *IAS* the pheromone trail is over an upper bound τ_{max}, the pheromone trail is re-initialized as in [40]. The pheromone evaporation is used after the global pheromone update rule.

4   Experimental Method, Setting and Results

The ACO as an aML algorithm usually use *no* interaction. The ants walk around and update the global weights after each iteration. This procedure is repeated a distinct number of times. Following the iML-approach the human now can open the black-box and can manipulate this algorithm by changing the behavior of the ants. This is done by changing the pheromones, i.e. the human has the possibility to add or remove pheromones after each iteration.

4.1   Experimental Method

Based on the *Inner Ant System for TSP* this could be understood as adding or removing of pheromones on a track between cities. So the roads become more or less interesting for the ants and there is a high chance that they will consider road changes. In pseudocode we can write Algorithm 2.

For testing the Traveling Salesman Problem using iML we implemented an online tool with the following workflow:

⟶ Click on the empty field to add new cities.

⟶ Press "Start" to initialize the ants and to let them run.

⟶ With a click on "Pause/Resume" the algorithm will be paused.

⟶ Selection of two edges (first vertex and second vertex).

⟶ Between these two edges the pheromones can be now adjusted by the slider below.

⟶ With "Set Pheromone" changes of pheromones are written in the graph.

⟶ Another click on "Pause/Resume" continues the algorithm.

⟶ The steps above can be repeated as often as needed.

4.2   Implementation Details

The implementation is based on Java-Script. So it is a browser based solution which has the great benefit of platform independence and no installation is required.

For the test-setup we used 30 ants, 250 iterations. For the other parameters we choose fixed default values: $\alpha = 1$; $\beta = 3$; $\rho = 0.1$. The parameters are in the current prototype fixed, this makes it easier to compare the results.

When starting the application an empty map appears on the left side. By clicking on the map a new city is created. The script automatically draws the connections between all the cities. After starting the algorithm, a list of cities/numbers will appear in the control center (see Fig. 2).

Algorithm 2. Ant Colony Algorithm iML

Input : ProblemSize, m, β, ρ, σ, q_0
Output: $Pbest$
$Pbest \leftarrow$ CreateHeuristicSolution(ProblemSize);
$Pbest_{cost} \leftarrow$ Cost($Pbest$);
$Pheromone_{init} \leftarrow \frac{1.0}{ProblemSize \times Pbest_{cost}}$;
$Pheromone \leftarrow$ InitializePheromone($Pheromone_{init}$);
while $\neg StopCondition()$ **do**
    for $i = 1$ to m **do**
        $S_i \leftarrow$ ConstructSolution(Pheromone, ProblemSize, β, q_0);
        $Si_{cost} \leftarrow$ Cost(S_i);
        if $Si_{cost} \leq$ Pbest$_{cost}$ **then**
            Pbest$_{cost} \leftarrow Si_{cost}$;
            $Pbest \leftarrow S_i$;
        end
        LocalUpdateAndDecayPheromone(Pheromone, S_i, Si_{cost}, ρ);
    end
    GlobalUpdateAndDecayPheromone(Pheromone, $Pbest$, $Pbest_{cost}$, ρ);
    while $isUserInteraction()$ **do**
        GlobalAddAndRemovePheromone(Pheromone, $Pbest$, $Pbest_{cost}$, ρ);
    end
end
return P_{best};

After selecting two of them, the pheromones on the track between the cities can be adjusted with the slider. The current amount of pheromones is displayed as blue line with variance in the width for the amount of pheromones. After each iteration the current shortest path is calculated. If the new path is shorter than the old one, the green line will be updated. For the evaluation on testing process there are some pre-defined data sets. From these data sets the best solution is known. The original data sets can be found on [41].

The results of the pre-defined datasets can be compared with the optimal solution after finishing the algorithm by clicking on "Compare with optimal tour". The optimal tour is displayed with a red line.

It is also possible to extend the existing data sets by adding points. A deletion of points is currently not possible, but we are working on it, as this allows a lot of interesting experiments (perturbation of graph structures). Saving and loading modules brings the benefit that the user can store and share the results if he discovered something interesting. During the loading the saved data is maximized to the size of the window.

4.3 Experimental Results

The update of the pheromones on a path changes the ant's behavior. Because of human interaction such as adding pheromones the chances that an ant might

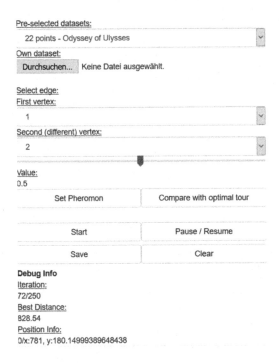

Fig. 2. The control-panel of our Java-Script code (Color figure online)

take that path become higher. Consequently, this is a direct interaction with the algorithm. The interaction could not be effective through the evaporation of pheromones if this happens the user has to set pheromones again.

The interaction only changes the probability that the path could be taken. It has no effect on the shortest path. So it is obvious that a change of the pheromones may not necessarily result in a better path. An increase of this probability that it has an effect can be done by increasing the numbers of Iterations. If we take a closer look at our data set "14 cities in Burma", Burma14.tsp, it is possible to see this effect. The path between city 1 and 10 is part of the shortest path (see Fig. 3).

If we start the algorithm without interaction the probability that the shortest path is taken is very low. If we now increase some of our parameters like colony size (from 20 to 40) and the number of iterations (from 250 to 500), the chances become higher, that the algorithm will return the shortest path. When we now do the same with human interaction (add pheromones to path 1–10 and decrease pheromones on the surrounding paths), after iterations 10, 60, 100 and 150, then there is a high probability that the shortest path can be found in 250 iterations (see Fig. 4).

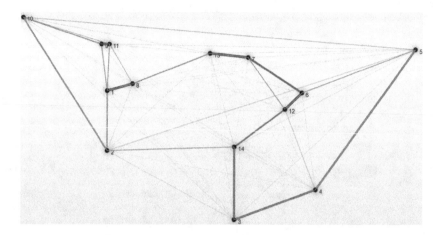

Fig. 3. Not optimal path of Burma14.tsp dataset using an ant algorithm without iML after 250 iterations and using twenty ants.

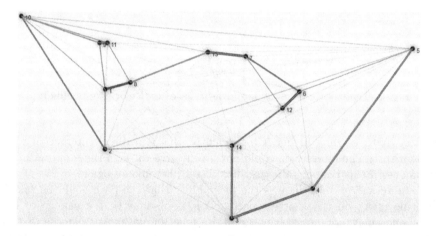

Fig. 4. Optimal path of Burma14.tsp dataset using iML, after 250 iterations including four human interactions and twenty ants for the ant algorithm.

5   Discussion and Future Research

As we see in the test results above, the iML-approach poses benefits, however, further evaluations must also answer questions regarding the cost, reliability, robustness and subjectivity of humans-in-the-loop. Further studies must answer questions including: "When is it going to be inefficient?" In the example above the number of iterations can be reduced from 500 to 250, by three human inter-actions. The benefit is that after a few iterations the user can intuitively observe whether and to what extent ants are on a wrong way. The best number of cities, for an intuitively decision, is between about 10 and 150. A number beyond 150 cities poses higher complexity and prevent a global overview. An increase of the cities is possible, if there is for example a preprocessing phase of subspace clustering [42].

Further challenges are in the transfer of our approach to other nature inspired algorithms which have a lot of potential for the support of solving hard problems [43].

iML can be particular helpful whenever we are lacking large amounts of data, deal with complex data and/or rare events where traditional aML-algorithms suffer due to insufficient training samples. A doctor-in-the-loop can help where human expertise and long-term experience is useful, however, the optimal way will be in hybrid solutions in combining the "best of two worlds", following the HCI-KDD approach [17,44].

In the future it is planned to use gamification [45] and crowdsourcing [46], with the grand goal to make use of many humans to help to solve hard problems.

6   Conclusion

We demonstrated that the iML approach [5] can be used to improve current TSP solving methods. With this approach we have enriched the way the human-computer interaction is used [47]. This research is in-line with other successful approaches. Agile software paradigms, for example, are governed by rapid responses to change and continuous improvement. The agile rules are a good example on how the interaction between different teams can lead to valuable solutions. Gamification seeks for applying the Games Theory concepts and results to non-game contexts, for achieving specific goals. In this case, gamification could be helpful by considering the human and the computer as a coalition. There are numerous open research directions. The challenge now is to translate these approach to other similar problems, for example on protein folding, and at the same time to scale up on complex software applications.

References

1. Dong, M., Tao, J., Mak, M.W.: Guest editorial: advances in machine learning for speech processing. J. Sig. Process. Syst. **82**, 137–140 (2016)
2. Aggarwal, C.C.: Ensemble-based and hybrid recommender systems. Recommender Systems: The Textbook, pp. 199–224. Springer International Publishing, Switzerland (2016)
3. Sofman, B., Lin, E., Bagnell, J.A., Cole, J., Vandapel, N., Stentz, A.: Improving robot navigation through self-supervised online learning. J. Field Robot. **23**, 1059–1075 (2006)
4. Holzinger, A.: Interactive machine learning (iml). Informatik Spektrum **39**, 64–68 (2016)
5. Holzinger, A.: Interactive machine learning for health informatics: when do we need the human-in-the-loop? Brain Inform. **3**, 119–131 (2016)
6. Akgul, C.B., Rubin, D.L., Napel, S., Beaulieu, C.F., Greenspan, H., Acar, B.: Content-based image retrieval in radiology: current status and future directions. J. Digit. Imaging **24**, 208–222 (2011)

7. Gigerenzer, G., Gaissmaier, W.: Heuristic decision making. Ann. Rev. Psychol. **62**, 451–482 (2011)
8. Atzmueller, M., Baumeister, J., Puppe, F.: Introspective subgroup analysis for interactive knowledge refinement. In: Sutcliffe, G., Goebel, R. (eds.) FLAIRS Nineteenth International Florida Artificial Intelligence Research Society Conference, pp. 402–407. AAAI Press (2006)
9. Papadimitriou, C.H.: Computational Complexity. Encyclopedia of Computer Science, pp. 260–265. Wiley, Chichester (2003)
10. Gigerenzer, G.: Gut Feelings: Short Cuts to Better Decision Making. Penguin, London (2008)
11. Holzinger, A.: iML (2016). http://hci-kdd.org/project/iml. Accessed 3 July 2016
12. Kieseberg, P., Malle, B., Frühwirth, P., Weippl, E., Holzinger, A.: A tamper-proof audit and control system for the doctor in the loop. Brain Inform. 1–11 (2016)
13. Kieseberg, P., Weippl, E., Holzinger, A.: Trust for the doctor-in-the-loop. Eur. Res. Consortium Inform. Math. (ERCIM) News: Tackling Big Data Life Sci. **104**, 32–33 (2016)
14. Wilson, A.G., Dann, C., Lucas, C., Xing, E.P.: The human kernel. In: Cortes, C., Lawrence, N., Lee, D., Sugiyama, M., Garnett, R. (eds.) Advances in Neural Information Processing Systems, NIPS 2015, vol. 28. pp. 2836–2844 (2015)
15. Wilson, A.G., Adams, R.P.: Gaussian process kernels for pattern discovery and extrapolation. In: International Conference on Machine Learning ICML 13. vol. 28, pp. 1067–1075. JMLR (2013)
16. Bernstein, A., Arbuckle, T., Roberts, D.V., M., Belsky, M.: A chess playing program for the IBM 704. In: Proceedings of the 6–8 May 1958 Western Joint Computer Conference: Contrasts in Computers, pp. 157–159. ACM (1958)
17. Holzinger, A.: Human-computer interaction and knowledge discovery (HCI-KDD): what is the benefit of bringing those two fields to work together? In: Cuzzocrea, A., Kittl, C., Simos, D.E., Weippl, E., Xu, L. (eds.) CD-ARES 2013. LNCS, vol. 8127, pp. 319–328. Springer, Heidelberg (2013)
18. Crişan, G.C., Nechita, E., Palade, V.: Ant-based system analysis on the traveling salesman problem under real-world settings. Combinations of Intelligent Methods and Applications. Smart Innovation, Systems and Technologies, vol. 46, pp. 39–59. Springer, Heidelberg (2016)
19. Crescenzi, P., Goldman, D., Papadimitriou, C., Piccolboni, A., Yannakakis, M.: On the complexity of protein folding. J. Comput. Biol. **5**, 423–465 (1998)
20. Macgregor, J.N., Ormerod, T.: Human performance on the traveling salesman problem. Percept. Psychophysics **58**, 527–539 (1996)
21. Crisan, G.C., Pintea, C.-M., Pop, P., Matei, O.: An analysis of the hardness of novel TSP Iberian instances. In: Martínez-Álvarez, F., Troncoso, A., Quintián, H., Corchado, E. (eds.) HAIS 2016. LNCS, vol. 9648, pp. 353–364. Springer, Heidelberg (2016). doi:10.1007/978-3-319-32034-2_30
22. Cook, W.: TSP (2016). www.math.uwaterloo.ca/tsp. Accessed 3 July 2016
23. Crişan, G.C., Pintea, C.M., Palade, V.: Emergency management using geographic information systems: application to the first romanian traveling salesman problem instance. Knowl. Inf. Syst. 1–21 (2016)
24. Cook, W.: In Pursuit of the Traveling Salesman: Mathematics at the Limits of Computation. Princeton University Press, Princeton (2012)
25. Dantzig, G.B.: Linear Programming and Extensions. Princeton University Press, Princeton (1998)
26. Papadimitriou, C.H., Steiglitz, K.: Combinatorial Optimization: Algorithms and Complexity. Courier Corporation, Mineola (1982)

27. Tucker, A.: On directed graphs and integer programs. In: Symposium on Combinatorial Problems, Princeton University (1960)
28. Dorigo, M., Birattari, M., Stuetzle, T.: Ant colony optimization - artificial ants as a computational intelligence technique. IEEE Comput. Intell. Mag. **1**, 28–39 (2006)
29. Sumpter, D.J.T., Beekman, M.: From nonlinearity to optimality: pheromone trail foraging by ants. Anim. Behav. **66**, 273–280 (2003)
30. Dorigo, M., Sttzle, T.: Ant colony optimization: overview and recent advances. Technical report, IRIDIA, Universite Libre de Bruxelles (2009)
31. Li, L., Peng, H., Kurths, J., Yang, Y., Schellnhuber, H.J.: Chaos-order transition in foraging behavior of ants. Proc. Nat. Acad. Sci. **111**, 8392–8397 (2014)
32. Colorni, A., Dorigo, M., Maniezzo, V.: Distributed optimization by ant colonies. Proc. First Eur. Conf. Artif. Life ECAL **91**, 134–142 (1991)
33. Gordon, D.M.: The rewards of restraint in the collective regulation of foraging by harvester ant colonies. Nature **498**, 91–93 (2013)
34. Yang, X.S.: Nature-Inspired Optimization Algorithms. Elsevier, Amsterdam (2014)
35. Brownlee, J.: Clever Algorithms: Nature-Inspired Programming Recipes. Jason Brownlee, Melbourne (2011)
36. Dorigo, M., Gambardella, L.M.: Ant colony system: a cooperative learning approach to the traveling salesman problem. Trans. Evol. Comput. **1**, 53–66 (1997)
37. Pintea, C., Dumitrescu, D., Pop, P.: Combining heuristics and modifying local information to guide ant-based search. Carpathian J. Math. **24**, 94–103 (2008)
38. Pintea, C.M., Dumitrescu, D.: Improving ant systems using a local updating rule. In: Proceedings of the Seventh International Symposium on Symbolic and Numeric Algorithms for Scientific Computing, pp. 295–299. IEEE Computer Society (2005)
39. Helsgaun, K.: An effective implementation of the Lin-Kernighan traveling salesman heuristic. Eur. J. Oper. Res. **126**, 106–130 (2000)
40. Stützle, T., Hoos, H.: Max-min ant system and local search for the traveling salesman problem. In: IEEE International Conference on Evolutionary Computation, pp. 309–314. IEEE (1997)
41. Gerhard Reinelt, U.H.: TSPLIB - Library of sample instances for the TSP (2008). http://comopt.ifi.uni-heidelberg.de/software/TSPLIB95/index.html. Accessed 23 June 2016
42. Hund, M., Böhm, D., Sturm, W., Sedlmair, M., Schreck, T., Ullrich, T., Keim, D.A., Majnaric, L., Holzinger, A.: Visual analytics for concept exploration in subspaces of patient groups: making sense of complex datasets with the doctor-in-the-loop. Brain Inform. 1–15 (2016)
43. Holzinger, K., Palade, V., Rabadan, R., Holzinger, A.: Darwin or lamarck? future challenges in evolutionary algorithms for knowledge discovery and data mining. In: Holzinger, A., Jurisica, I. (eds.) Interactive Knowledge Discovery and Data Mining in Biomedical Informatics. LNCS, vol. 8401, pp. 35–56. Springer, Heidelberg (2014)
44. Holzinger, A.: Trends in interactive knowledge discovery for personalized medicine: cognitive science meets machine learning. IEEE Intell. Inform. Bull. **15**, 6–14 (2014)
45. Ebner, M., Holzinger, A.: Successful implementation of user-centered game based learning in higher education: an example from civil engineering. Comput. Educ. **49**, 873–890 (2007)
46. Raykar, V.C., Yu, S., Zhao, L.H., Valadez, G.H., Florin, C., Bogoni, L., Moy, L.: Learning from crowds. J. Mach. Learn. Res. (JMLR) **11**, 1297–1322 (2010)
47. Amershi, S., Cakmak, M., Knox, W.B., Kulesza, T.: Power to the people: the role of humans in interactive machine learning. AI Mag. **35**, 105–120 (2014)

A Threat to Friendship Privacy in Facebook

Francesco Buccafurri[(✉)], Gianluca Lax, Serena Nicolazzo,
and Antonino Nocera

DIIES, University Mediterranea of Reggio Calabria, Via Graziella,
Località Feo di Vito, 89122 Reggio Calabria, Italy
{bucca,lax,s.nicolazzo,a.nocera}@unirc.it

Abstract. The rapid growth of social networks, primarily Facebook, has coincided with an increasing concern over personal privacy. This explains why more and more users personalize their Facebook privacy settings. As a matter of fact, the list of friends is often one of the profile sections kept private, meaning that this information is perceived as sensible.

In this paper, we study the robustness of this privacy protection feature, showing that it can be broken even in the less advantageous conditions for the adversary. To do this, we exploit both the potential information extracted from user alter accounts in Twitter and a social network property, recently demonstrated for Twitter, called interest assortativity. The preliminary experimental results reported in this paper, give a first evidence of the effectiveness of our attack, which succeeds even in the most difficult case that is when the information about the victim are minimum.

Keywords: Facebook privacy · Assortativity · Identity management

1 Introduction

Facebook's privacy setting gives a user the possibility to choose who is allowed to see their profile information. Hence, a user who wants not to reveal his friend list information to everyone can specify to hide such an information in the privacy setting page. By default, everyone can see the friends of a user. As a matter of fact, there are many Facebook users having a private list of friends, meaning that this information is often (reasonably) perceived as sensible. In this paper, we study the robustness of this privacy protection feature, showing that it can be broken even in the less advantageous conditions for the adversary. Obviously, if the adversary knows the victim in the real life or has information about the contexts in which the victim lives, he can easily guess some Facebook profiles owned by a real-life friend of the victim whose friend list is public. It is rather intuitive that only few seeds are enough to discover incrementally large portions of private friends, as usually friends form highly connected clusters. Therefore, this case is trivial. But we want to consider the most difficult case. The adversary has only the name of the victim and the link to his Facebook profile, he can

© IFIP International Federation for Information Processing 2016
Published by Springer International Publishing Switzerland 2016. All Rights Reserved
F. Buccafurri et al. (Eds.): CD-ARES 2016, LNCS 9817, pp. 96–105, 2016.
DOI: 10.1007/978-3-319-45507-5_7

guess only some general information about him (nationality, for example), but has no information about his real life, his job, his interests, etc. This case, for example, may occur in Web investigation. Again, the privacy of the list of friends can be broken once only a few friends (even one) is found with public profile. But, how to find them? Since guessable general information selects a very large portion of Facebook users, it would seem that the only way for the adversary is to try an infeasible guess-and-check attack. In this paper, we show that, by exploiting a social network property recently demonstrated for Twitter [9], a much more efficient attack is possible, allowing the adversary to break the privacy of the victim in the most cases. This short paper includes the first experimental evidence of this result, thus encouraging us to more deeply analyze this issue in the next future.

The plan of this paper is as follows. In Sect. 2, we present our approach to discover private friendships in Facebook. Section 3 describes the preliminary experimentation carried out to study the effectiveness of our technique. Section 4 deals with literature related to our work. Finally, in Sect. 5, we draw our conclusions.

2   Approach Formalization

In this section, we describe the technique we propose to discover (at least a part of) friends of a social network user who decided to make private his friend list. First, we observe that our approach works for social networks, such as Facebook, in which friendship relations are symmetric (that is, if the user u_1 is friend of u_2, then also u_2 is friend of u_1).

The intuition underlying our approach is that privacy setting of an account is indicated by the account owner, meaning that u_1 can choose to make private his friendship with u_2, whereas u_2 can choose to make public his friendship with u_1. Consequently, by looking at u_2's account, the friendship between u_1 and u_2 can be inferred even thought u_1 tries to hide it. It is worth noting that the mere execution of the strategy sketched above has a strong limitation that makes this trivial search unfeasible. Indeed, due to the huge number of social network accounts, the search space of possible friends is limitless. Moreover, this strategy returns at most one friend for each possible friend analyzed.

To overcome these drawbacks, we designed a technique more sophisticated than the above one to reach two important advantages. The first one is to provide a relatively limited number of accounts to analyze (say *candidates*), thus reducing the search space and making this solution feasible. The second advantage is that, thanks to a suitable selection of each candidate, the processing of each candidate account is able to return more friends of the initial account u_1 (to obtain this, we exploit the mechanism of friend community present in social networks).

The technique used to discover private friends basically relies on three procedures, *find alter accounts*, *select candidates*, and *find common friends*. For the sake of presentation, we describe at high level how our proposal works, whereas the detailed implementations of the above three procedures are provided in Sects. 2.1, 2.2 and 2.3, respectively.

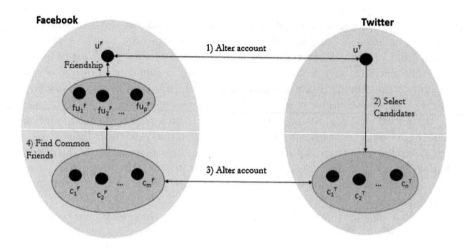

Fig. 1. Graphical representation of the approach.

The input of our technique is u^F, which is the account of the user u in a social network F that supports symmetric friendship relations. In the follow, we instantiate F with Facebook, the most popular social network. Clearly, the friend list of u^F is private. The output of our technique is a set of accounts $f_i u^F$ that are friends of u^F in Facebook. Our approach is schematized in Fig. 1 and consists of 4 steps.

1. In order to discover private friends of u^F, the first step we run is *finding alter accounts* of u^F. This step aims to identify a secondary account of u in another social network(how to perform this task is described in Sect. 2.1).

   It is well know that users register account on different social networks and use them for different purposes [8,26]. Among all the social networks in which u has registered an account, we are interested in his secondary account in Twitter: indeed, Twitter is a very famous and common social networks, which is used to exchange very short messages. At the end of this step, we obtain u^T, which is the account of the user u in Twitter.

2. Now, we run the second step of our technique, that is *select candidates*. This steps aims to identify Twitter accounts that are in the same community of u and that can lead to discover the private friends of u^F. Among the three steps, this is the core one and is deeply explained in Sect. 2.2. Let $c_1^T, \ldots, c_n^T$ be the set of candidates outputted at this step.

3. In this step, we run the procedure *finding alter accounts* for each candidate c_j^T, in order to discover his/her account on Facebook, say c_j^F. At the end of this step, we have found some accounts on Facebook that hopefully are in the same Facebook community of u^F (because they are alter accounts of users in the same community of u in Twitter).

4. In the last step, for each c_j^F, we run the procedure *finding common friends* in order to find the list of friends in common between c_j^F and u^F. This procedure,

which can appear *magic*, is instead provided by many social networks in order to give members the opportunity to find new friends. The detail on the implementation of this step is given in Sect. 2.3 At the end of this step, we obtain the set $f_i u^F$ containing some (hopefully all) private friends of u^F.

From the high-level description of how our technique works, it is clear we cannot guarantee that this approach is always able to break the privateness of friend list: indeed, it is necessary that alter accounts are found and friend community exists. However, as we will show in Sect. 3, we experimented that for many real-life accounts, the execution of this technique is able to discover at least a portion of private friend list.

In the next sections, we will describe the implementation of the three procedures used in our technique.

2.1 Finding Alter Accounts

Many social networks provide their users with the possibility to add in their own profiles a link toward one of their accounts in another social site or external website. This feature is typically enabled during the creation of the user profile. This information is extremely useful in our approach because it allows the identification of the accounts belonging to the same person in a multi-social network scenario.

Technically speaking, users who explicitly declare their alter accounts via social network tools, physically create special links among social networks. These special links are referred as me edges [10,22]. Information about these inter-social network links can be extracted in several ways. The basic strategy leverages the use of social network APIs, a set of methods and services, typically available for social network developers, allowing the interaction with social-network data and functionalities to create new software on top of them.

However, not all social networks provides APIs to extract this information. Therefore, another possibility to extract alter accounts relies on the XFN (*XHTML Friends Network*) standard, an HTML microformat to represent relationship among user accounts. This is obtained by empowering the set of values that the `rel` attribute of the HTML tag `<a>` (which represents a link) can assume. In particular, the value "me" (i.e., `rel='me'`) is used to indicate that the corresponding `<a>` link represents a me edge.

Finally, in cases in which users do not declare explicitly their alter accounts, several approaches proposed by the scientific community can be applied to detect missing me edges (see, for example, [12,19,27,33]).

In summary, alter accounts can be retrieved by using social network APIs, XFN, or techniques such as those defined in [12,19,27,33]. Observe that, in the case of Facebook and Twitter, XFN is adopted for declaring alter accounts.

2.2 Selecting Candidates

The approach we follow to obtain the set of candidates leverages the concept of *assortativity* in social networks. Assortativity is an empirical measure describing a positive correlation in personal attributes of people socially connected with each other [29]. Hence, if a network is assortative with respect to a given attribute, it means that the majority of its users tend to act as their friends when it comes of the aspect expressed by that particular attribute.

It is proved that Twitter shows assortative behavior with respect to user interests [11], where interest assortativity is defined as the preference for friends to share the same interest (e.g., sport, music). Indeed, in Twitter there exist accounts belonging to *public figures*, which, due to their influence w.r.t. a specific topic, act as a sort of representative for that topic [15]. This way, the abstract concept of interest (or topic) can be mapped to the concrete entity of a public figure.

Assortativity w.r.t. an interest I, say IA_I, is given by the difference between the fraction of the users interested in I having at least one friend interested in I measure in the real network, and that computed in the *random* graph corresponding to the real network, said *null model* [29]. Indeed, the random graph models the case in which no assortativity occurs and is obtained by preserving the nodes of the social network and replacing the deterministic occurrence of edges by a random variable in such a way that node degree distribution is unaltered. More in details, the fraction referred above has as numerator the number of nodes that: (1) follow a public figure associated with the interest I and (2) have at least a friend who is follower of any other public figure representative of I; the denominator is the total number of nodes following any public figures associated with I.

Thanks to the assortative behavior of Twitter users, we can find people belonging to his clique by searching on the neighbors of a public figure of interest for a given user, obtaining a set of suitable candidates for our technique.

2.3   Finding Common Friends

By following the reasoning described in Sect. 2.2, we can extract a set of Twitter accounts, which are potentially "close" to the user, say u, for whom we want to reconstruct the friend list. Now, for each of the candidates obtained we can adopt the strategy described in Sect. 2.1 to find their alter-accounts in Facebook, thus obtaining a set of Facebook-candidate accounts.

At this point, if these candidates have a public friend list, we can verify whether u is present in any of these lists. Each time we find an account in any of these lists, due to the bidirectional nature of Facebook friendships, we have discovered an element of the friend list of u. Because the set of candidates may be very big, it is very likely that we can reconstruct the entire friend list of u. However, this strategy would require a very large number of checks to verify the membership of u in any of the friend list of the candidates.

Fortunately, Facebook provides a very powerfull set of APIs, namely Graph API [1], that can give us some advantages in our objective. Graph APIs are a low-level HTTP-based APIs useful to retrieve data from Facebook.

Specifically, it is possible to discover the mutual friends between two Facebook users by performing an HTTPS request at the following link:

`https://www.facebook.com/friendship/<screen-name1>/<screen-name2>`

where the parameters `<screen-name1>` and `<screen-name2>` represent the string ids used to univocally identify the two users in Facebook. Interestingly, this API method works also if one of the two accounts (that of u in our case) has the friend list private. Due to the tendency of Facebook users to form cliques [31] the above API method allows us to discover a very large set of items of the friend list of u with a single call. This reduces the number of operations required to reconstruct the entire friend list.

3   Preliminary Evaluation

Our experiments were performed on a machine equipped with a 2 Quad-Core E5440 processor and 16 GB of RAM. The operating system was Linux Ubuntu Server 14.04.4 LTS, with kernel version 4.2.0-35, Java Virtual Machine version 1.8.0 45 (64-Bit) and Twitter4J [2] as external library for Twitter API support. We wrote our implementations in Java.

To obtain the initial set of Facebook profiles to test our approach performance, we could not rely on existing datasets as they do not provide information about me edges. To extract necessary data, we exploited the SNAKE system [14] which allows the extraction of profile contact information from a very large set of social networks. One of the main issues in this activity was the detection of the profiles showing the right features for our investigation (i.e., an alter account in Twitter and a private friend list). However, using one of the classical crawling technique [30] is not suitable for two main reasons:

1. First, the percentage of accounts with a me edge is very low [13], so it is extremely difficult to find these particular users. This implies that an almost complete visit should be performed to obtain necessary information. However, full structural information of the network is not needed, because we are interested only in Facebook users with an alter account in Twitter.
2. Secondly, a crawling technique may privilege the visit of some nodes with particular structural properties (i.e., very high degree) introducing some biases in our results.

As a consequence, we decided to perform uniform sampling. Although, uniform sampling is not a trivial task in general, for Facebook and Twitter, it is facilitated by how user identifiers are organized. Indeed, both social networks adopt 64-bit identifiers for user accounts. However, because we are looking for private Facebook accounts, we cannot start our sampling from Facebook. We started by uniformly sampling Twitter to collect accounts having a me edge towards Facebook[1]. In particular, the URL address of the profile page of Twitter has the following structure: http://twitter.com/account/redirect_by_id?id=xxx, where xxx is a 64-bit positive integer. Hence, to obtain a uniform sampling, we generated numbers uniformly at random in a suitable interval and then we checked if it

---

[1] Observe that, the direction of the me edge is not relevant for our objective, because we only need to know that the two accounts belong to the same person.

corresponds to a real account with a me edge towards Facebook and whose alter account in Facebook has a private friend list. From this sampling step we obtained a set of 355 accounts.

We proceeded by analyzing the set of Twitter friends for each of the accounts above, and we selected public figures among them. In our case, because the set of candidates (see Sect. 2) is a subset of followers of these public figures, we neglected those public figures who have a too high in-degree and considered only accounts with an in-degree ranging from 500 to 1500. Clearly, this choice was made only to guarantee computation feasibility, and did not affect the performance of our technique as will be shown in the following.

After this, we considered the Facebook alter accounts of the candidates, extracted in the previous step, and continued by calling the Graph API method described in Sect. 2.3 to verify whether we were able to reconstruct the private friend list of the original set of 355 users. As a result, we succeeded in 259 cases, thus obtaining a probability of success of 0.73.

4   Related Work

The more social networks take a central role in people everyday life, the more users privacy becomes a critical issue for researchers. As stated in [4], although a considerable part of Facebook users are not aware of privacy options or do not use them, there is an always increasing number of active users having more online privacy literacy.

Indeed, a number of studies [5,16,18,23,24,28] analyse users behaviour when it comes of privacy in social networks. In particular, the authors of [28] measure the disparity between what users desire and their actual privacy settings, and perform an analysis of problems emerging from a not proper management of privacy. They found that privacy settings match users' expectations only in 37 % of the time, exposing content to more users than expected. Hargittai et. al [23] examine how users privacy practices have changed over time according to modifications on Facebook privacy settings. However, concerning the problem faced in this paper, no change of privacy setting can affect neither the issue nor the solution. The study presented in [16] aims at exploring relationships between concern about mediated lurking and strategic ambiguity on Facebook, and Facebook privacy management. Moreover, the authors of [5,24] focus on privacy settings of adolescents on Facebook. As explained in [17] unintentional disclosure to friends and acquaintances on Facebook can led to bullying/meanness and unwanted contacts, especially among adolescents. Other work surveys users' awareness, attitudes, and privacy concerns towards profile visibility and show that only a minority of users change the default privacy preferences on Facebook [3,21].

From Facebook birth, privacy flaws have continued to keep appearing. For instance, in 2006 Facebook introduced a new functionality, called "News Feed", which tracks and displays the online activities of a user's friends on start pages of the user. Although none of the individual actions were private, users felt deprived of their sense of control over their information and began to form protest groups on Facebook [6]. Subsequently, Facebook introduced privacy controls that allowed users to determine what was shown on the news feed and to whom.

The information gained can be exploited for a number of reasons [21,25]. An attacker could, for instance, deduce social security numbers (which are often derived from name, gender, and date of birth) from the information posted on the user profiles

[7,21]. Moreover, data on relationships or common interests in groups can be exploited for phishing [25].

In order to mitigate privacy threats, authors of [20] propose a recommender system that suggests privacy settings automatically learned for a given profile (cluster) of users. Whereas, in [32] the authors investigate what strategies undergraduate students have developed in addition to the use of the default privacy settings, to protect their privacy on Facebook. These are excluding contact information, using the limited profile option, untagging and removing photographs, and limiting friendship requests from strangers.

Despite these attempts and in addition to the low level of users privacy awareness, there exist more complex ways to bypass privacy setting on Facebook. Indeed, our work shows how, leveraging Twitter data, a user can discover the private Facebook friend list of a victim. This combined use of multi-social network resources adds further privacy concerns to the above literature.

5   Conclusion

Although a considerable part of Facebook users is not aware of privacy options or do not use them, there is an always increasing number of active users who decide to protect their personal information by restricting the access to their profile. One of the most sensitive profile information is the friend list. In this paper, we described a possible attack on the privateness of the list of friends.

For this purpose, we started by the observation that if the adversary has information about the contexts in which the victim lives, he can easily guess some Facebook profiles owned by the victim real-life friends, and from them reconstruct some portions of the victim friend list (as usually friends form highly connected clusters).

Therefore, our attention moved toward the most difficult case: The adversary knows the minimum information that is only the name of the victim and his Facebook profile. In this scenario, it would seem that the only way for the adversary is to try an infeasible guess-and-check attack. In this paper, we showed that, a much more efficient strategy is possible, allowing the adversary to bypass Facebook privacy settings and break the privacy of the victim in most cases. Our attack exploits the concept of alter accounts combined with a recently studied property, named interest assortativity.

Starting from the victim Facebook profile, we first identify his alter account on Twitter (if any), and then, thanks to interest assortativity, we are able to select some suitable candidates that can lead to some public friends in common with the victim, thus breaking his privacy. The attack incrementally proceeds, by discovering the most of private friends.

This short paper includes the first experimental evidence of this result, thus encouraging us to more deeply analyze this issue in the next future.

Acknowledgment. This work has been partially supported by the Program "Programma Operativo Nazionale Ricerca e Competitività" 2007–2013, Distretto Tecnologico CyberSecurity funded by the Italian Ministry of Education, University and Research.

References

1. Facebook Graph API Documentation (2016). https://developers.facebook.com/docs/graph-api
2. Twitter4J (2016). http://twitter4j.org/
3. Acquisti, A., Gross, R.: Imagined communities: awareness, information sharing, and privacy on the facebook. In: Danezis, G., Golle, P. (eds.) PET 2006. LNCS, vol. 4258, pp. 36–58. Springer, Heidelberg (2006)
4. Bartsch, M., Dienlin, T.: Control your facebook: an analysis of online privacy literacy. Comput. Hum. Behav. **56**, 147–154 (2016)
5. Beldad, A.: Sealing one's online wall off from outsiders: determinants of the use of facebook's privacy settings among young dutch users. Int. J. Technol. Hum. Interact. (IJTHI) **12**(1), 21–34 (2016)
6. Boyd, D.: Facebook\'s privacy trainwreck. Convergence: Int. J. Res. New Media Technol. **14**(1), 13–20 (2008)
7. Buccafurri, F., Lax, G.: Implementing disposable credit card numbers by mobile phones. Electron. Commer. Res. **11**(3), 271–296 (2011)
8. Buccafurri, F., Lax, G., Nicolazzo, S., Nocera, A.: Comparing twitter and facebook user behavior: privacy and other aspects. Comput. Hum. Behav. **52**, 87–95 (2015)
9. Buccafurri, F., Lax, G., Nicolazzo, S., Nocera. A.: Interest assortativity in twitter. In Proceedings of the 13th International Conference on Web Information Systems and Technologies (WEBIST), WEBIST (2016)
10. Buccafurri, F., Lax, G., Nicolazzo, S., Nocera, A.: A model to support design and development of multiple-social-network applications. Inf. Sci. **331**, 99–119 (2016)
11. Buccafurri, F., Lax, G., Nocera, A.: A new form of assortativity in online social networks. Int. J. Hum. Comput. Stud. **80**, 56–65 (2015)
12. Buccafurri, F., Lax, G., Nocera, A., Ursino, D.: Discovering links among social networks. In: Flach, P.A., De Bie, T., Cristianini, N. (eds.) ECML PKDD 2012, Part II. LNCS, vol. 7524, pp. 467–482. Springer, Heidelberg (2012)
13. Buccafurri, F., Lax, G., Nocera, A., Ursino, D.: Moving from social networks to social internetworking scenarios: the crawling perspective. Inform. Sci. **256**, 126–137 (2014)
14. Buccafurri, F., Lax, G., Nocera, A., Ursino, D.: A system for extracting structural information from social network accounts. Softw. Pract. Experience **45**(9), 1251–1275 (2015)
15. Cha, M., Haddadi, H., Benevenuto, F., Gummadi, P.K.: Measuring user influence in twitter: the million follower fallacy. ICWSM **10**(10–17), 30 (2010)
16. Child, J.T., Starcher, S.C.: Fuzzy facebook privacy boundaries: exploring mediated lurking, vague-booking, and facebook privacy management. Comput. Hum. Behav. **54**, 483–490 (2016)
17. Christofides, E., Muise, A., Desmarais, S.: Risky disclosures on facebook the effect of having a bad experience on online behavior. J. Adolesc. Res. **27**(6), 714–731 (2012)
18. Debatin, B., Lovejoy, J.P., Horn, A.-K., Hughes, B.N.: Facebook and online privacy: attitudes, behaviors, and unintended consequences. J. Comput. Mediated Commun. **15**(1), 83–108 (2009)
19. Gani, K., Hacid, H., Skraba, R.: Towards multiple identity detection in social networks. In: Proceedings of the International Conference Companion on World Wide Web (WWW 2012 Companion), Lyon, France, pp. 503–504. ACM (2012)

20. Ghazinour, K., Matwin, S., Sokolova, M.: Yourprivacyprotector, a recommender system for privacy settings in social networks (2016). arXiv preprint arXiv:1602.01937

21. Gross, R., Acquisti, A.: Information revelation and privacy in online social networks. In: Proceedings of the 2005 ACM Workshop on Privacy in the Electronic Society, pp. 71–80. ACM (2005)

22. Gyongyi, Z.I.: Social affinity on the web, 15 October 2013. US Patent 8,560,605

23. Hargittai, E., et al.: Facebook privacy settings: who cares? First Monday **15**(8) (2010)

24. Hofstra, B., Corten, R., van Tubergen, F.: Understanding the privacy behavior of adolescents on facebook: the role of peers, popularity and trust. Comput. Hum. Behav. **60**, 611–621 (2016)

25. Jagatic, T.N., Johnson, N.A., Jakobsson, M., Menczer, F.: Social phishing. Commun. ACM **50**(10), 94–100 (2007)

26. Jain, P., Kumaraguru, P., Joshi, A.: @ i seek'fb. me': Identifying users across multiple online social networks. In: Proceedings of the 22nd International Conference on World Wide Web Companion, pp. 1259–1268. International World Wide Web Conferences Steering Committee (2013)

27. Korula, N., Lattanzi, S.: An efficient reconciliation algorithm for social networks. In: Proceedings of the International Conference on Very Large Data Bases (VLDB 2014), pp. 377–388, Hangzhou, Cina. VLDB Endowment (2014)

28. Liu, Y., Gummadi, K.P., Krishnamurthy, B., Mislove, A.: Analyzing facebook privacy settings: user expectations vs. reality. In: Proceedings of the 2011 ACM SIGCOMM Conference on Internet Measurement Conference, pp. 61–70. ACM (2011)

29. Newman, M.E.: Assortative mixing in networks. Phys. Rev. Lett. **89**(20), 208701 (2002)

30. Rao, N., Iyengar, S., DeSaussure, G.: The visit problem: visibility graph-based solution. In: Proceedings of the 1988 IEEE International Conference on Robotics and Automation, pp. 1650–1655. IEEE (1988)

31. Van Cleemput, K.: Friendship type, clique formation and the everyday use of communication technologies in a peer group: a social network analysis. Inf. Commun. Soc. **15**(8), 1258–1277 (2012)

32. Young, A.L., Quan-Haase, A.: Privacy protection strategies on facebook: the internet privacy paradox revisited. Inf. Commun. Soc. **16**(4), 479–500 (2013)

33. Zafarani, R., Liu, H.: Connecting users across social media sites: a behavioral-modeling approach. In Proceedings of the ACM SIGKDD International Conference on Knowledge Discovery and Data Mining, Chicago, IL, USA, pp. 41–49 (2013)

A Blockcipher Based Authentication Encryption

Rashed Mazumder[2]([✉]), Atsuko Miyaji[1,2,3], and Chunhua Su[1]

[1] Graduate School of Engineering, Osaka University, Osaka, Japan
{miyaji,su}@comm.eng.osaka-u.ac.jp
[2] Japan Advanced Institute of Science and Technology, Nomi, Japan
{miyaji,s1420213}@jaist.ac.jp
[3] Japan Science and Technology Agency (JST) CREST, Tokyo, Japan

Abstract. Authentication encryption (AE) is a procedure that satisfies both privacy and authenticity on the data. It has many applications in the field of secure data communication such as digital signatures, ip-security, data-authentication, e-mail security, and security of pervasive computing. Additionally, the AE is a potential primitive of security solution for IoT-end device, RfID, and constrained device. Though there are many constructions of AE, but the most important argument is whether the AE is secure under nonce-reuse or nonce-respect. As far our understanding, the McOE is the pioneer construction of nonce-reuse AE. Following that, many schemes have been proposed such as APE, PoE, TC, COPA, ElmE, ElmD, COBRA, and Minalphar. However, Hoang et al. (OAE1) claimed that the concept of nonce-reuse in the AE is not secure and proper. Hence, a door is re-opened for the nonce-respect AE. Moreover, the construction of AE should satisfies the properties of efficiency and upper security bound due to limitation of power and memory for the constrained device. Therefore, we propose a blockcipher based AE that satisfies upper privacy security bound $\left(\text{Priv} = O\left(2^{2n/3}\right)\right)$ and it operates in parallel mode. It doesn't need decryption oracle in the symmetric encryption module of the AE. The proposed construction satisfies padding free encryption. Furthermore, the efficiency-rate of the proposed scheme is 1.

Keywords: Blockcipher · Constrained device · Authentication · Compression function

1 Introduction

Authentication encryption (AE) is a procedure, where a sender sends data to a receiver in such a way that the receiver can identify whether the data is altered

This work is partially supported by the Grant-in-Aid for Scientific Research (C)(15K00183) and (15K00189) and Japan Science and Technology Agency, CREST and Infrastructure Development for Promoting International S&T Cooperation. C. Su — JSPS Grant-in-Aid for Young Scientists (15K16005).

F. Buccafurri et al. (Eds.): CD-ARES 2016, LNCS 9817, pp. 106–123, 2016.
DOI: 10.1007/978-3-319-45507-5_8

or not [1–3]. Additionally, the AE checks the originality of the sender including message. There are many applications of AE in the field of secure communication such as digital signatures, ip-security, data-authentication, e-mail security, and IoT [18–21]. Furthermore, the AE is a potential primitive of cryptographic solutions for resource constrained device, and IoT-end device [36–38]. For example, there are numerous bunch of senders and receivers in the domain of data communication [4–8]. Hence, it is infeasible and expensive to establish private network for all parties [2,3,6–8]. Under this circumstance, the only way is to implement such a security solution under public network that ensures the privacy and authenticity of the data. Generally, the AE has two components such as symmetric encryption (SE) and message authentication code (MAC) [1–3,7]. The grammar of SE is $SE\,(K, M) \to C$, where K, M, and C means key, message and ciphertext respectively [2,3,9,10,30]. Moreover, the MAC inherits tag (T) and verification such as $MAC\,(K, C) \to T$ and $\mathsf{Verf}\,(K, C, T) \to M$ or $\perp$. Usually, the symmetric encryption ensures the privacy of data. In addition, the authenticity of the data is preserved by MAC [2,3,30]. For example, a doctor $\mathcal{D}_1$ needs to send medical report of a patient ($\mathcal{P}$) to doctor $\mathcal{D}_2$ for consulting (Fig. 1). Under this circumstance, it is mandatory to protect the confidentiality of the patient's report and record. Moreover, the originality of doctor $\mathcal{D}_1$ is also needed to verify as a valid sender. The combined form of the two different components of AE can achieve both the goals. Therefore, the summery of the functions of AE are:

– receiver can perceive the altered data
– infeasible for adversary to get success in forgery
– infeasible for adversary to retrieve the entire message

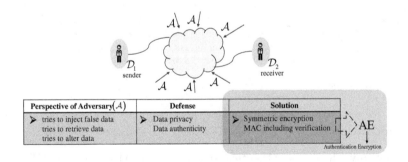

Fig. 1. Simple concept of AE

The AE is constructed through a scratch or blockcipher [2,3,16–19]. Usually, the blockcipher based AE is more suitable than the scratch based AE because of direct implementation of blockcipher rather than the encryption function [20–23]. Now-a-days, the applications of IoT-end device, RfID, and resource constrained device are increasing exponentially [11–15]. However, these devices have certain drawbacks of limited memory, power, and processor [7,12,12,20,21]. Therefore, the blockcipher based AE is more relevant due to light operation [21,24, 36,37]. On the contrary, there are certain ISO standards of cryptographic primitive for IoT-end device or resource constrained device such as ISO/IEC29192-1, ISO/IEC29192-2, ISO/IEC29192-3, ISO/IEC29192-4 [31–33]. In addition, the ISO standard of ISO/IEC29192-2 directs the blockcipher as a core cryptographic primitive for low-resource devices. Furthermore, a certain size of blockciphers, security parameters, and resource utilizations have been emphasized according to the above standardizations. Later, the standard of ISO/IEC 29192-5 emphasized the encrypted length as 80, 128, 160, 256 bits for IoT-end device and resource constrained device [32,33]. Usually, the traditional blockcipher and lightweight-cipher satisfies the above encryption size [31–33]. Thus, an efficient and upper security bounded construction of blockcipher based authentication encryption is required.

Table 1. Comparison study of the proposed scheme and others [18–26,35–38]

Scheme name	Mode	D.O.	FME	Padding	r	PRF. Security	$\#E$ blockciphers
McOE	S	Y	N	Y	1	$O\left(2^{n/2}\right)$	$a+m+1$
OTR	P	N	Y	N	1	$O\left(2^{n/2}\right)$	$a+m+2$
COPA	P	Y	N	Y	1/2	$O\left(2^{n/2}\right)$	$a+m+2$
PoE	P	Y	N	Y	1	$O\left(2^{n/2}\right)$	$a+m+1$
OAE1,2	S	Y	N	Y	1	$O\left(2^{n/2}\right)$	–
OCB	P	Y	Y	N	1	$O\left(2^{n/2}\right)$	$a+m+2$
COBRA	S	N	N	Y	1	$O\left(2^{n/2}\right)$	$m+5$
CLOC	S	N	N	Y	1	$O\left(2^{n/2}\right)$	$a+m+1$
SILC	S	N	N	Y	1	$O\left(2^{n/2}\right)$	$a+m+1$
Proposed	P	N	Y	N	1	$O\left(2^{2n/3}\right)$	$m+3$

FME: Flexible size of message encryption per iteration, r: Efficiency-rate
P, S: Parallel or Serial operational mode, D.O.: Decryption oracle
$\#E$: total number of used blockciphers, a, m: each block of associate data
and message
Y: Yes, N: No

1.1 Motivation

There are many schemes of authentication encryption (AE) such as McOE, OCB, OTR, COPE, PoE, OAE1,2, COBRA, CLOC, and SILC [18–24,34–37]. Among these, the OCB is one of the pioneer construction. It is based on blockcipher also [22]. The strong features of the OCB are parallel and efficiency ($r = 1$). The privacy security of this scheme is bounded by $O\left(2^{n/2}\right)$. However, the OCB needs decryption oracle which increases the overhead-cost of authentication encryption process [38]. Hence, the actual efficiency of the OCB has been decreased [38]. On the evaluation of OCB, Minematsu proposed a scheme of OTR [38] that overcomes the above drawback (decryption oracle) of the OCB. Furthermore, the OTR satisfies an upper efficiency-rate $(r = 1)$ including a reasonable privacy security bound $\left(\text{Priv} = O\left(2^{n/2}\right)\right)$. In addition, the OCB and OTR follows none-respecting construction. On the other hand, the McOE scheme brings a breakthrough in the domain of nonce reusing AE [21]. Thereafter, a bunch of schemes have been proposed based on the properties of the McOE such as COPA, PoE, APE, and ELmE [20,35]. However, Hoang et al. showed that the concept of nonce reusing is no more secure for any online authentication scheme [35]. In addition, Hoang et al. claimed that the online characteristic is a parameter of efficiency [35]. Therefore, a window is re-opened for off-line and nonce respecting AE. Furthermore, the McOE needs decryption oracle and it's privacy security is bounded by $O\left(2^{n/2}\right)$. Most recently, there are two more proposals such as CLOC and SILK [36,37]. The constructions of CLOC and SILK are good for short message. Additionally, these two schemes are free of decryption oracle. However, the operation mode of CLOC and SILK is serial.

According to Table 1 and the above discussions, the most of the authentication scheme's privacy security are bounded by $O\left(2^{n/2}\right)$. Furthermore, many schemes need decryption oracle. Additionally, a padding mechanism is necessary for symmetric encryption module of AE when message and blocklength is not equal. However, the padding technology itself has certain dis-advantages [2,3]. Usually, there is a common attack that is called length extension attack [2,3,26,27]. Therefore, we outline our motivations in the following way:

- higher efficiency and upper security bound
- competitive mode
- free of decryption oracle in encryption and decryption module
- allowed flexible size of message encryption
- no padding
- minimization of blockcipher calling
- efficient and low-cost primitive

1.2   Contribution

In this paper, we present a construction of authentication encryption. Our proposed scheme is based on blockcipher based compression function. Furthermore, our scheme is nonce respecting authentication encryption including associate data. The symmetric encryption module of the proposed scheme is a variant of OCB. Furthermore, the module of MAC follows a variant of PMAC plus. The achievements of the proposed scheme are listed below:

- ▶ efficiency-rate $= 1$
- ▶ parallel mode
- ▶ free of decryption oracle in encryption and decryption module
- ▶ allowed flexible size of message encryption (FME)
- ▶ no padding
- ▶ $\text{Priv} = O\left(2^{2n/3}\right)$
- ▶ supports less call of blockcipher calling
- ▶ blockcipher based compression function
- ▶ nonce respecting including associate data

1.3 Organization

We define preliminaries in Sect. 2. The propose scheme's definition and corresponding security notions are available in Sect. 3. We mention the security proof of the proposed construction in Sect. 4. Furthermore, the summaries are given in Sect. 5.

2 Preliminaries Including Security Notions

2.1 Fundamental Notations

Let X and Y are finite length of strings under the set of $\mathcal{X}$ and $\mathcal{Y}$. Additionally, $\mathcal{C}, \mathcal{T}$ are set of uniform distribution for the strings of ciphertext (C) and MAC $(T : \text{tag})$. Let N, AD, and $\mathcal{M}$ direct the space for Nonce, Associate data, and Message. Furthermore, K and n means key and block-length. In addition, there are certain operators used in the proposed authentication encryption such as $\oplus$ (XOR). Additionally, we use a defined function operator $CS\,(\cdot)$ in encryption and decryption module. The operation of $CS\,(\cdot)$ is complement including bitwise left-shift. For example, we generate α and β before encryption or decryption (Fig. 2). The value of α and β need to use in each iteration of encryption or decryption module. Furthermore, these values should be different in every iteration for tight security bound [18,19,22,38]. Thus, it can be used as counter or unique nonce and associate data. Literally, the function operator of $CS\,(\cdot)$ takes the value of α and returns one bit left-shift after complement when $i = 1 | i :$ number of iteration. If i increases then left-shift also will be increased bitwise according to the value of i. In each iteration, the output of $CS_i\,(\alpha)$ and $CS_i\,(\beta)$ are defined as p_i and q_i, where $i \leq l$ (Fig. 2). Our defined another parameter is τ, which is created as a by-product of encryption/decryption module. Generally, the τ_i is created in each iteration. Thereafter, the XOR values of all τ_i are used for tag generation (Fig. 3).

2.2 Blockcipher

A blockcipher (n, k) consists of a pair of algorithm such as $E = \{0,1\}^n \times \{0,1\}^k \rightarrow \{0,1\}^n$ and $E^{-1} = \{0,1\}^n \times \{0,1\}^k \rightarrow \{0,1\}^n (n, k :$ block and key length). Usually, query of blockcipher is (m, k) and output is c, where key is randomly permuted. Hence, a triplet is the combine form of m, k, and c as (m, k, c). Additionally, the blockcipher oracle doesn't permit for similar query or triplet in principle. For example, if $(m_1, k_1) = c_1$ is queried to oracle then $(c_1, k_1) = m_1$ is not permitted for asking to oracle. Let block (n, k) is the set of all blockciphers of (n, k) according to the ICM [28,29]. Generally, adversary $\mathcal{A}$ tries to explore encrypted plaintext under a given key. However, to retrieve the information of the desire plaintext using different key set is infeasible for adversary. Moreover, to find an actual plaintext or message is infeasible for $\mathcal{A}$ if blockcipher changes [28–30]. Usually, a PRP security comes from the property of blockcipher [22–24]. Hence, the PRP-security of a blockcipher block (n, k) is defined as the success probability of adversary, where $\mathcal{A}$ tries to distinguish between the output of blockcipher oracle and random permutation oracle [22–24, 28–30].

2.3 Authentication Encryption

The authentication encryption is noted as AE. Generally, there are two algorithms of encryption and decryption (MAC included for both the algorithms) under the AE. Furthermore, Algorithm 1 is noted as $\mathcal{E}$-AE and $\mathcal{E}$-DE. In addition, the algorithm of $\mathcal{E}$-AE consists of nonce and associate data including message and returns ciphertext. Moreover, the message exploration and tag verification process are executed under the module of $\mathcal{D}$-AE. If verification process is valid then return message or $\perp$. In this section, we define the basic encryption and decryption module only. Later, the modified version of $\mathcal{E}$-AE and $\mathcal{D}$-AE (Algorithm 1) will be used in symmetric encryption module of the proposed construction.

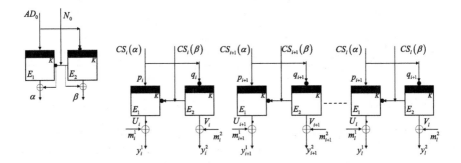

Fig. 2. Encryption procedure of AE

2.4 PRF Security

Let $F_K : K \times X \rightarrow Y$ be a pseudo-random function (keyed), where $K \xrightarrow{\$} \{0,1\}^k$ is a secret key space. On the contrary, a random function is defined as F_R, which is chosen randomly and uniquely from all functions of $X \rightarrow Y$ according to the similar domain-range of F_K. The PRF security is defined as the success probability of distinguishing between F_K and F_R. For example, there is a distinguish-er Dt that can can interplay with both the oracle of F_K and F_R. Hence, the advantage of PRF security of F_K over F_R is defined as follows:

$$\text{Adv}_{\text{PRF}}[\text{Dt}] = \Pr\left[\text{Dt}^{F_K} \Rightarrow 1\right] - \Pr\left[\text{Dt}^{F_R} \Rightarrow 1\right] \tag{1}$$

The first probability of (1) is based on $K \xrightarrow{\$} \{0,1\}^k$ and the second probability is taken over $F_R : X \xrightarrow{\$} Y$. Thus, F_K is PRF secure iff the advantage of Dt is small. Moreover, F_K and F_R are respectively considered as real and ideal world.

Algorithm 1. Encryption Module and Decryption Module (Basic Module)

1: Encrypt $\mathcal{M}$

2: partitioning $m_i^j \in \mathcal{M}$ s. t. $\left(m_1^1, m_1^2\right), \ldots, \left(m_l^1, m_l^2\right)$, where $j \in \{1,2\}, i \leq l$

3: initialization: $\alpha \leftarrow E_{AD_0 \oplus K_1}\left(\overline{N_0}\right) \oplus \overline{N_0}, \beta \leftarrow E_{\overline{AD_0} \oplus K_2}\left(N_0\right) \oplus N_0$

4: **for** $i = 1$ to l **do**

5:

$$U_i \leftarrow E_{CS_i(\alpha) \oplus K_1}\left(\overline{CS_i}\left(\beta\right)\right), V_i \leftarrow E_{\overline{CS_i}(\alpha) \oplus K_2}\left(CS_i\left(\beta\right)\right),$$
$$y_i^1 \leftarrow U_i \oplus m_i^1, y_i^2 \leftarrow V_i \oplus m_i^2$$

6: **end for**

7: $\mathcal{C} \leftarrow \left(y_i^1 \oplus y_i^2 \oplus \ldots \oplus y_l^1 \oplus y_l^2\right) \wedge$ return $\mathcal{C}$

8: Decrypt $\mathcal{C}$

9: partitioning $y_i^j \in \mathcal{C}$ s. t. $\left(y_1^1, y_1^2\right), \ldots, \left(y_l^1, y_l^2\right)$, where $j \in \{1,2\}, i \leq l$

10: initialization: $\alpha \leftarrow E_{AD_0 \oplus K_1}\left(\overline{N_0}\right) \oplus \overline{N_0}, \beta \leftarrow E_{\overline{AD_0} \oplus K_2}\left(N_0\right) \oplus N_0$

11: **for** $i = 1$ to l **do**

12:

$$U_i \leftarrow E_{CS_i(\alpha) \oplus K_1}\left(\overline{CS_i}\left(\beta\right)\right), V_i \leftarrow E_{\overline{CS_i}(\alpha) \oplus K_2}\left(CS_i\left(\beta\right)\right),$$
$$m_i^1 \leftarrow U_i \oplus y_i^1, m_i^2 \leftarrow V_i \oplus y_i^2$$

13: **end for**

14: $\mathcal{M} \leftarrow \left(m_i^1 \oplus m_i^2 \oplus \ldots \oplus m_l^1 \oplus m_l^2\right) \wedge$ return $\mathcal{M}$

2.5 PRP Security

Let blockcipher $\mathsf{block}(n, k)$ is a pseudo-random permutation, where $E = \{0,1\}^k \times \{0,1\}^n \to \{0,1\}^n$. Furthermore, $\{0,1\}^k \leftarrow^\$ K_E$ is a keyed and ideal permutation of blockcipher. On the other hand, there is a random permutation RP s. t. $RP \leftarrow^\$ \mathrm{Pm}(n) \mid \mathrm{Pm}$: Permutation. Therefore, the PRP security means the winning probability of differentiating between $\mathsf{block}(n, k)$ and RP. We assume that dT is a distinguish-er that can interact with the oracle of $\mathsf{block}(n, k)$ and RP. Thus, the advantage of PRP security is defined as follows:

$$\mathrm{Adv}_{\mathrm{PRP}}[\mathsf{dT}] = \Pr\left[\mathsf{dT}^{E(\cdot)} \Rightarrow 1\right] - \Pr\left[\mathsf{dT}^{RP(\cdot)} \Rightarrow 1\right] \tag{2}$$

The first probability depends on $\{0,1\}^k \leftarrow^\$ K_E$ and later one is based on $RP \leftarrow^\$ \mathrm{Pm}(n)$.

3 Proposed Authentication Encryption Scheme

We define our proposed construction of blockcipher based authentication encryption as AE_T^P (P: parallel, T : tag). The proposed AE_T^P has three modules of M_1, M_2, and M_3. The informal definition of M_1, M_2, and M_3 are respectively initialization of nonce and associate data, encryption including tag generation, and decryption including verification. Formally, the proposed scheme looks

$AE_T^p = (M_1|$ Initialization, $\mathcal{E}\text{-}AE_T^p, \mathcal{D}\text{-}AE_T^p)$. Furthermore, the key, nonce, associate data, message, ciphertext, and tag are respectively come from the spaces of $K_{AE_T^p}, N_{AE_T^p}, AD_{AE_T^p}, M_{AE_T^p}, C_{AE_T^p}$, and $T_{AE_T^p}$. On the contrary, our scheme is a variant of OCB, where symmetric key encryption module follows CTR mode using unique nonce and AD. Moreover, the tag generation or MAC function follows the variation of a PMAC plus construction.

We use three Algorithms of 2, 3, and 4 for the formal definition of M_1, M_2, and M_3. Additionally, the basic of encryption and decryption module comes from the Algorithm 1. In addition, we use two key sets of K_1 and K_2 for encryption and decryption module. Thereafter, K_3 and K_4 key sets are used in tag generation and verification process. Though, the decryption oracle doesn't need in the entire procedure of the proposed AE, but it needs for verification process of re-tag generation only.

3.1 Privacy Notion of AE_T^p

The privacy notion is based on $AE_T^p = (\mathcal{E}\text{-}AE_T^p, \mathcal{D}\text{-}AE_T^p)$. We assume an adversary $\mathcal{A}$ is unique nonce, AD based game and it has access to the encryption oracle and decryption oracle of AE_T^p. On the contrary, adversary $\mathcal{A}$ is

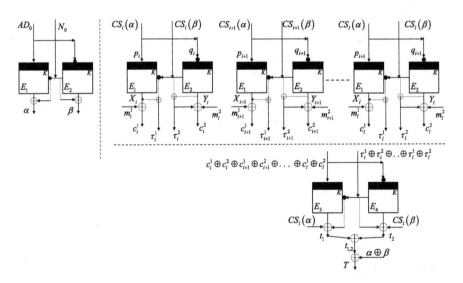

Fig. 3. Proposed construction of AE_T^p

Algorithm 2. Module $M_1(\alpha, \beta)$ of AE_T^p

1: initialization of N_0 and AD_0
2: $\alpha \leftarrow E_{AD_0 \oplus K_1}(\overline{N_0}) \oplus \overline{N_0}$
3: $\beta \leftarrow E_{\overline{AD_0} \oplus K_1}(N_0) \oplus N_0$
4: return (α, β)

Algorithm 3. Module $M_2(C,T)$ of $\mathcal{E}\text{-AE}_T^p$: Encryption and tag Generation

1: Input $\mathcal{M}|$set of message
2: Call M_1 s. t. $M_1 \rightarrow (\alpha, \beta)$
3: $M_i^j \in \mathcal{M}$ s. t. $\left(M_1^1, M_1^2\right), \ldots, \left(M_l^1, M_l^2\right)$, where $j \in \{1,2\}, i \leq l$
4: **for** $i = 1$ to l **do**
5:

$$\begin{cases} X_i \leftarrow E_{CS_i(\alpha) \oplus K_1} \left(\overline{CS}_i(\beta)\right), \\ Y_i \leftarrow E_{\overline{CS}_i(\alpha) \oplus K_2} \left(CS_i(\beta)\right) \end{cases}$$
$$C_i^1 \leftarrow X_i \oplus M_i^1, C_i^2 \leftarrow Y_i \oplus M_i^2,$$
$$\tau_i^1 \leftarrow X_i \oplus \overline{CS}_i(\beta), \tau_i^2 \leftarrow Y_i \oplus CS_i(\beta)$$

6: **end for**
7: $\mathcal{C} \leftarrow C_i^1 \oplus C_i^2 \oplus \ldots \oplus C_l^1 \oplus C_l^2$
8: $\gamma \leftarrow \tau_i^1 \oplus \tau_i^2 \oplus \tau_{i+1}^1 \oplus \tau_{i+1}^2 \oplus \ldots \oplus \tau_l^1 \oplus \tau_l^2$
9: $t_1 \leftarrow E_{\mathcal{C} \oplus K_3}(\bar{\gamma}) \oplus \bar{\gamma} \oplus CS_l(\alpha), t_2 \leftarrow E_{\overline{C} \oplus K_4}(\gamma) \oplus \gamma \oplus CS_l(\beta)$
10: $t_{1,2} \leftarrow t_1 \oplus t_2$
11: $T \leftarrow t_{1,2} \oplus (\alpha \oplus \beta)$
12: return $(\mathcal{C}, T)$

Algorithm 4. Module $M_3 (M$ or $\perp)$ of $\mathcal{D}\text{-AE}_T^p$: Decryption including Verification

1: Call M_1 s. t. $M_1 \rightarrow (\alpha, \beta)$
2: Call M_2 s. t. $M_2 \rightarrow (\mathcal{C}, T)$
3: $C_i^j \in \mathcal{C}$ s. t. $\left(C_1^1, C_1^2\right), \ldots, \left(C_l^1, C_l^2\right)$, where $j \in \{1,2\}, i \leq l$
4: **for** $i = 1$ to l **do**
5:

$$X_i \leftarrow E_{CS_i(\alpha) \oplus K_1} \left(\overline{CS}_i(\beta)\right) \oplus \overline{CS}_i(\beta),$$
$$Y_i \leftarrow E_{\overline{CS}_i(\alpha) \oplus K_2} \left(CS_i(\beta)\right) \oplus CS_i(\beta)$$
$$M_i^1 \leftarrow X_i \oplus C_i^1, \; M_i^2 \leftarrow Y_i \oplus C_i^2$$
$$\tau_i^1 \leftarrow X_i \oplus \overline{CS}_i(\beta), \; \tau_i^2 \leftarrow Y_i \oplus CS_i(\beta)$$

6: **end for**
7: $\mathcal{M} \leftarrow M_i^1 \oplus M_i^2 \oplus \ldots \oplus M_l^1 \oplus M_l^2$
8: $\gamma \leftarrow \tau_i^1 \oplus \tau_i^2 \oplus \tau_{i+1}^1 \oplus \tau_{i+1}^2 \oplus \ldots \oplus \tau_l^1 \oplus \tau_l^2$
9: $t'_1 \leftarrow E^{-1}{}_{\mathcal{C} \oplus K_3}(\bar{\gamma}) \oplus \bar{\gamma} \oplus CS_l(\alpha), t'_2 \leftarrow E^{-1}{}_{\overline{C} \oplus K_4}(\gamma) \oplus \gamma CS_l(\beta)$
10: $t'_{1,2} \leftarrow t'_1 \oplus t'_2$
11: $T' \leftarrow t'_{1,2} \oplus (\alpha \oplus \beta)$
12: **if** $T = T'$ **then**
13:     return $\mathcal{M}$ is valid and explore
14: **else**
15:     $\perp$
16: **end if**

---

inclusively bounded for encryption oracle ($\mathcal{E}\text{-AE}_T^p$) and random-bits oracle. Thus the encryption oracle takes input as $(N, A, M) \in N_{\text{AE}_T^p} \times AD_{\text{AE}_T^p} \times M_{\text{AE}_T^p}$ and returns $(C, T) \leftarrow \mathcal{E}\text{-AE}_T^p (N, A, M)$. The random-bits oracle and \$ oracle inherit $(N, A, M) \in N_{\text{AE}_T^p} \times AD_{\text{AE}_T^p} \times M_{\text{AE}_T^p}$, where the output is $(C, T) \leftarrow^\$ \{0, 1\}^{|M|+T}$. Therefore, the privacy advantage is defined as follows:

$$\text{Adv}_{\text{AE}_T^p}^{\text{priv}} (\mathcal{A}) = \Pr\left[\mathcal{A}^{\mathcal{E}\text{-AE}_T^p (\cdot, \cdot, \cdot)} = 1\right] - \Pr\left[\mathcal{A}^{\$(\cdot, \cdot, \cdot)} = 1\right],$$

where the first probability comes from $K \leftarrow^\$ K_{\text{AE}_T^p}$ and second one is based on random-bits oracle including randomness of $\mathcal{A}$. Furthermore, adversary is based on unique nonce and associate data. In principle, adversary can't make duplicate query.

3.2   Authenticity Notion of AE_T^p

The authenticity notion is based on $\text{AE}_T^p = (\mathcal{E}\text{-AE}_T^p, \mathcal{D}\text{-AE}_T^p)$. Let adversary $\mathcal{A}$ has access on encryption and decryption oracle of $\mathcal{E}\text{-AE}_T^p$ and $\mathcal{D}\text{-AE}_T^p$. The input of encryption oracle is $(N, A, M) \in N_{\text{AE}_T^p} \times AD_{\text{AE}_T^p} \times M_{\text{AE}_T^p}$. Thus the output is $(C, T) \leftarrow \mathcal{E}\text{-AE}_T^p (N, A, M)$. Furthermore, the decryption oracle invokes $(N, A, C, T) \in N_{\text{AE}_T^p} \times AD_{\text{AE}_T^p} \times C_{\text{AE}_T^p} \times T_{\text{AE}_T^p}$. Hence, the feedback is $M \leftarrow \text{AE}_T^p (N, A, C, T)$ or $\perp$. The advantage of authenticity is defined as follows:

$$\text{Adv}_{\text{AE}_T^p}^{\text{auth}} (\mathcal{A}) = \Pr\left[\mathcal{A}^{\mathcal{E}\text{-AE}_T^p, \mathcal{D}\text{-AE}_T^p} \text{ forges}\right],$$

where the probability is taken from $K \leftarrow^\$ K_{\text{AE}_T^p}$ and randomness of $\mathcal{A}$. Furthermore, $\mathcal{A}$ forges if decryption oracle returns message strings for a query (N, A, C, T), when (C, T) didn't part of encryption oracle. More specifically, adversary gets success for the condition of $(N_i, A_i, C_i, T_i) \neq (N_j, A_j, C_j, T_j)$. In principle, adversary doesn't make query (N', A', C', T') to decryption oracle if $(C', T') \leftarrow (N', A', M')$ was feedback of encryption oracle. Additionally, adversary is based on unique nonce and AD.

4   Security Analysis

4.1   Privacy Security Analysis

Privacy of AE_T^p is defined as the success probability of distinguish between the ciphertext and uniform distribution of string by adversary $\mathcal{A}$. Furthermore, $\mathcal{A}$ is based on unique nonce and associated data. The privacy security is formalized through a set of games. Thereafter, we take a pair of games for each segment. Gradually, we forward by taking pair of games and find the success probability of distinguish between two games. Thus we will show that the difference between two oracles are nominal. Let $\mathcal{A}$ be an adversary that makes q queries such as $(N_1, A_1, M_1) \ldots (N_l, A_l, M_l)$. Moreover, $\mathcal{A}$ is nonce-respecting and unique AD based adversary. The total length of message is σ_{2l}, where l is the number of iteration (two blocks message/iteration). In principle, we follow the proof technique of [22–24, 39] according to our scheme properties.

Theorem 1. *Let* AE_T^p *be the proposed authenticated encryption including encryption algorithm* $\mathcal{E}$-AE_T^p, *where* $n \geq 1$. *An adversary* $\mathcal{A}$ *is allowed to access random-bits oracle and* $\mathcal{E}$-AE_T^p. *Furthermore, adversary* $\mathcal{A}$ *can query upto* q. *The total message length is* σ_{2l}. *Thus the advantage of* $\mathcal{A}$ *is to distinguish between* $\mathcal{E}$-AE_T^p *from random oracle-bits and* $\$$. *Hence, the advantage is of adversary is bounded as follows:*

$$\mathrm{Adv}_{\mathrm{AE}_T^p}^{\mathrm{priv}}(\mathcal{A}) \leq \sigma\left(\sigma + 1\right)\Big/2^{2n} + 3/2^n$$

Proof. We use certain sequential games that have different targets and goals. In addition, the final goal is to locate the advantage of adversary for privacy of the proposed AE. Our approach is very simple such as to implement a game $\mathcal{G}_{\mathcal{A}}$, which performs the proposed scheme AE_T^p. Moreover, our final game is $\mathcal{G}_{\mathrm{E}}$. The task of $\mathcal{G}_{\mathrm{E}}$ is to inherit random oracle. We move forward by taking pair of consecutive games. Our target is to distinguish the pair of games. The success probability of distinguishing the two consecutive games is defined as the advantage of adversary. In this way, we reach into the final game of $\mathcal{G}_{\mathrm{E}}$. Thus, we show that the adversarial advantage of distinguishing the most recent game and the last game is nominal. Moreover, we take the all probability values of success. Thereafter, we calculate the union bound of these values and get the provable privacy security bound of the proposed scheme.

Our construction is based on blockcipher compression function. Therefore, the output of each iteration including input should be unique. If current output collides with previous entry then the adversary wins. Furthermore, an event is created as $\mathcal{WIN}$ in the aspect of adversarial win. Moreover, the new and fresh value comes from the random oracle if $\mathcal{WIN}$ occurs. In addition, the collide data/value needs to eliminate from the oracle of the proposed scheme AE_T^p. Thereafter, the success probability of the event $(\mathcal{WIN})$ indicates the advantage of adversary for distinguishing the consecutive pair of games. Additionally, we use PRF/PRP switch method in the given security proof [34].

On the contrary, we use a variant of PMAC-plus for MAC generation [23]. Therefore, two blockciphers are used to generate a tag (T). For better security, we actually use two sets of key under two blockciphers. The generation of MAC depends on the ex-or values of all ciphertext (C_i) and XOR values of all τ_i. Actually, these two are used as input of blockcipher. Thereafter, the output (size: $2n$-bits) is produced and XOR with the most recent values of $CS(\cdot)$. Thus, the security can be achieved better than the birthday bound. Generally, the collision resistance of blockcipher is defined as to find a similar output for different two input is infeasible for adversary [1–3]. Under this section, we play with the games through pairwise. Furthermore, the success probability of the adversary is given by the event of $\mathcal{WIN}$. At first, we take the proposed scheme and game $\mathcal{G}_{\mathcal{A}}$.

GAME $\mathcal{G}_{\mathcal{A}}$. $\mathcal{G}_{\mathcal{A}}$ inherits the proposed scheme AE_T^p. Moreover, $\mathcal{G}_{\mathcal{A}}$ invokes N, A, M as parameter of input. Thus, the corresponding responses are C, T. On the contrary, the queries of AE_T^p uses random function. Therefore,

$$\Pr\left[\mathcal{A}_{RP}^{\text{AE}_T^{\text{P}}} = 1\right] = \Pr\left[\mathcal{A}^{\mathcal{G}_A} = 1\right] \tag{3}$$

GAME $\mathcal{G}_B$. Let the queries of RP belongs to random function. Thus, the game $\mathcal{G}_B$ provides random output. However, the uniqueness of output can't be confirmed due to random function. Furthermore, if any collision occurs with previous any response then an event $\mathcal{WIN}$ is called. Therefore, the advantage of adversary is to distinguish between the game $\mathcal{G}_B$ and $\mathcal{G}_A$. The success probability of the event $\mathcal{WIN}$ is the advantage of adversary. All queries of RP for AE_T^{P} are stored in the database of $D_{\text{AE}_T^{\text{P}}}$, where RP is queried by σ times by AE_T^{P}. Therefore, the advantage of adversary is:

$$\Pr\left[\mathcal{A}^{\mathcal{G}_B} = 1\right] - \Pr\left[\mathcal{A}^{\mathcal{G}_A} = 1\right] \leq {}^{\sigma}\!/_{2^n} \tag{4}$$

GAME $\mathcal{G}_C$. In this section, the proposed scheme AE_T^{P} inherits random function. Furthermore, the database $D_{\text{AE}_T^{\text{P}}}$ is updated and synchronized. Therefore, the game $\mathcal{G}_C$ and $\mathcal{G}_B$ are in-distinguishable in the aspect of adversary. As a result, the advantage of adversary is as follows:

$$\Pr\left[\mathcal{A}^{\mathcal{G}_C} = 1\right] = \Pr\left[\mathcal{A}^{\mathcal{G}_B} = 1\right] \tag{5}$$

GAME $\mathcal{G}_D$. We will use PRF/PRP switch theme [34] in this section. The ciphertext should be indistinguishable in respect of random oracle. According to our AE construction definition, the ciphertext is created by the ex-or values of blockcipher compression output and message. Though, adversary can control message, but it can't control the output of blockcipher output. In addition, the nonce and associate data are unique. Therefore, there are four cases for collision occurred (Figs. 4 and 5). If collision occurs then an event $(\mathcal{WIN})$ is re-called in the respect of adversary.

▶ Case-1. In this section, we evaluate the probability of collision under blockcipher output. For example, the pair of output is X_i and Y_i ($i \leq l$). Thus, two types of collision can be occurred such as query of double and single query.
  • SubCase-1 (query of double). The requirements of collision under this SubCase are two different queries for the iteration of i, j ($i \geq j$) and similar output for input of any two queries. For example, the output are X_i and Y_i for the iteration of i. In addition, X_j and Y_j are the output of j-th iteration. Thus, there is a chance to collide with $X_i = X_j, Y_j$ or $Y_i = X_j, Y_j$ (Fig. 4). If collision occurs then an event is called. Moreover, the random and uniform values come from the set of $\mathcal{X}$ and $\mathcal{Y}$. Thereafter, these new values are replaced by collide values. The success probability of the event $\mathcal{WIN}$ is:

$$\begin{aligned} \Pr\left[\mathcal{WIN}\right] &= \Pr\left[\mathcal{WIN}_1 \vee \mathcal{WIN}_2 \vee ...\mathcal{WIN}_\sigma\right] \\ &\leq \Pr\left[\mathcal{WIN}_1\right] + \Pr\left[\mathcal{WIN}_2\right] + ...\Pr\left[\mathcal{WIN}_\sigma\right] \\ &\leq \sigma\left(\sigma - 1\right)/2^{2n} \end{aligned} \tag{6}$$

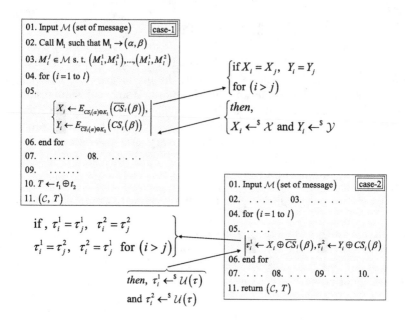

Fig. 4. Under the game $\mathcal{G}_D$

- SubCase-2 (single query). The output of i-th iteration are X_i and Y_i. Therefore, there is a chance to make a collision between $X_i = Y_i$. Thereafter, an event $\mathcal{WIN}$ is called in the aspect of adversarial success. Moreover, the collide values are replaced by the random and uniform values (Fig. 4). For example, $X_i \leftarrow \mathcal{X}$, $Y_i \leftarrow \mathcal{Y}$. The success probability of $\mathcal{WIN}$ under this SubCase is:

$$\begin{aligned}
\Pr[\mathcal{WIN}] &= \Pr[\mathcal{WIN}_1 \vee \mathcal{WIN}_2 \vee ...\mathcal{WIN}_\sigma] \\
&\leq \Pr[\mathcal{WIN}_1] + \Pr[\mathcal{WIN}_2] + ... \Pr[\mathcal{WIN}_\sigma] \\
&\leq \sigma \cdot (1/2^n)
\end{aligned} \tag{7}$$

▶ Case-2. According to our construction definition, the nonce is unique for each iteration. Thus, the ex-or values blockcipher output and nonce is random. However, there is a chance to occur collision such as $\tau_i^1 = \tau_j^1, \tau_i^2$ and $\tau_i^2 = \tau_j^1, \tau_j^2$. The event $\mathcal{WIN}$ is defined if collision occurs. Thereafter, the collide values are replaced by random and uniform distribution of $\mathcal{U}(\tau)$ (Fig. 4). So, the success probability of the event $\mathcal{WIN}$ is:

$$\begin{aligned}
\Pr[\mathcal{WIN}] &= \Pr[\mathcal{WIN}_1 \vee \mathcal{WIN}_2 \vee ...\mathcal{WIN}_\sigma] \\
&\leq \Pr[\mathcal{WIN}_1] + \Pr[\mathcal{WIN}_2] + ... \Pr[\mathcal{WIN}_\sigma] \\
&\leq 2\sigma/2^{2n}
\end{aligned} \tag{8}$$

▶ Case-3. This section is responsible for evaluation of tag collision. Generally, two different blockciphers including two unique key sets are used to generate tag. For example, the random value of ciphertext ($\mathcal{C}$) and most recent $CS(\cdot)$

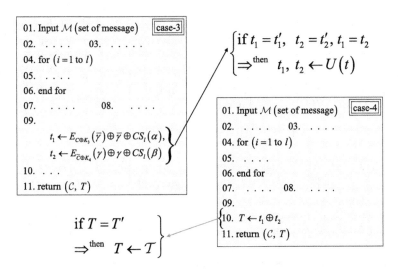

Fig. 5. Under the game $\mathcal{G}_\mathcal{D}$

value are used to generate tag. Therefore, there is a chance to collide between t_1 and t_2 (Fig. 5). If collision occurs then an event is defined as $\mathcal{WIN}$. The advantage of adversary is to find the probability of the event $\mathcal{WIN}$. Therefore, the advantage is:

$$\Pr\left[\mathcal{WIN}\right] = 2/2^n \tag{9}$$

▶ Case-4. The final tag is produced by the ex-or values of t_1, t_2 and $(\alpha \oplus \beta)$. If t_1 and t_2 are random then the ex-or output of T is also random. However, there is a chance to make collision such as $T = T'$. Hence, the probability of the event $\mathcal{WIN}$ is:

$$\Pr\left[\mathcal{WIN}\right] = 1/2^n \tag{10}$$

Adding the value of 6, 7, 8. 9 and 10, we get the advantage of distinguishing the game of $\mathcal{G}_\mathcal{C}$ and $\mathcal{G}_\mathcal{D}$.

GAME $\mathcal{G}_\mathrm{E}$. The $\mathcal{G}_\mathrm{E}$ simulates the random oracle model. The database $D_{\mathrm{AE}_T^p}$ is updated and synchronized after the operation of game $\mathcal{G}_\mathcal{D}$. Therefore, the current all entries are random and uniformly distributed. Hence, the game of $\mathcal{G}_\mathcal{D}$ and $\mathcal{G}_\mathrm{E}$ are identical in the aspect of adversary. So, the advantage of the adversary to distinguish the game of $\mathcal{G}_\mathrm{E}$ and $\mathcal{G}_\mathcal{D}$ is:

$$\Pr\left[\mathcal{A}^{\mathcal{G}_\mathrm{E}} = 1\right] = \Pr\left[\mathcal{A}^{\mathcal{G}_\mathcal{D}} = 1\right] \tag{11}$$

Therefore, taking the union bound of 4, 6, 7, 8, 9, and 10, Theorem 1 satisfies.

4.2 Authenticity Security Analysis

The authenticity of AE_T^p scheme is based on both oracle of encryption and decryption. The authenticity is said to be broken when adversary can inject under the condition of N', A', C', T' $(N', A', C', T') \neq (N, A, C, T)$. For example, encryption queries are $(N_1, A_1, M_1), \ldots, (N_q, A_q, M_q)$. Moreover, list of decryption queries are $(N'_1, A'_1, C'_1, T'_1) \ldots (N'_q, A'_q, C'_q, T'_q)$. The total length of message for encryption and decryption are respectively σ^{2l} and $\sigma^{2l'}$. Let there is an experiment $\mathcal{EXP}^{\mathrm{p}}_{\mathrm{auth}}$, which outputs 1 iff the adversary successfully forges N', A', C', T' for $M'|M \neq M'$. Therefore,

$$\mathrm{Adv}^{\mathrm{auth}}_{\mathrm{AE}^{\mathrm{p}}_T}(\mathcal{A}) = \Pr\left[\mathcal{EXP}^{\mathrm{p}}_{\mathrm{auth}}(\mathcal{A}) = 1\right] \tag{12}$$

Theorem 2. *Let* AE^{sim}_T *be the proposed authenticated encryption, where* $\mathcal{E}$-$\mathrm{AE}^{\mathrm{sim}}_T$ *and* $\mathcal{D}$-$\mathrm{AE}^{\mathrm{sim}}_T$ *be the encryption and decryption algorithm. Furthermore, adversary* $\mathcal{A}$ *is allowed to access both the oracles. Thus the advantage of* $\mathcal{A}$ *is success probability of injecting false data instead of valid data through the defined experiment* $\mathcal{EXP}$. *Therefore, the advantage of adversary is bounded as follows:*

$$\mathrm{Adv}^{\mathrm{auth}}_{\mathrm{AE}^{\mathrm{p}}_T}(\mathcal{A}) \leq \sigma\left(\sigma + 1\right)\Big/ 2^{2n} + 5/2^n + \sigma^2/2^{n+1}$$

5   Conclusion

In this paper, we have studied the familiar constructions of authentication encryption (AE). Moreover, the applications of AE have been evaluated. Recently, the AE has been considered as an important cryptographic tool/primitive for the security solution of IoT-end device, RfID, and resource constrained device. Thus, the AE should satisfies the properties of efficiency and better security. Though there are many constructions such as OCB, OTR, CLOC, SILK, APE, McOE, PoE, COPA, and COBRA but most of the scheme's privacy security are bounded by $O\left(2^{n/2}\right)$. Moreover, decryption oracle is necessary for all constructions except the OCB, OTR, CLOC, and SILK. Therefore, we have presented a blockcipher based AE that satisfies upper privacy security bound $\left(\mathrm{Priv} = O\left(2^{n/2}\right)\right)$. Our proposed scheme operates without decryption oracle in the module of encryption and decryption. Furthermore, the efficiency-rate is 1 and the operation mode is parallel. Moreover, the proposed construction can support flexible message encryption without padding. Our proposed scheme is a variant of OCB. More specifically, the symmetric encryption module follows the CTR mode and the MAC module follows the PMAC Plus construction. However, the proposed scheme can't support small domain encryption including format preserving encryption. Furthermore, decryption module is not online. Therefore, our target is to overcoming these limitations in future.

References

1. Rogaway, P.: Evaluation of Some Blockcipher Modes of Operation (2011). http://web.cs.ucdavis.edu/rogaway/papers/modes.pdf
2. Menezes, A.J., van Oorschot, P.C., Vanstone, S.A.: Handbook of Applied Cryptography, 5th edn. CRC Press, Boca Raton (2001)

3. Stallings, W.: Data & Computer Communications, 10th edn. Pearson, Boston (2013)
4. Hanaoka, G., Zheng, Y., Imai, H.: LITESET: a light-weight secure electronic transaction protocol. In: Boyd, C., Dawson, E. (eds.) ACISP 1998. LNCS, vol. 1438, pp. 215–226. Springer, Heidelberg (1998)
5. Kim, H., Kim, T.: Design on mobile secure electronic transaction protocol with component based development. In: Laganá, A., Gavrilova, M.L., Kumar, V., Mun, Y., Tan, C.J.K., Gervasi, O. (eds.) ICCSA 2004. LNCS, vol. 3043, pp. 461–470. Springer, Heidelberg (2004)
6. Cao, L.-C.: Improving security of SET protocol based on ECC. In: Gong, Z., Luo, X., Chen, J., Lei, J., Wang, F.L. (eds.) WISM 2011, Part I. LNCS, vol. 6987, pp. 234–241. Springer, Heidelberg (2011)
7. Lorenz, M.: Authentication and transaction security in e-business. In: Fischer-Hübner, S., Duquenoy, P., Zuccato, A., Martucci, L. (eds.) The Future of Identity in the Information Society, vol. 262, pp. 175–197. Springer, Heidelberg (2008)
8. Bailey, D.V., Brainard, J., Rohde, S., Paar, C.: Wireless authentication and transaction-confirmation token. In: Obaidat, M.S., Filipe, J. (eds.) ICETE 2009. CCIS, vol. 130, pp. 186–198. Springer, Heidelberg (2011)
9. Subpratatsavee, P., Kuacharoen, P.: Transaction authentication using HMAC-based one-time password and QR code. In: Park, J.J.J.H., Stojmenovic, I., Jeong, H.Y., Yi, G. (eds.) Computer Science and Its Applications. LNEE, vol. 330, pp. 93–98. Springer, Heidelberg (2015)
10. Zhang, L., Wu, W., Wang, P.: Extended models for message authentication. In: Lee, P.J., Cheon, J.H. (eds.) ICISC 2008. LNCS, vol. 5461, pp. 286–301. Springer, Heidelberg (2009)
11. Atzori, L., Iera, A., Morabito, G.: The internet of things: a survey. Comput. Netw. **54**(15), 2787–2805 (2010). Elsevier
12. Zhou, Z., Tsang, K.F., Zhao, Z., Gaalou, W.: Data intelligence on the Internet of Things. Pers. Ubiquit. Comput. **20**, 277–281 (2016). doi:10.1007/s00779-016-0912-1. Springer
13. Coppola, P., Mea, V.D., Gaspero, L.D., Lomuscio, R., Mischis, D., Mizzaro, S., Nazzi, E., Scagnetto, I., Vassena, L.: AI techniques in a context-aware ubiquitous environment. In: Hassanien, A.E., Abawajy, J.H., Abraham, A., Hagras, H. (eds.) Pervasive Computing. Computer Communications and Networks. Springer, Heidelberg (2009)
14. Zhao, K., Ge, L.: A survey on the internet of things security. In: 9th CIS, pp. 663–667. IEEE (2013). ISBN 978-1-4799-2548-3
15. Mennink, B.: Embedded security for internet of things. In: 2nd NCETACS, pp. 1–6. IEEE (2011). ISBN 978-1-4244-9578-8
16. Zanella, A., Bui, N., Castellani, A., Vangelista, L., Zorzi, M.: Internet of things for smart cities. IEEE Internet Things J. **1**(1), 22–32 (2014)
17. Özen, O., Stam, M.: Another glance at double-length hashing. In: Parker, M.G. (ed.) Cryptography and Coding 2009. LNCS, vol. 5921, pp. 176–201. Springer, Heidelberg (2009)
18. Andreeva, E., Bogdanov, A., Luykx, A., Mennink, B., Tischhauser, E., Yasuda, K.: Parallelizable and authenticated online ciphers. In: Sako, K., Sarkar, P. (eds.) ASIACRYPT 2013, Part I. LNCS, vol. 8269, pp. 424–443. Springer, Heidelberg (2013)

19. Andreeva, E., Bilgin, B., Bogdanov, A., Luykx, A., Mennink, B., Mouha, N., Yasuda, K.: APE: authenticated permutation-based encryption for lightweight cryptography. In: Cid, C., Rechberger, C. (eds.) FSE 2014. LNCS, vol. 8540, pp. 168–186. Springer, Heidelberg (2015)

20. Abed, F., Fluhrer, S., Forler, C., List, E., Lucks, S., McGrew, D., Wenzel, J.: Pipelineable on-line encryption. In: Cid, C., Rechberger, C. (eds.) FSE 2014. LNCS, vol. 8540, pp. 205–223. Springer, Heidelberg (2015)

21. Fleischmann, E., Forler, C., Lucks, S.: McOE: a family of almost foolproof on-line authenticated encryption schemes. In: Canteaut, A. (ed.) FSE 2012. LNCS, vol. 7549, pp. 196–215. Springer, Heidelberg (2012)

22. Rogaway, P.: Efficient instantiations of tweakable blockciphers and refinements to modes OCB and PMAC. In: Lee, P.J. (ed.) ASIACRYPT 2004. LNCS, vol. 3329, pp. 16–31. Springer, Heidelberg (2004)

23. Yasuda, K.: A new variant of PMAC: beyond the birthday bound. In: Rogaway, P. (ed.) CRYPTO 2011. LNCS, vol. 6841, pp. 596–609. Springer, Heidelberg (2011)

24. Naito, Y.: Full PRF-secure message authentication code based on tweakable block cipher. In: Chakraborty, S. (ed.) ProvSec 2015. LNCS, vol. 9451, pp. 167–182. Springer, Heidelberg (2015). doi:10.1007/978-3-319-26059-4_9

25. Yau, A.K.L., Paterson, K.G., Mitchell, C.J.: Padding Oracle attacks on CBC-mode encryption with secret and random IVs. In: Gilbert, H., Handschuh, H. (eds.) FSE 2005. LNCS, vol. 3557, pp. 299–319. Springer, Heidelberg (2005)

26. Lee, T., Kim, J.-S., Lee, C.-H., Sung, J., Lee, S.-J., Hong, D.: Padding oracle attacks on multiple modes of operation. In: Park, C., Chee, S. (eds.) ICISC 2004. LNCS, vol. 3506, pp. 343–351. Springer, Heidelberg (2005)

27. Paterson, K.G., Yau, A.K.L.: Padding oracle attacks on the ISO CBC mode encryption standard. In: Okamoto, T. (ed.) CT-RSA 2004. LNCS, vol. 2964, pp. 305–323. Springer, Heidelberg (2004)

28. Black, J.A., Rogaway, P., Shrimpton, T.: Black-box analysis of the block-cipher-based hash-function constructions from PGV. In: Yung, M. (ed.) CRYPTO 2002. LNCS, vol. 2442, pp. 320–335. Springer, Heidelberg (2002)

29. Black, J.A., Rogaway, P., Shrimpton, T., Stam, M.: An analysis of the blockcipher-based hash functions from PGV. J. Cryptol. **23**, 519–545 (2010)

30. Miyaji, A., Mazumder, R.: A new (n, 2n) double block length hash function based on single key scheduling. In: AINA, pp. 564–570. IEEE (2015)

31. Hirose, S., Ideguchi, K., Kuwakado, H., Owada, T., Preneel, B., Yoshida, H.: A lightweight 256-bit hash function for hardware and low-end devices: lesamnta-LW. In: Rhee, K.-H., Nyang, D.H. (eds.) ICISC 2010. LNCS, vol. 6829, pp. 151–168. Springer, Heidelberg (2011)

32. Shirai, Taizo, Shibutani, Kyoji, Akishita, Toru, Moriai, Shiho, Iwata, Tetsu: The 128-bit blockcipher CLEFIA (Extended Abstract). In: Biryukov, Alex (ed.) FSE 2007. LNCS, vol. 4593, pp. 181–195. Springer, Heidelberg (2007). IACR archive, https://www.iacr.org/archive/fse2007/45930182/45930182.pdf

33. Yoshida, H.: On the standardization of cryptographic application techniques for IoT devices in ITU techniques for IoT devices in ITU-T and ISO/IEC JTC 1 T and ISO/IEC JTC1 (2015). https://www.ietf.org/proceedings/94/slides/slides-94-saag-2.pdf,

34. Bellare, M., Rogaway, P.: The Security of Triple Encryption and a Framework for Code-Based Game-Playing Proofs. In: Vaudenay, S. (ed.) EUROCRYPT 2006. LNCS, vol. 4004, pp. 409–426. Springer, Heidelberg (2006)

35. Hoang, V.T., Reyhanitabar, R., Rogaway, P., Damian, V.: Online authenticated-encryption and its nonce-reuse misuse-resistance. In: Gennaro, R., Robshaw, M. (eds.) Advances in Cryptology – CRYPTO 2015. LNCS, vol. 9215, pp. 493–517. Springer, Heidelberg (2015)
36. Iwata, T., Minematsu, K., Guo, J., Morioka, S.: CLOC: authenticated encryption for short input. In: Cid, C., Rechberger, C. (eds.) FSE 2014. LNCS, vol. 8540, pp. 149–167. Springer, Heidelberg (2015)
37. Iwata, T., Minematsu, K., Guo, J., Morioka, S., Kobayashi, E.: SILC: SImple Lightweight CFB. DIAC Competitions. https://competitions.cr.yp.to/round2/silcv2.pdf
38. Minematsu, K.: Parallelizable rate-1 authenticated encryption from pseudorandom functions. In: Nguyen, P.Q., Oswald, E. (eds.) EUROCRYPT 2014. LNCS, vol. 8441, pp. 275–292. Springer, Heidelberg (2014)
39. Chang, D., R., S.M., Sanadhya, S.K.: PPAE: practical parazoa authenticated encryption family. In: Au, M.-H., Miyaji, A. (eds.) ProvSec 2015. LNCS, vol. 9451, pp. 198–211. Springer, Heidelberg (2015). doi:10.1007/978-3-319-26059-4_11

An Efficient Construction of a Compression Function for Cryptographic Hash

Rashed Mazumder[2]([✉]), Atsuko Miyaji[1,2,3], and Chunhua Su[1]

[1] Graduate School of Engineering, Osaka University, Osaka, Japan
{miyaji,su}@comm.eng.osaka-u.ac.jp
[2] Japan Advanced Institute of Science and Technology, Nomi, Japan
{s1420213,miyaji}@jaist.ac.jp
[3] Japan Science and Technology Agency (JST) CREST, Tokyo, Japan

Abstract. A cryptographic hash (CH) is an algorithm that invokes an arbitrary domain of the message and returns fixed size of an output. The numbers of application of cryptographic hash are enormous such as message integrity, password verification, and pseudorandom generation. Furthermore, the CH is an efficient primitive of security solution for IoT-end devices, constrained devices, and RfID. The construction of the CH depends on a compression function, where the compression function is constructed through a scratch or blockcipher. Generally, the blockcipher based cryptographic hash is more applicable than the scratch based hash because of direct implementation of blockcipher rather than encryption function. Though there are many $(n, 2n)$ blockcipher based compression functions, but most of the prominent schemes such as MR, Weimar, Hirose, Tandem, Abreast, Nandi, and ISA09 are focused for rigorous security bound rather than efficiency. Therefore, a more efficient construction of blockcipher based compression function is proposed, where it provides higher efficiency-rate including a satisfactory collision security bound. The efficiency-rate (r) of the proposed scheme is $r \approx 1$. Furthermore, the collision security is bounded by $q = 2^{125.84}$ (q = numer of query). Moreover, the proposed construction requires two calls of blockcipher under single iteration of encryption. Additionally, it has double key scheduling and it's operational mode is parallel.

Keywords: Cryptographic hash · Collision resistance · Constrained device

1 Introduction

A cryptographic hash (CH) is defined as to proceed data from an arbitrary domain to a fixed domain [1,2,6–8,10]. The applications of CH are enormous.

This work is partially supported by the Grant-in-Aid for Scientific Research (C)(15K00183) and (15K00189) and Japan Science and Technology Agency, CREST and Infrastructure Development for Promoting International S&T Cooperation. C. Su—JSPS Grant-in-Aid for Young Scientists (15K16005).

F. Buccafurri et al. (Eds.): CD-ARES 2016, LNCS 9817, pp. 124–140, 2016.
DOI: 10.1007/978-3-319-45507-5_9

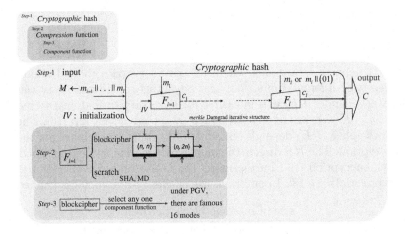

Fig. 1. Basic concept of cryptographic hash [2,6,8,34]

Generally, the CH is used in message verification, password verification, pseudo-random generation, and message authentication [1–3,7]. Furthermore, the cryptographic hash is an efficient primitive of security solution for IoT-end device, RfID, and resource constrained device [35–39,44]. Usually, the internal construction of CH depends on compression function [16,17]. The compression function is based on scratch or blockcipher [6,8,16,17,31]. The blockcipher based compression function is a combination of component functions (Fig. 1). The component functions depend on the 16 modes of PGV construction so far [8,16,17]. Additionally, a classical structure of Merkle Damgrad is used for message encryption of the cryptographic hash, if message size is bigger than the blocksize [1–3]. According to Fig. 1, message (M) is multiple of blocklength. Hence, message is partitioned as $M|m_{i=1}||. . .||m_l$. Thereafter, partitioned message injects as input with initial vector value (IV). The function F_i is called compression function, which is built by blockcipher or scratch. Usually, one of the PGV modes needs to select as a component function of compression function [8,16,17]. On the contrary, the generic of blockcipher compression function is more suitable than that of the scratch for encryption of a constrained device, IoT-end device because of implementation of blockcipher rather than the encryption function [5,6,13,14].

Usually, the blockcipher based compression function is classified as single block-length ($\mathcal{SBL}$) and double block-length ($\mathcal{DBL}$). Due to short size of output, the application of $\mathcal{SBL}$ is limited now [2,9,33]. On the other hand, the $\mathcal{DBL}$ is more reliable construction due to its better resistance against birthday attack [2,13,16,18,21,28]. Moreover, the $\mathcal{DBL}$ is categorized as (n,n) and $(n,2n)$ blockcipher (base is key size). The $(n,2n)$ blockcipher is better due to upper security bound (larger key space) [6,8,13,20,23]. Generally, there are certain parameters that indicate the strength of blockcipher based compression function such as:

– security bound (CR : collision and PR : preimage resistance)
– efficiency-rate (r)

- number of calling blockcipher ($\#E$)
- key scheduling (KS)
- operational mode (OM)

The CR is defined as a game, where an adversary tries to find similar output under two different input, but the advantage of adversary is very limited [6,13,21]. Under PR, it is infeasible for adversary to find any m (message) such that $y = F(m)$, where y is predefined by the adversary [2,6,16]. The number of blockcipher ($\#E$) depends on number of calling blockcipher per message-block encryption. The KS directs the number of key requirement for single message block encryption [16]. Furthermore, the OM stands for operational mode (parallel or serial) [17,18]. In addition, the efficiency-rate [6,15] is defined as:

$$r = \frac{\text{size of message block/per iteration}}{(\text{number of blockcipher call}) \times \text{block-length}}$$

Table 1. Result of existing familiar schemes

Name	CR	KS	r	$\#E$	OM
MR [23,31]	$O(2^n)$	1	1/2	2	Parallel
Weimar [6]	$O(2^n)$	2	1/2	2	Parallel
Hirose [13]	$O(2^n)$	1	1/2	2	Parallel
Tandem [6,14]	$O(2^n)$	2	1/2	2	Parallel
Abreast [6,14]	$O(2^n)$	2	1/2	2	Parallel
Nandi [20]	$O(2^{\frac{2n}{3}})$	3	2/3	3	Serial
ISA09 [21]	$O(2^n)$	3	2/3	3	Serial

CR: Collision resistance, KS: Key Scheduling, r: Efficiency rate
$\#E$: Number of blockcipher calls,
OM: Operational mode

Motivation. The parameters of CR, PR, r, $\#E$, OM, and KS are vital for any satisfactory scheme of blockcipher based compression function [1,6–8,13,21]. Firstly, certain gaps are identified from the current familiar schemes based on the above parameters. Thus, the importance of the findings are shown in the field of efficient and secure communication. For example, the key scheduling cost is analysed in respect of construction of compression function. Usually, 176 bytes are needed for operating of single key scheduling [27]. Hence, minimization of key scheduling is a common practice. Additionally, the operation mode is very crucial for resource limited devices, where the parallel mode can provide maximum support in respect of memory system [29,30]. Moreover, the efficiency-rate needs to reach the landmark ($r = 1$) [6,13,15,21]. There are some well-known schemes of blockcipher compression function such as MR, Weimar, Hirose,

Tandem, Abreast, Nandi, and ISA09 (Table 1). For example, the CR of MR scheme is bounded by $q = 2^{126.70}$ but the r is $1/2$ (q : number of queries). The scheme of Weimar-DM provides tight security bound such as $q = 2^{126.23}$ [6]. Moreover, it follows double key scheduling including $1/2$ efficiency-rate. The scheme of Hirose delivers marginal security bound as $q = 2^{124.55}$ but it ensures a single key scheduling. However, the CR and PR bound of the Tandem-DM and Abreast-DM are not satisfactory as that of the MR, Weimar, and Hirose [23]. Moreover, the efficiency-rate of Tandem-DM and Abreast-DM is $1/2$ like MR, Weimar, and Hirose [6,11,12]. Though the scheme of Nandi is bounded by $q = O\left(2^{2n/3}\right)$ but it provides higher efficiency-rate ($r = 2/3$) [20]. Additionally, the construction of ISA09 provides better efficiency-rate ($r = 2/3$) [21]. According to the above discussions and Table 1, most of the existing schemes have rigorous security margin. However, the efficiencies are low for the constructions of MR, Weimar, Hirose, Tandem and Abreast. On the other hand, the schemes of Nandi and ISA09 satisfies higher efficiency-rate. Moreover, the constructions of Nandi and ISA09 satisfies $KS = 3$ and $\#E = 3$ [20,21]. On the contrary, the OM is serial for Nandi and ISA09 schemes. Thus, the overall efficiencies are not adequate for the ISA09 and Nandi schemes.

Now-a-days, the importance of an efficient blockcipher compression function are enormous [6,8,13,33,34,40,41,44]. The blockcipher is one of the important cryptographic primitive for the security solution of IoT environment according to certain standards such as ISO/IEC29192-1, ISO/IEC29192-2, ISO/IEC29192-3, and ISO/IEC29192-4, [42–44]. Generally, IoT-end device, RfID, and constrained device are used in IoT environment [39–42]. Furthermore, these devices need to operate fast but the major draw-backs are limited memory, power, and processor [37,38,42–44]. Therefore, the cryptographic solution scheme should satisfies the property of better efficiency. In summary, the targets for an efficient blockcipher compression function are as follows:

- higher efficiency-rate
- reasonable key scheduling
- less number of calling blockcipher ($\#E$)
- operational mode
- satisfiable security bound

Contribution. In this paper, a blockcipher based compression function is proposed. The component function of the proposed construction follows one of the secure modes of PGV. The contributions of the proposed construction are as follows:

- efficiency rate, $r = 0.996$
- $KS = 2$
- $\#E = 2$
- Parallel mode
- CR security bound, $q = 2^{125.84} | q$: number of query

Table 2. Comparison: the proposed scheme and existing familiar schemes [6,14,15,20, 21,23]

	CR	r	KS	$\#E$	OM
MR	$2^{126.70}$	$r = 0.5$	1	2	P
Weimar	$2^{126.23}$	$r = 0.5$	2	2	P
Hirose	$2^{124.55}$	$r = 0.5$	1	2	P
Tandem	$2^{120.87}$	$r = 0.5$	2	2	P
Abreast	$2^{124.42}$	$r = 0.5$	2	2	P
proposed scheme	$2^{125.84}$	$r = 0.996$	2	2	P
Nandi	$O(2^{2n/3})$	$r = 0.66$	3	3	S
ISA09	$O(2^n)$	$r = 0.66$	3	3	S
MDC-2	$O(2^n)$	$r = 0.5$	2	2	P
MDC-4	$O(2^n)$	$r = 0.5$	4	4	SP

P: Parallel, S: Serial, SP: Semi-Parallel

In addition, a comparative study of the proposed construction and current familiar schemes is given through Table 2.

Outline. The basic preliminaries are provided in Sect. 2. The technical details of the proposed scheme are given in Sect. 3. Section 4 is responsible for the analysis of security bound. Furthermore, the result analysis is given including performance analysis in Sect. 5. Finally, the conclusions and future works are provided in Sect. 6.

2 Preliminaries

2.1 Ideal Cipher Model (ICM)

In ideal cipher model, a blockcipher is defined as $\mathcal{B}(n,k)$ where n means block-length and k means key-length. The operation of $\mathcal{B}(n,k)$ is $\mathcal{E} = \{0,1\}^n \times \{0,1\}^k \rightarrow \{0,1\}^n$. The reply of forward $(\mathcal{E})$ and backward $(\mathcal{E}^{-1})$ query is random and independent permutation of $\mathcal{K} \in \{0,1\}^k$. Let $\mathcal{BLOCK}_n^k$ is the set of all block-ciphers $\mathcal{B}(n,k)$. Under ideal cipher model, $\mathcal{E}$ is chosen randomly from $\mathcal{BLOCK}_n^k$. Actually, $\mathcal{E}$ invokes key and plaintext as input and returns ciphertext as output. On the contrary, input of $\mathcal{E}^{-1}$ are key and ciphertext. Then output is plaintext. Usually, the query and response through $\mathcal{E}$ and $\mathcal{E}^{-1}$ are stored as k_i, x_i, y_i. Moreover, the adversary is not allowed to make any duplicate query [17,22].

2.2 Security Definition

There are certain properties, which are responsible for analysing the security issue of blockcipher compression function. For example, collision resistance (CR), preimage resistance (PR), padding oracle attack, and initial value (CV) attack are the most familiar properties [6,13,23,24]. In this section, the collision and preimage resistance of the blockcipher compression function are briefly discussed [16–19].

Collision Resistance of Compression Function. The adversary $\mathcal{A}$ is allowed for accessing to the blockcipher oracle $\left(\mathcal{E} \in \mathcal{BLOCK}_n^k\right)$. Hence, the output of compression function are (α_1, β_1, m_1) and (α_2, β_2, m_2). Furthermore, an experiment is defined as Exp-coll$_{f_{\mathcal{E}}}(\mathcal{A})$. The output of the experiment is 1 iff following condition satisfies.

$$f_{\mathcal{E}}(\alpha_1, \beta_1, m_1) = f_{\mathcal{E}}(\alpha_2, \beta_2, m_2) \wedge \{(\alpha_1, \beta_1, m_1) \neq (\alpha_2, \beta_2, m_2)\},$$

where $f_{\mathcal{E}}$ is a blockcipher compression function and α, β are chaining values including $m|$ message. The advantage of adversary for finding a collision under $f_{\mathcal{E}}$ is defined below. Let, $\mathrm{Adv}_{f_{\mathcal{E}}}^{\mathrm{coll}}(\mathcal{A}) = \Pr\left[\text{Exp-coll}_{f_{\mathcal{E}}}(\mathcal{A}) = 1\right]$, where coll stands for collision. The advantage of adversary $\mathcal{A}$ is quantified by the number of queries that are allowed to ask blockcipher oracle. Therefore, $\mathrm{Adv}_{f_{\mathcal{E}}}^{\mathrm{coll}}(q) = \max_{\mathcal{A}} \left\{\mathrm{Adv}_{f_{\mathcal{E}}}^{\mathrm{coll}}(\mathcal{A})\right\}$, where the maximum is taken over all adversaries that ask at most q oracle queries [16,19].

Preimage Resistance of Compression Function. The adversary $\mathcal{A}$ has access on blockcipher oracle $\left(\mathcal{E} \in \mathcal{BLOCK}_n^k\right)$. Furthermore, $\mathcal{A}$ selects value of α, β randomly before making any query to blockcipher oracle. Let the feedback of oracle are α' and β' in respect of adversarial query. In addition, assume an experiment Exp-pre$_{f_{\mathcal{E}}}(\mathcal{A})$, where pre stands for preimage. Hence, the output of the defined experiment is 1 iff:

$$f_{\mathcal{E}}(\alpha_1, \beta_1, m_1) = (\alpha, \beta),$$

where $f_{\mathcal{E}}$ is a blockcipher compression function and α_1, β_1 are chaining values including $m|$ message. The advantage of adversary for finding a preimage under $f_{\mathcal{E}}$ is defined by $\mathrm{Adv}_{f_{\mathcal{E}}}^{\mathrm{pre}}(\mathcal{A}) = \Pr\left[\text{Exp-pre}_{f_{\mathcal{E}}}(\mathcal{A}) = 1\right]$. Moreover, the advantage of $\mathcal{A}$ is evaluated through the total number of queries. Therefore, $\mathrm{Adv}_{f_{\mathcal{E}}}^{\mathrm{pre}}(q) = \max_{\mathcal{A}} \left\{\mathrm{Adv}_{f_{\mathcal{E}}}^{\mathrm{pre}}(\mathcal{A})\right\}$, where the maximum is taken over all adversaries that ask q oracle queries [16,19].

3 Proposed Scheme

Usually, the efficiency-rate can be increased by using three calls of blockcipher. The above method is used in Nandi and ISA09 [20,21]. Furthermore, a method of using a pair of chaining values including message in the two blockciphers is also useful. Such kind of method is used in MDC-2 and later in MDC-4 [4,9,32,45].

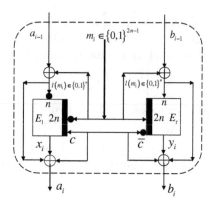

Fig. 2. Proposed Scheme (Variant of MDC-2, 4)

The proposed construction is actually inspired and followed by the construction of MDC-2 and MDC-4 [4,9,45]. However, in respect of security there is a drawback for these (MDC-2, 4) kind of construction. In MDC-2, two chaining values are used as input, where message is common for two blockciphers. There is no dependency between two chaining values as input. On the contrary, it can be said that the computations of the two block ciphers used in the compression function are completely isolated. For example, given the input and output $(x_1, y_1 \rightarrow x_2, y_2)$, if the input is swapped then the new output will be swapped values of the old output $(y_1, x_1 \rightarrow y_2, x_2)$. It actually suffers for symmetric property. Therefore, certain changes are occurred in the proposed construction (Fig. 2). For example, one constant bit 0 and 1 is used to each of the block ciphers as part of the key for the proposed scheme (trivial practice in cryptography, [14]). Hence, the attacker can't predict the output of the chaining values which is given under the assumption where the attacker can freely alter the input of chaining values and message. This premise is used for breaking the symmetric property of the proposed scheme, where $x||y$ and $y||x$ will be treated as two different values. Moreover, the scheme is secured under a generic attack because of the ideal cipher model primitive [26]. Additionally, the MDC-2, MDC-4 are (n, n)-bit $\mathcal{DBL}$ hash functions with efficiency-rate $1/2$ and $1/4$ [24], where the proposed scheme is based on $(n, 2n)$ blockcipher. Furthermore, a different component function is used in respect of the MDC-2 and MDC-4. The proposed scheme can compress $4n$ bits into $2n$ bits, where MDC-2 and MDC-4 can compress $3n$ bits to $2n$ bits. Furthermore, the proposed scheme satisfies type-1 (from Stam's conjecture), where two blockciphers $\mathcal{E}_l$, $\mathcal{E}_r$ are distinct and independent under the ICM [8,16]. In general, the proposed scheme is defined as variant of the MDC-2 and MDC-4.

Definition 1. Let $\mathcal{E} \in \mathcal{BLOCK}_n^k$ be a block cipher taking a set of k-bit key and n-bit block-length such that $\mathcal{E}_{l,r} = \{0,1\}^k \times \{0,1\}^n \rightarrow \{0,1\}^n$. $\mathcal{E}^{dbl} = \{0,1\}^k \times \{0,1\}^{2n} \rightarrow \{0,1\}^{2n}$ is defined as a double block length (dbl) cipher and parallel calling of two independent blockciphers of $\mathcal{E}_{1,r}$ such that,

$$x_i \leftarrow \mathcal{E}_{1,(\overline{m}_i||c)}\left(\overline{a_{i-1} \oplus l(m_i)}\right)$$
$$y_i \leftarrow \mathcal{E}_{r,(m_i||\bar{c})}\left(b_{i-1} \oplus l(m_i)\right)$$

where parameters are defined as $m_i \in \{0,1\}^{2n-1}, (a,b,x,y) \in \{0,1\}^n$ and $l(m_i) = \text{lsb of } m_i \in \{0,1\}^n, c = \{1\}$. Thus, the final output is $f_{\mathcal{E}}(a_i, b_i)$ where,

$$\begin{cases} a_i \leftarrow x_i \oplus (a_{i-1} \oplus l(m_i)) \oplus c \\ b_i \leftarrow y_i \oplus (b_{i-1} \oplus l(m_i)) \oplus \bar{c} \end{cases}$$

Definition 2. Let $f_{\mathcal{E}} = \{0,1\}^k \times \{0,1\}^{2n} \to \{0,1\}^{2n}$ be a blockcipher based compression function such as $(a_i, b_i, m_i) = f(a_i, b_i, m_i)$, where, $a_i \in \{0,1\}^n$, $b_i \in \{0,1\}^n$, $m_i \in \{0,1\}^{2n-1}$, and $c = \{0,1\}$. Therefore, $f_{\mathcal{E}}$ consists of ideal blockcipher $(\mathcal{E})$ such as:

$$\left[\begin{array}{l} a_i = f_1\left(\overline{a_{i-1} \oplus l(m_i)}, \overline{m}_i||c\right) \oplus (a_{i-1} \oplus l(m_i)) \oplus c \leftarrow \\ \mathcal{E}_1\left(\overline{a_{i-1} \oplus l(m_i)}, \overline{m}_i||c\right) \oplus (a_{i-1} \oplus l(m_i)) \oplus c \end{array} \right]$$

$$\left[\begin{array}{l} b_i = f_r\left(b_{i-1} \oplus l(m_i), m_i||\bar{c}\right) \oplus (b_{i-1} \oplus l(m_i)) \oplus \bar{c} \leftarrow \\ \mathcal{E}_r\left(b_{i-1} \oplus l(m_i), m_i||\bar{c}\right) \oplus (b_{i-1} \oplus l(m_i)) \oplus \bar{c} \end{array} \right]$$

4   Security Analysis

The security proof of the proposed scheme follows an ICM [16,17], where $\mathcal{A}$ is not allowed to make any duplicate query. For example, the query of $\mathcal{E}(k,x) = y$ isn't being executed by the adversary, if $\mathcal{E}^{-1}(k,y) = x$ query is already in the query storage $(\mathcal{Q})$. The adversary $\mathcal{A}$ searches for a collision under a pair of different inputs (query) through the blockcipher oracle. Additionally, $\mathcal{A}$ tries to find an output of compression function for making collision with initial chaining value. Moreover, the preimage attack means: Adversary $\mathcal{A}$ selects α', β' randomly and tries to find $f(\alpha, \beta, m) = \alpha', \beta'$. In addition, the advantage of $\mathcal{A}$ is very limited to get the above success.

4.1   Collision Security Analysis

An adversary $\mathcal{A}$ has access to a blockcipher oracle for finding a collision. The query is Q_i and corresponding response is triplet as $(m : \text{mesage}, k : \text{key}, c : \text{ciphertext})$. For any i-th iteration $(i \leq q)$, the query process looks either $Q_i \in \{(m,k) = c\}$ or $Q_i \in \{(c,k) = m\}$. The Q_i stores in $\mathcal{Q} \in (Q_1, Q_2, ..., Q_i)$ for each iteration of i where $\mathcal{Q}$: query storage. Under this circumstance, adversary $\mathcal{A}$ has target to find,

$$f_{\mathcal{E}}(m_i, k_i, c_i) = f_{\mathcal{E}}(m_j, k_j, c_j)| \because (m_i, k_i, c_i) \neq (m_j, k_j, c_j) \wedge (i \neq j) \quad (1)$$

According to the definition of proposed scheme, 1 is re-defined as:

$$f_{\mathcal{E}}(a_i, b_i, m_i) = f_{\mathcal{E}}(a_j, b_j, m_j)| \because (a_i, b_i, m_i) \neq (a_j, b_j, m_j) \wedge (i \neq j) \quad (2)$$

Theorem 1. *Let $f_{\mathcal{E}}$ be a double block-length compression function (Definitions 1 and 2). An adversary, $\mathcal{A}$ is assigned for finding a collision (coll) under the $f_{\mathcal{E}}$ after q pairs of queries. Hence, the advantage of $\mathcal{A}$ is bounded by,*

$$Adv_{f_{\mathcal{E}}}^{coll}(q) \leq \frac{6q^2 - 2q}{(2^n - q)^2}$$

Proof. An adversary $\mathcal{A}$ makes a relevant query to the blockcipher oracle, where the number of query is limited by q queries. For any i-th query, the reply of x_i and y_i randomly selects by the adversary from the blockcipher oracle. The main difficulty is to find out the set size of an oracle from where these fresh value come. There are three possible incidents that are responsible for collision-hit under any i-th iteration. In the beginning, the three incidents are clarified through two targets ($\mathcal{TAR}1$, $\mathcal{TAR}2$). The goal of the first incident is to find a collision for two distinct queries ($j < i$) where $\mathcal{TAR}1$ represents the responsibilities of the first incident. The $\mathcal{TAR}2$ is responsible for second and third incident. Since $\mathcal{A}$ has target to find a collision through single query. Furthermore, $\mathcal{A}$ investigates for a collision against initial chaining values. Finally, three phases of $\mathcal{QUERY}$, $\mathcal{RESPONSE}$, and $\mathcal{CHECK}$ have been defined under $\mathcal{TAR}1$ and $\mathcal{TAR}2$. Let adversary $\mathcal{A}$ is allowed to ask query to blockcipher oracle at $\mathcal{QUERY}$ phase. Moreover, corresponding feedback assign under $\mathcal{RESPONSE}$ phase. In addition, a collision is checked in the phase of $\mathcal{CHECK}$.

Algorithm 1. $\mathcal{TAR}1$ (for notations follow Definitions 1 and 2)

1: $\mathcal{Q}$: Query storage, q: query, $\mathcal{A}$: Adversary, $^{\mathcal{TAR}1}\mathcal{C}_i$: event, m : message
2: **for** each node $(i < q)$ **do**
3:    $\mathcal{QUERY}$: $\left(\mathcal{E} \leftarrow \mathcal{BLOCK}_n^k\right) \leftarrow \mathcal{A}^{\mathcal{E},\mathcal{E}^{-1}}$
4:    $\mathcal{RESPONSE}$:
5:    $q_{i,1} \leftarrow \left(x_i = \mathcal{E}_{(m_i||c)}\left(\overline{a_{i-1} \oplus l(m_i)}\right)\right) \wedge q_{i,2} \leftarrow y_i$
6:    $\mathcal{CHECK}$:
7:    **if** $(q_{i,1}, q_{i,2}){=}(q_{j,1}, q_{j,2})$, where $j < i$ **then**
8:        1. Call: $^{\mathcal{TAR}1}\mathcal{C}_i \wedge$ terminate
9:    **else**
10:        write the value of $q_{i,1}, q_{i,2}$ to $\mathcal{Q}$
11:    **end if**
12: **end for**

Collision probability based on the first incident ($\mathcal{TAR}1$). Under an iteration of i, a pair of query is executed that returns two distinct outputs. According to Algorithm 1, there is a chance to make collision through two different query-pairs after any i-th ($j < i < q$) iteration. For example, a query pair of j-th iteration are:

$$\begin{bmatrix} a_j \leftarrow \mathcal{E}_{1,\bar{m}_j||c}\left(\overline{a_{j-1} \oplus l(m_j)}\right) \oplus (a_{j-1} \oplus l(m_j)) \oplus c, \\ b_j \leftarrow \mathcal{E}_{\mathrm{r},m_j||\bar{c}}\left(a_{j-1} \oplus l(m_j)\right) \oplus (a_{j-1} \oplus l(m_j)) \oplus \bar{c} \end{bmatrix}$$

Moreover, the query responses are $a_i \leftarrow E_{1,\bar{m}||c}\left(\overline{a_{i-1} \oplus l\,(m_i)}\right) \oplus (a_{i-1} \oplus l\,(m_i))$ $\oplus c$ and $b_i \leftarrow E_{r,m||\bar{c}}\,(a_{i-1} \oplus l\,(m_i)) \oplus (a_{i-1} \oplus l\,(m_i)) \oplus \bar{c}$ on the i-th $(j < i)$ iteration. Let $^{T\mathcal{AR}1}\mathcal{C}_i$ be an event, where adversary tries to find a collision through different two iterations $(j < i \leq q)$. Thus, Eq. 2 is re-defined as:

$$\begin{cases} \{a_i \leftarrow (c \oplus a_{i-1} \oplus l\,(m_i) \oplus x_i)\} \\ \{a_j \leftarrow (c \oplus a_{j-1} \oplus l\,(m_j) \oplus x_j)\} \end{cases} = \vee \begin{cases} \{a_i \leftarrow (c \oplus a_{i-1} \oplus l\,(m_i) \oplus x_i)\} = \\ \{b_j \leftarrow (\bar{c} \oplus b_{j-1} \oplus l\,(m_j) \oplus y_j)\} \end{cases}$$
(3)

$$\begin{cases} \{b_i \leftarrow (\bar{c} \oplus b_{i-1} \oplus l\,(m_i) \oplus y_i)\} = \\ \{a_j \leftarrow (c \oplus a_{j-1} \oplus l\,(m_j) \oplus x_j)\} \end{cases} \vee \begin{cases} \{b_i \leftarrow (\bar{c} \oplus b_{i-1} \oplus l\,(m_i) \oplus y_i)\} = \\ \{b_j \leftarrow (\bar{c} \oplus b_{j-1} \oplus l\,(m_j) \oplus y_j)\} \end{cases}$$
(4)

From $3 \wedge 4$, the probability of collision hit under the event of $^{T\mathcal{AR}1}\mathcal{C}_i$ is $\frac{2(i-1)}{(2^n - (i-1))^2}$ (when $j < i \leq q$). Therefore, the probability of single event under the $T\mathcal{AR}1$ is:

$$\Pr\left[^{T\mathcal{AR}1}\mathcal{C}\right] = 2\,(i-1)\Big/\left(2^n - (i-1)\right)^2$$

If $^{T\mathcal{AR}1}\mathcal{C}$ be the events of all colliding pairs under the $f_\mathcal{E}$ for q pairs of queries. Hence,

$$\Pr\left[^{T\mathcal{AR}1}\mathcal{C}\right] = \Pr\left[^{T\mathcal{AR}1}\mathcal{C}_2 \vee .. \vee {}^{T\mathcal{AR}1}\mathcal{C}_q\right]$$

$$\leq \sum_{i=2}^{q} \Pr\left[^{T\mathcal{AR}1}\mathcal{C}_i\right] \leq \frac{2 \times 2 \times (i-1)}{(2^n - i)^2} = \frac{2q^2 - 2q}{(2^n - q)^2}$$
(5)

Collision probability based on the second and third incident $(T\mathcal{AR}2)$. Let a_i, b_i be the output of compression function $(i < q)$, where

$$\{(a_i \leftarrow x_i \oplus (a_{i-1} \oplus l\,(m_i)) \oplus c)\,, (b_i \leftarrow y_i \oplus (b_{i-1} \oplus l\,(m_i)) \oplus \bar{c})\}$$

Hence, there is a probability to make collision when $a_i = b_i$. Let $^{T\mathcal{AR}2}\mathcal{C}_i$ be a collision event for the above condition under the check phase of $i < q$. Furthermore, there is an option to make a collision with initial chaining values. For example, the output pair of the proposed scheme a_i, b_i collides with the initial chaining values (a_0, b_0) at any phase of query process. Therefore, the conditions of collision-hit under the initial key attack are $\{a_i = (a_0)\,, (b_0)\} \vee \{b_i = (a_0)\,, (b_0)\}$.

Hence, the probability of collision under two incidents is at most $1/(2^n - i) \times 2 \times 2/(2^n - i)$. Finally, the probability of these two incidents under the event of $^{T\mathcal{AR}2}\mathcal{C}$ for q pairs of queries is:

$$\Pr\left[^{T\mathcal{AR}2}\mathcal{C}\right] = \Pr\left[^{T\mathcal{AR}2}\mathcal{C}_1 \vee .. ^{T\mathcal{AR}2}\mathcal{C}_q\right]$$

$$\leq \sum_{i=1}^{q} \Pr\left[^{T\mathcal{AR}2}\mathcal{C}_i\right] = \sum_{i=1}^{q} \frac{1}{(2^n - i)} \times \frac{2 \times 2}{(2^n - i)} \leq \frac{q}{(2^n - q)} \times \frac{2 \times 2 \times q}{(2^n - q)} = \frac{4q^2}{(2^n - q)^2}$$
(6)

Adding the values of 5 and 6, Theorem 1 satisfies.

Algorithm 2. (for $\mathcal{TAR}2$)

1: $\mathcal{TAR}2$: line 2 to 7 is replaced of $\mathcal{TAR}1$ (from line 4)
2: **if** $(q_{i,1} = q_{i,2})$ **then**
3:     create the event $\left({}^{\mathcal{TAR}2}\mathcal{C}_i\right) \wedge$ terminate
4:     "AND"
5:     **if** $(q_{i,1}, q_{i,2}) = (q_{0,1}, q_{0,2})$ **then**
6:         create the event $\left({}^{\mathcal{TAR}2}\mathcal{C}_i\right) \wedge$ terminate
7:     **end if**
8: **end if**

4.2 Preimage Security Analysis

A standard proof technique of Armknecht et al. is used for the preimgae security proof of the proposed scheme [14]. The PR security bound of MR, Weimar, Hirose, Tandem and Abreast is also based on [14]. The two important concepts are adopted such as query: super, normal and adjacent query-pair from [6,14]. Let $\mathcal{A}$ randomly picks the output value of compression function (a', b'). Now $\mathcal{A}$ has target to find a probability for preimage-hit through $f_{\mathcal{E}}^{\mathrm{p}}(a_i, b_i, m) = (a', b')$ condition, where a_i, b_i, m : input of compression function and $a_i \neq b_i$.

Theorem 2. *Let $f_{\mathcal{E}}$ be a double block-length compression function. An adversary $\mathcal{A}$ is defined for finding a preimage-hit under the $f_{\mathcal{E}}$ after q pairs of queries. Hence, the advantage of $\mathcal{A}$ is bounded by,*

$$Adv_{f_{\mathcal{E}}}^{pre}(q) \leq 8q \Big/ N^2 + 8q \Big/ (N-q)^2$$

Proof. An adversary $\mathcal{A}$ keeps a query database in the form of,

$$\left[\begin{array}{l} \left\{ a_i \leftarrow \mathcal{E}_{1,\overline{m}||c}\left(\overline{a_{i-1} \oplus l\,(m_i)}\right) \oplus (a_{i-1} \oplus l\,(m_i)) \oplus c \right\} \\ \text{and} \left\{ b_i \leftarrow \mathcal{E}_{\mathrm{r},m||\bar{c}}\,(b_{i-1} \oplus l\,(m_i)) \oplus (b_{i-1} \oplus l\,(m_i)) \oplus \bar{c} \right\} \end{array} \right]$$

In such a fashion, when the oracle size reaches $N/2$ (N : Oracle size (2^n)), the rest of the queries under the key-set reaches the adversary as free query [6,14,25]. This free set of queries exist in the domain which is called the super query database ($\mathcal{SQD}$). On the other hand, the first $N/2$ is defined as a normal query database ($\mathcal{NQD}$) [14]. Additionally, the free queries are asked by the adversary non-adaptively in the super query database ($\mathcal{SQD}$). Therefore the successful conditions of a preimage-hit are:

$$\left\{ \begin{array}{l} a_i \leftarrow \mathcal{E}_{1,\bar{m}_i||c}\left(\overline{a_{i-1} \oplus l\,(m_i)}\right) \oplus (a_{i-1} \oplus l\,(m_i)) \oplus c \right\}, \\ a_j \leftarrow \mathcal{E}_{1,\bar{m}_j||c}\left(\overline{a_{j-1} \oplus l\,(m_j)}\right) \oplus (a_{j-1} \oplus l\,(m_j)) \oplus c \right\} = \{(a')\,,(b')\} \end{array} \right. \tag{7}$$

$$\left\{ \begin{array}{l} b_i \leftarrow \mathcal{E}_{\mathrm{r},m||\bar{c}_i}\,(b_{i-1} \oplus l\,(m_i)) \oplus (b_{i-1} \oplus l\,(m_i)) \oplus \bar{c} \right\}, \\ b_j \leftarrow \mathcal{E}_{\mathrm{r},m||\bar{c}_j}\,(b_{j-1} \oplus l\,(m_j)) \oplus (b_{j-1} \oplus l\,(m_j)) \oplus \bar{c} \right\} = \{(a')\,,(b')\} \end{array} \right. \tag{8}$$

Algorithm 3

1: **procedure** PREIMAGE TARGET
2:     **for** $i < N/2$ **do** (for normal query)
3:         run $\mathcal{QUERY} \wedge \mathcal{RESPONSE} \wedge \mathcal{CHECK}$
4:     **end for**
5:     **for** $N/2 < i < N$ **do** for super query
6:         $(\mathcal{QUERY} \wedge \mathcal{CHECK})$
7:     **end for**
8: **end procedure**

Equations 7 and 8 can occur in either in the domain of a normal query win ($\mathcal{NQW}$) or super query win ($\mathcal{SQW}$). Therefore, the probability of the preimage-hit is $\Pr[\mathcal{NQW}] + \Pr[\mathcal{SQW}]$.

Probability of $\mathcal{NQW}$. The adversary $\mathcal{A}$ makes any relevant query independently and receives a_i, b_i. Furthermore, $\mathcal{A}$ executes until the oracle set size reaches to $N/2$ [6,14]. According to the above mentioned conditions (7, 8), the hitting probability is $2 \times 2 \big/ (2^n - q)$.

If $\mathcal{A}$ makes a query $\mathcal{E}_{1,\overline{m}_i||c}\left(\overline{a_{i-1} \oplus l\,(m_i)}\right)$ (left block) then the answer of a right block provides as free query to $\mathcal{A}$ because of the adjacent query pair [6,14]. Thereafter, the set size is $(2^n - q)/2$ which outfits the probability as $2\big/(2^n - q)$. Thus, the probability of the normal query is:

$$\Pr[\mathcal{NQW}] = q \times 2 \times 2/(2^n - q) \times 2/(2^n - q) = {}^{8q}\big/(2^n - q)^2 \qquad (9)$$

Probability of $\mathcal{SQW}$. The concept of a super query oracle is very simple [6,14]. If the query oracle reaches at the point of $N/2$, then the rest of the queries set as free to the adversary [6,14]. Later these queries are asked by the adversary non-adaptively [14] for finding a preimage-hit (Algorithm 3). Moreover, the preimage-hit is notified either in this domain ($\mathcal{SQD}$) or not. Thus, the probability is either $2/N$ or 0 for any output value of a_i/b_i. Now a pair of conditions under $\mathcal{SQW}$ are:

$$\{a_i \leftarrow (l\,(m_i) \oplus a_{i-1} \oplus x_i) \oplus c\} = (a')\,,(b') \qquad (10)$$

$$\{b_i \leftarrow (l\,(m_i) \oplus b_{i-1} \oplus y_i) \oplus \overline{c}\} = (a')\,,(b') \qquad (11)$$

According to 10, the answer of a_i has a possibility to come from the set size of $N/2$. Hence, the probability is $2/N$. Recalling the concept of an adjacent query pair (free query) [6,14], where the answer of another block (right block) comes from the set size of $N/2$. As a result, the probability of 10 is in total $4/N^2$. In similar way, the probability of 11 is $4/N^2$. Now, the final probability of the $\mathcal{SQW}$ is evaluated based on the the number of points for a $\mathcal{SQW}$, the cost of $\mathcal{SQW}$ and the probability of obtaining preimgae-hit such as:

$$\Pr[\mathcal{SQW}] = q/(N/2) \times (N/2) \times 2 \times \left(4/N^2\right) = 8q/N^2 \qquad (12)$$

Adding the values of 9 and 12, Theorem 2 satisfies.

5   Result Analysis

5.1   Collision Resistance Analysis

Theorem 1 provides a probability of collision hit under the given adversary $\mathcal{A}$. The number of queries (q) is important for finding an upper bound of the collision security. Hence, the value of q is required to investigate when the adversarial advantage is $1/2$ (birthday attack).

Let, $N = 2^n$ and $\mathrm{Adv}_{f_E}^{\mathrm{coll}}(\mathcal{A}) \leq \frac{6q^2 - 2q}{(2^n - q)^2}$ [Theorem 1], where $n = 128$. According to the birthday attack [1, 6, 13, 20, 21], $\mathrm{Adv}_{f_{\mathcal{E}}}^{\mathrm{coll}}(\mathcal{A}) = \frac{1}{2}$. Thus, the number of queries are $q = 2^{125.84}$.

5.2   Efficiency-rate

The efficiency-rate of a blockcipher based compression function is defined as $r = \frac{|m|}{(n \times \#E)}$, where $|m| = $ length of message, $n = $ blocklength and $\#E = $ number of blockcipher calls. According to the definitions (Definitions 1 and 2) of the proposed scheme, the efficiency-rate is $r = 0.996 \Rightarrow r \approx 1$. In Fig. 3, the proposed scheme is compared with the existing schemes in respect of efficiency-rate.

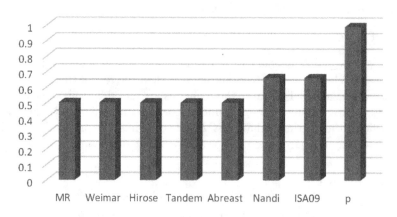

Fig. 3. Comparison of efficiency-rate

5.3   Performance Analysis

In this section, a comparison study is given for the proposed scheme in respect of memory resources. It is known that 176 bytes of memory is required for single key scheduling [27]. For example, a $2n$-bit size of message is taken for encryption. Therefore, the following Tables 3 and 4 are made based on the characteristics of

Table 3. Required memory for key scheduling [20, 21, 27]

Name	KS	Required memory (in byte, B)
Proposed scheme	2	$2 \times 176\,\text{B}$
Nandi [20]	3	$3 \times 176\,\text{B}$
ISA09 [21]	3	$3 \times 176\,\text{B}$

Table 4. Required memory for key scheduling [6, 23, 27]

Name	KS	l	B	$\mathcal{V}$	$B + \mathcal{V}$
Proposed scheme	2	$l = 1$	$\mathfrak{a} \leftarrow 2 \times 176\,\text{B}$	γ	$\mathfrak{a}$
MR [23]	1	$l = 2$	$\mathfrak{b} \leftarrow 1 \times 176\,\text{B}$	γ	$\mathfrak{b} + \gamma$
Weimar [6]	2	$l = 2$	$\mathfrak{c} \leftarrow 2 \times 176\,\text{B}$	γ	$\mathfrak{c} + \gamma$
Hirose [13]	1	$l = 2$	$\mathfrak{d} \leftarrow 1 \times 176\,\text{B}$	γ	$\mathfrak{d} + \gamma$
Tandem [12]	2	$l = 2$	$\mathfrak{e} \leftarrow 2 \times 176\,\text{B}$	γ	$\mathfrak{e} + \gamma$
Abreast [11]	2	$l = 2$	$\mathfrak{f} \leftarrow 2 \times 176\,\text{B}$	γ	$\mathfrak{f} + \gamma$

l: number of iteration for processing $2n$-bit message
B: required memory for key scheduling in byte
$\mathcal{V}$: memory require for storing output ($\gamma = 2n$ bit)
$B + \mathcal{V}$: total required memory for key scheduling, when message $= 2n$

Table 5. Required memory for key scheduling, when $m = tn$

Name	l	$\mathcal{V}$	$B + \mathcal{V}$
Proposed scheme	$l = tn/2n$	γ	$\mathfrak{a} + \gamma$
MR	$l = tn/n$	γ	$\mathfrak{b} + \gamma$
Weimar	$l = tn/n$	γ	$\mathfrak{c} + \gamma$
Hirose	$l = tn/n$	γ	$\mathfrak{d} + \gamma$
Tandem	$l = tn/n$	γ	$\mathfrak{e} + \gamma$
Abreast	$l = tn/n$	γ	$\mathfrak{f} + \gamma$

$\mathfrak{a}, \mathfrak{b}, \mathfrak{c}, \mathfrak{d}, \mathfrak{e}, \mathfrak{f}$: these values come from
the Table 4 (column B)

the current familiar schemes and the proposed scheme. For any $\mathcal{DBL}$ compression function, the output is $2n$-bit. Therefore, assume that the minimum $2n \rightarrow \gamma$ bit is required to store the output value (denoted as $\mathcal{V}$) of i-th iteration. In Table 4, the message size is $2n$-bit for example. Hence, the memory resource doesn't need to store the output for the proposed scheme. Next, the above cost (Table 4) is generalized including the number of iterations (l) for tn-bit message ($t > 2$) in Table 5. Additionally, the proposed scheme is faster than that of the MR, Weimar, Tandem, Abreast (if, $m > 2n$) in certain cases.

6   Conclusion

This paper studied the gap between security bound and efficiency of compression function for the cryptographic hash. Additionally, study result introduces that the blockcipher based compression function is more suitable than the scratch based construction for security solution of IoT-end devices, RfID, and constrained devices. Thus, a better efficient compression function (blockcipher based) is proposed in this paper. Additionally, the proposed scheme provides improved efficiency-rate, less call of blockcipher, and reasonable security bound. It satisfies two calls of $2n$-bit key property, where two block ciphers are independent. The proof technique of this scheme depends on the ICM tool. The proposed scheme has a provision of fixed size message encryption property. Therefore, this property opens a window for new applications, where a variable length of the message can be encrypted without padding. Finally, the proposed scheme is secure under one of the modes of PGV which can be extended to make the scheme secure under all modes of the PGV [17–19].

References

1. Bogdanov, A., Leander, G., Paar, C., Poschmann, A., Robshaw, M.J.B., Seurin, Y.: Hash functions and RFID tags: mind the gap. In: Oswald, E., Rohatgi, P. (eds.) CHES 2008. LNCS, vol. 5154, pp. 283–299. Springer, Heidelberg (2008)
2. Menezes, A.J., van Oorschot, P.C., Vanstone, S.A.: Handbook of Applied Cryptography, 5th edn. CRC Press, Boca Raton (2001)
3. Kaps, J.-P., Sunar, B.: Energy comparison of AES and SHA-1 for ubiquitous computing. In: Zhou, X., Sokolsky, O., Yan, L., Jung, E.-S., Shao, Z., Mu, Y., Lee, D.C., Kim, D.Y., Jeong, Y.-S., Xu, C.-Z. (eds.) EUC Workshops 2006. LNCS, vol. 4097, pp. 372–381. Springer, Heidelberg (2006)
4. Wang, X., Lai, X., Feng, D., Chen, H., Yu, X.: Cryptanalysis of the hash functions MD4 and RIPEMD. In: Cramer, R. (ed.) EUROCRYPT 2005. LNCS, vol. 3494, pp. 1–18. Springer, Heidelberg (2005)
5. Wang, X., Yin, Y.L., Yu, H.: Finding collisions in the full SHA-1. In: Shoup, V. (ed.) CRYPTO 2005. LNCS, vol. 3621, pp. 17–36. Springer, Heidelberg (2005)
6. Fleischmann, E., Forler, C., Lucks, S., Wenzel, J.: Weimar-DM: a highly secure double-length compression function. In: Susilo, W., Mu, Y., Seberry, J. (eds.) ACISP 2012. LNCS, vol. 7372, pp. 152–165. Springer, Heidelberg (2012)
7. Lee, J., Kapitanova, K., Son, S.H.: The price of security in wireless sensor networks. Comput. Netw. **54**(17), 2967–2978 (2010). Elsevier
8. Özen, O., Stam, M.: Another glance at double-length hashing. In: Parker, M.G. (ed.) Cryptography and Coding 2009. LNCS, vol. 5921, pp. 176–201. Springer, Heidelberg (2009)
9. Lee, J., Stam, M.: MJH: a faster alternative to MDC-2. In: Kiayias, A. (ed.) CT-RSA 2011. LNCS, vol. 6558, pp. 213–236. Springer, Heidelberg (2011)

10. Lai, X., Massey, J.L.: Hash functions based on block ciphers. In: Rueppel, R.A. (ed.) EUROCRYPT 1992. LNCS, vol. 658, pp. 55–70. Springer, Heidelberg (1993)
11. Lee, J., Kwon, D.: The security of abreast-DM in the ideal cipher model. IEICE Trans. **94-A**(1), 104–109 (2011)
12. Lee, J., Stam, M., Steinberger, J.: The collision security of Tandem-DM in the ideal cipher model. In: Rogaway, P. (ed.) CRYPTO 2011. LNCS, vol. 6841, pp. 561–577. Springer, Heidelberg (2011)
13. Hirose, S.: Some plausible constructions of double-block-length hash functions. In: Robshaw, M. (ed.) FSE 2006. LNCS, vol. 4047, pp. 210–225. Springer, Heidelberg (2006)
14. Armknecht, F., Fleischmann, E., Krause, M., Lee, J., Stam, M., Steinberger, J.: The preimage security of double-block-length compression functions. In: Lee, D.H., Wang, X. (eds.) ASIACRYPT 2011. LNCS, vol. 7073, pp. 233–251. Springer, Heidelberg (2011)
15. Mennink, B.: Optimal collision security in double block length hashing with single length key. In: Wang, X., Sako, K. (eds.) ASIACRYPT 2012. LNCS, vol. 7658, pp. 526–543. Springer, Heidelberg (2012)
16. Black, J.A., Rogaway, P., Shrimpton, T.: Black-box analysis of the block-cipher-based hash-function constructions from PGV. In: Yung, M. (ed.) CRYPTO 2002. LNCS, vol. 2442, pp. 320–335. Springer, Heidelberg (2002)
17. Black, J., Rogaway, P., Shrimpton, T., Stam, M.: An analysis of the blockcipher-based hash functions from PGV. J. Cryptol. **23**, 519–545 (2010)
18. Hirose, S., Kuwakado, H.: Collision resistance of hash functions in a weak ideal cipher model. IEICE Trans. **95A**(1), 251–255 (2012)
19. Liskov, M.: Constructing an ideal hash function from weak ideal compression functions. In: Biham, E., Youssef, A.M. (eds.) SAC 2006. LNCS, vol. 4356, pp. 358–375. Springer, Heidelberg (2007)
20. Nandi, M., Lee, W.I., Sakurai, K., Lee, S.-J.: Security analysis of a 2/3-Rate double length compression function in the black-box model. In: Gilbert, H., Handschuh, H. (eds.) FSE 2005. LNCS, vol. 3557, pp. 243–254. Springer, Heidelberg (2005)
21. Lee, J., Hong, S., Sung, J., Park, H.: A new double-block-length hash function using feistel structure. In: Park, J.H., Chen, H.-H., Atiquzzaman, M., Lee, C., Kim, T., Yeo, S.-S. (eds.) ISA 2009. LNCS, vol. 5576, pp. 11–20. Springer, Heidelberg (2009)
22. Shannon, C.E.: Communication theory of secrecy systems. Bell Syst. Tech. J. **128**(4), 656–715 (1949)
23. Miyaji, A., Mazumder, R.: A new (n, 2n) double block length hash function based on single key scheduling. In: IEEE Explore, AINA, pp. 564–570 (2015)
24. Abed, F., Forler, C., List, E., Lucks, S., Wenzel, J.: Counter-*b*DM: a provably secure family of multi-block-length compression functions. In: Pointcheval, D., Vergnaud, D. (eds.) AFRICACRYPT. LNCS, vol. 8469, pp. 440–458. Springer, Heidelberg (2014)
25. Coron, J.-S., Dodis, Y., Malinaud, C., Puniya, P.: Merkle-Damgård revisited: how to construct a hash function. In: Shoup, V. (ed.) CRYPTO 2005. LNCS, vol. 3621, pp. 430–448. Springer, Heidelberg (2005)
26. Dodis, Y., Puniya, P.: On the relation between the ideal cipher and the random oracle models. In: Halevi, S., Rabin, T. (eds.) TCC 2006. LNCS, vol. 3876, pp. 184–206. Springer, Heidelberg (2006)
27. Joan, D., Vincent, R.: The Design of Rijndael, AES-The Advanced Encryption Standard. Springer, Heidelberg (2002). ISBN: 978-3-662-04722-4
28. Kuwakado, H., Hirose, S.: Hashing mode using a lightweight blockcipher. In: Stam, M. (ed.) IMACC 2013. LNCS, vol. 8308, pp. 213–231. Springer, Heidelberg (2013)

29. Burak, D.: Parallelization of a block cipher based on chaotic neural networks. In: Rutkowski, L., et al. (eds.) ICAISC 2015, Part II. LNCS(LNAI), vol. 9120, pp. 191–201. Springer, Switzerland (2015)

30. Bos, J.W., Özen, O., Stam, M.: Efficient hashing using the AES instruction set. In: Preneel, B., Takagi, T. (eds.) CHES 2011. LNCS, vol. 6917, pp. 507–522. Springer, Heidelberg (2011)

31. Mazumder, R., Miyaji, A.: A new scheme of blockcipher hash. IEICE Trans. **99–D**(4), 796–804 (2016)

32. Knudsen, L.R., Mendel, F., Rechberger, C., Thomsen, S.S.: Cryptanalysis of MDC-2. In: Joux, A. (ed.) EUROCRYPT 2009. LNCS, vol. 5479, pp. 106–120. Springer, Heidelberg (2009)

33. Miyaji, A., Mazumder, R., Sawada, T.: A new (n, n) blockcipher hash function: apposite for short messages. In: IEEE Explore, Asia JCIS, pp. 56–63 (2014)

34. Mazumder, R., Miyaji, A.: A single key scheduling based compression function. In: Lambrinoudakis, C., Gabillon, A. (eds.) CRiSIS 2015. LNCS, vol. 9572, pp. 207–222. Springer, Switzerland (2015)

35. Barreto, L., Celesti, A., Villari, M., Fazio, M., Puliafito, A.: An authentication model for IoT clouds. In: IEEE Explore, ASONAM, pp. 1032–1035 (2015)

36. Riahi, A., Natalizio, E., Challal, Y., Mitton, N., Iera, A.: A systemic and cognitive approach for IoT security. In: IEEE Explore, ICNC, pp. 183–188 (2014)

37. Lee, J.Y., Huang, Y.H.: A lightweight authentication protocol for internet of things. In: IEEE Explore, ISNE, pp. 1–2 (2014)

38. Jing, Q., Vasilakos, A.V., Wan, J.: Security of the internet of things: perspectives and challenges. Wirel. Netw. **20**(8), 2481–2501 (2014). Springer

39. Abomhara, M., Kien, G.M.: Security and privacy in the internet of things: current status and open issues. In: IEEE Explore, PRIMS, pp. 1–8 (2014)

40. Zanella, A., Bui, N., Castellani, A., Vangelista, L., Zorzi, M.: Internet of things for smart cities. IEEE Internet Things J. **1**(1), 22–32 (2014)

41. Xu, L.D., He, W., Li, S.: Internet of things in industries: a survey. IEEE Trans. Ind. Inf. **10**(4), 2233–2243 (2014)

42. Hirose, S., Ideguchi, K., Kuwakado, H., Owada, T., Preneel, B., Yoshida, H.: A lightweight 256-Bit hash function for hardware and low-end devices: Lesamnta-LW. In: Rhee, K.-H., Nyang, D.H. (eds.) ICISC 2010. LNCS, vol. 6829, pp. 151–168. Springer, Heidelberg (2011)

43. Shirai, T., Shibutani, K., Akishita, T., Moriai, S., Iwata, T.: The 128-bit Blockcipher CLEFIA, IACR archive, Extended Abstract. https://www.iacr.org/archive/fse2007/45930182/45930182.pdf

44. Yoshida, H.: On the standardization of cryptographic application techniques for IoT devices in ITU techniques for IoT devices in ITU-T and ISO/IEC JTC 1 T and ISO/IEC JTC1 (2015). https://www.ietf.org/proceedings/94/slides/slides-94-saag-2.pdf

45. Fleischmann, E., Forler, C., Lucks, S.: The collision security of MDC-4. In: Mitrokotsa, A., Vaudenay, S. (eds.) AFRICACRYPT 2012. LNCS, vol. 7374, pp. 252–269. Springer, Heidelberg (2012)

Visualization Model for Monitoring of Computer Networks Security Based on the Analogue of Voronoi Diagrams

Maxim Kolomeets, Andrey Chechulin, and Igor Kotenko$^{(\boxtimes)}$

Laboratory of Computer Security Problems,
St. Petersburg Institute for Informatics and Automation (SPIIRAS),
39, 14 Liniya, St. Petersburg, Russia
{kolomeec, chechulin, ivkote}@comsec.spb.ru

Abstract. In this paper we propose an approach to the development of the computer network visualization system for security monitoring, which uses a conceptually new model of graphic visualization that is similar to the Voronoi diagrams. The proposed graphical model uses the size, color and opacity of the cell to display host parameters. The paper describes a technique for new graphical model construction and gives examples of its application along with traditional graph based and other models.

Keywords: Visual analytics · Visualization of security data · Graphical models · Computer networks · Voronoi diagrams

1 Introduction

Computer networks are rapidly growing today. Meanwhile, the more devices are in the network, the harder it is to ensure its security. This problem is met by operators of security systems of corporate level (e.g., security information and event management systems, SIEM systems), when the analyzed computer network is measured not only by hundreds of employees' workplaces and high order technical equipment, but also by smart doors, servers, various sensors of climate, security, etc.

To cope with the control of growing networks we need to apply systems for monitoring network security, which give us possibility to visualize the computer network and parameters of its state in a simple and efficient manner. But, as a rule, in such systems the network is presented with the application of rather traditional graphical models, for example, in the form of graphs or tables, that are difficult to understand in the case of large networks and display of a variety of parameters. In order to cope with this problem it is necessary to improve the efficiency of visualization means by complex use of various graphical models such as graphs, matrices, treemaps, parallel coordinates, etc. in the framework of the multiple view concept [1]. At the same time it is necessary to increase the efficiency of visualization of particular graphic models.

In the case of visualization of computer networks and their security, different techniques are developed that allow clustering of segments of the network (e.g., based on clustering of graph elements) or encapsulation of the state parameters [2].

F. Buccafurri et al. (Eds.): CD-ARES 2016, LNCS 9817, pp. 141–157, 2016.
DOI: 10.1007/978-3-319-45507-5_10

Yet another solution to the problem is to develop conceptually new graphical models, which are able to present information in a form that is new for the user and that allows to increase the efficiency of the user's work.

The novelty of this paper is to use a conceptually new graphic visualization model similar to the Voronoi diagrams, which allows to increase the effectiveness of visual analysis for the computer network security, for example, as one of functions of the SIEM system. It is expected that this model will be used in the developed visualization system in the framework of the supported multiple view concept.

The main contribution of the paper lies in the fact that it offers a new technique of visualization of network security, as well as reveals the theoretical and practical side of how this technique can be used in SIEM systems. The organization of the paper is as follows. Section 2 analyzes existing graphical models that can be used to visualize parameters of computer network security with description of their advantages and disadvantages. In Sect. 3 we describe the developed conceptually new graphical model. Section 4 discusses the developed system for visualization of computer network security and provides examples of application of the proposed graphical model in the framework of this system. In Sects. 5 and 6 the proposed graphical model is evaluated, as well as its comparison with other graphical models is performed. Section 7 discusses conclusions and future research directions.

2 Review of Computer Network Visualization Techniques

Within the developed computer network visualization system, graphs, matrices, and treemaps were mainly used to realize the multiple view concept. The listed graphical model (Fig. 1) have different advantages and disadvantages [3], which can also be expressed in terms of informativity and ease of perception and use.

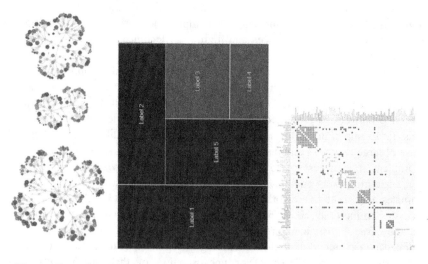

Fig. 1. Examples of graphical models (left to right): graphs, treemaps and matrices

Informativity can be represented as the detailization level, which is expressed in the compliteness of simultaneously displayed data. Ease of perception and use can be represented in the form of speed and simplicity of user interactions with displayed data. It is obvious that different graphical models have different ratio of informativity and ease of perception and use. Thus, often increase of the informativity due to the resulting congestion of the graphical model negatively affects the ease of perception and use, and vice versa. Some examples are an informative but difficult to read table, and an uninformative, but easy to understand semaphore shown in Fig. 2.

Input Packet Length	Input Rate	Input Media Overhead (Ethernet)	Total Input Port bytes	MAC removed bytes (including CRC)	Other PP/MAC/FR AMER removed bytes	PP Packet add bytes (to fabric and peer PP)	Switch Port Packet Size	Switch Port effective Input Rate
64	1.00E+10	20	84	24	0	12	72	8.57E+09
128	1.00E+10	20	148	24	0	12	136	9.19E+09
256	1.00E+10	20	276	24	0	12	264	9.57E+09
1500	1.00E+10	20	1520	24	0	12	1508	9.92E+09

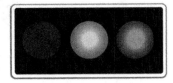

Fig. 2. Examples of a table and a semaphore

Let us consider from this point of view the graphic models [4, 5], which are most often used to visualize the security of computer networks. Matrices [6] (Fig. 1, right) are efficient in displaying the relations of elements of a small computer network that has complex topology and where each host has many connections. Security parameters, determined based on network traffic, can be set using the color and transparency of cells, located at intersections of rows and columns. However, the size of the cells depends on the dimension of the matrix, which is set by the number of network hosts. With the increase in the number of rows and columns of the matrix, the size of a particular cell goes to one pixel, the perception of the color tone and the more transparency of which is difficult. Inefficient use of space of matrices should be noted, when most of the cells remains blank, which has negative effect on the users' perception of parameters, especially when large computer networks are visualized. It is also worth considering that the matrices can visualize the links parameters, but not the parameters of the computer network hosts.

On the other hand, matrices efficiently display clusters of network, and they can be used to construct attack graphs [7] (Fig. 3, left) and to analyze entire segments of the network, rather than individual hosts.

Matrices can also be expanded by displaying multidimensional data in 3D space. For example, the 3D analogue of a matrix is the dispersion chart [8], which is represented as a cube which axes are local IP addresses, global IP addresses and port numbers, and the color of the dot shows successful and unsuccessful attempts to establish TCP connections (Fig. 3, right). Thus, the presence of long lines or planes, consisting of the points on the dispersion chart, can inform about network scanning.

For efficient visualization of host parameters (for example, the data of the vulnerability scanners [6] (Fig. 4, left), assessment of criticality of assets, etc.) of a computer network, one can also use treemaps [9] (Fig. 1, in the center). Treemaps are efficient to display parameters, as they can handle the color, depth and size. It should be noted that in the presence of cells of large area, one can also use transparency as an

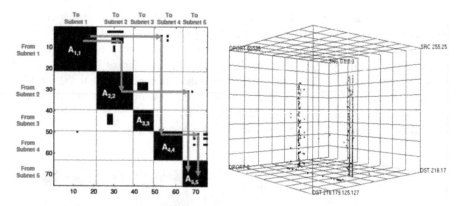

Fig. 3. Usage of a matrix to visualize attack graphs (left) and as the dispersion chart (right)

additional parameter. However, treemaps are suitable to visualize purely hierarchical networks and are unable to visualize the interaction parameters. However, along with matrices, treemaps can be expanded, for example, for constructing attack graphs [10], when the steps of the intruder are displayed by directed edges (Fig. 4, right).

Graphs [11], as the most common way to visualize computer networks, are efficient for topology visualization and can display parameters of hosts using the vertices of the graph, as well as interaction parameters using edges. However, like matrices, graphs inefficiently use space, leaving large empty areas. However, graphs are often used to display the network topology, when host type is used as vertices (Fig. 5).

For visualization of parameters vertices of graphs can be replaced by glyphs [12]. Glyphs can be represented in a pie chart in which the number of equal sized segments depends on the number of displayed parameters (Fig. 6). The parameters themselves can be expressed in the form of segments' color and their transparency. The glyphs can be augmented by the ring with the same number of segments that display the previous parameter value. Due to this, it is possible to produce a historical analysis.

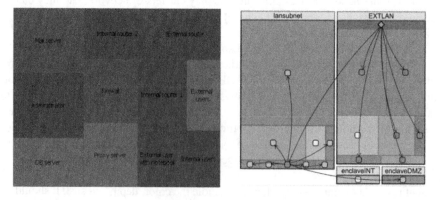

Fig. 4. Visualization of security vulnerabilities (left) and attack graph (right) using treemaps

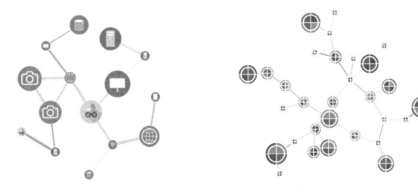

Fig. 5. A graph displaying host type   **Fig. 6.** A graph, augmented by glyphs

The disadvantage of glyphs is that when they are used the graphical model becomes overloaded, thereby ease of perception deteriorates. It is worth saying that the graphs have many variations of how they are built and used. For example, graphs can be used for visual analysis of granting access to resources [13] with the role access system that supports hierarchies or groups of users, to visualize patterns of network traffic [14], for visualizing logs of financial transactions [12], for visualization of computer attacks [15, 16], etc.

At the analysis of existing graphic models the features were outlined that allow the user to efficiently analyze information. First, the user perceives better spatial mapping (plane and spacial figures), while the color and shape of figures are optional parameters. It is easy to demonstrate: the most important security parameters in treemaps (Fig. 4) are displayed with size of the planes; graphs (Figs. 5 and 6) operate with the sizes of the vertices; and at rendering in the form of a matrix (Fig. 3) the operator most often searches for and analyzes structures in the form of planes and lengthwise lines, consisting of individual cells. Second, it can be concluded that to visualize the links parameters it is better to use matrices, but they are unable to visualize hosts. For visualization of hosts parameters it is better to use treemaps, but they are unable to visualize links. In the case when it is necessary to visualize both hosts and links one needs to use graphs. Thus, the analysis of the advantages and drawbacks of existing graphical models showed that the simultaneous display of parameters of hosts and links is only possible with the use of graphs. However, if the vertices in the graphs are displayed in the form of planes, the operator will be able to analyze the information faster. Thus, analysis of relevant works showed that the creation of graphical models that will allow to effectively display both parameters (as in the treemaps) and the topology (as in graphs) is a perspective approach.

3   The Proposed Graphical Model

For monitoring of computer network security a graphical model is proposed [17], which visually resembles Voronoi diagram [18], however, it is not the same from a mathematical point of view (Fig. 7). The main idea is to integrate capabilities of graphs to visualize the topology of the computer network and treemaps to visualize

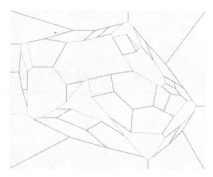

Fig. 7. The proposed graphical model

Fig. 8. Planar graph   **Fig. 9.** The construction of the convex hull

parameters. The solution appeared from the representation of network hosts in the form of cells, and links between hosts in the form of links between these cells. At the same time in the graphical model there are separators (dark grey in Fig. 7) which divide the cells that are next to each other, but have no links. For ease of understanding, we can present an analogy in the form of a maze: cells-polygons that represent hosts can be interpreted as the maze rooms; the links of the cells that represent the relationship between hosts can be interpreted as doors between the maze rooms; the separators that represent the lack of links can be interpreted as the maze walls.

The algorithm for constructing the proposed graphical model is more complex than the algorithms for constructing graphs, matrices or treemaps, and consists of four steps: (1) building of the convex hull of a given planar graph; (2) implementation of the restricted Delaunay triangulation [18]; (3) formation of cells, based on triangulation; (4) selection of separators.

Let us consider the algorithm for constructing the proposed graphical model in more detail, on the example of the implemented software tool that provides a visual interface to display the security parameters of computer networks.

The proposed graphical model is implemented on the basis of the graph adjacency matrix. The first step builds a planar graph, which is supplemented by the convex hull. The convex hull is required for obtaining the convex figure, which is used to perform the next step. Graph which will be used in this example, and the result of the first step are shown in Figs. 8 and 9 respectively.

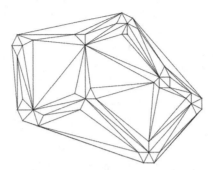

Fig. 10. The graph and its triangulation

In the next step for the resulting figure we should produce a restricted Delaunay triangulation [18]. It is worth noting the importance of implementing exactly limited triangulation, as it allows to triangulate the figures taking into account already existing relations and to avoid crossing of edges. The result of this step is shown in Fig. 10. The next step is to form the cells that will serve as the basis of the graphical model. For this we need to associate a subset of the triangles, obtained as the result of triangulation, with the corresponding vertex of the graph.

For each vertex of the host (in Fig. 11 it is selected as a light grey circle) we find a subset of triangles (in Fig. 11 they are highlighted in gray) that includes this vertex. Next for triangles of this subset the weight centers are determined (in Fig. 12 they are shown as light gray points), union of which gives the desired polygon (in Fig. 12 it is highlighted in light gray edges).

The resulting polygon corresponds to the host, based on which we defined the subset of triangles of the triangulation. The result of the step is shown in Fig. 13, where the edges of the figure resulting from the triangulation are black, and the edges of the desired cells are red (in Fig. 13 it is light grey).

The next step is to outline the separators. Since each cell corresponds to a specific host, the edges of the cells-hosts, with which there is a link, can be designated a certain color, for example gray. All other edges will be separators and will have an appropriate

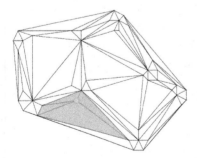

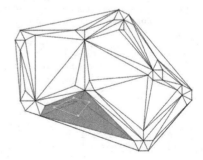

Fig. 11. The determination of triangles required to build a cell

Fig. 12. The construction of the cell

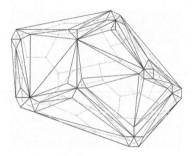

Fig. 13. The result of building the cells of the graphical model

color (e.g. red in Fig. 14). To obtain a figure of a certain shape (e.g. rectangle as in Fig. 14) we can also add points to the cells of the convex hull, or move these points to the required positions. In Fig. 14 the resulting shape is depicted with addition of new points, and Fig. 15 shows a figure with relocation of the common points of the polygons-hosts of the convex hull.

Therefore, the graphical model allows to display hosts in the form of planes, and the links between the hosts – in the form of contact planes. The formal description of the algorithm to build the presented graphical model can be represented as the following pseudo code:

```
// step 1 - making the convex hull of planar graph
graph = getPlanarGraph(adjacencyMatrix)
graph = addConvexHullToGraph(graph)
//step 2 - making the constrained Delaunay triangulation
listOfTriangles = makeConstrainedDelaunayTriangulation(graph)
listOfPolygons
//step 3 - making cells based on triangulation
for each dot from graph {
        listOfTrianglesThatContainsDot = getTriangles(dot,
listOfTriangles);
        polygon
        for each triangle from listOfTrianglesThatContainsDot{
                triangleCenter = getCenterOfTriangle(triangle)
                addPontToPolygon(polygon, triangleCenter)
        }}
//step 4 - making separators
for each polygon from listOfPolygons{
        for each line from polygon{
                connectedPolygon = getConnectedPolygon(line, polygon)
                connectionIsExist = isConnectionExist(polygon,
connectedPolygon, graph)
                if connectionIsExist == true{
                        color = grey
                }else{
                        color = red }
                setLineColor(line, color)
        }}
// the end of algorithm is drawing of cells
draw(listOfPolygons)
```

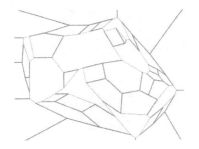 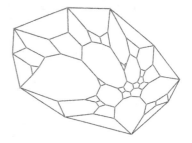

Fig. 14. Adding new points to the polygons   **Fig. 15.** Relocation of points of the polygons

It should be noted that from the mathematical point of view [18], the proposed model is not a Voronoi diagram, despite the visual similarity, since the Voronoi diagram has the different mathematical meaning, and existing algorithms for its construction do not allow to visualize the computer network topology when constructing the chart based on vertices of the graph.

4   Examples of Application of the Proposed Graphical Model

The proposed graphical model can be used to visualize the security parameters of a computer network or to analyze the behavior of the attacker. It may be required when informing the operator of SIEM system about the threats of a security breach or by visual analysis of computer network security. Let us consider examples of application of the proposed graphical model in the framework of implementation of the visualization system in more details.

4.1   Description of the Visualisation System

To analyze the security of a computer network the visualization system is developed, which supports the display of the computer network using both the classical methods of visualization, such as graphs, graphs augmented with glyphs, treemaps and matrices and the graphical model, proposed in this paper. The example of dashboard of the developed visualization system is depicted in Fig. 16.

The system includes the ability to manage data sources, aggregation and correlation of data collected from sources and tools for visual analytics of computer network security. Tabs to navigate to the relevant controls are at the top of the dashboard in Fig. 16.

In the left part of the dashboard in Fig. 16 there is enumeration of representations of computer networks formed on the basis of data from different sources.

The central part of the dashboard is the implementation of the multiple view concept, when the data is displayed in different views: as graph; as the graph augmented with glyphs; charts and diagrams; treemaps; matrices and as graphical model, formed as the analogue of Voronoi diagrams, presented in this paper.

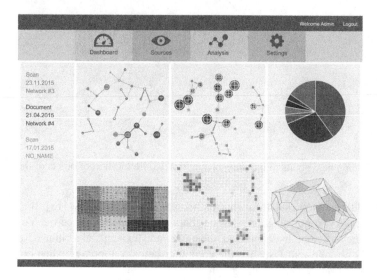

Fig. 16. The dashboard of the developed visualization system

In various usage scenarios, the user selects the graphical model, which is capable to visualize data the user needs at the moment most efficiently. In the following sub-sections the examples of scenarios of using the developed graphical model in comparison with the graphs will be presented.

4.2 Description of the Source Data

Data of a computer network (Fig. 17), which consists of 9 segments, will be used as source data for visualization.

The segment, which consists of external users who have remote connection to the computer network via the Internet, is represented in block 1. Block 2 displays the web server for remote connectivity, as well as hosts needed to operate the web server. Block

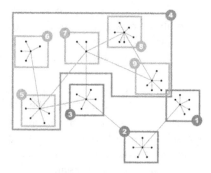

Fig. 17. Segments of a computer network

3 represents the security system located between the web server and the demilitarized zone (DMZ). The demilitarized zone is shown by block 4 and includes segments of the internal network of the company. Block 5 and block 9 are the computers of the internal network users. Block 6 displays the devices connected to the network through Wi-Fi connection. Block 7 is the server of storing and processing data. Block 8 corresponds to the virtualization server, together with the virtual machines placed on it.

4.3   Example 1. Visualization of the State of Computer Network Security

To visualize the security of a computer network for each host the indicators of protection from attacks and possible damage in case of compromise of this host are calculated. In the proposed graphical model the security level against attacks can be represented in the form of a polygon color – hosts that have passed the threshold are in red color (in Fig. 18 – dark grey), and possible damage is shown as the size of the polygon (area of polygon). We shall also consider the example of visualization based on the graph, where the security is represented by vertex color, and the possible damage – as the radius of the vertex. Let us consider two variants.

In the first case (Fig. 18) the vulnerable hosts are red (dark grey in Fig. 18) are strongly scattered. Almost every network segment has vulnerable hosts. Despite the fact that damage at their compromise a small, scatteredness gives greater variability of actions for the attacker due to the presence of many potential hosts from which attack may occur.

Figure 19 shows the corresponding visualization based on the graph, where the value of the possible damage in case of compromise is outlined by radius of vertex, and the presence of vulnerability is marked in red color (in Fig. 19 light gray, as they are almost invisible, they are indicated by arrows). It is obvious that the proposed graphical model allows us to more quickly identify vulnerable hosts and produce visual analysis of the damage done when they are compromised.

In another case (Fig. 20), it is clear that virtualization platform is under vulnerability, and therefore all machines, located on it, as well as some computers of internal users are also under vulnerability. Corresponding visualization based on the graph is shown in Fig. 21. As in the previous case, visual analysis of potential damage and identifying the vulnerable segment are more efficient when using the proposed model.

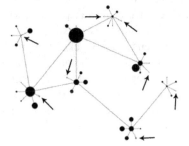

Fig. 18. Scattered unprotected hosts are presented on the basis of the proposed model

Fig. 19. Scattered unprotected hosts are presented on the basis of the graph

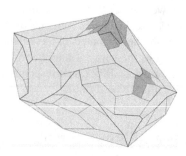

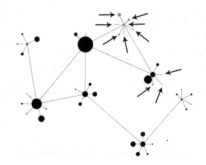

Fig. 20. Two segments of the network with unprotected hosts, presented on the basis of the proposed model

Fig. 21. Two segments of the network with unprotected hosts, presented on the basis of the graph

4.4 Example 2. Visualization of the Attack Route

Visualization of the route of the attack (Fig. 22) may be noted as another example of using the proposed graphical model.

Fig. 22. Visualization of the attack route

The host from which an attacker carries out an attack is one of the computers of internal users. This host can be denoted in blue (dark gray in Fig. 22). All hosts, to which the actions of the attacker were recorded, can be also displayed in blue, however with different degree of transparency, which will depend on the intensity of the actions of the attacker. Thus it is possible to analyze which segment of the network is affected by the attack and if the attacker compromised the most important hosts or not. One can also estimate how close the attacker came to certain hosts for subsequent selection of protection strategies. In Fig. 22 it is seen that in such a scenario only some elements of the network will be affected (virtualization platform and servers for storing and processing data), however the potential damage from compromise is unreasonably great.

5   Evaluation of the Proposed Graphical Model

In order to evaluate the proposed graphical model two groups of indicators were identified – performance indicators and functionality indicators.

Functionality indicators define the set of scenarios that the proposed graphical model is able to visualize, such as network connectivity, network size, abilities to display topology, possibility to display the parameters of hosts and links between hosts. Performance indicators define the efficiency of user's perception of information and ease of working with data, for example: the efficiency of indicators perception, efficiency of finding a way to attack, efficiency of analysis of network segments.

The evaluation of the proposed graphical model was carried out in comparison with the visualization of a computer network as a graph.

The evaluation was performed using a survey of experts. All experts note that in a scenario, when the computer network is a non-planar graph, application of the proposed graphical model is impossible, which is the main drawback of the proposed graphical model. In some scenarios, when non-planar graphs are rarely used or not used at all, the proposed graphical model is by an order more efficient. It is also noted that the proposed graphical model is not efficient in visualization of small computer networks, and to visualize them it is more efficient to use matrices and graphs.

Thus, the graphical model is most appropriate to be used when rendering a medium to large scale computer networks. High computational complexity of the algorithm is also a disadvantage, however this can be shortened by using a client-server architecture, when only coordinates of the cells will be transferred to the thin client.

As a whole experts agree in opinion that the proposed graphical model has more options for visualizing metrics and network segments in comparison with the classical methods of visualization that are based on graphs, matrices and treemaps.

Thus, the proposed graphical model is an alternative to visualization of computer networks in the form of graphs, treemaps and matrices. The use of human spatial perception (the location of the cell-computers relative to each other) and the absence of necessity of edges provides a number of advantages at the cognitive level of perception of visualization. On the other hand, a disadvantage of the presented graphical model is that it can help to visualize exclusively planar graphs, which reduces the usage scope. However, in some scenarios, when graphs are not planar, are rarely used or not used at all, the proposed graphical model is by order more efficient. It is also worth noting that the use of the proposed graphical model is applicable for visualization of any object that can be represented as a planar graph.

It is supposed that the proposed graphical model can improve the efficiency of visual analytics using the graphical models to visualize the computer networks within the multiple view concept in SIEM systems.

6   Discussion

Based on the evaluation of the proposed graphical model a comparative table (Table 1) was built with three other graphical models – graphs, treemaps and matrices. It should be noted that graphical models are considered in the minimum version, i.e. without additions and excluding the presentation of information in the form of text and sig-natures. The table shows the display capabilities and the number of simultaneously displayed parameters of security of network hosts, network connections, possibility of extension of graphical models for visualization in 3D space, possibility of visualization of topological parameters and possibility of display of networks of different topological types. The cells contain evaluations of the efficiency of parameters display perception in one way or another. Four estimations are outlined: (1) does not support – graphical model does not support this method of visualization; (2) supports – graphical model supports this method of visualization, but with restrictions; (3) good – graphical model supports this method of visualization; (4) fine – graphical model supports this method of visualization, the efficiency of the perception is high and the user easily analyzes the information.

Graphs are not restricted in display of size and color of vertices, size and color of connections, clustering, and can also display any topological types. Graphs have a limit

Table 1. Comparison of the possibilities of graphs, treemaps, matrices, and the proposed model

		Graphs	Treemaps	Matrices	The proposed model
Hosts parameters display	size	good	fine	does not support	fine
	color	good	fine	does not support	fine
	transparency	supports	good	does not support	good
Display of parameters of links	size	good	does not support	does not support	good
	color	good	does not support	good	good
	transparency	supports	does not support	supports	good
	shape	supports	does not support	supports	supports
Possibilities of extension for display in 3D		supports	does not support	supports	supports
Display of topology parameters	hosts clasterization	good	good	fine	good
	incapsulation of hosts (nestness)	does not support	fine	does not support	fine
Display of different topological types	hierarchical	good	fine	good	fine
	planar	good	does not support	good	fine
	non-planar	good	does not support	fine	does not support

on the transparency of the elements, as with the transparency of less than 30 % the item will be hard to read. Graphs also can display hosts and connections by a limited set of geometric shapes to be visualized in 3D, provided that clustering of the vertices is done. The only thing that graphs do not support is display of nesting.

Treemaps do well with display of hosts using the size and color of planes. It is the use of planes that allows the user to efficiently analyze information. With it, treemaps have no restrictions in the display of hosts with transparency, because even at minimal transparency the outlines of the plane are kept, and the user cannot miss it, as it would be in the case of graphs. However, treemaps cannot display the parameters of the links and cannot be displayed in 3D. But at the same time they do not have restrictions on clustering of hosts and perfectly display nesting, as it is the basis of the very concept of the treemaps. However, because of the nesting treemaps allow to display exclusively hierarchical networks.

Matrices cannot display hosts, but allow to visualize them when using the cells' colors and their transparency. Matrices cannot operate with cells' sizes. Transparency of the matrix cells have the same restriction as graphs (at least 30 % transparency), but they have no restrictions in colors. Cells themselves can also be represented as a limited set of geometric shapes and can be displayed in 3D. Matrices cannot visualize nesting of the hosts, however, with the help of links they can efficiently display the network's clusters that will be represented in the form of planes (Fig. 1, right part). Matrices can display without limitations any topological types, however they are most efficient in finding clusters in complex non-planar networks.

The proposed graphical model uses the size, color and opacity of the cell for displaying of parameters of the host, as in the trees of maps, so their estimations coincide. To display the links' parameters it uses size, color and transparency of edges of cells. Edges are visualized as lines like in graphs, therefore their estimations are also identical, except for the transparency – in the proposed model, even at zero transparency the contour of lines is preserved. The proposed graphical model can be represented in the form of a 3D polyhedron, where the edges will correspond to the cells. The graphical model also has the capability of clustering, as shown in Fig. 18, and through the use of planes, inside which one can place similar planes, it supports nesting. The proposed graphical model also supports the display of hierarchical and planar networks, but does not support non-planar network.

Thus, we can see that the proposed model in some cases (in the hierarchical and planar network topologies) can provide an alternative to graphs, treemaps or matrices, or be used as a supplement to graphical models within the multiple view concept, based on which the dashboard of security systems are built.

The development of the presented graphical model is been continued. At the moment the development of the algorithm of the polymorphism of cells is performed, in order to be able to change the size and shape of the cells without violating the topology. The development of the algorithm of display of proposed graphical model in 3D is carried out, this can be achieved by imposing points of the graphical model on the sphere, and then to draw cross-sections of the sphere at the points that correspond to the cells.

Another direction for future research is to analyze the possibility and efficiency of using the proposed graphical model for visualization of processes associated with information security, but which are not associated with computer networks. Any process that is currently visualized using planar graphs (some examples are displayed in Sect. 2), can be visualized with the proposed graphical model. Thus, despite the fact that in the implemented system the proposed model is used to find vulnerabilities, risk assessment and other parameters of a computer network, the scope and possibility of application to ensure information security are much wider.

7   Conclusion

In this paper the analysis of existing visualization methods was performed and the new graphical model based on the analogue of Voronoi diagrams was presented. We demonstrated that the proposed graphical model of visualization of computer networks allows in some cases to display data more efficiently, compared to already existing graphical models. The developed visualization system was presented used to analyze the security of computer networks, and examples of visual analysis of the computer network state were provided. The estimation of the proposed model for visualizing the security parameters of computer network was done, and the comparison of its efficiency with graphs, matrices and treemaps was performed. Directions of future research based on the use of the proposed graphical model were presented, in particular the development of algorithms for polymorphism and nesting of cells, display in 3D and using the proposed model for visual analytics of processes and objects, which were previously represented as graphs.

Acknowledgements. This research is being supported by the Ministry of Education and Science of The Russian Federation (contract 14.604.21.0137, unique contract identifier RFMEFI 60414X0137) in SPIIRAS.

References

1. Wang, M., Woodruff, A., Kuchinsky, A.: Guidelines for using multiple views in information visualization. J. Adv. Vis. Interfaces, 110–119 (2000)
2. Shi, L., Liao, Q., Sun, X., Chen, Y., Lin, C.: Scalable network traffic visualization using compressed graphs. In: Proceedings of the IEEE International Conference on Big Data (BigData 2013), Santa Clara, CA (2013)
3. Tufte, E.: Visual Explanations. Graphics Press, Cheshire (1997)
4. Klyshinskij, J., Rysakov, S., Shihov, A.: Review of the methods of multidimensional data visualization. J. New Inf. Technol. Autom. Syst., 519–530 (2014)
5. Marty, R.: Applied Security Visualization. Addison Wesley Professional, Reading (2009)
6. Kwan-Liu, M.: Cyber security through visualization. In: Asia Pacific Symposium on Information Visualisation, Tokyo, Japan (2006)
7. Noel, S., Jajodia, S.: Understanding complex network attack graphs through clustered adjacency matrices. In: 21st Annual Computer Security Applications Conference (ACSAC 2005). IEEE Computer Society (2005)
8. Lau, S.: The spinning cube of potential doom. Commun. ACM **47**(6), 24–26 (2004)

9. Harrison, L., Spahn, R., Iannacone, M., Downing, E., Goodall, J.: Nessus vulnerability visualization for the web. In: VizSec 2012, Seattle, WA, USA (2012)
10. Williams, L., Lippmann, R., Ingols, K.: GARNET: a graphical attack graph and reachability network evaluation tool. In: Goodall, J.R., Conti, G., Ma, K.-L. (eds.) VizSec 2008. LNCS, vol. 5210, pp. 44–59. Springer, Heidelberg (2008)
11. McGuffin, M.: Simple algorithms for network visualization: a tutorial. J. Tsinghua Sci. Technol. 17(4), 383–398 (2012)
12. Novikova, E., Kotenko, I.: Analytical visualization techniques for security information and event management. In: 21st Euromicro International Conference on Parallel, Distributed and network-based Processing (PDP 2013), Belfast (2013)
13. Montemayor, J., Freeman, A., Gersh, J., Llanso, T., Patrone, D.: Information visualisation for rule-based resource access control. In: International Symposium on Usable Privacy and Security (SOUPS) (2006)
14. Glatz, E., Mavromatidis, S., Ager, B., Dimitropoulos, X.: Visualizing big network traffic data using frequent pattern mining and hypergraphs. In: Proceedings of the First IMC Workshop on Internet Visualization (WIV 2012), Boston, MA, USA (2012)
15. Mansmann, F., Fischer, F., Keim, D.A., North, S.C.: Visual support for analyzing network traffic and intrusion detection events using treemap and graph representations. In: Proceedings of the Symposium on Computer Human Interaction for the Management of Information Technology (CHiMiT 2009), vol. 3, pp. 19–28 (2009)
16. Kotenko, I., Chechulin, A.: Common framework for attack modeling and security evaluation in SIEM systems. In: 2012 IEEE International Conference on Green Computing and Communications, Conference on Internet of Things, and Conference on Cyber, Physical and Social Computing, Besançon, France (2012)
17. Kolomeec, M., Chechulin, A., Kotenko, I.: Methodological primitives for phased construction of data visualization models. J. Internet Serv. Inf. Secur. (JISIS) 5(4), 60–84 (2015)
18. Aurenhammer, F., Klein, R., Lee, D.: Voronoi Diagrams and Delaunay Triangulations. World Scientific Publishing Co., Singapore (2013)

Modeling Cyber Systemic Risk
for the Business Continuity Plan of a Bank

Angelo Furfaro$^{(\boxtimes)}$, Teresa Gallo, and Domenico Saccà

University of Calabria, P. Bucci, 41, 87036 Rende, CS, Italy
{a.furfaro,t.gallo,sacca}@dimes.unical.it

Abstract. The pervasive growth and diffusion of complex IT systems, which handle critical business aspects of today's enterprises and which cooperate through computer networks, has given rise to a significant expansion of the exposure surface towards cyber security threats. A threat, affecting a given IT system, may cause a ripple effect on the other interconnected systems often with unpredictable consequences. This type of exposition, known as cyber systemic risk, is a very important concern especially for the international banking system and it needs to be suitably taken into account during the requirement analysis of a bank IT system. This paper proposes the application of a goal-oriented methodology (GOReM), during the requirements specification phase, in order to consider adequate provisions for prevention and reaction to cyber systemic risk in banking systems. In particular, the context of the Italian banking system is considered as a case study.

Keywords: Business Continuity · Disaster Recovery · Systemic risk · Cyber threat · Goal-Oriented Methodology · Requirements Engineering

1   Introduction

During the last few years, the diffusion of cyber threats has seen a steep growth at a rate which is predicted to increase in the near future [13]. Cyber security threats include events such as accidental cyber-related incidents or deliberate actions coming from external entities such as hacker attacks and virus/worm/malicious software infiltrations [17]. These threats might directly affect industrial control systems and processes and need to be properly managed [22]. The effects of a threat exploit on a given system, may propagate through communication networks causing damages to other interconnected systems and giving rise to a ripple effect. This phenomenon, where a threat triggers a knock-on effect among different enterprises, is known as *systemic risk* and has been the subject of many studies in the financial and economic domains [16].

Provisions against the cyber systemic risk are usually directed to establish a strategy for circumscribing negative effects, e.g. by activating alternative solutions to the damaged systems, and to slow down, and possibly to stop the propagation towards the other interconnected systems.

© IFIP International Federation for Information Processing 2016
Published by Springer International Publishing Switzerland 2016. All Rights Reserved
F. Buccafurri et al. (Eds.): CD-ARES 2016, LNCS 9817, pp. 158–174, 2016.
DOI: 10.1007/978-3-319-45507-5_11

Nowadays, a big-enterprise IT system is usually geographically distributed, pervasive and ubiquitous for its internal and external users. Therefore, each of such systems consists of a network of subsystems where the cyber systemic risk must be reduced as much as possible. Cyber security risk has to be continuously monitored, while real-time recovery and support procedures, assuring an enough degree of system availability, have to be provided [1,4]. Systemic effects have to be reduced and global collaboration among all stakeholders, both public and private, should be provided for an effective proactive prevention of a cyber shock of our global, not only financial, networked systems [21].

In a recent white paper [5], the Depository Trust & Clearing Corporation (DTCC) affirms that a global cyber systemic risk could become less dangerous if the defense is both collective and coordinated, otherwise the failure is quite sure. The last DTCC report on systemic risk [14] is very alarming on the cyber risk for the worldwide financial markets. Therefore, instead of providing specific cyber risk defenses for each system, a global cyber systemic risk [26,27] strategy should be devised and enforced by means of the adoption of shared rules, regulations and common approaches.

This paper focus on the banking context and, specifically on the business continuous plan (BCP) and its disaster recovery plan (DRP), as regulated by the Bank of Italy for the banking operators located in Italy [6]. However, each Bank operating in the European Union must provide similar guidelines for BCP and DRP of their banking operators.

The definitions of BCP and DRP are driven worldwide by many sectoral rules and regulations [25], without any global coordination. A supervising institution, having the authority to push and actually drive the different BCPs, would be able to manage the global systemic risk by a coordinated strategy. Moreover, the 2016 edition of "The Global Risks Report" [11], by the World Economic Forum, outlines the need for cooperation among stakeholders for risk management and cites some tests performed in Germany.

We model, by means of a goal oriented methodology [23] named GOReM [18], the requirements for the cyber systemic risk treatment for a bank operating in Italy. All Italian banks follow rules and regulations delivered by the Bank of Italy. However, each European Nation has a central banking institution which establish similar guidelines for the local banks. Then, the developed models might be applied, with small adaptations, to whichever bank in Europe.

In particular, the models obtained using GOReM, follow what established by Bank of Italy in the guidelines [6]. Those models allowed to easily highlight how a BCP has two different ways to handle the cyber systemic risk. The first includes critical processes which might develop contagion only to the internal stakeholders of the bank (including counterparts cooperating to the business of the bank). In this case the ripple effect of an incident is treated at the bank level and the Bank of Italy is only notified. The second cyber systemic risk treatment is related to the safeguard of systematically important processes of the payment systems and of the access to financial markets. In this case, both BCP and the handling of a possible ripple effect of an incident on other banks and, more generally, on external entities, is strongly centralized by the Bank of Italy. The latter is a hierarchical control, although with rigid response time, which might introduce delays in the tentative to slow down or stop contagion in the European and even worldwide financial system [16].

GOReM has already been successfully employed in the context of some industrial research projects, involving enterprises such as ACI Informatica [7] and Poste Italiane [10]. The numerous GOReM practical models in different contexts, including that of system security compliance in cloud [19], allowed to improve the methodology potentialities and to achieve a very good satisfaction of the many stakeholders, which are different in backgrounds and for desired goals.

The rest of the paper is structured as follows: Sect. 2 describes an overview of GOReM; the requirements specification of a Cyber Systemic Risk in Bank is presented in Sect. 3. Finally, results and conclusions are drawn in Sect. 4.

2   An Overview of GOReM

This description of GOReM is a small overview which we use often with the aim to give a mean to understand the models hereafter introduced. GOReM uses the UML notation [9]. As a consequence, it is easy to employ and it simplifies the concept sharing among a wide variety of stakeholders [15]. The resulting requirements modeling activity has been recognized by the users to be easy and effective. Typical activities of requirements engineering (RE) [23], i.e. elicitation of requirements, analysis, validation, verification and management, are expressed in GOReM mainly in term of: (i) stakeholders and their goals, (ii) use cases and involved processes and (iii) work-product documentations. The methodology consists of three main phases, each of which is devoted to modeling specific aspects of a RE process: Context Modeling, Scenario Modeling and Application Modeling (see Fig. 1).

Context Modeling aims at clearly representing the reference domain. The work-products of this phase are: a *Stakeholder Diagram*, which shows a, often hierarchical, specification of all the stakeholders involved in the specific context; each stakeholder is in turn characterized by a set of *Softgoals* [20] they intend to pursue; a *Softgoal Dependency Diagram*, which shows the relationships between the stakeholders and the softgoals, as well as the relationships among softgoals (i.e., contributes, hinders, includes, extends, specializes); moreover, the *Rules and Regulations* that govern the context are individuated and analyzed in a work-product.

Scenario Modeling specifies different business scenarios in terms of *Roles* that are played by the involved stakeholders, their specific *Goals*, and the specific *Rules and Regulations* that govern the business scenario. A *SWOT* Analysis (Strengths, Weaknesses, Opportunities and Threats) is often performed with the aim to guide decisions on future work.

Application Modeling defines application scenarios in order to specify the functionalities which should be provided by a single business scenario resulting

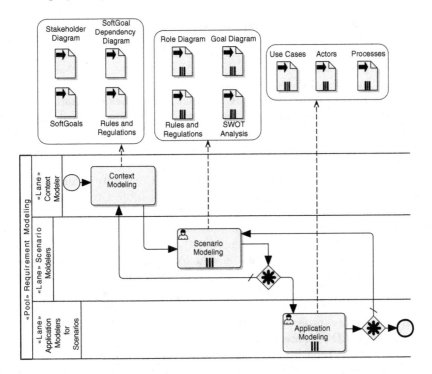

Fig. 1. Reference process model of GOReM and work products

from the previous phase. Each application scenario is characterized by functionalities that are modeled by UML-based *Use Cases*, *Actors* and possibly *Processes*.

These phases are repeated iteratively and feedback among them is allowed in order to support an incremental refinement process. Furthermore, scenarios and applications are specified concurrently. A BPM model [3] of the reference process for GOReM, along with its main work-products, is reported in Fig. 1.

3   Modeling the Banking Cyber Systemic Risk

This Section describes a comprehensive subset of the requirements specification of the business continuity for Italian banks, as established by Bank of Italy in its guidelines in [6], as it has been worked out, employing GOReM, in the context of the project [10].

The context model of the business continuity in a bank and the description of one of the possible business scenarios, that is the risk treatment in bank, are first described. Then, one specific application scenario, concerning the treatment of cyber systemic risk for the so called "systematically important processes" [6] of a bank, is modeled in terms of actors, use cases and processes.

3.1   The Context Model: Banking Business Continuity

The banking system has a complex organizational infrastructure. In the following, we model a small subset with the only objective to give an idea of the effectiveness and powerfulness of employing GOReM for this purpose.

The term *Business Continuity* (BC) refers to all of the organizational, technical and staffing measures employed in order to: (i) ensure the continuation of core business activities in the immediate aftermath of a crisis and (ii) gradually ensure the continued operation of all business activities in the event of sustained and severe disruption [2].

To this end, each bank must define a Business Continuity Plan (BCP), i.e. a formal document stating the principles, setting the objectives, describing the procedures and identifying the resources for business continuity management concerning critical and systemically important corporate process [6]. The bank must also use internal audit, testing activity and continuously improvement implementations of its BCP, with the aim to: (i) analyze well the exposure to risks, (ii) identify vulnerabilities, and (iii) evaluate, implement and maintain updated, appropriate BC and Disaster Recovery (DR) solutions. A critical part of the BCP is the Disaster Recovery Plan (DRP), i.e. a document establishing the technical and organizational measures to cope with events that put electronic data processing (EDP) centers out of service.

Despite suitable tools and countermeasures are constantly in action to prevent their occurrence, unfortunately accidents happen. In this cases, it is essential that a BCP is promptly put in operation, to ensure the continuity of services. Hence, the appropriated Disaster Recovery procedures, as specified by the DRP, have to begin immediately.

Figure 2 shows a GOReM diagram that depicts the stakeholders which were identified for this context, their softgoals and the dependencies among them.

The main stakeholders are: the **Bank of Italy**; **Banking System Operator**, which can be of two different types, i.e. **Operator of technological infrastructures or networks**, and **operating companies**, i.e. wholesale markets in government securities, multilateral wholesale trading facilities in government securities, multilateral deposit trading systems, securities settlement systems, central counterparties and central securities depositories, with registered offices and/or operational headquarters in Italy; **Bank personnel**, i.e. people, including corporate bodies, which work internally in the bank; **Service Provider**, i.e. external stakeholders that provide IT services and other commodities, by stipulating specific contracts with the bank; **Selling Net**; **Shareholder** and **Customer**.

Each stakeholder is associated to a set of softgoals as it can be seen from Fig. 2. The identified softgoals are resumed in the following.

SG1: Supervising the non-interruption of the bank's services.
SG2: Every operator has to put into execution the suitable provisions, according to the BCP, for ensuring business continuity and disaster recovery in reaction to threats.

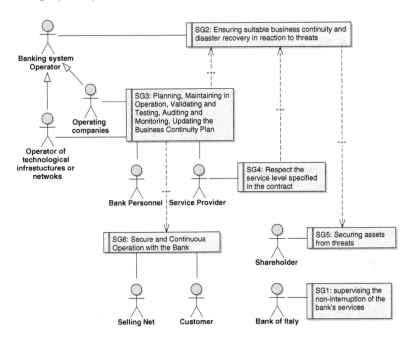

Fig. 2. Context model: the banking business continuity's softgoals and dependencies diagram

SG3: Planning, keeping into operation, validating and testing, auditing and monitoring, updating the BCP. This softgoal is shared by all kinds of considered bank operators.

SG4: Guaranteeing the service level specified in the contract (i.e. external providers must stipulate a contract with the bank that specifies a service level agreement among the parties and that has to be compliant to the business continuity needs).

SG5: Safeguarding assets from threats. Shareholders need to be ensured about the safety of their financial assets.

SG6: Guaranteeing secure and continuous operation of the bank. Both customers and selling nets need always working and safe banking services.

Figure 2 also outlines the existing dependencies among Softgoals. In particular, the achievement of SG3 and SG4 contributes to SG2. Similarly, reaching SG2 has a positive effect on SG5 and analogously the same holds for SG3 on SG6.

3.2   Scenario Model: Risk Treatment

The scenario we choose to model is about the treatment of risks coming from bank defaults, financial and market crashes, human mistakes, cyber threats and so on. This scenario includes situations such as: destruction or inaccessibility of important structures, unavailability of critical information systems, unavailability of human resources essential to corporate processes, interruption of operation of infrastructure (e.g. electricity, telecommunications, interbank networks, financial markets), alteration or loss of critical data and documents.

According to the Bank of Italy guidelines [6], operators must define, monitor, test and maintain updated, a BCP for coping with the above situations of crisis involving the operators or significant counterparts as, other group members, major suppliers, prime customers, specific financial markets, clearing, settlement and guarantee systems.

An important step in applying GOReM is the identification of the roles played by each involved stakeholder. Each Stakeholder, while playing a given role, has some specific goals he want to reach inside the scenario. The stakeholders-roles mapping alongside the role-specific goals are resumed by the diagram reported in Fig. 3.

Table 1 details each goal of the considered scenario while Table 2 lists a subset of the rules and regulations of interest for the scenario of Risk treatment. A unique identifier is associated to each rule/regulation and some relationships of warning with respect to others rules/regulations is given (column W) for indicating the need of a deeper analysis when applied in practice.

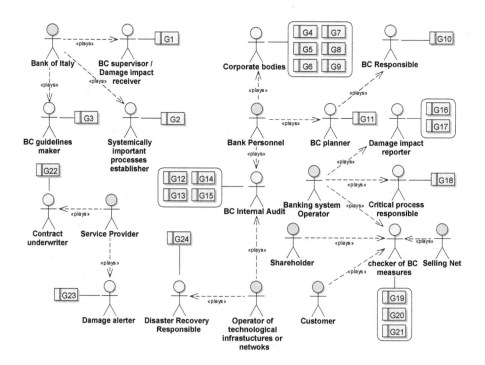

Fig. 3. Scenario model for risk treatment: softGoals-roles-goals diagram

Table 1. Scenario model for risk treatment: role and goal description

Stakeholder	Role	Goal	Description
Bank of Italy	BC supervisor / Damage impact receiver	G1	Each operator has its suitable Business Continuity Plan and the impact of possible damages undergone by its Banks for specific systemically important processes, is managed
	Systemically important processes establisher	G2	Systematically important processes are individuated and assigned for being protected by a suitable operator
	BC guidelines maker	G3	Each operator refers to guidelines for business continuity aligned with the actual European level of risk knowledge
Bank personnel	Corporate bodies, i.e. considered part of the bank personnel	G4	Establish objectives and strategies for BCP of the bank
		G5	Assign human, technological and financial resources sufficient to attain the objectives of the BCP
		G6	Approve the BCP and successive modifications resulting from technological and organizational adjustments and formally accept the residual risks not covered by the BCP
		G7	Control the results of checks on the adequacy of the BCP and of its measures, done at least once a year
		G8	Designate the person responsible for business continuity planning
		G9	Promote the development and regular checking of the BCP and its adaptation to any significant organizational, technological or infrastructural innovations and in the case of detection of shortcomings or the materialization of new risks
	BC Responsible	G10	Supervise the planning of the BCPs by means of the coordination of every involved BC planner
	BC Planner	G11	Establish the BCP for the operator, compliant to the guidelines provided by Bank of Italy
	BC Internal Audit	G12	Check, at fixed times, the BCP and its updating by examining the test programs, taking part in the tests and checking the results, and suggesting changes to the BCP on the basis of the shortcomings found
		G13	Analyze the criteria for escalation in the case of incidents, by evaluating the length of time required to declare the state of crisis

(Continued)

Table 1. *(Continued)*

Stakeholder	Role	Goal	Description
		G14	Test the BCPs of the outsourcers and other critical suppliers and may decide to rely on the controls performed by the structures of the latter if they are deemed professionally capable, independent and transparent
		G15	Examine the outsourcing contracts to make sure that the level of safeguards conforms the corporate objectives and standards
Banking System Operator	Damage Impact reported	G16	Produce an impact analysis, preliminary to the drafting of the BCP and regularly update the impact analysis, with the aim to determine the level of risk for each corporate process and highlight the repercussions of a service outage. The impact analysis considers, in addition to operational risks, also such other risks as market and liquidity risk
		G17	Document the residual risks, not handled by the BCP, which must be explicitly accepted by the competent corporate bodies
	Critical process responsible	G18	Identify relevant processes relating to corporate functions whose non-availability, owing to the high impact of the resulting damage, necessitates high levels of business continuity to be achieved through preventive measures and BC solutions activated in case of incident
	Checker of BC measures	G19	Shareholders, together with the bank system operators and the selling net, as well as with customers, cooperate in defining the procedures for testing the planned business continuity measures in real crisis scenarios
		G20	Determine an appropriate frequency of the testing task for each measures
		G21	Write down and notify the results of tests to the competent corporate bodies and transmit, for the matters under their respective competence, to the operational units
Service provider	Contract underwriter	G22	Ensure the service levels agreed with the operators, as formally state in the signed contract, in the case of crisis and ensure the continuity provisions to be put in place in keeping with attainment of corporate objectives and with the indications of the Bank of Italy
	Damage alerter	G23	Notify promptly the operator of any incident, in order to allow immediate activation of the BC procedures
Operator of technological infrastructures or networks	Disaster Recovery Responsible	G24	Define and maintain updated the DRP, with reference to central and peripheral information systems

Table 2. Scenario model for risk treatment: rules and regulations diagram

Id	Rules and regulations	Type	Location/ Adopter	W
A	CPMI-IOSCO consultative paper "Guidance on cyber resilience for financial market infrastructure", November 2015	Best practice	EU	B, C
B	Opinion of the European Central Bank of 25 July 2014 on a proposal for a directive of the European Parliament and of the Council concerning measures to ensure a high common level of network and information security across the Union (CON/2014/58)	Policy	EU	A, C
D	Guidelines on business continuity for market infrastructures	Best practice	Italy	A,B, E, F
E	Legislative Decree 385/1993 (the Consolidated Law on Banking)	Law	Italy	A, B, G
F	Legislative Decree 58/1998 (the Consolidated Law on Finance)	Law	Italy	A, B, H
G	Business continuity oversight expectations for systemically important payment systems, issued by Eurosystem in June 2006	Best practice	European Union	E, F, H
H	Principles for Financial Market Infrastructures, issued by Bank for International Settlements Committee on Payment and Settlement Systems (CPSS) and IOSCO Technical Committee, April 2012	Best practice	European Union	E, F, G

3.3 Application Model: Cyber Systemic Risk for Banks in Italy

The application model we consider is related to the Cyber Systemic Risk as dealt with by the Bank of Italy. This is one of the application models that might be derived from the above presented Risk Treatment scenario.

This application model deals with business continuity and safeguards for the so referred "Systematically Important Processes", which are identified and controlled directly by the Bank of Italy and which govern essential services in the payment system and in the access to the financial markets. A malicious exploitation of a cyber threat for these processes might evolve in a systemic crisis inside other operators and on the whole financial system. For those processes, the Bank of Italy controls, asks for updates, and manages every risk of crisis and incidents.

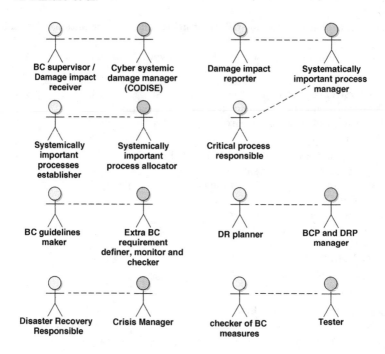

Fig. 4. Application model for cyber systemic risk: actor diagram

The Bank of Italy requires that the operators, involved in systematically important processes, work actively for adjustment of the BCP. These operators must comply with stricter business continuity requirements than those which normally apply to all operators. In particular, these requirements are concerned with the recovery time of systemically important processes, the location of standby facilities, and the resources allocated to crisis management (see Sect. 3 of [6]).

Figure 4 shows the Actors Diagram relevant to this application model, where scenario roles are mapped to actors, and Fig. 5 resumes the main use cases involving the identified actors.

Some use cases are extensions of some others which are supposed to be already defined in another application model, named "Business continuity management", where the constraints by the Bank of Italy are less stringent and related to critical processes which are not systematically important processes. A short description of these use cases is given below.

BCP adjustments and compliance monitoring (**eUCa**). This use case extends the use case **UCa** which is part of the use cases concerning critical processes which do not belong to the set of those considered *systematically important*. BC and DR plans, defined in the application model "Business Continuity Management", require some adjustments to become compliant with the stricter requirements defined by the Bank of Italy. The operator must also ensure continuous compliance with the special requirements and all this must be done by the responsible

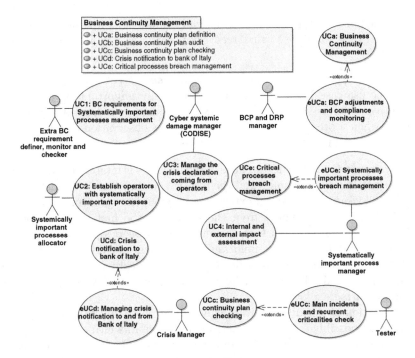

Fig. 5. Application model for cyber systemic risk: main use case diagram

for these activities (i.e. the actor "BC and DR plans requirement adjustment and compliance responsible").

Main incidents and recurrent criticality check (**eUCc**). This use case extends the use case **UCc** (*Business continuity plan checking*). The Bank of Italy requires at least one a year of test for the safeguards provided for the continuity of the systemically important processes. Operators must actively participate in tests and market-wide simulations, organized or promoted by authorities, by markets and by the main financial infrastructures. In addition, this use case prescribes the drafting of a yearly report about: the main features of the business continuity plan; the adaptations that have been made to it; the additions implemented during the year; the tests conducted on the main incidents and criticalities.

Managing crisis notification to and from Bank of Italy (**eUCd**). This use case extends the use case **UCd**, related to notification to Bank of Italy, when the blockage of essential infrastructures is related to internal critical processes. In this case, the actor "crisis manager" must instead communicates promptly to the Bank of Italy every cyber attack and state of crisis coming from some threat to its systemically important processes. Furthermore, the use case includes the sending of an assessment report, drafted according to **UC4**. In addition, this use case dictates that the "crisis manager" receives the notification, coming from the Bank of Italy, that other operators are subject to a cyber attack, which might cause contagion to some of its systematically important processes. Then, this actor should raise an alert so that recovery procedures may immediately begin (see **UC3**).

Systemically important processes breach management (**eUCe**). This use case extends the use case **UCe**. The actor "systematically important processes manager" activates immediately the recovery procedures as indicated by the BCP and DRP when a breach to some process under its observation occurs. As specified by the guidelines, these procedures govern:

(i) the recovery time that, if the cause of the blockage is internal to the operator, must not exceed four hours and the restart time must not exceed two hours. If the blockage is due to an external contagion, the operator must activate his DR within two hours from the restart of the first affected operator. For information systems with on line duplication of operational data the time between the recovery point and the incident should zeroed. In case of extreme situations, promptly recovery of systemically important processes, using protected off line PCs, faxes, and telephone contacts with selected counterparts, is allowed.

(ii) the location of standby facilities, which must be distant from their primary facilities, possibly outside the metropolitan area in which the primary facility is located and it must be served by utilities (i.e. telecommunications, electricity, water) different from those serving the primary facility.

(iii) the resources allocated to crisis management. Human, technological and logistical resources needed to keep systemically important processes operating are established in the BCP.

BC requirements the management of systematically important processes (**UC1**). Stricter BC requirements for systematically important processes are established by Bank of Italy. This use case directly controls the operators adjustment and the compliance of their BCPs to the evolving requirements imposed by the Bank of Italy.

Establish which operator has systematically important processes (**UC2**). The Bank of Italy is in charge to individuate the specific set of operators having systematically important processes.

Manage the crisis declaration coming from operators (**UC3**). For incidents that may have significant impact on systemically important processes, the declaration of the state of crisis is managed by CODISE, part of Bank of Italy, which begins this activity with an initial assessment of potentially damaged operators.

Internal and external impact assessment (**UC4**). In the occurrence of crisis, the actor "systematically important processes manager", prepares the assessment of the impact on operations of its central and peripheral structures and of the current relations with customers and counterparts.

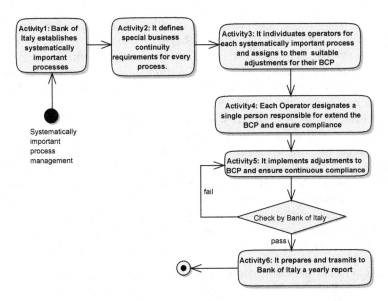

Fig. 6. Application model for cyber systemic risk: systemically important processes management process

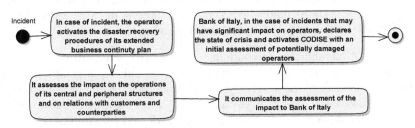

Fig. 7. Application model for cyber systemic risk: incident management process

Figures 6 and 7 report two activity diagrams that respectively model the process of handling cyber systemic risk for important banking processes and the process of managing the possible know-on effect of a cyber systemic incident inside the important processes of an operator.

4 Results and Conclusions

We tested the suitability of GOReM for modeling the context of business continuity in of a Bank and the requirements related to handling of the cyber systemic risk as regulated by the guidelines issued by the Bank of Italy. In the complex and touchy scenario of banking, the relevant models have been defined and graphically represented [15]. GOReM allowed to easily identify stakeholders, roles and specific goals from which the main use cases and processes, have been derived.

The result of this study is a requirements specification that may be employed as a good starting point for the devising a global approach towards the management of the cyber systemic risk in the financial and banking domain. In fact, it gives the adequate planning independence to the single bank, but under the riverbed of the constraints dictated by a supervisor authority, like the Bank of Italy for the Italian banking operators. Moreover, this vision could scale at the behavior of a node inside a bigger network, where other nodes are the other Bank of the other European Nations. In turn, this model might be applied to a coordinated European supervision institution, e.g. the European Systemic Risk Board [12]. Even more, it is also desirable to scale worldwide under the control of a global authority, which might coordinate business continuity and disaster recovery for preventing and managing a cyber systemic risk, for the global financial world.

As a final consideration, special attention should be paid to the time needed for a given operator to react to a cyber incident: be "promptly" might not be an adequate answer. Two observations come from this modeling experience:

(i) Cyber systemic effects are here handled by a central authority, which in this case is the Bank of Italy, that establishes the state of crisis and manages the know-on effect on other operators. This centralization may result in a waste of time even though prudential politics suggest that this is a good strategy.

(ii) Time of response to a state of crisis that is communicated after some "hours" (see use case **eUCe**) might be a very large interval of time, especially at a worldwide level, compared to the speed of cyber threats.

A possible solution might be in modifying the hierarchical organization in a more horizontal and collaborative one, which might come only from common decided rules and regulations [8]. However, Cyber Systemic Risk treatment in Europe and worldwide is nowadays urgent. According to [24], while business areas are already supervised, the supervision agreement for network and information security is still a work in progress. This is a big delay for cyber systemic risk that must be regained soon.

Acknowledgments. This work has been partially supported by the "National Operative Programme for Research and Competitiveness" 2007–2013, Technological District on Cyber Security (PON03PE_00032_2_02), funded by the Italian Ministry of Education, University and Research, and the Italian Ministry of Economic Development.

References

1. Business continuity oversight expectations for systemically important payment systems (SIPS). Report, Eurpean Central Bank (2006). https://www.ecb.europa.eu/pub/pdf/other/businesscontinuitysips2006en.pdf
2. ESCB definitions of major business continuity terms in relation to payment and securities settlement systems. European Central Bank, June 2007
3. Business Process Model and Notation^{TM} v. 2.0. Spec. formal/2011-01-03, Object Management Group (2011). http://www.omg.org/spec/BPMN/2.0/

4. Principles for financial market infrastructures. Press release ISBN 92-9197-108-1, Bank for International Settlements Committee on Payment and Settlement Systems (CPSS) and IOSCO Technical Committee (2012)
5. Cyber Risk a Global Systemic Threat: A White Paper to the Industry on Systemic Risk. White paper, Depository Trust & Clearing Corporation (DTCC), October 2014. http://www.dtcc.com/%7e/media/Files/Downloads/issues/risk/cyber-risk.pdf
6. Guidelines on business continuity for market infrastructure. guidelines, Bank of Italy (2014). https://www.bancaditalia.it/compiti/sispaga-mercati/codise/Guidelines_business_continuity_market_infrastructures.pdf
7. DICET-INMOTO - ORganization of Cultural HEritage for Smart Tourism and Real-time Accessibility (OR.C.HE.S.T.R.A.) - Project funded by the Italian Ministry of Education, University and Research (MIUR) - PON Project - Research and Competitiveness 2007–2013 (2015)
8. Market intermediary business continuity and recovery planning. Technical report FR32/2015, International Organization of Securities Commissions, December 2015. http://www.iosco.org/library/pubdocs/pdf/IOSCOPD523.pdf
9. Unified Modeling Language^{TM}, v. 2.5. Spec. formal/15-03-01, Object Management Group (2015). http://www.omg.org/spec/UML/2.5/
10. District of cyber security (2016). https://www.distrettocybersecurity.it
11. The global risks report 2016. Insight report, 11th edn. World Economic Forum (2016). http://www3.weforum.org/docs/Media/TheGlobalRisksReport2016.pdf
12. Handbook on the assessment of compliance with ESRB recommendations. European Systemic Risk Board (2016)
13. Internet Security Threat Report. vol. 21, Symantec, April 2016
14. Systemic risk barometer: results overview 2016–Q1. Press release, Depository Trust & Clearing Corporation (DTCC) (2016). http://www.dtcc.com/%7E/media/Files/PDFs/Systemic-Risk-Barometer-Q1-2016.pdf
15. Caire, P., Genon, N., Heymans, P., Moody, D.L.: Visual notation design 2.0: towards user comprehensible requirements engineering notations. In: 21st IEEE International Requirements Engineering Conference (RE 2013), Rio de Janeiro, Brasil, pp. 115–124, July 2013
16. Cerutti, E., Claessens, S., McGuire, P.: Systemic risks in global banking: What available data can tell us and what more data are needed? Working Paper 18531, National Bureau of Economic Research, November 2012. http://www.nber.org/papers/w18531
17. Chaudhary, R., Hamilton, J.: The five critical attributes of effective cybersecurity risk management - white paper. Technical report, Crowe Horwath LLP (2015)
18. Citrigno, S., Furfaro, A., Gallo, T., Garro, A., Graziano, S., Saccà, D.: Mastering concept exploration in large industrial research projects. In: INCOSE Italia Conference on Systems Engineering (CIISE 2014), Rome, Italy, pp. 26–37, 24-25 November 2014
19. Furfaro, A., Gallo, T., Garro, A., Saccà, D., Tundis, A.: Requirements specification of a cloud service for cyber security compliance analysis. In: Proceedings of the 2nd International Conference on Cloud Computing Technologies and Applications (CloudTech 2016), IEEE, Marrakesh, 24–26 May 2016
20. Glinz, M.: On non-functional requirements. In: 15th IEEE International Requirements Engineering Conference (RE 2007), pp. 21–26. IEEE, New Delhi, October 2007
21. Goldsmith, D., Siegel, M.: Systematic approaches to cyber insecurity. Technical report, MIT Sloan School of Management1 - ECIR Working Paper (2012)

22. Kosub, T.: Components and challenges of integrated cyber risk management. Zeitschrift für die gesamte Versicherungswissenschaft **104**(5), 615–634 (2015)
23. van Lamsweerde, A.: Goal-oriented requirements enginering: a roundtrip from research to practice [enginering read engineering]. In: 12th IEEE International Requirements Engineering Conference, Kyoto, Japan, pp. 4–7, September 2004
24. Nouy, D.: Single supervisory mechanism after one year: the state of play and the challenges ahead. In: Bank of Italy Conference on Micro and Macroprudential Banking Supervision in the Euro Area, Milan, Italy, 24 November 2015. https://www.bankingsupervision.europa.eu/press/speeches/date/2015/html/se15 1124.en.html
25. Rissman, D.: US regulators issue guidance on disaster recovery and business continuity planning for hedge funds (2013). http://aceits.net/us-regulators-issue-guidance-on-disaster-recovery-and-business-continuity-planning-for-hedge-funds/
26. Sommer, P.: Reducing systemic cybersecurity risk. Oecd/ifp project on future global shocks, Information Systems and Innovation Group, London School of Economics and Ian Brown, Oxford Internet Institute, Oxford University (2011). https://www.oecd.org/gov/risk/46889922.pdf
27. Tendulkar, R.: Cyber-crime, securities markets and systemic risk. Joint staff working paper, IOSCO Research Department and World Federation of Exchanges (2013). http://www.iosco.org/research/pdf/swp/Cyber-Crime-Securities-Markets-and-Systemic-Risk.pdf

Differentiating Cyber Risk of Insurance Customers: The Insurance Company Perspective

Inger Anne Tøndel[✉], Fredrik Seehusen, Erlend Andreas Gjære,
and Marie Elisabeth Gaup Moe

SINTEF ICT, Trondheim, Norway
inger.a.tondel@sintef.no

Abstract. As a basis for offering policy and setting tariffs, cyber-insurance carriers need to assess the cyber risk of companies. This paper explores the challenges insurance companies face in assessing cyber risk, based on literature and interviews with representatives from insurers. The interview subjects represent insurance companies offering cyber-insurance in a market where this is a new and unknown product. They have limited historical data, with few examples of incidents leading to payout. This lack of experience and data, together with the need for an efficient sales process, highly impacts their approach to risk assessment. Two options for improving the ability to perform thorough yet efficient assessments of cyber risk are explored in this paper: basing analysis on reusable sector-specific risk models, and including managed security service providers (MSSPs) in the value chain.

Keywords: Cyber-insurance · Risk management · Risk modeling

1 Introduction

Cyber-insurance has been defined in literature as *"the transfer of financial risk associated with network and computer incidents to a third party"* [9]. It can take many forms, offering third party or first party coverage, and covering a variety of threat types [8,24]. The demand for this insurance product is increasing [35,36]. Although cyber-insurance has been around in some form for several decades, the cyber-insurance products are still relatively immature. This is underlined by statements such as *"cyber policies are still the Wild West of insurance policies"* [11] and *"products are untested, pricing appears arbitrary and experimentation in contract writing is commonplace"* [4]. Academic research on cyber-insurance has identified a number of challenges and knowledge gaps [4,24,40], some of which are related to assessing cyber risk.

Taking on cyber in their product portfolio is associated with a greater risk for insurance companies than other traditional covers, which is reflected in the product's pricing. According to a UK study, the cost of cyber-insurance relative to the limit purchased is typically three times the cost of cover for more

Published by Springer International Publishing Switzerland 2016. All Rights Reserved
F. Buccafurri et al. (Eds.): CD-ARES 2016, LNCS 9817, pp. 175–190, 2016.
DOI: 10.1007/978-3-319-45507-5_12

established general liability risks, and six times higher than for property insurance [18]. The UK study additionally points out that cyber-insurance has a lower price differentiation across customers, something that may be due to a lack of historical data in underwriting or inappropriate means of assessing the cyber risk of potential customers. This is concerning as it undermines the role that insurance can have in increasing the security posture of insurance buyers, since they will not see any benefit in terms of lower insurance cost [18].

As a basis for offering policy and setting tariffs, cyber-insurance carriers need to assess the cyber risk of companies. Insurance companies do this to differentiate between potential clients, thus reducing the risk of adverse selection [34]. This paper explores the challenges insurance companies face in assessing cyber risk, based on literature (Sect. 2) and interviews with representatives from insurance companies (Sect. 3). Section 4 outlines two options for improving the ability to perform thorough, yet efficient assessments of cyber risk: basing analysis on reusable sector-specific risk models, and including managed security service providers (MSSPs) in the value chain. Section 5 discusses the contribution of the paper and provides suggestions for further work. Section 6 concludes the paper.

2   Known Challenges for Assessing Cyber Risk of Insurance Customers

A large number of standards, guidelines and research papers suggest methods for information security risk assessments [39]. Though they have their differences, the methods tend to include similar steps: characterisation of the system; threat and vulnerability assessment; risk determination; control identification, and; evaluation and implementation of controls [15]. Figure 1 provides an overview of the risk assessment process and key challenges for insurance companies, identified through searches in academic literature as well as non-academic sources, such as news articles, technical reports and white papers (see Tøndel et al. [40] for more details on the method used for the literature study).

The cyber risk of an organisation depends on various internal and external conditions, including the organisation's assets, the technology they are using and its vulnerabilities, the security awareness and competence of the employees, routines relevant for cyber security, the security of the organisation's vendors, vulnerabilities in common infrastructure which the organisation relies on, and the motivation of potential attackers. With all these factors to consider, and limited knowledge of the impact of the various factors on the organisation's overall risk, risk is complex to understand and evaluate, and it is impossible to verify that the risk estimation is correct [24]. This is true for the organisation itself, but also for an insurance company offering cyber-insurance to the organisation. The premium paid by all insurance holders should cover any payouts plus return profit to the insurance company. To limit their own risk exposure, the insurers seek a mix of customers which provide a sufficient premium income compared to the overall risk portfolio, and a steady flow of payouts.

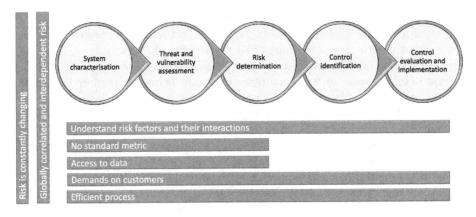

Fig. 1. The risk assessment process and challenges

The question of what constitutes "good IT security" has not been answered conclusively [13]. Research and practice on measuring information security has progressed, and there are many indicators and measurement frameworks available, see e.g. Herrmann [17] and ISO/IEC 27004 [20]. Still, there is no agreed set of metrics to predict information security risk in the general case [41]. Setting security baselines, or providing rewards for companies with documented security best practices, is difficult due to lack of knowledge about the effect of different security controls [26]. Simple metrics, like the number of records lost, does not always correlate with the total cost of the breach [30]. Currently, different insurance carriers evaluate risk in different ways, and they consider a variety of risk factors, covering both technical and organisational aspects [26,27].

The lack of robust actuarial data has been pointed out by various sources as a reason for limited success of the cyber-insurance market [5,13,14,41]. Several sources of historical cyber-incident information exist, e.g. from CERTs, security companies or researchers [13]. Examples of surveys that provide relevant data on costs of cyber-incidents are a NetDiligence survey of insurance payouts related to cyber liability [30] and Ponemon's Cost of Data Breach Study [37]. However, it is not easy to determine which sources of information should be relied upon more than others [13]. Barriers for information sharing include reluctance by firms to reveal details on security incidents [5,16,41], and limited ability to quantify costs associated with such incidents [41]. Toregas and Zahn make the following claim: *"Given that many companies are either unaware of a cyber attack or unwilling to disclose such attacks, and added to the fact that those attacks are hard to quantify, actuarial data for the cyber-insurance market is missing and unlikely to be available in the near future"* [41]. Insurance carriers are also reluctant to share incident information, due to a competitive market, and because they fear that they would ultimately *"give more than they get"* [26]. The significant information asymmetries currently present require insurance companies to perform costly state verification and upfront risk assessments [8].

Carriers engage clients heavily during the underwriting process. Historically they used extensive questionnaires [3,27], but it is becoming more common to speak directly with clients to understand their vulnerabilities and risk management controls [27]. In this process customers may need to share a potentially large amount of information with the insurance company. It has been pointed out that in a competitive environment, potential customers may favour insurance companies with less demanding assessment processes [26]. Likewise, potential clients may not like being dictated by the insurance company on how to mitigate cyber risks [28]. Insurance companies are however also interested in having an efficient assessment process, illustrated by quotes such as *"carriers typically don't spend weeks with potential insureds reviewing every single aspect of an organization to see what's happening with its implementation of information security policies"* [26] and *"cybersecurity insurance underwriting essentially tries to weed out the 20 percent of companies who have no clue about cybersecurity from the pool of potential insureds"* [27]. Despite this need to have an efficient process, from the viewpoints of both customers and providers, it should be pointed out that the upfront risk assessment performed by insurance companies can have positive side-effects on increased self-protection, and the consulting and risk assessment services provided by the insurance company is one central driver of product value [8].

The experienced cyber risk may change rapidly based on technology changes, discovery of vulnerabilities, political actions etc. There is a need to understand how to take these changes into account when it comes to cyber-insurance. Organisational resilience, i.e. the capability of recognizing, adapting to and coping with the unexpected [42] is relevant for this. In the safety domain, research has progressed on measuring organisational resilience through risk awareness, response capacity and support [32], and such a measurement framework has been adapted to the ICT domain [7]. Rapid changes are additionally a challenge for collecting reliable actuarial data, as changes in technology and attacker profiles can cause empirical information on incidents to quickly become outdated [8,24,26].

According to Böhme and Schwartz [9], cyber risk is characterised by both interdependent security and correlated risk; the security of a node is dependent on the security of other nodes and incidents may strike in a correlated fashion. Interconnected nodes [3,9] and dominant products [3] are key causes for this interdependency. An incident in one organisation may thus cause or increase the likelihood of incidents in another organisation. This risk comes in addition to the potential impact of an incident on third parties, up and down in the supply chain [10]. For insurance companies, these characteristics increase risk of concurrent claims [3]. Additionally, cyber incidents may cause pay-outs on a number of different insurance policies [22].

Table 1 gives a summary of key points from the literature related to these challenges.

3 Study of Insurance Companies

In addition to studying relevant literature, we have performed a study of experiences and practices of insurance companies when it comes to their cyber risk assessment of customers. The study reported in this paper is part of a bigger ongoing study with the overall goal of identifying what type of decision support and information is needed for evaluating cyber-insurance offerings, both from the perspectives of insurance companies and prospective customers.

3.1 Method

We have performed a study among key insurance companies offering cyber-insurance products in the Nordic market. The study included interviews performed in October/November 2015 and examination of relevant documentation. Relevant insurance companies for the study were identified by studying the web sites of such companies operating in the Nordic market, and the decision on which actors to approach for the study was based on the goal of covering the main actors in one country. The semi-structured interviews were carried out at the insurance companies' premises by one or two researchers, and the interviews were audio recorded and transcribed. The interview guide included the following topics: role of the interviewee; details of the cyber-insurance products offered; process for getting in touch with customers, evaluating risk and communicating policy terms to customers, and; future plans regarding cyber-insurance products. We talked with one representative from each company, and these were in underwriter or manager roles. Each interview lasted about one hour. All transcripts were thematically coded, and organised into thematic networks [2]. As the Nordic cyber-insurance market is small with a limited number of providers, we do not give any further details about the insurance companies that participated, in order to preserve anonymity. However, we point out that the number of companies interviewed is small, but still comprise the main actors in one of the Nordic countries. Regarding the context of the study, it should be noted that cyber-insurance is a relatively new product in the Nordics, and it is only the last few years that pure cyber-insurance products have been marketed here. Many Nordic companies are still unaware of cyber-insurance products' existence.

3.2 Results

The insurance companies we have studied seem to have relatively similar approaches to differentiate insurance customers in terms of risk. In general, they seem confident that their current approach and evaluation is good enough. At the same time they experience challenges and constraints in evaluating prospective customers' cyber risk. Figure 2 provides an overview of the central themes that came up in the interviews related to assessment of risk. In the following we go into these in more detail. An overview of the findings, related to the challenges identified in literature, can be found in Table 1.

Table 1. Overview of identified challenges from literature and interviews

Challenge	Overview of state of the art	Interview study
Understand risk factors and their interaction;no standard metric	• Uncertainty in what factors are most important for risk [13, 24–26, 41].	• No clear priorities on what risk factors are most important.
	• Challenging to achieve good measures of cyber risk [25, 33].	• Do not have the competence in-house (use external security experts to perform assessments)
	• Insurers lack experience and standards [24].	
	• Metrics considered by insurance companies are varied [3, 26, 27].	
Access to data	• Lack of robust actuarial data is one reason for limited success of the cyber-insurance market [5, 13, 14, 41].	• Cyber-insurance is a new product, i.e. having limited historical data to build on.
	• Companies can be reluctant and unable to share reliable data on incidents [5, 16, 24, 25, 41].	• Getting hold of reliable data from customers can be challenging.
	• Cyber-incident cost is not clearly defined and hard to measure [5, 10, 24].	
	• A competitive environment hinders information sharing among providers [26, 27].	
	• Challenges of information asymmetry [3, 8, 9, 24].	
Demands on customers; efficient process for customers and insurance companies	• Clients may not like being dictated on how to mitigate cyber risk [24, 28], and may choose carriers with less stringent assessment practices [26].	• Implementation of basic security measures is required, and risk assessment may introduce further requirements.
	• Insurance companies aim to reduce effort of assessments [3, 26, 27].	• Large customer base is needed, thus also efficient risk assessment processes.
		• The sales process needs to be quick with a clear and easy-to-understand message.
Risk is constantly changing	• Rapid technological development and changes in attacker profiles may cause historical data to become outdated quickly [8, 24–26].	• It is challenging to stay updated in the field, things change quickly.
Globally correlated and interdependent risk	• Interdependent security and correlated risk; the security of a node is dependent on the security of other nodes and incidents may strike in a correlated fashion [3, 9, 24].	• When concerned about catastrophic incidents, this impacts policy terms (become more risk averse).
	• Cyber incidents may cause pay-out on a number of different insurance policies [22].	

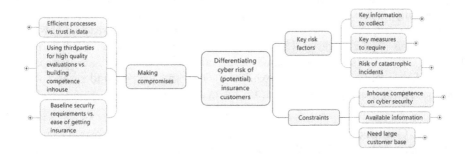

Fig. 2. Thematic network showing how insurance companies differentiate between potential customers.

Key Risk Factors. The interviewees did not provide any clear priorities on which risk factors they consider most important, except that commonly used factors include revenue and other metrics of the size of the business, as well as the organisation's operating sector. Instead, the insurance companies address a broad range of factors (e.g. based on the ISO/IEC 27001 standard [21]). They put some requirements on basic security measures that need to be in place for all customers, but they can also pose more specific requirements on individual customers. The criteria for deciding which security measures should be required from customers were not laid out by any of the interviewees.

Some of the interviewees are concerned about what could be called catastrophic risk, i.e. the risk of incidents which impact the majority of their customers at the same time. The interviews however give no indication of factors being considered most important to understand and address such risk.

Constraints. An interviewee explained how they find it challenging to stay updated on the field of cyber security. This may in part be related to the fact that cyber-insurance is a new product where they have limited experience and actuarial statistics to build on. But it is also pointed out that cyber security is an area where things change quickly, depending on the creativity of various threat actors.

Access to data is one challenge often experienced. The information most commonly collected (such as revenue and business sector) is easily obtained and trusted. However, other types of information (data protection is particularly mentioned) may be more difficult to get hold of. The interviewees mentioned a number of reasons for this: competence available in the business on cyber security and privacy; availability of the right people that have the competence, and; unwillingness to share information. In addition comes the risk of getting erroneous answers to the questions asked related to risk.

Insurance companies need to have a large customer base for their cyber-insurance products. This means that they need to be able to handle a large number of customers in an efficient manner, but also that the sales process and the steps needed to become a customer is easy enough, not to hinder adoption.

Additionally, the requirements regarding implementation of security measures must not be too strict. Currently, new customers are primarily reached through two channels (and this varies a bit between the insurance companies): insurance brokers and in-house sales personnel. Especially when in-house sales personnel are used, it seems important to exhibit a clear and easy-to-understand sales message and a quick process to sign up for cyber-insurance.

Making Compromises. Today, insurance companies make several compromises in the process of evaluating risk, agreeing on policies and setting premiums. The following key areas came up in the interviews.

To get a large customer base, the insurance companies need to have efficient processes for evaluating risk and it must be easy for customers to buy insurance. At the same time, insurance companies need to be able to trust the assessments they make regarding cyber risk of customers, and thus need to get hold of a range of data related to risk. The collection process should ensure that data can be trusted. To achieve a balance between these needs, the insurance companies today differentiate their customers, and only perform thorough analysis of companies that are considered high risk. Differentiation is mainly done based on size, either of the company or of the amount insured. Small sized companies will have to answer only a very limited number of questions, ensuring the ability of the insurance company to reach and handle a mass of customers. For larger sized companies, a more thorough analysis is made, but also here some compromises have to be made to ensure an efficient collection process. Approaches made to data collection include questionnaires filled out by company representatives, interviews and security testing. Use of questionnaires requires less effort from the insurance company, but potentially at the cost of trust in the data. There is also the issue of how often to re-evaluate risk. The insurance companies are aware that cyber risk is dynamic over time. At the same time, they have limited capacity to re-evaluate risk on a regular basis.

The insurance companies in our study use third parties (cyber security experts) to perform the evaluation of company risks. Some interviewees state that a key reason for this is limited competence on cyber risk management in-house. The use of third party experts allows for high quality evaluations, and also opens possibility for learning from the third parties and thus gradually building more competence in-house. The insurance companies currently seem very dependent on the evaluations made by these third parties.

The insurance companies do put some baseline security requirements on their customers. As one interviewee states: "We don't want to insure a burning house!" At the same time, the companies want a volume of users, and to achieve this they cannot raise the bar too high for their customers. Currently, requirements on having anti-virus software and firewalls are common, either for becoming a customer or as part of the insurance terms. Insurance companies may have more strict requirements for larger customers, based on the results of the risk evaluation.

4   Approaches to Efficient and Thorough Risk Assessments

The results from our interview study supports the current literature on risk assessment challenges for cyber-insurance carriers. The interview subjects all represent insurance companies offering cyber-insurance in a market where this is a new and unknown product. They have limited historical data to build on, and there has not been many incident cases yet. This lack of experience and data and the need for an efficient sales process highly impacts their approach to risk assessment. In the following we explore two options for being able to perform a thorough, and yet efficient assessment of risk in this context.

4.1   Reusable Sector-Specific Risk Models

As part of the process of differentiating cyber risk, insurance companies collect information from customers in a structured and repeatable manner, for instance through reusable questionnaires. We do, however, get the impression that the process of determining the appropriate risk level based on the collected information is not always structured, and can be based on expert judgement alone, which may result in arbitrary and poorly documented decisions. A common alternative to expert judgement is to use a *risk model*. A risk model is often specified in a modeling language that provides a precise and well-documented way of determining/calculating the risk level based on the information in the model. Creating risk models, however, can be time consuming, and making a new model from scratch for every assessment may not be feasible for insurance companies. One way of mitigating this problem is to create a generic risk model which captures some common knowledge and which can be reused in each assessment. Furthermore, the reusable risk model may be used as a basis for determining what kind of information should be collected from the customers.

In many settings, building a reusable risk model may not be worth it because the risk models vary too much across different assessments. However, in the setting of differentiating cyber risk insurance customers, several factors suggest that the use of reusable risk models may be appropriate: (1) The risk assessments have to be performed in a relatively short period of time, and the duration does not vary greatly from customer to customer. (2) The type of risks considered in each risk assessment are similar. These risks may for instance precisely correspond the type of cyber risks that are to be insured and which have precise legal definitions in the cyber-insurance terms and conditions, e.g. *Data Breach*, *Material Interruption*, or *System Failure*. (3) The information needed in each risk assessment is often collected from the customer in a structured manner and the type of information collected is similar across different customers.

In the field of risk assessment, several kinds of risk modeling techniques exists. These often build on tree-based and graph-based notations. Fault tree analysis (FTA) [19], event tree analysis (ETA) [1] and attack trees [38] are examples of the former and provide support for reasoning about the sources and consequences of unwanted incidents, as well as their likelihoods. Cause-consequence analysis

(CCA) [31], CORAS [23], and Bayesian networks [6] are examples of graph-based notations.

None of the above mentioned techniques have dedicated support for risk model reusability. In our opinion, for a risk modeling technique to support reusability, it should at a minimum: (1) Clearly distinguish between the information in the risk model which is *parameterized* (i.e. information that may vary across different risk model instances) and static information which should stay the same across different instances. (2) Provide clear guidelines for how the reusable risk model may be instantiated, i.e. how the parameterized information should be replaced with information specific to the instantiation domain.

Although none of the above mentioned risk modeling techniques have dedicated support for reusability, all of them can be extended to support this. One straightforward procedure for doing this in the setting of cyber risk insurance is as follows: (1) Make a risk model capturing general cyber attacks and cyber-insurance risks. (2) Identify and clearly mark which estimates in the risk model that are to be parameterized. (3) For each parameterized estimate, formulate a natural language question whose answer will allow the estimate to be determined for a given instantiation of the risk model.

By following the above steps, we obtain a set of questions in addition to a general risk model whose parametrized estimates are marked. To instantiate the risk model for a given cyber-insurance customer, we can give the questions to the customer, then determine the values of the parameterized estimates based on the answers to the questions, and finally determine the risk level using the guidelines of the risk modeling technique.

As an example, consider the reusable risk model shown in Fig. 3 specified in the CORAS risk modeling language. A CORAS risk model is a graph whose nodes describe the occurrence of events, and whose edges describe causal relationships between events represented by the nodes. Nodes may be annotated with likelihood values specifying how often events occur, and edges may be annotated with conditional likelihood values specifying the likelihood that one event leads to another event given that the former event has occurred. Consequences may

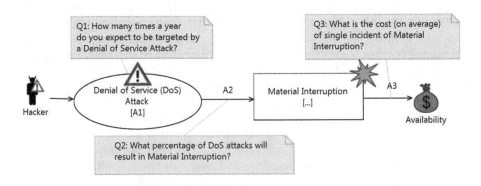

Fig. 3. Example of a reusable risk model specified in CORAS

also be specified. In CORAS, this is done by including special nodes called *assets* (the money bag in Fig. 3). The consequence that a node has on the asset may then be specified by drawing an edge from the node to the asset and labelling the edge with a consequence value. The meaning of the risk model specified in Fig. 3 is: Threat *Hacker* initiates the threat scenario *Denial of Service (DoS) Attack* with likelihood $A1$ which leads to the unwanted incident *Material Interruption* with conditional likelihood $A2$ which impacts the asset *Availability* with consequence $A3$.

The CORAS modeling language does not have explicit support for specifying parameterized values. However, in Fig. 3, we have indicated the parameterized values by the variables $A1$, $A2$, and $A3$. In addition, we have specified questions that may help estimate these values. In particular, question $Q1$ will help estimate the likelihood $A1$ of DoS attacks, question $Q2$ will help determine the conditional likelihood $A2$ that a DoS attack will cause Material Interruption given that the attack is initiated, and $Q3$ will help estimate the consequence $A3$ of the Material Interruption risk if it occurs.

In general, mapping an answer to an estimate may not be straightforward. However, in the current example, this is fairly straightforward since the questions have been identified based on the risk model (as opposed to building an appropriate risk model from a set of questions). To make matters even easier (for the insurance company), the answers to the questions could be constrained such that they can be directly replaced with the estimates they help determine in the risk model. For instance, the possible answers to question $Q1$ could be a choice between the likelihood values *Low, Medium,* or *High,* whose values have been given a precise meaning, e.g. *Low* could mean less than one time per ten years. Note that the likelihood estimate of the unwanted incident Material Interruption in Fig. 3 is not parameterized. However, this likelihood value can be calculated based on the other likelihood estimates in the diagram using the CORAS likelihood calculation rules. Using the CORAS calculation and verification rules will not be an issue, since we are only interested in using these rules on *instances* of the reusable model after the parametrized estimates have been replaced by actual values.

Although there may be clear advantages of using reusable risk models to differentiate cyber risk of insurance customers, more research is needed to determine how well this would work in practice. A particular concern is the feasibility of providing estimates that are sufficiently precise to determine an accurate risk level. If this proves to be infeasible, a possible solution is to only use qualitative estimates, or to have an explicit representation of uncertainty in the risk model if quantitative estimates are used. Another concern is how often the models need to be updated or the risk re-assessed, due to the dynamic nature of cyber threats.

4.2   A Role for Managed Security Service Providers

Involving companies known as *managed security service providers* (MSSPs) can potentially reduce the footprint and improve the quality of cyber risk assessments for insurance companies. MSSPs are security companies who provide a range of security products and services, often including 24/7 monitoring, analysis and detection of malicious network traffic. In addition to having clear knowledge of implemented security controls at their customers' site, MSSPs notify their customers about incidents as they happen and sometimes they assist customers further with incident response services. At the MSSP the incidents are continuously being documented over time, through a range of incident categories, both aggregated and on a per-incident basis.

From a perspective where the insurance company wants to assess risk of the customer when calculating a premium, we believe an MSSP engaged by the customer can provide very specific input in an effective manner, compared to existing alternatives and practices. The MSSPs have already insight into their customer's security architecture, strengths and weaknesses, and in particular the historical information on incidents and how these are handled. Such involvement mitigates the challenge on access to data, as identified in Table 1. In addition, MSSPs need to stay updated on general security and threat research, developing knowledge on the overall threat landscape including both public information as well as threat intelligence collected through monitoring their other customers, and through threat intelligence sharing channels. A partnership with an MSSP could help an insurance company better understand cyber risk, make the assessment process more efficient using previously collected knowledge, and staying up-to-date in terms of risk for the particular customer, general trends and globally correlated risks which may accumulate to catastrophic incidents.

For MSSPs and insurance companies to collaborate, incentives are needed for the customer organisation to allow information sharing between them. The MSSP holds very sensitive and detailed data about their customers, although some of this information can be made less sensitive through e.g. aggregation, anonymization or generalisation. Since MSSPs have their own security and risk experts in-house, the process of creating a risk map of their customer could for instance be offered as a service to the insurance company, without disclosing all of the underlying details. The result would still provide a reliable – and much richer – basis for the insurance company to assess risk, than simply relying on a self-evaluation by the customer.

While this approach limits the need for a potential insurance customer to expose sensitive information any further than already done, it also reduces their own workload related to obtaining insurance offers/coverage. It could also increase the likelihood that MSSP customers obtain a lower insurance premium as a result of implemented security measures, due to larger transparency for the insurance company and documented controls in form of the implemented security services by the MSSP. At the same time, selling this particular service provides an incentive for MSSPs to get involved in the value-chain, along with the potential upside for MSSPs on selling incident response services through insurance companies whenever this serves as coverage. Finally, this process reduces costs for the insurance company since it would be less cost-demanding than employing another third party assessment from someone without previous knowledge of the potential customer's security architecture, controls and incident history.

If the MSSP industry were able to agree with the insurance companies on a standard for disclosing risk information about their customers, we believe a win-win situation could arise for all parties involved. In practice this is a matter of agreeing on a level of detail and a format of the information to be shared between the MSSPs and the insurance companies, and a portofolio of products they can collaborate on. It is an open question to insurance companies whether more transparency should automatically incur lower premiums. There could also be implemented mechanisms where the MSSP automatically alerts the insurance company directly about incidents at the insured company in a timely and standardised manner, making it easier for the insurance company to provide the right assistance in less time, and at an earlier stage, which may help in limiting costs of incident handling. One could also imagine that the MSSP would be directly authorised by the insurance company in these situations to implement mitigations within agreed coverage limits, which would likely be more effective than using a third party without a day-to-day relationship with the insured company.

5 Discussion

In this paper we have presented practice and challenges regarding assessing cyber risk of cyber-insurance customers, from the viewpoint of insurance companies. Practice and challenges have been identified by studying literature, and through a study of insurance companies in the Nordic market. It needs to be noted that the study of insurance companies reported in this paper only include a few companies, due to the size of the Nordic market, and in order to maintain their anonymity we do not provide any specific details on these companies. As a consequence of these limitations, we do not claim that our results are generalizable to all insurance companies. However, we believe the validity of our results is strengthened when considered together with known challenges identified in literature.

Table 1 compares the main results from the literature study with our study of insurance companies. The results are very much in line; the same challenges that are described in literature are experienced by the insurance companies we have studied. However, what is more of a concern for the companies that we have studied, compared to the emphasis it has been given in the literature, is the need for an easy to understand product and an efficient sales process. As already mentioned, the Nordic market for cyber-insurance is characterised by this being a new and unknown product. This impacts the approach taken to risk assessments. In addition to the need for an efficient sales process, the insurance companies have limited experience with the product and little historical data to build on, though they can to some extent use experiences from cyber-insurance in other markets.

To improve cyber risk insurers' ability to have efficient, yet thorough analysis of cyber risk we have proposed two ways forward: reusable sector specific risk-models and including MSSPs in the value chain. These are not completely new ideas; the potential for developing a generic modeling structure for use with cyber-insurance has been discussed in a roundtable event organised by Department of Homeland Security [29] as part of their work with building a repository for sharing incident data [12], and in these discussions the potential role of security companies came up regularly when it comes to providing incident information [26–29]. The study we have performed further underlies the need for improved approaches, and in this paper we have provided more details on how one could go about building such re-usable models, and strengthen the input to the models by including MSSPs in the risk assessment process.

There is a need for more research in order to better understand how cyber risk assessments could be improved related to cyber-insurance. We have only studied this topic from the viewpoint of insurance companies, but other actors also have important roles in this respect; customers, brokers and third-party risk assessors. Further, the approaches we have outlined that can potentially improve current practice need to be evaluated to assess whether or not they will have the desired effect.

6   Conclusion

Insurance companies need to be able to assess cyber risk of prospective cyber-insurance customers. Many challenges related to performing such analysis have been identified in literature, and our study of insurance companies offering cyber-insurance to the Nordic market shows that these challenges described in the literature are relevant for insurers that operate in a market where cyber-insurance is a new and relatively unknown product. In such a market, the need for an efficient sales process and a clear sales message further constrains how insurance companies perform assessments of cyber risk. In this paper we have proposed two possible approaches to improve insurers' ability to perform efficient, yet thorough analysis of cyber risk: building reusable sector-specific risk models and collaborating with MSSPs.

Acknowledgments. This research has been performed as part of the inSecurance project, which is a strategic and internally funded research project at SINTEF ICT. We would like to thank the representatives from the insurance companies that participated in the interviews for sharing their experiences with us. We would also like to thank our colleagues Per Håkon Meland and Aida Omerovic for taking part in discussions leading up to this paper and for commenting on the interview guide, and our colleague Bjørnar Solhaug for performing and transcribing the interviews.

References

1. IEC 60300-3-9 Dependability management Part 3: Application guide Section 9: Risk analysis of technological systems Event Tree Analysis (ETA)
2. Attride-Stirling, J.: Thematic networks: an analytic tool for qualitative research. Qual. Res. **1**(3), 385–405 (2001)

3. Baer, W.S., Parkinson, A.: Cyberinsurance in IT security management. IEEE Secur. Priv. **5**(3), 50–56 (2007)
4. Bandyopadhyay, T., Shidore, S.: Towards a managerial decision framework for utilization of cyber insurance instruments in IT security. In: AMCIS 2011 Proceedings - All Submissions (2011)
5. Bandyopadhyay, T., Mookerjee, V.S., Rao, R.C.: Why IT managers don't go for cyber-insurance products. Commun. ACM **52**(11), 68–73 (2009)
6. Ben-Gal, I.: Bayesian networks. In: Encyclopedia of Statistics in Quality and Reliability (2007)
7. Bernsmed, K., Tøndel, I.A.: Forewarned is forearmed: indicators for evaluating information security incident management. In: 2013 Seventh International Conference on IT Security Incident Management and IT Forensics (IMF), pp. 3–14. IEEE (2013)
8. Biener, C., Eling, M., Wirfs, J.H.: Insurability of cyber risk: an empirical analysis. Geneva Pap. Risk Insur. Issues Pract. **40**(1), 131–158 (2015)
9. Böhme, R., Schwartz, G.: Modeling cyber-insurance: towards a unifying framework. In: Workshop on the Economics in Information Security (WEIS) (2012)
10. Cashell, B., Jackson, W.D., Jickling, M., Webel, B.: The economic impact of cyber-attacks. Technical report, CRS Report for Congress, April 2004
11. .Chickowski, E.: 10 things IT probably doesn't know about cyber insurance, 23 September 2014
12. Department of Homeland Security: Enhancing resilience through cyber incident data sharing and analysis: The value proposition for a cyber incident data repository. Technical report (2015)
13. ENISA: Incentives and barriers of the cyber insurance market in europe. Technical report, 28 June 2012
14. EY: Mitigating cyber risk for insurers, part 2: Insights into cyber security and risk. Technical report, Ernst Young Global Limited (2014)
15. Fenz, S., Ekelhart, A.: Verification, validation, and evaluation in information security risk management. IEEE Secur. Priv. **2**, 58–65 (2010)
16. Gordon, L.A., Loeb, M.P., Sohail, T.: A framework for using insurance for cyber-risk management. Commun. ACM **46**(3), 81–85 (2003)
17. Herrmann, D.S.: Complete Guide to Security and Privacy Metrics. Auerbach Publications, Boca Raton (2007)
18. HM Government UK, Marsh Ltd., UK cyber security: The role of insurance in managing and mitigating the risk. https://www.gov.uk/government/publications/uk-cyber-security-the-role-of-insurance
19. International Electrotechnical Commission: IEC 61025 Fault Tree Analysis (1990)
20. International Organization for Standardization: ISO/IEC 27004: Information technology - Security techniques - Information security management - Measurement. ISO (2009)
21. International Organization for Standardization: ISO/IEC 27001: Information technology - Security techniques - Information security management systems - Requirements. ISO (2013)
22. Lloyd's, Cambridge Centre for Risk Studies: Business blackout - the insurance implications of a cyber attack on the us power grid. Technical report, Lloyd's (2015)
23. Lund, M.S., Solhaug, B., Stølen, K.: Model-Driven Risk Analysis: The CORAS Approach. Springer, Heidelberg (2010)

24. Marotta, A., Martinelli, F., Nanni, S., Yautsiukhin, A.: A survey on cyber-insurance. Technical report IIT TR-17/2015, Ubstutyti du Ubfirnatuca e Telematica (2015)

25. Meland, P.H., Tøndel, I.A., Solhaug, B.: Mitigating risk with cyberinsurance. IEEE Secur. Priv. **6**, 38–43 (2015)

26. Protection, N., Directorate, P.: Cybersecurity insurance workshop readout report. Technical report, U.S. Department of Homeland Security (2012)

27. Protection, National, Directorate, Programs: Cyber risk culture roundtable readout report. Technical report, Department of Homeland Security (2013)

28. Protection, National, Directorate, Programs: Cyber insurance roundtable readout report - health care and cyber risk management: Cost/benefit approaches. Technical report, Department of Homeland Security (2014)

29. Protection, National, Directorate, Programs: Insurance industry working session readout report. Technical report, Department of Homeland Security (2014)

30. NetDilgence: Netdiligence cyber claims study 2014. Technical report, NetDilligence (2014)

31. Nielsen, D.S.: The cause/consequence diagram method as a basis for quantitative accident analysis. Technical report, Danish Atomic Energy Commission, Risoe. Research Establishment (1971)

32. Øien, K., Massaiu, S., Tinmannsvik, R., Strseth, F.: Development of early warning indicators based on resilience engineering. In: International Probabilistic Safety Assessment and Management Conference, PSAM 2010, pp. 7–11 (2010)

33. Oppliger, R.: Quantitative risk analysis in information security management: a modern fairy tale. IEEE Secur. Priv. **6**, 18–21 (2015)

34. Pal, R., Hui, P.: On differentiating cyber-insurance contracts a topological perspective. In: 2013 IFIP/IEEE International Symposium on Integrated Network Management (IM 2013), pp. 836–839. IEEE (2013)

35. Perlroth, N., Harris, E.A.: Cyberattack insurance a challenge for business, 8 June 2014

36. Ponemon: Managing cyber security as a business risk: Cyber insurance in the digital age. Technical report, Ponemon Institute LLC, August 2013

37. Ponemon: 2014 cost of data breach study: Global analysis. Technical report, Ponemon Institute LLC, May 2014

38. Schneier, B.: Attack trees. Dr. Dobbs J. **24**(12), 21–29 (1999)

39. Sulaman, S.M., Weyns, K., Höst, M.: A review of research on risk analysis methods for IT systems. In: Proceedings of the 17th International Conference on Evaluation and Assessment in Software Engineering, pp. 86–96. ACM (2013)

40. Tøndel, I.A., Meland, P.H., Omerovic, A., Gjære, E.A., Solhaug, B.: Using cyber-insurance as a risk management strategy: Knowledge gaps and recommendations for further research. Technical report SINTEF A27298, SINTEF (2015)

41. Toregas, C., Zahn, N.: Insurance for cyber attacks: The issue of setting premiums in context. Technical report, The George Washington University, 7 January 2014

42. Woods, D.D.: Essential Characteristics of Resilience. Resilience Engineering: Concepts and Precepts, pp. 21–34. Ashgate, Aldershot (2006)

Special Session on Privacy Aware Machine Learning for Health Data Science (PAML 2016)

Data Anonymization as a Vector Quantization Problem: Control Over Privacy for Health Data

Yoan Miche[1]([⊠]), Ian Oliver[1], Silke Holtmanns[1], Aapo Kalliola[1,4],
Anton Akusok[3], Amaury Lendasse[2], and Kaj-Mikael Björk[3]

[1] Bell Labs, Nokia, Finland
yoan.miche@nokia-bell-labs.com
[2] Department of Mechanical and Industrial Engineering
and the Iowa Informatics Initiative, The University of Iowa, Iowa City, USA
[3] Arcada University of Applied Sciences, Helsinki, Finland
[4] Aalto University, Espoo, Finland

Abstract. This paper tackles the topic of data anonymization from a vector quantization point of view. The admitted goal in this work is to provide means of performing data anonymization to avoid single individual or group re-identification from a data set, while maintaining as much as possible (and in a very specific sense) data integrity and structure. The structure of the data is first captured by clustering (with a vector quantization approach), and we propose to use the properties of this vector quantization to anonymize the data. Under some assumptions over possible computations to be performed on the data, we give a framework for identifying and "pushing back outliers in the crowd", in this clustering sense, as well as anonymizing cluster members while preserving cluster-level statistics and structure as defined by the assumptions (density, pairwise distances, cluster shape and members...).

1 Introduction

In this paper, we limit ourselves to the problem of user re-identification from a dataset. We decide to focus on two very specific questions: given a set of records with no obvious information that would allow for easily identifying a single person from the dataset, (i) can we make sure that no one is easily identifiable from the data (and identify it), and (ii) if some individuals are easy to identify, can we modify the data so as to "blend them in" while retaining the key characteristics of the data statistics? The approach we take is to consider the data fields (over a set of records) as separate entities and try to build clusters of records based on metric proximity: if the records have similar values across several vector elements, they are likely to be grouped together. We assume then that if such a group is large enough and that the records inside that group have been "stirred" enough, identification of a single individual becomes impossible. One of the main assumption in this paper is that whatever further processing is to be performed on the anonymized data, is relying on these "group statistics/properties" to be

F. Buccafurri et al. (Eds.): CD-ARES 2016, LNCS 9817, pp. 193–203, 2016.
DOI: 10.1007/978-3-319-45507-5_13

as intact as possible. The proposed "stirring" of the data implies that global data statistics and structures will be preserved, but local ones are disturbed. We basically want to preserve the underlying manifold structure (in terms of the cluster of data that it is composed of) as much as possible, while locally shuffling the data around. In order to clarify some of the notions presented, we introduce here an example data set of health-related information in Table 1. We consider for the purpose of this example that this represents the full health records from a certain medical institution.

Table 1. Example of Health Data records from a medical institution.

ID	Non-sensitive			Sensitive
	Zip code	Age	Nationality	Condition
01	13053	28	Russian	Heart disease
02	13068	29	American	Heart disease
03	13068	21	Japanese	Viral infection
04	13053	23	American	Viral infection
05	14853	50	Indian	Cancer

The records from Table 1 show no obvious easily identifiable information when considering single fields. Nevertheless, relationships between the non-sensitive fields in this data can probably make it relatively easy to identify some individuals: within a zip code, the nationality and the age allow someone to restrict the set of possible individuals dramatically. The last individual in the table is even more striking as her age, nationality and zip code surely make her stand out of the rest.In such a situation, the proposed approaches in this paper seek to "blend in" this last individual from Table 1 with the rest of the records, as well as making sure that all the records get "shuffled" (regarding each of the fields) so as to make the data anonymized. In effect, we want here to actively modify the data values, not by changing their nature (as would hashing the values do, e.g.) or by omitting them, but really by modifying the values to realistic ones (belonging to the same category/set) in a way that preserves some of the information.

2   High-Level Motivation for Data Privacy

In this section, we propose a high level description of the problem tackled in this paper. The next sections then describe the proposed means of doing so. In an ideal situation, data mining and classification or partition of data, in particular for health and medical data [6], can be made in an unambiguous manner; meaning that, for example, a classification of the data can be made and the number of border cases is minimal. Application of algorithms that increase the privacy (or the entropy) of a system distort this in some known manner, in terms of the direct effects on the data fields. For example κ-anonymity [2] and ℓ-diversity [8] reduce the distribution and amounts of unique values in the discrete valued cases; differential privacy [4] adds noise in the continuous valued cases, for example, speeds, distances etc. A privacy function distorts a system such that classification and/or mining either cannot be made or becomes difficult to make in a reasonable manner [5].

In this work, we consider the case of such privacy functions that modify the data in such a way as to avoid changing the "format" of the data, and thus the underlying space in which the data lies. Indeed, another way to consider this is that the privacy functions usually alter the underlying space or topology of the space rather than moving the elements themselves. This altering of the topology in the best case involves continuous (in the sense of metric preserving or homotopy preserving) stretching and shrinking, but may also include non-continuous tearing and creasing of the space such that the resolution of the original metric function is no longer possible. The challenge here is then to avoid this deformation of the underlying space, by attempting to shuffle and move the data around in the best manner (regarding increasing the privacy and minimising the distortions on the data). The work in this paper is aimed at this problem: proposing several practical solutions to the identification problem from Table 1. We first define in the next section, some notations and assumptions on the structure of the data, and first look at the problem of moving a single sample (or a group of them) back into bigger clusters. We then tackle the problem of increasing the privacy for the samples within a cluster so as to make sure that re-identification, even within a cluster, is more difficult.

3   Methodology for Data Anonymization in a Data Clustering Context

3.1   Some Notational Details

Traditionally in the data privacy literature, one defines a table $\mathbf{T}$ of N records as $\mathbf{T} = \{\mathbf{t}_1, \ldots \mathbf{t}_N\}$, with attributes $\{A_1, \ldots, A_d\}$. We have that $\mathbf{T} \in \Omega$, the set of all possible records (samples), and $\mathcal{A} = \{A_1, \ldots, A_d\}$ is the set of all possible d attributes (in this case, all possible attributes are used in table $\mathbf{T}$). Typically, one denotes the value of a certain attribute A_j for sample $\mathbf{t}_i$ as $\mathbf{t}_i[A_j]$. In this paper, and for the developments below, we take the liberty to note $\mathbb{X}^{(j)}$ the set of all possible values for a certain attribute A_j. Referring to Table 1 for our example case, if A_j is the attribute for the Zip Code of the patients, this means that $\mathbb{X}^{(j)}$ represents the set of all possible Zip Codes (possibly limited to the existing ones that make sense within the context of this table, e.g. limited to a country).

We then assume that it is possible to define a distance function $d^{(j)} : \mathbb{X}^{(j)} \times \mathbb{X}^{(j)} \longrightarrow \mathbb{R}_+$ over this set $\mathbb{X}^{(j)}$. Note that the metric space $\mathcal{X}^{(j)} = (\mathbb{X}^{(j)}, d^{(j)})$, defined by these two entities need not be Euclidean. Some considerations on such distance functions over non-Euclidean spaces are detailed in the following Sect. 3.2. Departing slightly from the data privacy notations and denoting by $\mathbf{T} = [\mathbf{t}_1, \ldots, \mathbf{t}_N]^T$, the matrix of N samples holding the health records. A record $\mathbf{t}_i$ is now defined as $\mathbf{t}_i = [a_{i,1}, a_{i,2}, \ldots, a_{i,d}]$, $a_{i,j} \in \mathbb{X}^{(j)}$, with $\mathbb{X}^{(j)}$ the set considered as part of the metric space $\mathcal{X}^{(j)} = (\mathbb{X}^{(j)}, d^{(j)})$.

With these extended notations, we can see the column $[a_{1,j}, \ldots, a_{N,j}]^T \in \mathbb{X}^{(j) \, N \times 1}$ as a discrete random variable (or a set of realizations of the underlying random variable, more precisely) over $\mathcal{X}^{(j)}$. The following section discusses the previous assumption of being able to define a distance function over a potentially non-Euclidean space.

3.2 Distance Functions Over Non-Euclidean Spaces

The argument for considering the use of distances over non-Euclidean spaces in this work, is that it is possible to tweak and modify such non-Euclidean distances so that their distribution and properties will be "close enough" to that of the original Euclidean distance. Most of the developments in this paper rely on having "meaningful and consistent" distance functions across all the dimensions, so that they can be at least compared, even if this means re-mapping the distribution of its values.

More formally, let us assume that we have two metric spaces $\mathcal{X}^{(i)} = (\mathbb{X}^{(i)}, d^{(i)})$ and $\mathcal{X}^{(j)} = (\mathbb{X}^{(j)}, d^{(j)})$, with $\mathcal{X}^{(i)}$ the canonical Euclidean space (i.e. $\mathbb{X}^{(i)} = \mathbb{R}^d$ and $d^{(i)}$ the Euclidean norm) and $\mathcal{X}^{(j)}$ a non-Euclidean metric space endowed with a non-Euclidean metric. Drawing uniformly samples from the set $\mathbb{X}^{(j)}$, we form $\mathbf{x}^{(j)} = \left[x_1^{(j)}, \ldots, x_n^{(j)} \right]$, a set of values (realizations of the underlying random variable), with $x_l^{(j)} \in \mathbb{X}^{(j)}$. Denoting then by $f_{d^{(j)}}$ the distribution of pairwise distances over all the samples in $\mathbf{x}^{(j)}$, we assume that it is possible to modify the distribution of the values of the non-Euclidean metric $d^{(j)}$ (into a distribution $f_{d^{(j)}}^{\mathrm{map}}$) such that

$$\lim_{n \to \infty} f_{d^{(j)}}^{\mathrm{map}} = f_{d^{(i)}}, \tag{1}$$

where $f_{d^{(i)}}$ is the distribution of the Euclidean distances $d^{(i)}$ over the Euclidean space $\mathcal{X}^{(i)}$ and $f_{d^{(j)}}^{\mathrm{map}}$ is a non-linear transformation of the original distribution $f_{d^{(j)}}$ by a certain function.

The limit here is over n as the distribution $f_{d^{(j)}}$ is considered to be estimated using a limited number n of realizations of the random variables, and we are interested in the limit case where we can "afford" to draw as many samples as possible to be as close to the Euclidean metric as possible. That is, that we can make sure that the non-Euclidean metric behaves over its non-Euclidean space, as would a Euclidean metric over a Euclidean space. This assumption is "theoretically reasonable", as it comes down to being able to transform a distribution $f_{d^{(j)}}$ into another $f_{d^{(j)}}^{\mathrm{map}}$, given both. And while this may not be simple nor possible using linear transformation tools, most Machine Learning techniques are able to fit a continuous input to another different continuous output (this is basically the well-known Universal Function Approximator property [3]). It can be noted that using such tools, the mapping will not be perfect (as we will work with discrete versions of the distributions) and will not result in the equality case from Eq. 1. Nevertheless, we assume in this paper that this is sufficient for our needs. With this assumption in mind, we come to the problem of addressing Differential Privacy approaches as a Vector Quantization matter.

4   Considering Differential Privacy as a Vector Quantization Problem

Using the previous notations introduced, Differential Privacy aims at finding sets or clusters (groups) C_l of samples

$$C_l = \{\mathbf{t}_i, \mathbf{t}_j \in \mathbf{T} | \forall i, j \in [\![1, N]\!], i \neq j, \forall k \in [\![1, d]\!],$$
$$d^{(k)}(a_{i,k}, a_{j,k}) \leq \varepsilon_k \}, \tag{2}$$

with ε_k the maximum radii of the cluster C_l (each dimension k can have a separate radius, thus). The total number of clusters C is here determined by the choices made for the maximum radii of them, i.e. the ε_k. Intuitively, these C_l are clusters of samples that are "not too distant from each other". If all the metric spaces (across all dimensions) were Euclidean, Eq. 2 would simply define the sets of samples that have pairwise Euclidean distance smaller than a certain epsilon. In this respect, we are considering similarity between groups of sample as a defined by cluster density across all dimensions. In our case, we generalize this definition by potentially having a different distance function for each dimension, thus bounded by different ε_k. Note that samples that are "alone" in their cluster basically represent outliers in terms of the data they hold (and thus, individuals): they might be very easy to identify/recognize out of the rest of the records, as they do not "fit with others". This observation can be generalized to clusters that have "few samples" in the ball they define. "Few" has to be defined, in this case. This is directly related to the κ in κ-anonymity.

Denoting by m, the previous "few", if $|C_{l1}| \leq m$, there are not enough records in the cluster: They might be easy to identify, or represent too obvious a group. The goal is then to modify as few dimensions as possible (so as to minimize distortion of the data) to bring these records in the nearest cluster C_{l2} which respects $|C_{l2}| > m$ or so that $|C_{l1}| + |C_{l2}| > m$. To be able to find which nearby cluster is the most fitting for such a lonesome sample, we decide to rely on centroids. We thus need to calculate a centroid (or representative) of the clusters such that $|C_l| > m$. Note that as the sets $\mathbb{X}^{(j)}$ across which the data is defined do not necessarily have any implied order, we have to use solely the distances between samples to calculate the most fitting centroid.

This comes to determining the centroid c_l of cluster C_l with only inter-records distances (pairwise distances for all samples within one cluster):

$$c_l^{(j)} = \arg \min_{a_{k,j} \in \mathbb{X}^{(j)}} \left[\sum_{a_{i,j} \in C_l} d^{(j)}(a_{i,j}, a_{k,j}) \right], \tag{3}$$

where $c_l^{(j)}$ denotes the j-th coordinate of the centroid c_l of cluster C_l, and Eq. 3 has an abuse of notations in the summation index to avoid too heavy notations: the summation is made over the j-th coordinate $a_{i,j}$ of all the samples $\mathbf{t}_i$ in cluster C_l. This is to avoid defining the set of samples in the cluster formally. From Eq. 3, it can be seen that the centroid coordinates are picked from the sets $\mathbb{X}^{(j)}$, and not calculated as some mean value over the samples present in the cluster. This would not have any sense in the case of discrete $\mathbb{X}^{(j)}$, so this definition is more practical for the general purpose.

We do not discuss in this paper the algorithmic means of finding such centroids based on this definition from Eq. 3. With the centroids of each cluster estimated, we can then decide how to move samples that are lonesome and too easy to identify.

4.1   Moving Samples to Nearby Clusters

The task of moving a sample (or a small enough group of them) into a near cluster first requires the determination of the most suitable cluster for each of these samples.

Identifying the Most Suitable Cluster. Intuitively, and in order to preserve data as much as possible, the most suitable cluster C_l for this application is such that the total distortion, approximated in this case by how much the outlier $\mathbf{t}_o$ is moved across all dimensions, is minimal. Thus, denoting by $\mathbf{t}_o = [a_{o,1}, \ldots, a_{o,d}]$ an outlier, $\mathcal{C} = \{C_k\}_{1 \leq k \leq C}$ the set of all the clusters (which have a sufficient amount of samples in them), and by $d_{\mathrm{map}}^{(j)}$ the mapped version of the distance function $d^{(j)}$ (so that the distribution of its values matches that of an Euclidean metric, see Sect. 3.2), we get

$$C_l = \arg \min_{C_k \in \mathcal{C}} \left[\sum_{j=1}^{d} d_{\mathrm{map}}^{(j)} \left(a_{o,j}, c_k^{(j)} \right) \right]. \tag{4}$$

One argument for using the mapped distances $d_{\mathrm{map}}^{(j)}$ in this determination of the suitable cluster, is that we have to make a decision over all the dimensions at once, regarding the distortion generated by moving the outlier into a cluster. Therefore, in order to quantify this distortion across all dimensions at once, it is important that the distances are all within similar ranges and following similar distributions (otherwise, some dimensions will be "favoured" by the sum, possibly unjustly). Actual weighting of the distances in order to artificially favour some dimensions is the subject of further work.

Moving the Sample to the Decided Cluster. Once the most suitable cluster C_l for outlier t_o has been determined (note that there might not be a unique solution to this cluster determination), the problem is to move the outlier within that cluster so as to modify the actual values of the outlier as little as possible. We identify three ways to do this in practice, out of which the first is probably the best in terms of low distortion, but also the most difficult — and thus probably not achievable in real cases. In all the following three cases, the following steps are applied:

$$\forall k \in [1, d], \begin{cases} a_{o,k} = a_{o,k}^{\text{new}} \text{ if } d^{(k)}(a_{o,k}, c_l^{(k)})' > \\ \qquad \max_{a_{i,k} \in C_l} \left[d^{(k)}(a_{i,k}, c_l^{(k)}) \right] , \\ a_{o,k} \qquad \text{unchanged otherwise} \end{cases} \tag{5}$$

where $a_{o,k}^{\text{new}}$ is the new value to be given to the k-th coordinate of the outlier t_o, and $\max_{a_{i,k} \in C_l} \left[d^{(k)}(a_{i,k}, c_l^{(k)}) \right]$ is in fact the maximum intra-cluster distance between cluster elements and the centroid c_l of the cluster C_l. Thus, we ensure that the modification of this specific dimension does not modify too much the intra cluster distances. We then propose three approaches to determine the new $a_{o,k}^{\text{new}}$ value: (a) Setting it to the centroid value, and adding some noise; (b) Setting it to the centroid value only; (c) Setting it to an existing cluster element value.

(a) Centroid and Noise. In this case, we set the new value of the outlier coordinate $a_{o,k}^{\text{new}}$ as

$$a_{o,k}^{\text{new}} = c_l^{(k)} + r, \tag{6}$$

where r is randomly drawn from a certain distribution such that the distribution of the distances from the cluster samples to the cluster centroid is not modified too much. More precisely, with $f_{d_{C_l}}$ the distribution of the distances between the samples in cluster C_l and its centroid, and $f_{d_{C_l}}^{\text{new}}$ the same distribution after modifying the outlier coordinate $a_{o,k}$, we want to make sure that $\text{KL}(f_{d_{C_l}}, f_{d_{C_l}}^{\text{new}}) \leq \varepsilon$, where $\text{KL}(\cdot, \cdot)$ stands for the Kullback-Leibler divergence between the two distributions [7]. In practice, other metrics could be used in this place, such as the Earth-Mover Distance [1,9], e.g. This approach, as said before, although probably very desirable, is rather difficult to achieve practically, as drawing the noise value r in such a way as described above is difficult.

(b) Flattening to Centroid. This case is a direct simplified version of the previous one. Here, we set the new value of $a_{o,k}^{\text{new}}$ as

$$a_{o,k}^{\text{new}} = c_l^{(k)}. \tag{7}$$

While this approach has a very clear advantage of being simple, it might lead to moving the outlier "too close" to the centroid. Remember here that the centroid is likely not an actual sample from the data, and we are thus inserting a sample with unseen before coordinates, in this cluster.

(c) Flattening to a Cluster Element Value. Finally, this third approach is probably a good compromise of simplicity of execution and low distortion of the data. Here, we set the new value of $a_{o,k}^{\text{new}}$ as

$$a_{o,k}^{\text{new}} = a_{i,k} \text{ with } a_{i,k} \text{ drawn at random from } C_l. \tag{8}$$

In this case, we thus draw from the existing sample values from this cluster for this specific dimension. This ensures that we avoid disturbing too much the existing samples within the cluster, while moving effectively the outlier within the cluster. Once we have the outlier(s) moved back into the most appropriate cluster, we can assume that the isolated individuals these samples were representing are no longer as easy to re-identify as before. We can move on to the second part of this work: anonymizing the data within a cluster.

4.2   Anonymizing the Data Within a Cluster

The idea behind this approach is to provide some methods to anonymize the data (by modifying its inherent values) while retaining, as in the previous sections, the structure of it — in the same data clustering sense as in the rest of the paper. For this, we propose two approaches that aim at anonymizing the data within a cluster (and not the whole cluster in itself), so that samples (individuals) within a cluster cannot be re-identified easily. The two approaches are relatively destructive on purpose, in order to provide a means of destroying "intelligently" the data for some specific data fields. The first one relies on flattening the required dimensions: if a specific data field is deemed sensitive, it can be summarized, for a single cluster, by a single value. The second approach is a lot less destructive, and tries to preserve the overall cluster statistics as much as possible, by randomizing the values within a cluster for all the samples so that the cluster remains similar.

Flattening Dimensions. Referring back to Table 1, it is for example likely that the data in the "Sensitive" field, namely the Condition, would need to be modified before this data is released. For such cases where destructive data alterations are desirable or even needed, it would be possible to replace the sensitive values by empty or unusable ones. This would effectively destroy some of the data statistics and structures within the cluster considered. But in the cases where one would want to preserve some of this information in order to keep some structure within the cluster, the question becomes: how do we modify this data so that it is as close to destroying it as possible, while maintaining the cluster structure/statistics? The proposed straightforward way to do this is to "flatten" the sensitive field (dimension) to the value of the centroid. The effect of collapsing a specific dimension is illustrated on Fig. 1. In effect, what happens for each cluster C_l is

$$\forall k \in \mathcal{S}, \ \forall \mathbf{t}_i \in C_l, a_{i,k} = c_l^{(k)}, \tag{9}$$

where $\mathcal{S}$ is the set of the considered sensitive fields to be anonymized "destructively". While this approach effectively destroys the data structure within the

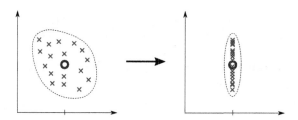

Fig. 1. Example of collapsing of one dimension to the centroid value. This obviously breaks cluster distribution and distances to the centroid.

cluster to some extent, there is a risk that the cluster is already initially as on Fig. 1; this could likely happen if the initial clustering of the data samples is efficient already in the first place. The flattening procedure proposed here would then have no effect and one could argue that the anonymization is not carried out.

This is unlikely to happen for all clusters at the same time, although this is obviously highly data-dependent. For this reason, we propose the second method, also considered as destructive regarding the data values, but "safer" in this respect.

Shuffling Data Around. This second method is about preserving the intra-cluster data structure as much as possible, while still modifying the sample values as much as possible. This approach is the most costly in terms of computations and general costs. In this case, we shuffle the samples (on one dimension at a time only) around the centroid. In effect, for a cluster C_l,

$$\forall k \in \mathcal{S},\ \forall \mathbf{t}_i \in C_l, a_{i,k} = a_{i,k}^{\text{new}}\ \text{s.t. KL}(f_{d_{C_l}}, f_{d_{C_l}}^{\text{new}}) \leq \varepsilon, \tag{10}$$

where, as before, $f_{d_{C_l}}$ is the distribution of the distances between the samples in cluster C_l and its centroid, and $f_{d_{C_l}}^{\text{new}}$ the same distribution after modifying the coordinate $a_{i,k}$, and $a_{i,k}^{\text{new}} \in \mathbb{X}^{(k)}$ is the new value for the coordinate k of sample $\mathbf{t}_i$ in C_l. This approach is illustrated on Fig. 2, where one can see that

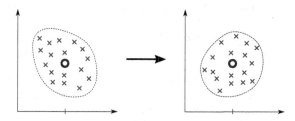

Fig. 2. Example of re-distributing the samples within a cluster (or adding noise to them in a controlled fashion): The distribution of the distances to the centroid is preserved and the overall cluster structure is preserved.

the overall effect is to "shuffle around" within the cluster, while preserving the distances between the samples in the cluster and the cluster centroid.

Note in this case that we do not try to preserve explicitly the pairwise distances between the samples within a cluster. Such distances will, at the whole cluster level, be preserved somewhat in any case, by preserving the distances to the centroid.

5   Conclusions and Future Work

In this paper, we propose an early version of a data anonymization framework, focusing on making individual re-identification difficult, while preserving clusters/group statistics and structure, over any type of data field (provided it can be abstracted as a metric space). We first develop the means of identifying outliers in terms of clustering the data, and propose ways to modify the data so as to "push back" this outlier with the rest of the crowd. We then propose several methods to "stir" the data within a cluster, effectively modifying the data values completely, but retaining the internal structure of the clusters. This to allow for further data processing at a somewhat global level, while ensuring the privacy of individuals. As can be noted, some of the data alterations proposed in this work are relatively computationally heavy, and currently require many iterations to converge to an acceptable solution (e.g. the case from Sect. 4.2 where one shuffles data around within a cluster so as to minimize the distortions on the distances distributions). Current and future work will focus on developing efficient algorithms to perform the proposed anonymization tasks, and experiment the proposed framework over large data sets composed of very different data fields.

References

1. Bogachev, V.I., Kolesnikov, A.V.: The Monge-Kantorovich problem: achievements, connections, and perspectives. Russian Math. Surveys **67**, 785–890 (2012)
2. Ciriani, V., di Vimercati, S.C., Foresti, S., Samarati, P.: κ-anonymity. In: Secure Data Management in Decentralized Systems, vol. 33, Advances in Information Security, pp. 323–353. Springer US (2007)
3. Cybenko, G.: Approximations by superpositions of sigmoidal functions. Math. Control Sig. Syst. **2**(4), 303–314 (1989)
4. Dwork, C.: Differential privacy: a survey of results. In: Agrawal, M., Du, D.-Z., Duan, Z., Li, A. (eds.) TAMC 2008. LNCS, vol. 4978, pp. 1–19. Springer, Heidelberg (2008)
5. Kieseberg, P., Hobel, H., Schrittwieser, S., Weippl, E., Holzinger, A.: Protecting anonymity in data-driven biomedical science. In: Holzinger, A., Jurisica, I. (eds.) Interactive Knowledge Discovery and Data Mining in Biomedical Informatics. LNCS, vol. 8401, pp. 301–316. Springer, Heidelberg (2014)
6. Kieseberg, P., Malle, B., Frühwirt, P., Weippl, E., Holzinger, A.: A tamper-proof audit and control system for the doctor in the loop. In: Brain Informatics, pp. 1–11 (2016)

7. Kullback, S., Leibler, R.A.: On information and sufficiency. Ann. Math. Stat. **22**(1), 79–86 (1951)
8. Machanavajjhala, A., Gehrke, J., Kifer, D., Venkitasubramaniam, M.: ℓ-diversity: privacy beyond κ-anonymity. In: International Conference on Data Engineering (ICDE), pp. 24 (2006)
9. Mallows, C.L.: A note on asymptotic joint normality. Ann. Math. Stat. **43**(2), 508–515 (1972)

An Open-Source Object-Graph-Mapping Framework for Neo4j and Scala: Renesca

Felix Dietze[1], Johannes Karoff[2], André Calero Valdez[1(✉)], Martina Ziefle[1], Christoph Greven[3], and Ulrik Schroeder[3]

[1] Human-Computer Interaction Center, RWTH Aachen University,
Campus Boulevard 57, Aachen, Germany
{dietze,calero-valdez,ziefle}@comm.rwth-aachen.de
[2] RWTH Aachen University, Aachen, Germany
johannes.karoff@rwth-aachen.de
[3] Learning Technologies Research Group, RWTH Aachen University,
Ahornstr. 55, Aachen, Germany
{greven,schroeder}@cs.rwth-aachen.de

Abstract. The usage and application of graph databases is increasing. Many research problems are based on understanding relationships between data entities. This is where graph databases are powerful. Nevertheless, software developers model and think in object-oriented software. Combining both approaches leads to a paradigm mismatch. This mismatch can be addressed by using object graph mappers (OGM). OGM adapt graph databases for object-oriented code, to relieve the developer. Most graph database access frameworks only support table-based result outputs. This defeats one of the strongest purposes of using graph databases. In order to harness both the power of graph databases and object-oriented modeling (e.g. type-safety, inheritance, etc.) we propose an open-source framework with two libraries: (1) *renesca*, which is a graph database driver providing graph-query-results and change-tracking. (2) *renesca-magic*, a macro-based ER-modeling domain specific language (DSL). Both were tested in a graph-based application and lead to dramatic improvements in code size (factor 10) and extensibility of the code, with no significant effect on performance.

Keywords: Graph databases · Scala · Neo4j · REST API · Object-graph-mapper · OGM

1 Introduction

An increasing amount of today's applications uses graph-based data structures. Social Network Analysis [1], bibliometrics [2], biomedical data [3], recommender

---

The framework is available at https://github.com/renesca/.

Published by Springer International Publishing Switzerland 2016. All Rights Reserved
F. Buccafurri et al. (Eds.): CD-ARES 2016, LNCS 9817, pp. 204–218, 2016.
DOI: 10.1007/978-3-319-45507-5_14

systems, and neural networks are just some of the research fields that use graph-based data structures (e.g. railroad-planning [4], remote sensing [5]). Even software development itself can benefit from the power of graph databases [6]. Graph databases differ from other forms of databases as they rely on graph-based data storage internally. This comes with the benefit of naturally modeling data that derives meaning from structure and relations. Another benefit of graph databases is their performance in local search tasks that are based on relationships of the stored data. This is particularly helpful when using social network data [7].

On the other hand a lot of software development today is done using the object-oriented software paradigm. Object-oriented modeling and programming allows an intuitive organization of code as it allows the developer to think in *object* terms that are natural to the human mind.

Holzschuher and Peinl [8] investigated the benefits of graph databases in comparison to Apache Shinding that uses a relational database backend. They state that using graph-based databases comes with little performance overhead and more readable code.

1.1 Object-Graph Mapping

Naturally, vendors have come up with Object-Graph Mapping tools that are already in use. Neo4j comes with an OGM[1] that is currently in release 2. But also third party vendors provide OGM for Neo4j. Hibernate is a very popular example. Hibernate OGM[2] also supports Neo4j and several other databases like NoSQL but also relational Databases (ORM). A similar solution is provided by Spring Data Neo4j[3] that uses AspectJ for advanced mapping features. The NoSQL database OrientDB also comes with a type-safe property-graph model that is ensured by the database itself[4]. The framework Structr[5] provides a Graph-Database and an Object Schema, but is aimed mostly at enterprise data management and comes with graphical editing tools. To the best of our knowledge there is no OGM that supports graph-query results, hyper-graphs and multiple-inheritance at our time of development.

1.2 Neo4j and Scala

We picked Neo4j as it is the graph database that outperforms many of its competitors [9,10]. Neo4j can be used as an embedded database or over the network via a REST API. In the embedded case the data is stored in the file system and is accessed by using Neo4j as a library. This allows to work imperatively with the complete graph to traverse and modify nodes as well as relations or to declaratively query data with the Cypher query language. The REST API provides access to nodes and relations via REST calls or Cypher queries.

---

[1] https://neo4j.com/docs/ogm-manual/current/.
[2] http://hibernate.org/ogm/.
[3] http://projects.spring.io/spring-data-neo4j/.
[4] http://orientdb.com/docs/last/Schema.html.
[5] https://structr.org.

Traditional relational databases have table data structures and the queries always result in a table form. Query results coming from the Neo4j REST API can be graphs and tables. At the time of development, the existing Scala Neo4j REST libraries imitated ORMs (Object Relational Mapper) and were therefore limited to list or table structures of nodes and relations. This is neither convenient to work with nor does it fit the purpose of a graph database, especially when using hypergraph data structures.

2   Our Contribution

We present the framework renesca for handling graph database query results using a new paradigm. With renesca, the result data structure can be a graph instead of a table. Changes to the data can be cumulatively applied (c.f. *Unit of Work* [11]).

On top of this paradigm we present the framework and DSL renesca-magic for describing graph database schemata. The DSL is implemented with Scala macros which generate code for using renesca in a type-safe way. This allows to interpret graph results with regards to a schema (see Fig. 1). Furthermore, the framework allows to realize hyperrelations, which means connecting relations with nodes.

The whole renesca framework (i.e. renesca and renesca-magic) is implemented in Scala as a lightweight (approx. 3,200 LOC + 6,500 LOC tests) OGM which can be used as two separate libraries.

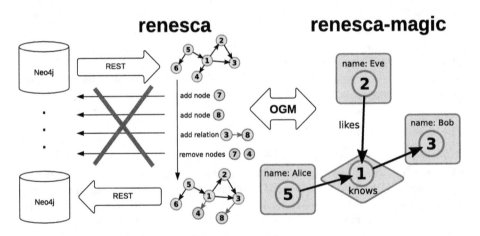

Fig. 1. The renesca-framework uses two libraries: renesca is an abstraction layer that allows to handle graphs over the REST-API of Neo4j. Changes can be done locally and persistence can be deferred as a Unit of Work. renesca-magic is a type-safe wrapper for the low-level property-graph model of Neo4j.

3   Accessing Neo4j Using Renesca

Renesca provides the query interface to the Neo4j REST API. It manages submission of prepared statements and returns the results in appropriate data structures. The data is handled using the following concepts:

3.1   Treat Query Results as Graphs Instead of Tables

Like the embedded version of Neo4j, with renesca it is possible to query a subgraph from the database and get the result as a graph *or* table data structure. The graph can be traversed like a Scala collection and properties are represented as hashmaps on nodes and relations. The property values can be casted to the expected type. The resulting graph consists of three classes: Node, Relation (startNode, endNode) and Graph (nodes, relations).

3.2   Track Changes and Persist Later as One Unit of Work

When modifying, creating and deleting nodes as well as connecting them with relationships, it is very expensive to submit a REST request for each change. In renesca we track changes and apply all of them at once when persisting the whole graph, with as few queries as possible. This takes fewer REST requests and leaves room for optimization. Changes to properties are also tracked and persisted. This approach allows to pass around the graph structure in the code and after all changes have been applied, persist once.

3.3   Example Code

Listing 1.1. Usage example of renesca

```scala
// establishing the database connection is left out in this
    example

db.query("CREATE (:ANIMAL {name:'snake'})-[:EATS]->(:ANIMAL
    {name:'dog'})")

val tx = db.newTransaction

// query a subgraph from the database
implicit val graph = tx.queryGraph("MATCH (n:ANIMAL)-[r
    ]->() RETURN n,r")

// access the graph like scala collections
val snake = graph.nodes.find(_.properties("name").
asInstanceOf[StringPropertyValue] == "snake").get

// useful methods to access the graph (requires implicit
    val graph in scope)
```

```
15 // e.g.: neighbours, successors, predecessors, inDegree,
        outDegree, degree, ...
  val name = snake.neighbours.head.properties("name").
  asInstanceOf[StringPropertyValue].value
  println("Name of snake neighbour:" + name) // prints "dog"

20 // changes to the graph are tracked
  snake.labels += "REPTILE"
  snake.properties("hungry") = true

  // creating a local Node
25 // (a Node the database does not know about yet)
  val hippo = Node.create

  // changes to locally created Nodes are also tracked
  hippo.labels += "ANIMAL"
30 hippo.properties("name") = "hippo"

  // add the created node to the Node Set
  graph.nodes += hippo

35 // create a new local relation
  // from a locally created Node to an existing Node
  graph.relations += Relation.create(snake, "EATS", hippo)

  // persist all tracked changes to the database
40 // and commit the transaction
  tx.commit.persistChanges(graph)
```

4   The Graph-Object Impedance Mismatch

The renesca framework provides graph query results which return object-graphs that can be worked with procedurally. Usually, entities in the business logic of an application directly correspond to records in the database – these are nodes in the context of graph databases. The abstraction layer renesca-magic generates boilerplate code for Node, Relation and Hyperrelation objects using a high level Scala DSL. This wraps the pure data-graph in an object-graph.

4.1   The Renesca-Magic Abstraction Layer

When only working with renesca, it is natural to write wrappers for specific nodes that correspond to objects, as these objects always have specific properties. So, instead of looking up in the property hashmap and casting every time, we write a wrapper class which implements typed getters and setters for the needed properties. Relations between objects can be implemented by wrapping the graph traversal with an appropriate getter. Therefore, we extended renesca with simple schema helpers to wrap nodes, relations and graphs.

For large models it can be very error prone to change the model and therefore refactor the boilerplate code. This issue leads to the idea of generating the boilerplate based on a compactly described model. The code generator is implemented as a set of Scala macros which transform a class-based ER-model DSL to work with the graph database in a type safe way.

Scala macros are hygienic macros and therefore work on abstract syntax trees instead of strings of code. The trees which are read from the schema definition are transformed and directly compiled. The macros analyze the multiple inheritance hierarchies and relation graph of the ER-Model to decide which labels to set on nodes and which getters / setters to generate. This is the heart of renesca-magic. Explaining it here is beyond the scope of this article. The interested reader can examine the code online[6].

The following subsections explain how renesca-magic transforms the model definition in order to map it to the property-graph model used by the database.

Labels. The names of the node and relation definitions are directly translated to labels and relation-types of the property graph model.

Properties. Renesca-magic generates wrapper classes and factories for nodes and relations. Both can have properties which can be primitives or optional primitives. The properties can be immutable by writing them with a *val* and mutable by using a *var*. Default values can be specified with an assignment of an expression which is evaluated on creation. The classes are generated with getters and setters, taking mutability and optionality into account. The factories provide methods to wrap existing nodes or relations and methods to create new instances with the required properties and the optional ones as default parameters.

Graphs. There is a wrapper for the whole graph, which provides access to the different types of nodes and relations contained in the graph. This graph can be persisted like the graph from renesca.

Relations and Neighbors. The wrapper for relations takes two additional parameters. The start node and the end node of the directed relation. This triggers the generation of accessors in the start node and end node wrappers to access neighbors over this relation in both directions.

Multiple Inheritance. When using the same property over and over again on different types of nodes it makes sense to define it only once in a trait and compose it into all the needed nodes by inheritance[7]. This helps to keep the schema definition DRY (Don't repeat yourself). The name of the trait is added to the list of labels. Like in OOP (Object oriented programming), all children of

---

[6] https://github.com/renesca/renesca-magic.
[7] Scala allows for multiple inheritance by using traits.

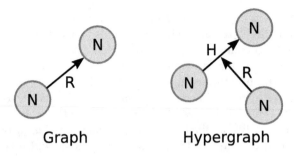

Graph   Hypergraph

Fig. 2. *left:* A regular graph connects two nodes (N) using a relation (R). *right:* A hypergraph allows for hyperrelations (H) which can be connected to a Node (N) itself by a regular relation (R). (H) and (R) together form a hyperedge in mathematical terms.

the trait can be handled as the same type. This allows to work with collections of nodes sharing the same properties. There are also traits for relations with the same functionality.

Hyperrelations. Hyperedges in mathematical terms are edges which connect an arbitrary set of vertices. In renesca-magic we define Hyperrelations as relations which get all characteristics of a node. They can be used as a drop-in replacement for nodes and relations. Hyperrelations can therefore connect two nodes and be connected with other nodes (see Fig. 2). So this is a specialized form of the mathematical definition. Internally in the generated code they are represented by a node with an incoming and outgoing relation.

4.2   Example Boilerplate Code

Since these benefits are hard to imagine without examples we demonstrate the benefits of using renesca-magic in a short artificial example (see Listing 1.7 in the appendix). We want to have a simple two node-type graph with one relationship. A class *Animal* has a relationship *Eats* with a class *Food*. Each class has getter and setters to access its neighbors and its properties. We omitted any comments in the generated code to not blow up the code unintentionally, yet we get 50 lines of boilerplate.

The amount of boilerplate needed to represent and access such a simple relationship is far too large. Using a Scala-Macro we can reduce the 50 lines of code to a mere 13 lines of code — including comments (see Listing 1.2).

Listing 1.2. Macro code for our example (Animal)-[eats]->(Food)

```
import renesca.schema.macros

@macros.GraphSchema
object ExampleSchemaWrapping {
```

```
5   // Nodes get their class name as uppercase label
    @Node class Animal { val name: String }
    @Node class Food {
      val name: String
      var amount: Long
10  }
    // Relations get their class name as uppercase
        relationType
    @Relation class Eats(startNode: Animal, endNode: Food)
    }
```

This short example also shows how to use properties that are immutable (using *val*) and mutable (using *var*). Accessing this graph is now equally simple (see Listing 1.3).

Listing 1.3. Creation of objects and changing properties

```
1 val snake = Animal.create("snake")
  val cake = Food.create(name = "cake", amount = 1000)
  val eats = Eats.create(snake, cake)

5 cake.amount -= 100
```

4.3   Additional Features Provided by Renesca-Magic

Wrapping Induced Subgraphs. The framework renesca-magic supports wrapping of induced subgraphs from a schema. By using such a wrapper (i.e. by using graph) renesca-magic automatically generates accessors for each node and relation. This comes with the benefit of traversing an induced sub-graph with methods of the object itself. In our example (see Listing 1.4) we can see that the relations between specified nodes will be induced.

Listing 1.4. Wrapping an induced subgraph

```
1 import renesca.schema.macros

  @macros.GraphSchema
  object ExampleSchemaSubgraph {
5   @Node class Animal { val name: String }
    @Node class Food {
      val name: String
      var amount: Long
    }
10  @Relation class Eats(startNode: Animal, endNode: Food)

    // Subgraph induction
    @Graph trait Zoo { Nodes(Animal, Food) }
  }
15
```

```
// Usage begins here
import ExampleSchemaSubgraph._

val zoo = Zoo(db.queryGraph("MATCH (a:ANIMAL)-[e:EATS]->(f:
    FOOD) RETURN a,e,f"))
val elefant = Animal.create("elefant")
val pizza = Food.create(name = "pizza", amount = 2)
zoo.add(Eats.create(elefant, pizza))
zoo.animals // provides Set(elefant)
zoo.relations // provides Set(elefant eats pizza)
db.persistChanges(zoo)
```

4.4   Traits and Relations to Traits

Since Scala allows for multiple inheritance using traits, we can map our relations
to traits instead of classes. This allows for polymorphic relations between nodes
that share common traits (see Listing 1.5, line 15).

Listing 1.5. Multiple inheritance using traits

```
@macros.GraphSchema
object ExampleSchemaTraits {
  // Inheriting Nodes receive their name as additional
      label
  @Node trait Animal { val name: String }

  // Node with labels FISH and ANIMAL
  @Node class Fish extends Animal
  @Node class Dog extends Animal

  @Relation trait Consumes {val funny:Boolean}

  // Relations can connect Node traits
  // instead of defining separate relations
  // for Fish and Dog explicitly
  @Relation class Eats(startNode: Animal, endNode: Animal)
      extends Consumes
  @Relation class Drinks(startNode: Animal, endNode: Animal
      ) extends Consumes

  // Zoo contains all Animals (Animal expands to child
      nodes)
  @Graph trait Zoo { Nodes(Animal) }
}
```

4.5   Hyperrelations

We can use hypergraphs in renesca-magic by masquerading a node as a hyperrelation (see Fig. 2). In our example (see Listing 1.6, line 13) we model an online

document system where articles are annotated with tags. The relation *tags* relates an article and a tag. The relation itself can now be in a relation *supports*, which can store who is supporting which tagging-action — thus a (tag, taggable)-tuple.

Listing 1.6. Multiple inheritance using traits

```
1 @macros.GraphSchema
  object ExampleSchemaHyperRelations {
    @Node trait Uuid { val uuid: String = java.util.UUID.
      randomUUID.toString }
    @Node trait Taggable
5   @Node class Tag extends Uuid { val name:String }
    @Node class User extends Uuid { val name:String }
    @Node class Article extends Uuid with Taggable { val
      content:String }

    // A HyperRelation is a node representing a relation:
10  // (n)-[]->(hyperRelation)-[]->(m)
    // It behaves like node and relation at the same time
    // and therefore can extend node and relation traits
    @HyperRelation class TaggingAction(startNode: Tag,
      endNode: Taggable) extends Uuid
    // Because these are nodes, we can connect a
      HyperRelation with another Node
15  @Relation class Supports(startNode: User, endNode:
      TaggingAction)
  }
```

5 Performance Evaluation

In order to asses the impact of using an additional abstraction layer on top of Neo4j, we measure runtimes of the usage example from the renesca documentation.

In the benchmark example the database already contains two nodes connected by one edge. The example consists of two transactions. In the first transaction we query both nodes and set an additional label and property on one of them. Then we create another node and connect it to the previously modified node. In the second transaction we query one node and add a property. The first trial uses change tracking provided by the renesca library, while the native implementation uses explicit Cypher-Queries to do the same reads and modifications to the database[8].

---

[8] The Benchmark is available at: https://github.com/renesca/renesca-benchmark.

5.1   Method

We run both implementations 2000 times on the same hardware with a local Neo4J 3.0.3 instance. We measure runtime and compare results using a Welch unpaired sample test. We report results using 95 % confidence interval and test-result against a significance level of $\alpha = .05$. This means that we have a 95 % chance of missing an existing difference in our sample. Since runtime data is often not normally distributed, we also apply BCa bootstrapping to verify our test results.

5.2   Results

After 2000 trials we could not detect a significant difference (see Fig. 3) in performance using a Welch two-sample test comparing means in required time $(t(3683.2) = -0.09142, p = .9272, \text{n.s.})$. Renesca has an average runtime of $M_R = 0.02894985s$ $(SD_R = 0.0165216S)$, while the native implementation has a mean runtime of $M_N = 0.02900663s$ $(SD_N = 0.02232678s)$.

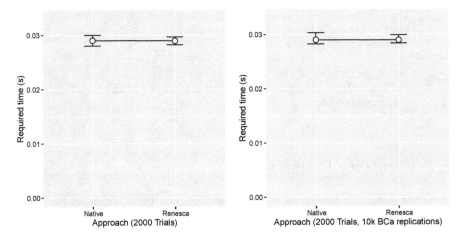

Fig. 3. Performance evaluation of renesca against a native implementation. Error bars denote 95 % confidence intervals. The left image shows means and CI, the right image shows bootstrapped means and CIs with 10,000 BCa [12] replications.

The bootstrapped results confirm our results, even for our heavily skewed sample (i.e. long-tail distribution). Uncertainty only shifts to longer times.

5.3   Discussion

We evaluate our frameworks with very simplistic means, to ensure no dramatic overhead is generated from them. We can show that no meaningful overhead comes from using renesca in our examples. This benchmark is by far not extensive, yet only explorative in nature. But it is necessary to keep in mind that for any given abstraction layer a benchmark can be generated that brings the benefits of the layer to a halt. Direct API access is always faster than through any abstraction layer. The benefits are more sought in clever optimization (i.e. removing redundant operations on higher levels of abstraction), maintainability and increases in developing speed. The trade-off on different aspects in efficiency (runtime vs. development) must be balanced to attain an effective abstraction layer.

6 Fields of Application

We see potential of using renesca in applications with complex data models which are not easily represented with ORMs. For example:

- cliques of Entities where each entity can be related to any other entity in the clique. This usually results in an quadratic amount of N:M relations in relational models.
- Relations to other Relations (Hyperrelations)

These examples describe advantages of graph databases in contrast to relational databases in general. They are not limited to renesca-magic, but the boilerplate generation allows to handle them with the same usability as ORMs for relational databases.

6.1 Argument Mapping Systems

Using all the features of renesca we implemented a real-life online discussion system that relies on a hypergraph-based data structure to organize its data. The system uses tags (similar as in Listing 6) to organize tagging and voting. The db-schema required to write 266 lines of code (LOC) including comments. Using renesca-magic it generated 2,739 LOC of boilerplate code without comments. This shows that we can reduce code size to a tenth using renesca-magic.

7 Conclusions and Future Work

In this paper we introduced two frameworks that improve the usability of the Neo4j database with Scala. The framework renesca implements access to the REST API of Neo4j and is the foundation of renesca-magic. The latter implements macros that allow object-graph-mapping (OGM). The amount of written code can be reduced by factor of 10. This improves both maintainability and extensibility. It also improves code-readability and facilitates Scala's power to use multiple inheritance.

Since cypher queries are not type safe, queries can create and retrieve data that does not match an existing object model. This is a source of common pitfalls for developers. Adding a query-parser that ensures type-safety in the query language at compile time could alleviate this burden off the user. At this time of writing Neo4j 3.0.0 is already released. It brings a high performance binary protocol called Bolt as an alternative to the REST API to access the database over a network. We plan to integrate this binary protocol into renesca to reduce the protocol overhead. We also plan to evaluate renesca using the methodology presented by Jouili and Vansteenberghe [10]. Naturally using an OGM will increase processing time, but determining under which circumstance this plays a role must be identified.

Acknowledgments. We would like to thank the anonymous reviewers for their constructive comments on an earlier version of this manuscript. The authors thank the German Research Council DFG for the friendly support of the research in the excellence cluster "Integrative Production Technology in High Wage Countries".

Appendix

A   Boilerplate Code Example

Listing 1.7. Full boilerplate code required to access a single relationship (Animal)-[eats]->(Food)

```scala
import renesca.graph._
import renesca.parameter._
import renesca.parameter.implicits._

case class Animal(node: Node) {
  val label = Label("ANIMAL")
  def eats: Set[Food] = node.outRelations.filter(_.
      relationType == Eats.relationType).map(_.endNode).
      filter(_.labels.contains(Food.label)).map(Food.wrap)
  def name: String = node.properties("name").asInstanceOf[
      StringPropertyValue]
}

object Animal {
  val label = Label("ANIMAL")
  def wrap(node: Node) = new Animal(node)
  def create(name: String): Animal = {
    val wrapped = wrap(Node.create(List(label)))
    wrapped.node.properties.update("name", name)
    wrapped
  }
}

case class Food(node: Node) {
  val label = Label("FOOD")
```

```scala
    def rev_eats(implicit graph: Graph): Set[Animal] = node.
        inRelations.filter(_.relationType == Eats.relationType
        ).map(_.startNode).filter(_.labels.contains(Animal  .
        label)).map(Animal.wrap)
    def name: String = node.properties("name").asInstanceOf[
        StringPropertyValue]
25  def amount: Long = node.properties("amount").asInstanceOf[
        LongPropertyValue]
    def 'amount_='(newValue: Long) { node.properties.update("
        amount", newValue) }
}

object Food {
30  val label = Label("FOOD")
    def wrap(node: Node) = new Food(node)
    def create(amount: Long, name: String): Food = {
     val wrapped = wrap(Node.create(List(label)))
     wrapped.node.properties.update("amount", amount)
35   wrapped.node.properties.update("name", name)
     wrapped
    }
}

40 case class Eats(startNode: Animal, relation: Relation,
       endNode: Food)

object Eats {
    val relationType = RelationType("EATS")
    def wrap(relation: Relation) = {
45   Eats(Animal.wrap(relation.startNode), relation, Food.wrap
        (relation.endNode))
    }
    def create(startNode: Animal, endNode: Food): Eats = {
     wrap(Relation.create(startNode.node, relationType,
        endNode.node))
    }
50 }
```

References

1. Dev, H.: Privacy preserving social graphs for high precision community detection. In: Proceedings of the 2014 ACM SIGMOD International Conference on Management of Data, pp. 1615–1616. ACM (2014)
2. Holzinger, A., Ofner, B., Stocker, C., Calero Valdez, A., Schaar, A.K., Ziefle, M., Dehmer, M.: On graph entropy measures for knowledge discovery from publication network data. In: Cuzzocrea, A., Kittl, C., Simos, D.E., Weippl, E., Xu, L. (eds.) CD-ARES 2013. LNCS, vol. 8127, pp. 354–362. Springer, Heidelberg (2013)

 3. Singh, M., Kaur, K.: Sql2neo: Moving health-care data from relational to graph databases. In: 2015 IEEE International on Advance Computing Conference (IACC), pp. 721–725. IEEE (2015)
 4. Mpinda, S.A.T., Bungama, P.A., Maschietto, L.G.: Graph database application using neo4j (railroad planner simulation). Int. J. Eng. Res. Technol. **4**, 999–1002 (2015). ESRSA Publications
 5. Lampoltshammer, T.J., Wiegand, S.: Improving the computational performance of ontology-based classification using graph databases. Remote Sens. **7**(7), 9473–9491 (2015)
 6. Urma, R.G., Mycroft, A.: Source-code queries with graph databases-with application to programming language usage and evolution. Sci. Comput. Program. **97**, 127–134 (2015)
 7. Angles, R., Prat-Pérez, A., Dominguez-Sal, D., Larriba-Pey, J.L.: Benchmarking database systems for social network applications. In: First International Workshop on Graph Data Management Experiences and Systems, p. 15. ACM (2013)
 8. Holzschuher, F., Peinl, R.: Querying a graph database-language selection and performance considerations. J. Comput. Syst. Sci. **82**(1), 45–68 (2016)
 9. Beis, S., Papadopoulos, S., Kompatsiaris, Y.: Benchmarking graph databases on the problem of community detection. In: Bassiliades, N., Ivanovic, M., Kon-Popovska, M., Manolopoulos, Y., Palpanas, T., Trajcevski, G., Vakali, A. (eds.) New Trends in Database and Information Systems II. AISC, vol. 312, pp. 3–14. Springer, Heidelberg (2015)
10. Jouili, S., Vansteenberghe, V.: An empirical comparison of graph databases. In: 2013 International Conference on Social Computing (SocialCom), pp. 708–715. IEEE (2013)
11. Fowler, M.: Patterns of enterprise application architecture. Addison-Wesley Longman Publishing Co., Inc., Reading (2002)
12. Davison, A.C., Hinkley, D.V.: Bootstrap Methods and Their Application, vol. 1. Cambridge University Press, Cambridge (1997)

Publishing Differentially Private Medical Events Data

Sigal Shaked$^{(\boxtimes)}$ and Lior Rokach

The Department of Information Systems Engineering,
Ben-Gurion University, Beersheba, Israel
{shaksi,liorrk}@post.bgu.ac.il

Abstract. Sequential data has been widely collected in the past few years; in the public health domain it appears as collections of medical events such as lab results, electronic chart records, or hospitalization transactions. Publicly available sequential datasets for research purposes promises new insights, such as understanding patient types, and recognizing emerging diseases. Unfortunately, the publication of sequential data presents a significant threat to users' privacy. Since data owners prefer to avoid such risks, much of the collected data is currently unavailable to researchers. Existing anonymization techniques that aim at preserving sequential patterns lack two important features: handling long sequences and preserving occurrence times. In this paper, we address this challenge by employing an ensemble of Markovian models trained based on the source data. The ensemble takes several optional periodicity levels into consideration. Each model captures transitions between times and states according to shorter parts of the sequence, which is eventually reconstructed. Anonymity is provided by utilizing only elements of the model that guarantee differential privacy. Furthermore, we develop a solution for generating differentially private sequential data, which will bring us one step closer to publicly available medical datasets via sequential data. We applied this method to two real medical events datasets and received some encouraging results, demonstrating that the proposed method can be used to publish high quality anonymized data.

Keywords: Data synthetization · Privacy preserving data publishing · Markov model · Clustering · Sequential patterns · Differential privacy · Medical events

1 Introduction

A large amount of sequential medical event data has been gathered in the recent years. Studies based on this data can help address challenges in the medical field

---

This work was supported in part by Deustche Telekom Labs.

F. Buccafurri et al. (Eds.): CD-ARES 2016, LNCS 9817, pp. 219–235, 2016.
DOI: 10.1007/978-3-319-45507-5_15

and may lead to new discoveries. Unfortunately, the publication of sequential data is accompanied by a real threat to users' privacy. Even when such data is not widely published as it might be in an academic study, shared datasets such as AOL's web querying history and Netflix's movie ratings (containing information which is publicly available to users of the services), have been vulnerable. Users have been identified based on linking the published data with externally available data. Since data owners prefer to avoid this type of risk, the collected data remains inaccessible to scientists.

The work of De Montjoye et al. [10] emphasizes the magnitude of the privacy risk, as based on human mobility data spanning 15 months among 1.5 million users, the authors show that human mobility traces are somewhat "unique in the crowd", by demonstrating that four randomly chosen locations in an hour rounded resolution are enough to re-identify 95 % of the users. Since four events can be obtained using very little outside information, their study represents a major threat to individuals' privacy.

There are two main traditional privacy models regarding record linkage, where the attacker reveals the owner of a record. The first aims at preventing an attacker from linking to a record owner, based on some quasi identifying attributes (QID) that were gained from external sources. K-anonymity [12] is usually adopted for this privacy model, demanding that each record is indistinguishable from at least $k-1$ other records with respect to the QID. [7,8] place a human agent for defining the background knowledge of the hypothetical enemy.

The second privacy model, differential privacy [4] aims to ensure that by using the published data the attacker gains as less additional knowledge as possible. It checks that the removal or addition of a single record does not significantly affect results of the querying function. Typically, differential privacy is achieved by adding noise to the outcome of a query. A randomized algorithm satisfies $\varepsilon-$differential privacy if the ratio between the probability that the algorithm outputs any output on a dataset and the probability that it outputs the same output on a dataset that differ by exactly one record, is bounded by a constant.

Some methods have been suggested for anonymizing sequential data such as that used in the previously mentioned cases. Ghasemzadeh et al. [6] anonymize sequential data using a probabilistic flow graph, which is a tree representing transition probabilities between pairs of time and location. Violating sequences are suppressed in order to achieve LK-privacy. The inclusion of time in each state might worsen the model's sparsity. While this might be necessary for effective passenger flow analysis, it is unnecessary for simpler analysis tasks. Pensa et al. [11] use a prefix tree of transitions between states and a pruning technique to ensure k-anonymity in sequential data. Each pruned trajectory propagates an increase in the support of the most similar trajectory in the prefix tree. The last two methods use tree-based techniques, which do not scale well to large domains (complexity increases quadratically with the number of transitions). Furthermore, these approaches are built based on partition-based privacy models and therefore provide limited privacy protection. We prefer to apply differential privacy that makes no assumptions about the attacker's existing knowledge.

Chen et al. [3] propose a sanitization algorithm to generate differentially private sequential data by making use of a noisy prefix tree based on the underlying variable-length n-gram model behind the data. Each node holds the count of sequences described by the nodes in the current branch, and Laplace noise is added to these counts. Their method lacks some features that are required in order for it to be applied in certain domains, such as medical events. First, input sequences are truncated to a predefined length, since the method does not perform well for long sequences. Second, the input data does not include a time dimension; this method can therefore neither support the generation of occurrence times, nor take into account possible dependencies of the sequential patterns with some other attributes that appear in the data.

Our suggested method addresses these gaps. We suggest a new privacy preservation method for sequential data, which generates differentially private synthetic data while preserving the sequential patterns of the source data. Data quality is maintained by using an ensemble of Markovian models, each of which captures another level of periodicity that considers dependency with an influencing attribute. Privacy is provided by using only the models' elements that fulfill differential privacy. In order to support the generation of occurrence times, each model also maintains transition times. Long sequences are handled by being partitioned into shorter parts, which are then clustered, condensed, and anonymized. The original long sequences are eventually reconstructed using a secondary ensemble of Markovian models.

To the best of our knowledge, this is the first use of Markovian generators to help ensure privacy preservation. Markovian generators have been applied to the task of sequence generation in other domains; for text generation, music composition and wind speed prediction.

The main contribution of this work is twofold; (1) demonstrating the generation of a differentially private medical events dataset, and (2) overcoming gaps in existing methods for sequential data anonymization, by providing a solution that incorporates generation of the time dimension, handles anonymization of long sequences, and considers dependencies of the sequential patterns with some predefined influencing attributes.

We evaluated the suggested method based on real world medical events data and received some encouraging results regarding its use.

The rest of this paper is organized as follows: in Sect. 2 background information and basic definitions are provided. Section 3 describes the model, and Sect. 4 presents the algorithm. In Sect. 5 we analyze performance and discuss experimental results. Finally, Sect. 6 concludes this work.

2   Background and Basic Definitions

2.1   Sequential Data

Let $E = e_1, e_2, .., e_{|E|}$ be the universe of all possible states within a sequence, where the meaning of a state varies from one domain to another. A state in a sequence can be, for example, a charted event like a ventilator setting, or a laboratory value as appears in medical electronic chart data. Other examples of states in the medical events domain include procedures that appear in medical billing data, or a hospital unit that takes care of a patient within data that describes transfers of patients within different units in the hospital.

A transactional sequential dataset D contains records of the form $\langle O, t, e \rangle$. Each record indicates a state e that occurred at time t and is attributed to an object O.

In this work, we apply sequence reconstruction for gaining the sequences' anonymity while preserving their other features; we use Markovian generators for this task. As can be seen in (1), each state e_i adds a multiplication with the probability $Pr(e_i|e_{i-1})$ to transfer from the previous state to e_i. The probability of accurately reconstructing a sequence, therefore, decreases with the sequence's size:

$$p(S) = Pr(e_1)\Pi_{i=2}^{|S|}Pr(e_i|e_{i-1}) \tag{1}$$

It is also harder to apply differential privacy to long sequences, since the longer the sequence is, the less support it has. We therefore divide the original sequence of states S into several shorter sequences s_i.

Considering all states that are attached to a certain object as a single sequence S may yield long sequences; for example, when the data describes hourly resolution transactions for a specific patient over three years, the object is comprised of a sequence with around $3 * 365 * 24 = 26,280$ states. In order to avoid the shortcomings that come with long sequences, we initially split long sequences into shorter ones, as discussed in Subsect. 3.3. This results in several possible sequences per objects which necessitates the following revision to our dataset definition:

Definition 1. *(a sequential dataset): A sequential dataset D contains records of the form $\langle O, t, e \rangle$. Each record indicates a state e that occurred at time t and is attributed to sequence s of object O.*

Definition 2. *(a sequence): A sequence s is an ordered list of states $s = e_1 \rightarrow e_2 \rightarrow .. \rightarrow e_{|s|}$, where $e_i \in E$. Records in a sequential dataset that belong to a single sequence s_1 share the same sequence Id (s) and object Id (O), and their times t_i dictate the order of states e_i in the sequence. A transition exists between two records that are attached to the same sequence, and have sequential times t_i and t_{i+1}. The transition time, therefore, is equal to $t_{i+1} - t_i$.*

Consecutive states in a sequence can be identical (for example: $s = e_3 \rightarrow e_2 \rightarrow e_2$). For convenience, we denote the original long sequence with S and the divided shorter sequence with s.

2.2 Cluster of Sequences

Our suggested method is based on the assumption that input objects share some common sequential patterns. In order to recognize common patterns, we initially cluster parts of sequences into groups. We measure the similarity between sequences by applying MinHash [2], a locality sensitive hashing (LSH) method that is often used for reducing dimensionality. With LSH the similarity is measured as the ratio of common hashed tokens for the two compared sequences using a family of hash functions H; the w-shingling (n-grams) method σ converts a sequence into a set of tokens.

$$LSH(s_1, s_2) = \frac{count_{h \in H}[h(\sigma(s_1)) = h(\sigma(s_2))]}{|H|} \tag{2}$$

Using the MinHash technique, the hash signature of a sequence s, $h(s)$, is constructed of minimal hash values of the tokens in the sequence. Using θ to hash each shingle z, we can hash a sequence s as follows:

$$h(s) = \min_{\forall_{z \in \sigma(s)}} (\theta(z)) \tag{3}$$

The MinHash technique can be used to efficiently measure the distance between sequences of unfixed size. Its low complexity stems from the fact that only $|H|$ comparisons are eventually made in order to estimate the distance between two sequences.

Definition 3. *(a cluster of sequences): A cluster C is a group of similar sequences s_i, according to the LSH similarity measure; $C = s_1, s_2, ..s_n$.*

The cluster's centroid represents sequential patterns that are commonly made by members of this cluster. When the cluster's members are similar, the cluster's centroid can be used to maintain sequential patterns of a higher quality than those maintained based on unclustered data. A cluster's centroid is represented as two Markovian chains, one for the times and the other for the states, as described later in Subsect. 3.1. An object can be attached to several sequences and can therefore be attached to several different clusters.

Definition 4. *(the similarity between two sequential datasets): The similarity between an origin dataset D, and an anonymized dataset D' is measured as the mean LSH similarity between each sequence in D' and it's nearest neighbor in D. The distance is the complementary to one of the similarity.*

$$sim\left(D, D'\right) = \sum_{s' \in D'} \frac{max_{\forall s \in D}\left(LSH\left(s, s'\right)\right)}{|D'|} \tag{4}$$

2.3 Differential Privacy

The differential privacy model [5] guards against privacy breaches by ensuring that any computation made on the data by a randomized algorithm is insensitive to the presence of a single record. Applying this notion for sequential data, therefore, requires bounding the influence of each individual record.

Definition 5. *(differential privacy): A data generation method M provides a $\varepsilon-$ differential privacy if, for any two datasets D and D' that differ on a single record (state transition), and for any possible output $R \in range(M)$, the probability to achieve the same output may only differ by a constant:*

$$pr\left(M(D) = R\right) \; = Pr\left(M(D') = R\right) \times e^{\mathcal{E}} \tag{5}$$

According to the composition property of differential privacy, a sequence of differentially private computations also provides differential privacy:

Theorem 1. [5]: *Let M_i be an $\varepsilon - differential$ privacy computation, then a sequence of n computations over a dataset D provides $(\sum_{i=1}^{n} \mathcal{E}_i)$-differential privacy.*

We can therefore compose a data generation method from several computational phases. Each phase, though, adds another level of noise ε_i to the anonymized data, which might damage the quality of the data.

2.4   Markov Model

Predicting a sequence of states requires some heavy computations, especially when it comes to long sequences. A common approach is to adopt the Markov independence assumption. In an m-order Markov model, the probability for the appearance of a state in a sequence depends only the previous m states of the sequence. A 2-order Markov model has the lowest computational cost, since it only examines the previous state when predicting the current state.

$$Pr\left(e_{i+1}{=}a \mid e_1, e_2, .., e_i\right) {=} Pr\left(e_{i+1}{=}a \mid e_i\right) \tag{6}$$

In order to generate a sequence of states, frequencies of starting states and state transitions are collected; let F_D denote the frequency of a given term according to dataset D, so that:

$$StartProb\left(a\right) {=} \mathcal{F}_D\left(e_1{=}a\right) \tag{7}$$

$$TransitionProb(a,b) {=} \mathcal{F}_D\left(e_{i+1}{=}b \mid e_i{=}a\right) \tag{8}$$

3   The Model

3.1   State & Time Markovian Model (STMM)

Two Markovian chains are required in order to supply a solution that includes generation of occurrence times. While the first chain handles transitions between states, the second chain models navigation along the time dimension. The two chains are combined, since each time transition matches a specific state transition.

Definition 6. *(a state and time Markovian model (STMM)): a STMM model maintains statistics regarding a Markovian chain of transitions between states and its matching transition times according to dataset D.*

$$STMM(D) =$$
$$\left\{ \begin{array}{l} \forall a \in range(E) \mid StartStateFreq(a), \\ \forall t \in \{1..24\} \mid StartTimeFreq(t), \\ \exists T \leftarrow \left\{ \forall_{i=1}^{|D-1|} (e_i, e_{i+1}) \right\} \Rightarrow \forall a, b \in range\,(T) \mid TransitionProb(a,b) \end{array} \right\}$$
$$(9)$$

where T denotes transitions within dataset D, and the maintained statistics are as follows:

Two types of statistics regarding the start of the chain:

$$StartStateFreq(a) = \mathcal{F}_D\,(e_1 = a) \tag{10}$$

$$StartTimeFreq(t) = \langle \mathcal{F}_D\,(t_1 = t)\,, \mathcal{L}_D(t_1 = t)\rangle \tag{11}$$

e_1 *is the starting state, and* t_1 *is its occurrence time. StartStateFreq(a) is therefore the frequency of records in D that contain the state a, and StartTimeFreq(t) is the frequency of records in D that start at time t, as well as the estimated (mean and standard deviation of) duration* $\mathcal{L}_D$ *for transitions in D that start at time t.*

Another type of statistic is maintained regarding transitions along the chain:

$$Transition(a,b) = \langle \mathcal{F}_D(e_{i+1} = b \mid e_i = a), T_D(e_{i+1} = b \mid e_i = a)\rangle \tag{12}$$

where Transition(a, b) holds both the frequency $\mathcal{F}_D$ *of a transition* $a \to b$ *according to dataset D, and the (mean and standard deviation of) transition time* T_D *for* $a \to b$ *according to D.*

3.2 Modelling State Transitions

In order to generate an anonymized dataset of high quality, we attempt to capture as many characteristics of the data as possible, and to consider several optional periodicity levels that appear in the data. In order to accomplish this, we gather a number of models and design an ensemble based method; each model focuses on a certain trend at a specific level of accuracy. Let's clarify this by providing the two following definitions:

Definition 7. *(influencing factor): an influencing factor f is a direct or derived attribute within dataset D, which the sequence is assumed to depend upon. For each possible value of this attribute* $v \in range(f)$, *a model is trained to represent a specific sequential trend.*

We can assume, for example, that diverse sequential patterns exist on different weekdays, so that $f = weekday$ and $v \in \{Sun, Mon, Tue, Wed, Thu, Fri, Sat\}$.

Definition 8. *(support level): A support level l is a set of four possible categories $l \in \{cluster\&factor, factor, cluster, all\}$.*

The various categories will derive the homogeneity level of the trained model; categories with higher support level train more models in the ensemble, each addresses a smaller population with higher homogeneousness. The most accurate support level is *cluster&factor*; models at this level are trained based on members of a given cluster C, while considering dependencies with factor f. The consideration of dependencies with a factor means that a separated STMM is created for each value v of that factor. The following support level is *factor*; here the model is trained based on the entire population of D, while considering dependencies with factor f. The next support level is *cluster*, where the model is trained based on members of a given cluster C, while considering no influencing factors. The least accurate level is *all*, in which a single model is trained based on the entire population of D, while considering no influencing factors.

Definition 9. *(a state and time Markovian model ensemble (STE)): An ensemble of state and time Markovian models is the set of STMM models that were trained according to each support level ℓ, given a clustered sequential dataset D'', a set of clusters C, and a set of factors F.*

$$STE(D, \ell, C, F) =$$
$$\bigcup_{\forall l \in \ell} \begin{cases} \forall c \in C, v \in f, f \in F | STMM(D''_{cluster=c \cap f.value=v}) & l = c \times f \\ \forall v \in f, f \in F | STMM(D''_{f.value=v}) & l = factor \\ \forall c \in C | STMM(D''_{cluster=c}) & l = cluster \\ STMM(D'') & l = all \end{cases} \qquad (13)$$

3.3   Dividing Sequences into Shorter Parts

Existing methods for differentially private sequence generation only handle short sequences [1,3]. In these techniques the source sequences are initially truncated into a predefined length, and the truncated set is then used as an input for the sanitization process. In this work we address this gap and provide a solution that also suits long sequences. For this task we apply the concept of dividing long sequences into smaller parts and then reconnect the parts; in this approach most of the training work is performed on short sequences, including clustering, state transitions modeling, and model anonymization. By processing shorter sequences, our method obtains more homogenous clusters that better reflect common patterns within the data.

The division of a single long sequence into smaller sections can be performed artificially according to a predefined sequence length, but a more natural separation could take place by analyzing the input data. Dealing with data that includes a time dimension, for example, comes with the benefit of being able to estimate the natural separation into sections based on the distribution of transition times within the data. Transition time is the time it takes to reach from one state to another, which is actually derived from the difference between timestamps of two successive object's records. We assume that some regularity

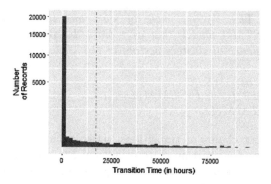

Fig. 1. A histogram of transition times for the *TRANSFERS* data, based on 25,000 sampled transitions; the red line indicates the recognized splitting point (16,800 h between transitions). (colour figure online)

in transition times or distances exists while a certain part of a sequence is active. Whenever the regularity seems to change drastically, we infer the occurrence of a stop, and therefore the sequence is split at this point.

Let's demonstrate this analytic process as it was conducted on the TRANS-FERS dataset that was used in our experiment (described in more detail later).

The histogram is based on the first 25,000 records in the data. As can be seen in Fig. 1, there seems to be some regularity of transition times that is distributed around the zero bar, diminishing at around 16,800 h. The small peaks after this regularity indicate the duration of various stops.

3.4   Reconstructing Divided Sequences

Processing shorter sequences facilitates the extraction of patterns with higher quality and enables their anonymization, but it requires an additional phase that connects the short sections into a whole sequence again. In order to reconnect sections of a divided long sequence, we use another Markovian chain that traverses from one section to another until connecting the entire original sequence back together. As mention before, each cluster represents some common sequential pattern. Assuming that members of each cluster are similar, by sampling a cluster we are able to ascertain (roughly) the pattern of a specific section of the sequence. The generation of a long sequence starts by sampling the initial cluster, according to which the first section of the sequence is generated. Each of the following sections of the sequence is then added to the sequence by sampling the transition to the following cluster and generating a short section of the sequence accordingly.

In order to strengthen our methods reconstruction ability, instead of modeling cluster transitions using a single Markovian chain, we suggest using an ensemble of such models that also takes into account some predefined factors. For this task we use another ensemble of STMMs which we call a cluster transitions ensemble (CTE).

Definition 10. *(CTE): An ensemble of state and time Markovian models, which is a set of STMM models that were trained according to each accuracy level ℓ, given a sequence of clusters per object $D_{clusters}$, and a set of factors F.*

$$CTE(D_{clusters}, \ell, F) =$$
$$\bigcup_{\forall l \in \ell} \begin{cases} \forall v \in f, f \in F | STMM(D_{clusters_{f.value=v}}) & l = factor \\ STMM(D_{clusters}) & l = all \end{cases} \qquad (14)$$

Since CTE represent chains of transitions between clusters, the state in this chain is the cluster. The starting state frequency $StartStateFreq(a)$ therefore represents the frequency of a specific starting cluster a and the estimated size of the starting sequence according to $D_{cluster}$; a minor difference from the use of STMM in STE is that in CTE we preserve statistics for the mean number of sections per sequence, while in STE we preserve statistics for mean duration per sequence. In a similar manner, $StartTimeFreq(t)$ is the frequency of sequences starting at time t.

The transition frequency $Transition(a, b)$ represents the frequency of transitioning from cluster a to cluster b, as well as the estimated time between the starting times of subsequent sequences in these two clusters, according to $D_{cluster}$.

3.5   Anonymizing the Model

As stated in Definition 5, a method M realizes differential privacy if it provides the same output as it would have provided in the absence of each possible input record.

Denoting the source data as D and the same data with one less record as D', differential privacy applies the following constraint to each possible calculation:

$$\frac{Pr\,(M(D) = R)}{Pr\,(M(D') = R)} \leq e^{\varepsilon} \qquad (15)$$

Applying differential privacy in our method, therefore, requires that all calculations in the model maintain this constraint. The pertinent statistics in our basic STMM model are frequencies of starting states, starting times, and transitions. By maintaining a count alongside the frequencies, we can easily check whether a given statistic meets the constraint; this is done by dividing the current frequency with the frequency achieved by removing a single record (from both numerator and denominator). For example, if the frequency of transition $a \rightarrow b$ is 0.3, based on three occurrences of this transition out of 10 transitions from a elsewhere, we must check the following constraint:

$$\frac{Pr\,(transition(D) = a \rightarrow b)}{Pr\,(transition(D') = a \rightarrow b)} = \frac{3/10}{(3-1)/(10-1)} \leq e^{\varepsilon}$$

The ε parameter calibrates the amount of the permitted difference between calculations with and without a single record; using higher ε values permits a greater difference and therefore reduces the anonymity level. In the current example, the constraint is supplied for $\varepsilon = 0.4$, but it is not supplied for $\varepsilon = 0.3$. If the ε parameter is predefined as 0.3, the transition $a \rightarrow b$ is suppressed from the model, and statistics are normalized and checked for the differential privacy constraint again; this continues until no further suppressions are made.

3.6   Additional Statistics

Some additional statistics are maintained in order to facilitate the data generation process. First, a list is compiled that, for each date maintains the number of starting objects, as well as the number of sections (mean and standard deviation) that form a starting object on this date. Next, some generic mean and standard deviation statistics are maintained for state transition time, cluster transition time, and sequence duration, as well as starting hour frequencies which are also kept. These statistics are held without the enforcement of differential privacy; it is possible to anonymize these statistics, but our assumption is that they are not considered sensitive.

However, other statistics are maintained, in adherence with differential privacy. For the sake of "fixing" a transition whenever relevant parts in the model were suppressed during the anonymization process, we maintain frequencies of neighbors for states, as well as for clusters. By using these statistics we can reach an indirect neighbor whenever no direct neighbor was found in the model. The frequency for each pair of states is based on the number of sequences that contain these two states (although not necessarily successively). In a similar manner, for each pair of clusters, the frequency is based on the number of objects that are attached to these two clusters.

4   Synthetic Data Generator

Our anonymization method adopts the sanitization-based approach. It trains a model, based on the assumption that input objects share some common sequential patterns, and generates data accordingly. We use the source sequential dataset as an input, and deliver an equivalent anonymized data as the output. Statistics and patterns can then be extracted from the output using various queries. This approach imposes no limitations on the analyzing capabilities, as opposed to techniques that anonymize data mining results.

The generation process includes three main phases: (1) sampling the daily number of new starting objects; (2) sampling start and end times for each section in the object's sequence, as well as an attached cluster, which represents the general pattern for this section; (3) filling these time slots with a sequence of state and occurrence time pairs.

Since we deal with an ensemble of models, it is possible that relevant models lead to the sampling of different values. For example, sampling a starting state which has two factors in the model (weekday and hour), requires the combination of two models. If the current generation point is Monday at 6:00, then the starting state' frequencies of the 6:00 model should be combined with those of Monday's model. We use weighted means for combining matching values within the various relevant models.

In order to emphasize the effect of less common trends, we manipulate the weights so that models with lower support gain more weight. In our example, when the Wednesday model has the support of 20,000 transactions, and the 6:00 model has the support of 100 transactions, we give more weight to the latter, since in this example, 6:00 is more specific. The inversion of the weights is calculated as one divided by the support of each model, with an additional step of normalizing the inverted weights so that their total sum is one.

5   Performance Analysis

We consider both quality and anonymity of the synthesized data while evaluating our suggested method. We use two quality measures; the first is the distance between two sequential datasets as presented in Definition 4. This measures the mean similarity between each object in the anonymized data and its nearest object in the source data. The second measure is the intersection of the top 20 frequent patterns in the two compared datasets (only 2-gram patterns were considered, as a fast estimation).

Anonymity is measured as the mean support for statistics in the model. We also consider the percentage of suppressed records in the model in order to gain a deeper understanding of the trade-off between quality and anonymity.

We applied our proposed method to two tables of the MIMIC-III (Medical Information Mart for Intensive Care III) database [9], which is a large, freely-available database comprising de-identified health-related data associated with over 40,000 patients who stayed in critical care units at Beth Israel Deaconess Medical Center between 2001 and 2012. The $TRANSFERS$ table contains physical locations for patients throughout their hospital stay. The $CPTEVENTS$ table contains current procedural terminology (CPT) codes, which facilitate billing for procedures performed on patients. A sample of patient data from each of the tables was used to evaluate our method, as described in Table 1.

The described methods were implemented in R and ran using AWS (community AMI ID: ami-753e7c10; instance type: m4.xlarge). The number of clusters was set to 15 % of the number of sequences. Sequence duration, weekday, and day hour were predefined as factors that are considered when generating a sequence of states, and weekday, month, and year were predefined as factors that are considered when re-constructing a long sequence from shorter sections. The separation into shorter sections was conducted according to transition times of at least 16,800 h in the $TRANSFERS$ data, as described in Subsect. 3.3. In the $CPTEVENTS$ data which contains no valid data in the time dimension, a fabricated time dimension was calculated according to the order of procedures ($ticketID\_seq$); splitting by transition times is irrelevant in this case. We examined the performance of our suggested method under different privacy budgets (as set by the ε parameter), as well as under different settings of the LSH similarity measure (number of hash functions and shingle size). The anonymization

Table 1. Attributes of the experimental data

Dataset	Objects	Sequences	Max records per object	Records	States	Defined state
TRANSFERS	4,370	4,655	138	24,996	85	*curr_warid+ eventtype* (unit+ operation)
CPTEVENTS	3,171	3,171	116	25,000	117	*cpt_cd* (procedure)

process was repeated ten times for each combination of four different values of the ε parameter (0.05, 0.35, 0.65, and infinity), three possible numbers of hash functions (100, 250, and 500), and three different shingle sizes (1, 2, and 3). The main characteristics for each of the experimental data samples are described in Table 1, including the number of objects, sequences, records, and states for each sample, and the maximal number of records per object. The defined state is also described.

Figures 2 and 3 report the quality of the anonymized data according to two quality measures: mean distance and top frequent patterns intersection rate. These measures are described under various privacy budgets, as well as various settings of the LSH distance measure.

As illustrated in Fig. 2, the higher the privacy budget (the ε parameter) is, the lower the mean distance which is obtained, indicating that the anonymized data is more similar to the source data using higher privacy budgets. This mainly occurs since as anonymity demands become more restrictive, uncommon trends are suppressed, and the common trends remain quite similar to their source form. 90 to 100 % similarity was obtained for the *CPTEVENTS* data, where higher support for common patterns exists, and 76 to 81 % similarity for the *TRANSFERS* data, where there is more pattern variety. We also examined the influence of different settings of the LSH distance measure; this measure was used for measuring similarity between sequences in the clustering phase. One shingle was found to provide lower distance according to the Friedman test (at a 95 % significance level). No additional significant difference was found within the various examined settings.

As presented in Fig. 3, there is no clear trend of the frequent patterns intersection rate measure with regard to the increase in privacy budget (the ε parameter). Moreover, no significant differences in this measure were found within the various examined settings of the LSH distance measure.

Figures 4 and 5 report the anonymity of the generated data according to the mean support rate measure and examine the tradeoff between quality and anonymity according to the suppression rate measure. These measures are described under various privacy budgets (the ε parameter), as well as various settings of the LSH distance measure (number of hash functions and shingle size).

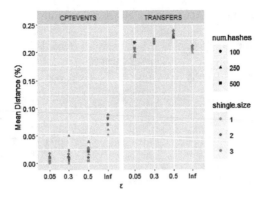

Fig. 2. Mean distances between source and anonymized data (y dimension) versus anonymity level as set by the ε parameter (x dimension) for the $CPTEVENTS$ and $TRANSFERS$ data (on the left and right, respectively). Three examined shingle sizes for the LSH distance measure are distinguished by color, and three examined number of hash functions used by the LSH are indicated by shape. One shingle was found to provide lower distance according to the Friedman test.

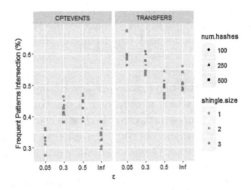

Fig. 3. Frequent patterns intersection rate between source and anonymized data (y dimension) versus anonymity level as set by the ε parameter (x dimension) for the $CPTEVENTS$ and $TRANSFERS$ data (on the left and right, respectively). Three examined shingle sizes for the LSH distance measure are distinguished by color, and three examined number of hash functions used by the LSH are indicated by shape.

As presented in Fig. 4, the higher the privacy budget (the ε parameter) is, the few records are suppressed. This demonstrates the tradeoff between anonymity and quality, since the suppression provides anonymity at the expense of damaging data quality. We also examined the influence of different settings of the LSH distance measure; smaller shingle sizes provides lower suppression rates; using 100 hash functions also decreases suppression rate. These findings are supported by Friedman tests (at a 95 % significance level).

As illustrated in Fig. 5, the higher the privacy budget (the ε parameter) is, the lower mean support is provided. This can be explained by the fact that as

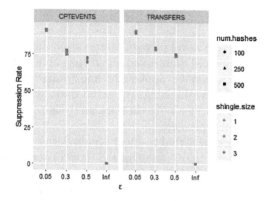

Fig. 4. Suppression rate between source and anonymized data (y dimension) versus anonymity level as set by the ε parameter (x dimension) for the $CPTEVENTS$ and $TRANSFERS$ data (on the left and right, respectively). Three examined shingle sizes for the LSH distance measure are distinguished by color, and three examined number of hash functions used by the LSH are indicated by shape. Lower shingle sizes, as well as smallest number of hash functions, were found to provide lower suppression rates.

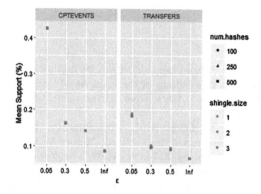

Fig. 5. Mean support between source and anonymized data (y dimension) versus anonymity level as set by the ε parameter (x dimension) for the $CPTEVENTS$ and $TRANSFERS$ data (on the left and right, respectively). Three examined shingle sizes for the LSH distance measure are distinguished by color, and three examined number of hash functions used by the LSH are indicated by shape. One shingle was found to provide higher mean support.

the privacy budget increases, less common trends (which tend to have lower support) influence. We also examined the influence of different settings of the LSH distance measure; one shingle provides higher mean support (supported by Friedman tests at a 95 % significance level).

6 Conclusions

In this paper, we proposed a novel privacy preservation approach for publishing differentially private sequential data based on an ensemble of Markovian models and demonstrated how it can be applied to anonymize medical events data. We designed a method for synthesizing sequential data, which allows published sequences to be used for a wider range of data analysis tasks, while preventing invasion or misuse of users' privacy.

Extensive experiments on actual medical events datasets demonstrated that our solution provides high quality anonymized data in terms of mean distance between the source and anonymized data. It also indicated that minimal performance demanding settings of the used similarity measure (one shingle and 100 hash functions) supply the best level of quality and anonymity, perhaps since using a more accurate distance measure results in less support for each pattern and increases the suppression rate.

Examining additional influencing factors such as patient attributes is essential in order to further improve the quality of the anonymized data and to refine our suggested method so it is applicable to additional datasets in the medical domain.

References

1. Bonomi, L., Xiong, L.: A two-phase algorithm for mining sequential patterns with differential privacy. In: Proceedings of the 22nd ACM International Conference on Conference on Information & Knowledge Management, CIKM 2013, pp. 269–278. ACM, New York (2013)
2. Broder, A.Z., Charikar, M., Frieze, A.M., Mitzenmacher, M.: Min-wise independent permutations. In: Proceedings of the Thirtieth Annual ACM Symposium on Theory of Computing, STOC 1998, pp. 327–336. ACM, New York (1998)
3. Chen, R., Acs, G., Castelluccia, C.: Differentially private sequential data publication via variable-length n-grams. In: Proceedings of the 2012 ACM Conference on Computer and Communications Security, CCS 2012, p. 638. ACM Press (2012)
4. Dwork, C.: Differential privacy. In: Bugliesi, M., Preneel, B., Sassone, V., Wegener, I. (eds.) ICALP 2006. LNCS, vol. 4052, pp. 1–12. Springer, Heidelberg (2006)
5. Dwork, C., McSherry, F., Nissim, K., Smith, A.: Calibrating noise to sensitivity in private data analysis. In: Halevi, S., Rabin, T. (eds.) TCC 2006. LNCS, vol. 3876, pp. 265–284. Springer, Heidelberg (2006)
6. Ghasemzadeh, M., Fung, B.C., Chen, R., Awasthi, A.: Anonymizing trajectory data for passenger flow analysis. Transp. Res. Part C: Emerg. Technol. **39**, 63–79 (2014)
7. Holzinger, A.: Interactive machine learning for health informatics: when do we need the human-in-the-loop? Brain Inform. **3**(2), 119–131 (2016)
8. Kieseberg, P., Malle, B., Frühwirt, P., Weippl, E., Holzinger, A.: A tamper-proof audit and control system for the doctor in the loop. Brain Inform. **3**, 1–11 (2016)
9. Lee, J., Scott, D.J., Villarroel, M., Clifford, G.D., Saeed, M., Mark, R.G.: Open-access MIMIC-II database for intensive care research. In: Conference Proceedings: Annual International Conference of the IEEE Engineering in Medicine and Biology Society, pp. 8315–8318 (2011)

10. de Montjoye, Y.A., Hidalgo, C.A., Verleysen, M., Blondel, V.D.: Unique in the Crowd: the privacy bounds of human mobility. Sci. Rep. **3**, 1376 (2013)
11. Pensa, R.G., Monreale, A., Pinelli, F., Pedreschi, D.: Pattern-preserving k-anonymization of sequences and its application to mobility data mining. In: CEUR Workshop Proceedings, vol. 397, pp. 44–60 (2008)
12. Samarati, P.: Protecting respondents identities in microdata release. IEEE Trans. Knowl. Data Eng. **13**(6), 1010–1027 (2001)

A Peer-to-Peer Protocol and System Architecture for Privacy-Preserving Statistical Analysis

Katerina Zamani, Angelos Charalambidis$^{(\boxtimes)}$, Stasinos Konstantopoulos,
Maria Dagioglou, and Vangelis Karkaletsis

Institute and Informatics and Telecommunications,
NCSR 'Demokritos', Agia Paraskevi, Greece
{kzam,acharal,konstant,mdagiogl,vangelis}@iit.demokritos.gr

Abstract. The insights gained by the large-scale analysis of health-related data can have an enormous impact in public health and medical research, but access to such personal and sensitive data poses serious privacy implications for the data provider and a heavy data security and administrative burden on the data consumer. In this paper we present an architecture that fills the gap between the statistical tools ubiquitously used in medical research on the one hand, and privacy-preserving data mining methods on the other. This architecture foresees the primitive instructions needed to re-implement the elementary statistical methods so that they only access data via a privacy-preserving protocol. The advantage is that more complex analysis and visualisation tools that are built upon these elementary methods can remain unaffected. Furthermore, we introduce RASSP, a secure summation protocol that implements the primitive instructions foreseen by the architecture. An open-source reference implementation of this architecture is provided for the R language. We use these results to argue that the tension between medical research and privacy requirements can be technically alleviated and we outline a research plan towards a system that covers further requirements on computation efficiency and on the trust that the medical researcher can place on the statistical results obtained by it.

Keywords: Privacy-preserving statistical analysis · Secure summation protocol · Statistical processing of health records

1 Introduction

The insights gained by the large-scale analysis of health-related data can have an enormous impact in public health and medical research, but access to such personal and sensitive data poses serious privacy implications for the data provider and a heavy data security and administrative burden on the data consumer. The discussion on what exactly it means to not disclose private data [4] and the

© IFIP International Federation for Information Processing 2016
Published by Springer International Publishing Switzerland 2016. All Rights Reserved
F. Buccafurri et al. (Eds.): CD-ARES 2016, LNCS 9817, pp. 236–250, 2016.
DOI: 10.1007/978-3-319-45507-5_16

discussion on policies for balancing between scientific advancement and privacy [7] are very relevant, but should be complemented by the equally relevant discussion of whether there is tension at all between data privacy and data-driven research. In other words, it is not straightforward if private data can be insulated from medical research workflows without compromising either.

As anonymization has been repeatedly proven to be inadequate [15], attention has turned to research in cryptography and distributed computation. These fields can provide methods for computing aggregates and statistics without revealing the specific data values involved in the computation, offering a much stronger guarantee of privacy than anonymization. However, from the perspective of the data mining practitioners and the medical researchers there is still a residue of functionality missing between their workflows over anonymized data and what is technically possible to achieve without accessing specific datapoints. Naturally, part of the workflow involves browsing data in order to formulate a hypothesis, and cannot possibly be performed over anything else but experimental data specifically collected and licensed to be shared. The scope of our discussion is, therefore, necessarily restricted to the data and processing required to empirically validate an already formulated hypothesis over a larger dataset than what can reasonably be made available to research.

To make this more concrete, we will assume use cases from *ambient assisted living (AAL)* environments. AAL covers a wide range of concepts, hardware and software products, and services that facilitate better, healthier and safer life outside formal health-care institutions. These environments emphasise the automatic collection of health data in one's own environment and the secure sharing of such data with medical care providers. In such a system, health data is shared between the following entities:

- The *AAL agent* that is the data management component of the AAL environment. The AAL agent has unrestricted access to its user's sensitive data. The management and security of the data held by the AAL agent is primarily within the scope of network security.
- The *health-care provider* that needs access to sensitive data of a small set of individuals on a need-to-know basis, depending on the medical condition that necessitates the monitoring of each individual. The management and security of the data held by the health-care provider is primarily within the scope of network security and access control.
- The *medical researcher* that needs access to aggregate values computed over the sensitive data of a large set of individuals, but does not need to know any specific individual's data. It is the data transfer protocols between this agent and the AAL agents that are within the scope of the work described here.

In the remainder of this paper, we first present the main approaches to privacy-preserving computation and discuss what requirements from our use case are not covered by the state of the art (Sect. 2). We then proceed to present a system architecture that exposes privacy-preserving computation functionality to tools (such as R) that are commonly used in medical research workflows (Sect. 3). We then present our peer-to-peer protocol that implements this privacy-preserving computation functionality based on the homomorphic property of composite secret sharing schemes (Sect. 4). We finally conclude and discuss future research direction (Sect. 5).

2   Related Work

We see in the literature three major approaches to privacy-preserving computation: *differential privacy*, *homomorphic encryption*, and *secure multiparty computation*. *Differential privacy* is based on the property that a result of a statistical value can be approximated even if random noise has been added to the data. *Homomorphic encryption* supports computations over cipher-texts, so that the result can be obtained without decrypting individual datapoints. Finally, *secure multiparty computation* is based on communication protocols between the agents to collaboratively compute a function over their private values without revealing the actual values.

Differential privacy preserves privacy by perturbing the datasets with randomized noise, such as symmetric exponential (Laplace) noise or with a use of a Geometric Distribution [18]. When the perturbed datasets are used in statistical analysis, knowledge of the distribution parameters of the noise applied allows approximating the analysis outcomes over the unperturbed data, but does not allow recovering any of the individual datapoints. To name an example, the PINQ data analysis platform [13] creates a differential privacy layer between the raw data and data analysis software. PINQ supplies the analyst with a set of transformations in operations like Where, Select, GroupBy and Join, in order to apply them to the data-set before applying operations for differential-privacy aggregations.

What should be noted about differential privacy is that it provides approximations and is only applicable where this is tolerated and where the datasets are large enough to allow for this approximation to be accurate enough for its purpose. In the analysis for medical data, it is often the case that datasets are not large enough to give tolerable error margins or that outliers can lead to important insights and should be highlighted rather than smoothed out.

The second major strain of privacy-aware computation protocols is based on *homomorphic cryptosystems*, cryptographic mechanisms with the property that certain operators (such as addition) can be computed directly within the encrypted space without requiring that the individual operands can be decrypted. One of the most prominent homomorphic cryptosystems is Paillier's cryptosystem [16], which allows computing the cipher of the sum of two numbers given the ciphers of these numbers. Paillier's cryptosystem requires that all numbers are encrypted using derivatives of the public part of a master key; these derivatives are such that they cannot decrypt the cipher of other derivative keys, but the master key can decrypt the cipher of the sum. This algorithmic basis can be extended to provide further numerical and categorical operators beyond summation; for example Kissner and Song [12] proposed an extension that supports union, intersection and element reduction.

Although data providers are perfectly protected from their peers, the main weakness of homomorphic systems is the trust that must be placed on the entity that issues the master key [10]. The typical summation protocol based on Paillier's cryptosystem has a master agent issue a master key and a number of data agents that exchange their encrypted values between them in order to send a total encrypted summation back to the master agent. Privacy from the master agent is only guaranteed by the fact the master agent only receives the cipher of the end-result. If the master agent colludes with one malicious data agent, they can use the private part of the master key to reveal the private value of the victim agent, the data agent that passes its encrypted data to the malicious agent.

To lift the requirement that the master agent must be trusted, Shi et al. [18] proposed a framework that can compute statistics on medical data with the use of an *untrusted* data aggregator, by encrypting values that can be decrypted with the sum of multiple cipher-texts under different user keys. Shi et al. propose a method where each agent encrypts periodically its data with its respective private key. The data of every agent includes its private value combined with white noise. The untrusted aggregator receives all the encrypted values from the agents and decrypts them with its private key and with the use of a correlation between the private keys of all agents and a specific hash function, that is based on the time series. The algorithm needs an initial trusted setup phase, which does not allow agents to join or leave the system dynamically. The proposed protocol is based on differential privacy and as an implication the resulted statistic is an approximation of the real one, which may cause problems in medical data. Moreover, as authors report, in order for their approach to work efficiently, the plain text space should be small.

There are many studies that combine their secure mechanism with the use of a trusted third party that works as the aggregator. In trusted third party protocols, there is an external trusted party which receives the private data of the agents and computes a function by using them. Hanmanthu et al. [5] propose an enhanced protocol that combines a technique which perturbs distributed data with the use of a third party. Specifically, they define a protocol for constructing a Naive Bayes classifier. In this protocol, each agent encrypts its perturbed data with its private key and sends it to a trusted third party. The trusted third party decrypts this data with the public key of the respective agent and constructs a perturbed Naive Bayes Classifier. Moreover, there are some studies that combine *secure multiparty computation (SMC)* systems with a trusted third party. Generally speaking, an SMC system deals with the computation of any function with any input in a distributed network, where the involved agents can learn only the total result and their own input. Thus, a common strategy to ensure trustworthiness is the use of a trusted third party. Ajmani et al. [1] present TEP, a trusted third party computation service that maintains generality. TEP offers flexibility because it fits in many SMC applications to guarantee privacy. However, this type of mechanism requires the existence of a trusted third party, so is inherently weaker than purely peer-to-peer networks.

Nevertheless, Sheikh et al. [17] proposed a SMC system that applies a secure summation protocol without the use of a trusted third party. The proposed protocol focuses on the increased computation complexity to avoid hacking. Each agent splits its data to a fixed number of segments and promotes a single segment to the next agent at each iteration. As an extension Sheikh et al. [17] define a master agent, which sets a random number during the initialization. Despite the fact that this protocol does not utilize a third trusted party, it is weak because if two neighbour agents collude, they can reveal the data value of the middle agent. Moreover, this technique imposes a considerable overhead in the communication between the agents.

Many recent research studies focus on privacy preserving on vertical and on horizontal partition of data. Our approach is oriented to horizontally distributed data, as each AAL agent keeps a private database with its values and each database contains the same set of attributes. Specifically, Karr et al. [8] propose a secure computation of linear regression for horizontally partitioned data without the use of a trusted third party. This is achieved by converting the linear regression equation to a summation form, where the quantities of each summation involve attribute values of the same agency. To protect data from the scope of the source and the values, they propose a SMC secure sum computation protocol. During the initialization of the protocol, a master agent adds his private value with a random number, that he previously produced, and forwards the summed value to the next agent. Each agent receives the aggregated value from the previous agent and forwards it to the neighbor agent, after the addition of his private value. The total summation result is returned back to the master agent, which removes his random number. This protocol is weak mostly because a private value of an agent can be revealed by the collusion of his neighbors. Also due to the circular mode of the algorithm, it can not be parallelised.

The study of Molina et al. [14] is closer to our approach. Specifically, they propose an application of homomorphic encryption to compute basic statistics on aggregated medical data which also guarantee the privacy of the medical data. Their SMC protocol preserves the privacy between the caregivers, where each one computes statistics for their corresponding patients. This is achieved with a double encryption, each one depending on a different public key — the public key of researcher and the public key of a caregiver chosen randomly to work as the aggregator. This approach can be mapped well in distributed systems because each caregiver can work in parallel to compute aggregates of their patients' data. However, privacy is relatively weak as the researcher and the aggregator can collude to reveal the plaintexts of each caregiver. Moreover, doubly homomorphic encryption schemes are not fully explored to define which statistics can be determined.

3   Privacy-Preserving Statistical Analysis

In this section we introduce our system architecture, and show how elementary statistical analysis methods can be implemented within this architecture in a way that essentially preserves the API of their conventional implementation. As a showcase, we assume the R language implementation of the t-test and show how the same interface can be implemented within our privacy-preserving architecture instead of by directly accessing data matrices. As the architecture assumes the existence of a privacy-preseving summation protocol to access the private data, we also discuss what characteristics are required from this protocol.

3.1   System Architecture

The system architecture can be perceived as a stack of three layers and each layer depends on the functionality provided from the layer at the lower stage. The upper layer, called the *Medical Researcher's interface*, accepts from the medical researcher the method with the initial parameters to be executed by the system. The purpose of this interface is to provide a familiar environment to the researcher and therefore in our current implementation this layer is developed in the R language. The initial parameters are transformed appropriately in order to be passed to the next layer, which is the *Compilation Layer*. At that stage, the high-level parameters and commands of the statistical method are transformed into low-level instruction for accessing the private databases of the agents. An instruction represents an aggregation over a selection of data. Currently, the aggregation operation is summation. However, the aggregations that are on one hand feasible by the system and on the other hand safe for preserving privacy depend on the secure protocol used. These instructions will be eventually evaluated by the lowest layer of the architecture, the *Privacy Protocol Layer*. Figure 1 depicts the system architecture and the information exchanged between the layers.

The Medical Researcher's Interface. The interface is developed in the R language since it offers a variety of plotting and analysis tools, while in parallel it is a familiar environment for statisticians. The researchers can execute the statistical method through the R environment by importing the *secure statistics* library. The purpose of this library is to expose high-level statistic methods (e.g. linear regression, t-test) as R functions.

The *secure statistics* library receive the same arguments as the conventional statistics functions in R. The only difference is that the data arguments are not matrices of values, but the parameters needed to make a distributed computation. The results of the statistics functions are, then, identical to those of the respective conventional functions over the same data.

The Compilation Layer. This layer is responsible for the communication between the two other layers. Specifically, it translates the arguments of the *secure statistic* to a suitable format, thus it defines the appropriate data that are going to be used for the statistic computation. Moreover, it converts the simple statistic equations to a set of summations; a compatible format to achieve the secure summation protocol. Therefore, a set of instructions is composed

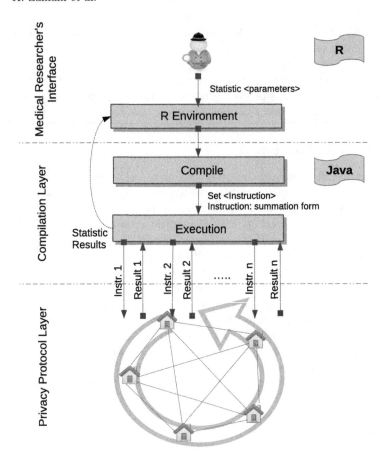

Fig. 1. The system's architecture

where each instruction represents a summation equation of the statistic with the appropriate parameters set for its computation. During the execution, the compilation layer gives to the privacy protocol layer a single instruction at a time and it receives its result. After the execution of the whole set, it computes the statistic and the analysis parameters. The statistic result is sent back to the Medical Researcher's interface layer.

The Aggregation Protocol. This layer executes the privacy protocol between the AAL agents, To deal with the concurrent computation of each instruction, we model our agents as actors. Each actor makes the appropriate computations with respect to the given instruction and its private data. These computations can easily be done since every AAL agent controls its corresponding health records. After the computation of the value, which represents the initial secret, the privacy protocol is executed. The protocol may involve all the actors to work collaboratively in order to compute the aggregation of their secrets without revealing the actual secrets to each other or the agent requesting the aggregation. The aggregated result is collected a designated actor. The selection of such actor is irrelevant and can be done randomly. Our proposed implementation for this layer is presented in more detail in Sect. 4.

Example. We will use a simple example to better demonstrate the proposed system. Suppose that a medical researcher needs to run a t-test to assess whether the means of two groups are statistically different from each other, that is to compute t in Eq. 1:

$$t = \frac{\bar{X} - \bar{Y}}{\sqrt{|X|^{-1}\sigma_X^2 + |Y|^{-1}\sigma_Y^2}} \tag{1}$$

where X and Y are the datapoints of the two groups, $\bar{X}$ and $\bar{Y}$ are their means, $|X|$ and $|Y|$ are their cardinalities, and σ_X^2 and σ_Y^2 their variances.

Assume, for instance, that a researcher wants to test the effect of medicine M_1 (Group 1) and medicine M_2 (Group 2) on blood pressure, with the further restriction that participants in Group 2 should be above 65 years old. A workflow using the R language would be:

- Select from a database the instances that match Group 1 criteria and store them in variable X
- Select from a database the instances that match Group 2 criteria and store them in variable Y
- Decide on the conditions of the T-test, such as the confidence level and alternation, and store them in variable C
- Pass X, Y, C as arguments to an implementation of t-test

Our architecture allows this workflow to remain essentially unaffected, except for the contents of X and Y. Instead of holding actual data arrays these now contain a representation of the Group 1 and Group 2 criteria, so that the selection can be executed in distributed manner. Using this representation, a privacy-aware implementation of t-test can produce the exact same result as the conventional implementation, except without ever accessing any individual data.

This representation declares a list of dependent variables and a list of eligibility criteria of the sample groups, as a set of (variable, operator, value) tuples. In our example, we assign to X and Y the criteria that we would have used to assign to them a value array if we had full access to the data:

- $X = [(\text{"medicine"}, =, \text{"M}_1\text{"})]$
- $Y = [(\text{"medicine"}, =, \text{"M}_2\text{"}), (\text{"age"}, >, \text{"65"})]$

The compilation layer converts the t-test implementation into a set of instructions. Recall that each instruction is an aggregation over the private data of each agent, under the given selection restrictions. Table 1 defines the instructions needed to implement the t-test (Eq. 1), which is then implemented using the following pseudo-code:

Table 1. Characteristic instructions provided by the RASSP Protocol.

Function	Definition
$\text{add}(C)$	$\sum_i s_i(C)$, where $s_i(C)$ is the secret value of the i-th AAL agent if condition C is satisfied, 0 otherwise
$\text{add}^2(C, k)$	$\sum_i (s_i(C) + k)^2$, where k is a constant and $s_i(C)$ is same as above
$\text{cnt}(C)$	$\sum_i c_i(C)$, where $c_i(C)$ is 1 if the i-th AAL agent satisfies condition C, 0 otherwise

1. $X = [(\text{"medicine"}, =, \text{"M}_1\text{"})];$
   X is a representation of the secret values of all AAL agents where medicine M_1 is used.
2. $Y = [(\text{"medicine"}, =, \text{"M}_1\text{"}), (\text{"age"}, >, \text{"65"})];$
   Y is a representation of the secret values of all AAL agents where medicine M_2 is used and age is above 65.
3. $N_1 = \text{add}(X); N_2 = \text{add}(Y);$
   N_1 is the sum of the secret values X and N_2 is the sum of the secret values Y.
4. $C_1 = \text{cnt}(X); C_2 = \text{cnt}(Y);$
   C_1 is the number of AAL agents with non-zero values in X and C_2 is the number of AAL agents with non-zero values in Y.
5. $\bar{X} = N_1/C_1; \bar{Y} = N_2/C_2;$
   This uses the values above to calculate means.
6. $\sigma_X^2 = \text{add}^2(X, -\bar{X}); \sigma_Y^2 = \text{add}^2(Y, -\bar{Y});$
   This uses the values above to calculate variances.
7. $T = (\bar{X} - \bar{Y}) / \text{sqroot}(\sigma_X^2/C_1 + \sigma_Y^2/C_2);$

Each instruction is executed with the use of the secure summation protocol, obtaining the aggregate values specified in the instruction without obtaining the values themselves. From the perspective of the R interface user, the t-test functions operate as if they had been passed the actual value matrices as parameters.

3.2   Reference Implementation

The system architecture that is described in Sect. 3.1 is implemented by the open source project at https://bitbucket.org/dataengineering/rassp

The project's source code is organized in three modules, each one implementing one of the layers in our architecture:

- proto implements the *aggregation protocol*
- stats is the implementation of statistical analysis primitives over an aggregation protocol, and implements the *compilation layer*
- RStats implements the R interface for the medical researcher over the compilation layer.

To execute the example immediately above using our implementation, the medical researcher executes the following code in the R interface:

```
# Describe the two groups in GroupStat structures:
group1 <- GroupStat(list(c("med","=","A")))
group2 <- GroupStat(list(c("med","=","B"), c("age",">","65")))
# Set dependent variables and groups in a Parameters structure:
p <- Parameters(list("bloodPr"), list(group1, group2))
# Execute the normal t-test using the Parameters structure p:
ttest(p, varEq=TRUE)
```

What is important to note in the example is that our implementation of the `ttest()` function presents an interface identical to the standard R implementation of the t-test. The underlying difference is that the `Parameters` structure does not point to actual data matrices but to instances of our `GroupStat` structure, which hold the information needed by the compilation layer in order to distribute the computation to the participating nodes.

3.3 Discussion

The proposed system architecture assumes that:

- The statistical analysis that is to be carried out can be implemented using the set of aggregation instructions provided by the aggregation protocol. In other words the algorithm should not depend on individual data points.
- A summation protocol exists that guarantees privacy.

The first assumption holds, since the most commonly used class of data mining algorithms can be expressed as an iteration of summation expressions [9]. If needed, categorical operators can be implemented based on summation [12].

Regarding the second assumption, we will now proceed to discuss the summation protocols that can be used in our architecture and, in Sect. 4, present the protocol we use in our reference implementation of the architecture.

Most of the related studies guarantee their privacy by utilising encryption or differential privacy techniques. These approaches do not fit in our problem, because we deal with medical history data that are distributed across AAL agents. In homomorphic techniques, a *master agent* shares a public key with the rest of the agents, in order to encrypt their data, and keeps a private key for the final decryption. Such a mechanism is privately weak in the case of collaborative computations, because if the medical researcher (master agent) and one AAL agent collude, they can learn another AAL agent's private value. This makes the technical protocol weak, as it places a heavy burden on non-technical policies and protocols to guarantee the integrity of the medical researcher. Since our main aim is to alleviate the need for non-technical policies and protocols and to make it easier for medical researchers to run statistics over datapoint they are not meant to access directly, homomorphism encryption does not cover our requirements.

In addition, differential privacy is also not applicable, from both the perspective of the medical researcher as well as from that of the AAL agent. From the perspective of the medical researcher, differential privacy computes *approximations*, which can be a problem as discussed in Sect. 2 above. From the perspective of the AAL agent, the secret value can be approximated by its repeated querying, since a different perturbation of the real secret needs to be computed for each query. The AAL agent cannot produce a single perturbed value and use this for all queries, since it needs to be re-computed to follow the distribution parameters requested by the medical researcher. This might be less of a problem in time-series data (such as power grid data or traffic data), but can result in substantial information leaking in static historical data, such as health records.

4   The Secure Summation Protocol

4.1   Background

Secret sharing schemes divide a secret into many *shares* which can be distributed to n mutually suspicious agents. The initial secret can be revealed if any k of these n agents combine their shares. We will call such schemes, (k, n)-threshold schemes. If such a scheme also possesses the *homomorphism* property, then multiple secrets can be combined by direct computation only on the shares. Such schemes are usually called *composite secret sharing schemes* [2].

More specifically, assume n mutually suspicious agents and each agent holds a secret s_i. The desired computation is combination into a super-secret s under an operation $\oplus$, namely $s = s_1 \oplus \cdots \oplus s_n$. Using a secret sharing scheme each s_i can be split into k shares $d_{i_1}, \ldots, d_{i_k}$ such that given a known function F_I it is the case that:

$$s_i = F_I(d_{i_1}, \ldots d_{i_k})$$

We will say the (k, n) threshold scheme has the $(\oplus, \otimes)$-homomorphism property if whenever $s = F_I(d_1, \ldots, d_k)$ and $s' = F_I(d'_1, \ldots d'_k)$ then

$$s \oplus s' = F_I(d_1 \otimes d'_1, \ldots, d_k \otimes d'_k)$$

The composition of the shares d_1, d'_1 yield a *super-share* $d_1 \otimes d'_1$. In other words, the $(\oplus, \otimes)$-homomorphism property implies that the composition of the shares under the operator $\otimes$ are shares of the composition under the operator $\oplus$.

Overall, the advantage of having a composite secret sharing scheme is that secret cannot be obtained, only if k or more agents collude and combine their sub-shares. In addition, this protocol is suitable to our approach from the AAL agent's point of view, because it does not use a trusted third party or depends on cryptographic assumptions, while at the same time it is k-secure. This approach represents a secure summation protocol that can easily be applied to collaborative agent systems.

Based on this mathematical foundation, we will now proceed to present the RASSP protocol, a $(+, +)$-homophorphic composite secret sharing scheme.

4.2 The RASSP Protocol

Assume that we have n AAL agents, where each one has its private value $v_i, i \in [1..n]$. Each AAL produces random breakdown of v_i into n terms $r_{ij}, j = 1..n$ such that $v_i = \sum_{j=1}^{n} r_{ij}$. These terms are computed by first producing $n - 1$ random terms $r_{ij}, j = 1..i - 1, i + 1..n$ and then setting

$$r_{ii} = v_i - \sum_{j \in [1..n] - \{i\}} r_{ij}$$

The r_{ij} terms are called *sub-shares* and are (except for r_{ii}) shared with the rest of the AAL agents, one per agent. In this manner, each AAL agent shares $n - 1$ values and receives $n-1$ values from the rest of the AAL agents. The *super-share* Y_i for each agent is defined as:

$$Y_i = r_{ii} + \sum_{k \in [1..n] - \{i\}} r_{ki} \tag{2}$$

Notice how the super-share of AAL agent i is the sum of the sub-share that it has not shared and of all the sub-shares that it has received from the other AAL agents. Finally, we define a function F_I as the sum of the super-shares:

$$F_I(Y_1, \ldots, Y_n) = \sum_{i=1}^{n} Y_i \tag{3}$$

It is straightforward to verify that $F_I(Y_1, \ldots, Y_n)$ is equal to the sum of all secrets. It is also straightforward to verify that only random numbers and obscured data values are shared between AAL agents and between AAL agents the researcher. Notice also that only if $(n - 1)$ AAL agents collude to merge their sub-shares can the private value of the n-th agent be revealed. Therefore, our system guarantees $(n - 1)$-security.

Figure 2 gives an example of the above description for a system of three AAL agents. In this example House1 has the private value v_1 and produces three numbers: r_{11}, r_{12}, r_{13}. Then, it shares r_{12} and r_{13} with House2 and House3, keeping r_{11} hidden. House1 receives two numbers (r_{21}, r_{31}) from the other AAL agents. In then shares the computed Y_1, so that F_I can be computed by summing all Y_i. $F_I(Y_1, Y_2, Y_3)$ computes the sum of all three AAL agents' secret values.

The described secure summation protocol is suitable for computing medical statistics and preserve privacy at the same time. The only constraint is that the resulted outcome is a sum of the private values, thus the statistic equations should be converted in a summation form. The summation form results in accurate values and not approximations, while simultaneously it can easily be parallelised [3]. Besides, medical researchers typically use descriptive statistics which utilise numerical descriptors such as mean and standard deviation. These descriptors can easily be converted into a summation form, thus they can be computed by our system.

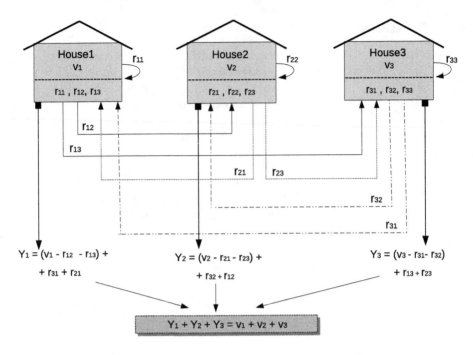

Fig. 2. The RASSP secure summation protocol.

5   Conclusions and Further Work

With this paper we experiment with privacy-preserving data mining that is accessed not through specialized APIs and tools, but through statistical analysis tools that are ubiquitous in data-driven research, such as the R language and its statistical analysis libraries. In this manner, we are targeting the uptake of our privacy-preservation infrastructure by the medical research community, as the discussion around privacy preservation is mute if the data cannot be efficiently and effectively used to achieve the medical research purpose.

Specifically, our first contribution is our architecture and its reference implementation. This architecture foresees the primitive *instructions* needed to reimplement the elementary statistical methods so that they only access data via a privacy-preserving protocol. The overall gist is that function arguments remain the same, except for substituting data matrices with a specification of how to select the data that each AAL agent will contribute to the distributed computation. The advantage is that more complex analysis and visualisation tools that are built upon these elementary methods can remain unaffected by replacing direct access to data with access via privacy-preserving protocols.

A further contribution is our review of *secure multiparty computation*, *differential privacy*, and *homomorphic encryption* approaches to justify and explain assuming the former as the most appropriate basis for our personal health record use case. Finally, we introduce RASSP, a secure summation protocol that computes sums within Benaloh's *composite secret sharing* framework for secure multiparty computation.

More complex instructions will be implemented as iterations of the primitive sum operator. As this is bound to reduce the run-time efficiency of the system, our next steps will be to integrate distributed computation concepts in order to parallelise the computation. Chu et al. [3] propose using the map-reduce framework to execute a variety of statistics, where the summation form of their equations facilitates the distribution of their calculations. This approach will be mapped to our architecture to improve the run-time efficiency of the system. A further optimization step will be to execute simultaneously instructions when there is no dependence between them. To achieve this, we will transfer from the programming languages and distributed computation literature optimization methods that can decide about the most efficient execution plan for a given program with multiple calls to the primitive instructions. We will also need to extend the current API of these instructions in order to allow multiple requests to be made to the distributed AAL agents with one network transaction.

Another relevant on-going discussion in the community is the involvement of humans in the data mining process itself [6] and when acting upon data mining results [11]. Given the responsibility of the medical practitioner when using data to make medical decisions, the uptake of our—and, in fact, any—privacy preserving protocol depends on the data consumers' ability to apply checks and bounds to the values that are allowed to participate in the computation. In this context, a more ambitious goal is to extend the RASSP protocol so that the medical researcher can specify what value ranges of the secret variables are reasonable or useful and to have this range restriction guaranteed without having to trust the AAL agents. To achieve this, we will experiment with variations of the current RASSP protocol where the AAL agents can to some extend also check whether their peers are (erroneously or maliciously) sharing sub-shares that add up to out-of-range values. Since such AAL agent behaviour can corrupt the result or obscure useful outliers, it undermines the trust that the researcher places on the result. Our goal is to devise a system of cross-checks that makes it unlikely that out-of-range values contribute to the sum undetected, but without compromising the privacy-preserving nature of the protocol.

Acknowledgements. The work described here was carried out in the context of the RADIO project. This project has received funding from the European Union's Horizon 2020 research and innovation programme under grant agreement No 643892. For more details, please visit the RADIO Web site http://www.radio-project.eu

References

1. Ajmani, S., Morris, R., Liskov, B.: A trusted third-party computation service. Technical report, MIT-LCS-TR-847, MIT (2001)
2. Benaloh, J.C.: Secret sharing homomorphisms: keeping shares of a secret secret. In: Odlyzko, A.M. (ed.) CRYPTO 1986. LNCS, vol. 263, pp. 251–260. Springer, Heidelberg (1987)

3. Chu, C., Kim, S.K., Lin, Y.A., Yu, Y., Bradski, G., Ng, A.Y., Olukotun, K.: Map-reduce for machine learning on multicore. In: Schölkopf, B., Platt, J.C., Hoffman, T. (eds.) Advances in Neural Information Processing Systems 19: Proceedings of the 21st Annual Conference on Neural Information Processing Systems (NIPS 2007), Vancouver, BC, Canada, pp. 281–288. MIT Press, 3-5 December 2007

4. Clifton, C., Kantarcioglu, M., Vaidya, J.: Defining privacy for data mining. In: Proceedings of the National Science Foundation Workshop on Next Generation Data Mining, Baltimore, USA, 1–3 November 2002

5. Hanmanthu, B., Ram, B.R., Niranjan, P.: Third party privacy preserving protocol for perturbation based classification of vertically fragmented data bases (2013). arXiv preprint arXiv:1304.6575

6. Holzinger, A.: Interactive machine learning for health informatics: when do we need the human-in-the-loop? Brain Inform. 3(2), 119–131 (2016)

7. Horvitz, E., Mulligan, D.: Data, privacy, and the greater good. Sci. Mag. 349, 253–255 (2015)

8. Karr, A.F., Lin, X., Sanil, A.P., Reiter, J.P.: Secure regression on distributed databases. J. Comput. Graph. Stat. 14(2), 263–279 (2005)

9. Kearns, M.: Efficient noise-tolerant learning from statistical queries. J. ACM (JACM) 45(6), 983–1006 (1998)

10. Kerschbaum, F.: Privacy-preserving computation. In: Preneel, B., Ikonomou, D. (eds.) APF 2012. LNCS, vol. 8319, pp. 41–54. Springer, Heidelberg (2014)

11. Kieseberg, P., Malle, B., Frühwirt, P., Weippl, E., Holzinger, A.: A tamper-proof audit and control system for the doctor in the loop. Brain Inform. 1–11 (2016)

12. Kissner, L., Song, D.: Privacy-preserving set operations. In: Shoup, V. (ed.) CRYPTO 2005. LNCS, vol. 3621, pp. 241–257. Springer, Heidelberg (2005)

13. McSherry, F.D.: Privacy integrated queries: an extensible platform for privacy-preserving data analysis. In: Proceedings of the 2009 ACM SIGMOD International Conference on Management of data (SIGMOD 2009), pp. 19–30. ACM (2009)

14. Molina, A.D., Salajegheh, M., Fu, K.: HICCUPS: health information collaborative collection using privacy and security. In: Proceedings of the First ACM Workshop on Security and Privacy in Medical and Home-Care Systems (SPIMACS 2009), pp. 21–30. ACM (2009)

15. Ohm, P.: Broken promises of privacy: responding to the surprising failure of anonymization. UCLA Law Rev. 57, 1701 (2010)

16. Paillier, P.: Public-key cryptosystems based on composite degree residuosity classes. In: Stern, J. (ed.) EUROCRYPT 1999. LNCS, vol. 1592, pp. 223–238. Springer, Heidelberg (1999)

17. Sheikh, R., Kumar, B., Mishra, D.K.: Privacy preserving k secure sum protocol (2009). arXiv preprint arXiv:0912.0956

18. Shi, E., Chan, T.H., Rieffel, E., Chow, R., Song, D.: Privacy-preserving aggregation of time-series data. In: Proceedings of the 18th Annual Network and Distributed System Security Symposium (NDSS 2011), vol. 2, pp. 1–17 (2011)

The Right to Be Forgotten: Towards Machine Learning on Perturbed Knowledge Bases

Bernd Malle[1,2], Peter Kieseberg[1,2], Edgar Weippl[2], and Andreas Holzinger[1(✉)]

[1] Holzinger Group HCI-KDD, Institute for Medical Informatics,
Statistics and Documentation, Medical University Graz, Graz, Austria
{b.malle,a.holzinger}@hci-kdd.org
[2] SBA Research gGmbH, Favoritenstrae 16, 1040 Vienna, Austria
PKieseberg@sba-research.org

Abstract. Today's increasingly complex information infrastructures represent the basis of any data-driven industries which are rapidly becoming the 21st century's economic backbone. The sensitivity of those infrastructures to disturbances in their knowledge bases is therefore of crucial interest for companies, organizations, customers and regulating bodies. This holds true with respect to the direct provisioning of such information in crucial applications like clinical settings or the energy industry, but also when considering additional insights, predictions and personalized services that are enabled by the automatic processing of those data. In the light of new EU Data Protection regulations applying from 2018 onwards which give customers the right to have their data deleted on request, information processing bodies will have to react to these changing jurisdictional (and therefore economic) conditions. Their choices include a re-design of their data infrastructure as well as preventive actions like anonymization of databases per default. Therefore, insights into the effects of perturbed/anonymized knowledge bases on the quality of machine learning results are a crucial basis for successfully facing those future challenges. In this paper we introduce a series of experiments we conducted on applying four different classifiers to an established dataset, as well as several distorted versions of it and present our initial results.

Keywords: Machine learning · Knowledge bases · Right to be forgotten · Perturbation · Anonymization · k-anonymity · SaNGreeA · Information loss · Structural loss · Cost weighing vector · Interactive machine learning

1 Introduction and Motivation for Research

Privacy aware machine learning [6] is an issue of increasing importance, fostered by anonymization concepts like k-anonymity [14], in which a record is

© IFIP International Federation for Information Processing 2016
Published by Springer International Publishing Switzerland 2016. All Rights Reserved
F. Buccafurri et al. (Eds.): CD-ARES 2016, LNCS 9817, pp. 251–266, 2016.
DOI: 10.1007/978-3-319-45507-5_17

released only if it is indistinguishable from k other entities in the data set. However, k-anonymity is highly dependent on spatial locality in order to effectively implement the technique in a statistically robust way, and in arbitrarily high dimensions data becomes sparse, hence, the concept of spatial locality is not easy to define. Consequently, it becomes difficult to anonymize the data without an unacceptably high amount of information loss [1]. Therefore, the problem of k-anonymization is on the one hand NP-hard, on the other hand the quality of the result obtained can be measured at the given factors: *k-anonymity* means that attributes are suppressed or generalized until each row in a database is identical with at least $k-1$ other rows [15]; *l-diversity* as extension of the k-anonymity model reduces the granularity of the data representation by generalization and suppression so that any given record maps onto at least k other records in the data [12]; *t-closeness* is a refinement of l-diversity by reducing the granularity of a data representation, and treating the values of an attribute distinctly by taking into account the distribution of data values for that attribute [11]; and *delta-presence*, which links the quality of anonymization to the risk posed by inadequate anonymization [13], but not with regard to the actual security of the data, i.e., the re-identification through an attacker. For this purpose, certain assumptions about the background knowledge of the hypothetical enemy must be made. In this work, we are going to measure the effects of the anonymization of knowledge bases on the performance of machine learning algorithms in order to give valuable feedback to data holders and anonymization providers.

Another challenge for data processing entities is increasingly imposed on them by the law. At least within the European Union, where a new Data Protection Reform will apply from 2018 onwards, customers are given a *right to be forgotten*, which means that an organization is obligated to remove a customer's personal data upon request. Since information in a modern, data driven infrastructure is not only usable for the customer herself, but also constitutes the basis for machine learning algorithms providing better insights and services, this information loss might be problematic, if only in competition with companies/organizations which do not fall under such jurisdiction. The ability to quantify the effects of information loss by erasure of sensitive data is therefore of great importance and the other core focus of our work.

2   Scenarios of Incurring Information Loss in Datasets

2.1   Selective Perturbation

Within a modern information infrastructure, several layers of data storage and processing might be affected by the *right to be forgotten*. The first and probably most benign impact would be the one on so-called *Front-End* databases; those are customer-facing databases on the backend which handle the bulk of day-to-day data transmissions and contain the customer's data in full detail. Erasing a data entry from this Front-end is therefore simple and of manageable consequences.

The second layer impacted by data erasure are archival and backup systems, which are necessary in case of failures on the Front-end. Although data erasure does not pose any technical problem here either, it is necessary to consider it on an organizational level in order to not inadvertently re-introducing already "forgotten" items.

Significant problems are to be expected when executing selective data erasure on statistical databases or knowledge bases prepared for machine-learning. Both kinds of DBs will usually not hold the original user information but merely statistically relevant fragments of it; this difficulty is compounded by the fact that in many cases it might not be technically necessary to even store a link to the original data. In such cases is it not only impossible to delete the relevant fragments from such data stores (not to mention the statistical/parametric results obtained by algorithms working on them), but the whole databases might have to be recreated upon every user deletion request. It is therefore absolutely crucial to have an insight into the results of potential data perturbation, if only to be able to redesign (parts of) an information infrastructure.

2.2 Tabular Anonymization

Figure 1 illustrates the original tabular concept of anonymization: Given an input table with several columns, we will in all probability encounter three different categories of data:

- **Personal identifiers** are data items which directly identify a person without having to cross-reference or further analyze them. Examples are first and last names, but even more so an (email) address or social security number (SSN). As personal identifiers are dangerous and cannot be generalized (see Fig. 2) in a meaningful way (e.g. one could generalize an email address by only retaining the mail provider fragment, but the result would not yield much usable information), this category of data is usually removed. The table shows this column in a red background color.
- **Sensitive data,** also called 'payload', which is the kind of data we want to convey for statistics or research purposes. Examples for this category would be disease classification, drug intake or personal income level. This data shall be preserved in the anonymized dataset and can therefore not be deleted or generalized. The table shows this column in a green background color.
- **Quasi identifiers (QI's),** colored in the table with an orange background, are data that in themselves do not directly reveal the identity of a person, but might be used in aggregate to reconstruct it. For instance, [16] mentioned that 87 % of U.S. citizens in 2002 had reported characteristics that made them vulnerable to identification based on just the 3 attributes *zip code, gender* and *date of birth*. But although this data can be harmful in that respect, it might also hold vital information for the purpose of research (e.g. zip code could be of high value in a study on disease spread). The actual point of all anonymization efforts is therefore to generalize this kind of information, which means to lower its level of granularity. As an example, one could generalize the ZIP codes 41074, 41075 and 41099 to an umbrella version 410**, as shown in Fig. 3.

Name	Age	Zip	Gender	Disease
Alex	25	41076	Male	Allergies
...	...	...	...	...

Fig. 1. The three types of data considered in (k-)anonymization

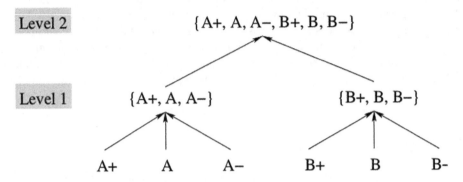

Figure 1: A possible generalization hierarchy for the attribute "Quality".

Fig. 2. Example of a typical generalization hierarchy

As described in [5], k-anonymization requires that in each data release every combination of values of quasi-identifiers must be identical to at least $k - 1$ other entries in that release, which can be seen as a clustering problem with each cluster's (also called *equivalence class*) quasi-identifier state being identical for every data point. This can be achieved via suppression and generalization, where suppression means simply deletion, whereas in generalization we try to retain some usable value.

The process of generalization works through a concept called *generalization hierarchies*, which form a tree, whose root denotes the most general value available for an attribute (usually the 'all' value) and then branches to more and more specific occurrences, with its leafs representing the set of exact, original values (see Fig. 2). In generalizing the original input value, one traverses the tree from the leaf level upwards until a prerequisite is fulfilled. Usually, this comes in the form of the k-anonymity requirement, so that we want to find a group of other data entries whose generalized QI's match the data point being processed.

Each level of generalization involves a certain cost in information loss, so we do not want to construct our clusters in any random sequence but minimize the overall information loss [2]. This makes k-anonymization an NP-hard problem due to an exponential number of possible generalized QI combinations.

Node	Name	Age	Zip	Gender	Disease
X1	Alex	25	41076	Male	Allergies
X2	Bob	25	41075	Male	Allergies
X3	Charlie	27	41076	Male	Allergies
X4	Dave	32	41099	Male	Diabetes
X5	Eva	27	41074	Female	Flu
X6	Dana	36	41099	Female	Gastritis
X7	George	30	41099	Male	Brain Tumor
X8	Lucas	28	41099	Male	Lung Cancer
X9	Laura	33	41075	Female	Alzheimer

Node	Age	Zip	Gender	Disease
X1	25-27	4107*	Male	Allergies
X2	25-27	4107*	Male	Allergies
X3	25-27	4107*	Male	Allergies
X4	30-36	41099	*	Diabetes
X5	27-33	410**	*	Flu
X6	30-36	41099	*	Gastritis
X7	30-36	41099	*	Brain Tumor
X8	27-33	410**	*	Lung Cancer
X9	27-33	410**	*	Alzheimer

Fig. 3. Tabular anonymization: input table and anonymization result

2.3 Graph (Social Network) Anonymization

Hitherto we were solely concerned with tabular data; however, as social networks have gained huge popularity over the previous decade, and are widely applicable in other areas as well, the question of how to efficiently anonymize networks has gained ever more significance over the years.

As a start, one could see a graph just as a collection of nodes, where each node contains some kind of feature vector, akin to the row in a data table. Adopting that view, we could be tempted to simply ignore the existence of edges and apply some kind of algorithm suitable to the anonymization of tabular data. The main problem with this however lies in the fact that the structural environment of a node (the constellation of its neighbors within the greater network) provides some additional information. That is, even if we successfully (k-)anonymize the feature vectors of a graph according to the methods described in the previous chapter, we still run the risk of too much information remaining in the form of a known local subgraph structure.

Consider Fig. 4 for example, in which the nodes of a graph have already been k-anonymized into groups of size 3 and 7, respectively. In this figure, local subgraphs (b) and (c) are actually (3)-anonymized, because as each node has the exact same local neighborhood structure, the additional information of a node possessing a degree of 0 (or 2) is of no additional value. For local subgraphs (a) and (d) on the other hand, the additional information of a node being of degree (x) has the potential to reveal its identity, meaning it is not indistinguishable from its neighbors within the equivalence class any more.

Several methods have been proposed to make re-identification of nodes in anonymized social graphs harder. [4] for example introduce the idea of vertex addition to labeled and unlabeled datasets. While an algorithm on the former remains NP complete, they provide an efficient ($O(nk)$) algorithm for unlabeled data. Experimenting on several well known datasets, they show that commonly-studied structural properties of the network, such as clustering coefficient, are only minorly distorted by their anonymization procedure.

Person re-identification is both a hard and important problem in many different domains and is challenging. Most approaches aim to model and extract

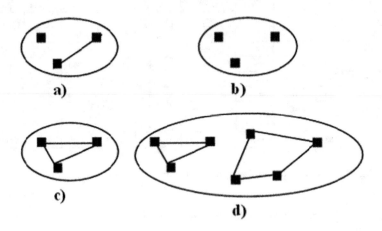

Fig. 4. Local subgraph neighborhoods as additional anonymization obstacle.

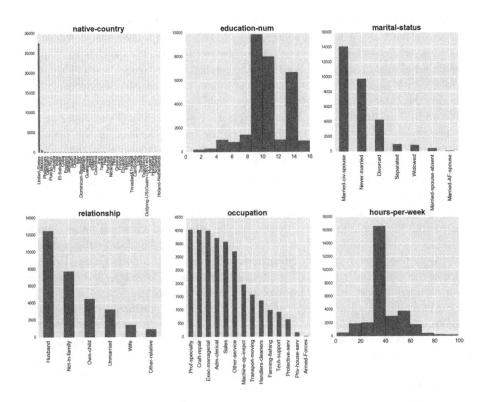

Fig. 5. Initial distribution of six selected data columns of the adult dataset.

distinctive and reliable features. However, seeking an optimal and robust similarity measure that quantifies a wide range of features against realistic conditions from a distance is still an open and unsolved problem for person re-identification techniques [17].

In order to develop protection techniques in social networks it is necessary to consider three aspects [18]: (1) the privacy information which may be under attack; (2) the background knowledge that an adversary may use to attack the privacy of target individuals; and (3) a specification of the usage of the published social network data so that an anonymization method can try to retain the utility of the data as much as possible whilst the privacy is preserved.

The authors of [9] take the approach of adding edges to an edge-labeled graph like the Netflix movie database (with users and movies being nodes and edge weights representing movie ratings). They define tables as bipartite graphs and prove NP-hardness for the problems of neighborhood anonymity, i-hop anonymity and k-symmetry anonymity.

Campan [3], whose local subgraph problem we already encountered, proposed a solution in the form of a greedy clustering algorithm which takes into account not only the information loss incurred by generalizing features of nodes, but also introducing a structural loss function based on the local neighborhood within an equivalence class (and between them). The author of this thesis implemented that approach utilizing GraphiniusJS and will demonstrate the algorithm in Sect. 3.2 as well as the anonymized results in Sect. 4.

3   Experiments

The following sections will describe our series of experiments in detail, encompassing the data source selected, the algorithm used as well as a description of the overall process employed to obtain our results.

3.1   Data

As input data we chose the adults dataset from the UCI Machine Learning repository which was generated from US census data of 1994 and contains approximately 32,000 entries; from those 30,162 were selected after preprocessing. Of the attributes (data columns) provided only one was deleted because it was also represented by a column containing its numerical mapping (education => education_num). Figure 5 shows the attribute value distribution of the original input dataset with the exception of the sample weights.

As one can see, there are several attributes with one value clearly dominating the others; *native-country* being the most prominent example with the entry for the United States dwarfing all other countries (which comes as no surprise given the data origin). As anonymization generalizes different countries together if necessary, it was interesting for the author to see how these distributions would change under a relatively large k-factor. Figure 6 shows the same attribute distribution with its values anonymized by a factor of $k = 19$. Although the

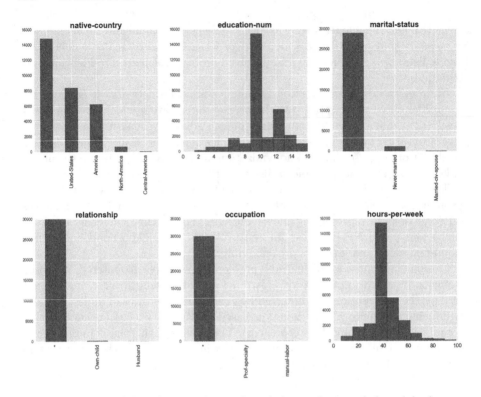

Fig. 6. Anonymized distribution of six selected data columns of the adult dataset, anonymization factor of k=19, equal weight for each attribute.

dominance of the United states was successfully "broken" by this method, in several instances the *generalized-to-all*-value (*) now skews the data set even more. Apart from the expected generalization information loss this is another reason why one would assume worse results from a machine learning classifier applied to an anonymized dataset.

3.2   Algorithm

SaNGreeA stands for *Social network greedy clustering* and was introduced by [3]. In addition to'clustering' nodes of a graph according to the minimum general information loss (GIL) incurred as described in Sect. 2.2, this algorithm also considers the structural information loss (SIL) incurred in assigning a node to a certain cluster. The SIL quantifies the probability of error when trying to reconstruct the structure of the initial graph from its anonymized version.

$$\text{GIL}(cl) = |cl| \cdot \left(\sum_{j=1}^{s} \frac{size(gen(cl)[N_j])}{size(min_{x\epsilon N}(X[N_j]), max_{x\epsilon N}(X[N_j]))} \right.$$

$$\left. + \sum_{j=1}^{t} \frac{height(\Lambda(gen(cl)[C_j]))}{height(H_{C_j})} \right)$$

where:
- $|cl|$ denotes the cluster cl's cardinality;
- $size([i1, i2])$ is the size of the interval $[i1, i2]$, i.e., $(i2 - i1)$;
- $\Lambda(w), w\epsilon H_{C_j}$ is the sub-hierarchy of H_{C_j} rooted in w;
- $height(H_{C_j})$ denotes the height of the tree hierarchy H_{C_j};

The total generalization information loss is then given by:

$$\text{GIL}(G, S) = \sum_{j=1}^{v} \text{GIL}(cl_j)$$

And the normalized generalization information loss by:

$$\text{NGIL}(G, S) = \frac{\text{GIL}(G, S)}{n \cdot (s + t)}$$

The SIL is composed of two different components: (1) the intra-cluster structural loss, signifying the error probability in trying to reconstruct the original edge distribution within an equivalence class (= anonymized cluster), and (2) the inter-cluster structural loss which represents the error probability in trying to reconstruct the original configuration of edges between two equivalence classes.

For the exact mathematical definitions of SIL & NSIL the reader is kindly referred to the original paper. Because the structural information loss cannot be computed exactly before the final construction of clusters, the exact computations were replaced by the following distance measures:

Distance between two nodes:

$$\text{dist}(X^i, X^j) = \frac{|\{l | l = 1..n \wedge l \neq i, j; b_l^i \neq b_l^j|}{n - 2}$$

Distance between a node and a cluster:

$$\text{dist}(X, cl) = \frac{\sum_{X^j \epsilon cl} \text{dist}(X, X^j)}{|cl|}$$

The algorithm starts with initializing a first cluster by a randomly choosing a node. Then, for every new node encountered, the weighted sum of the above two information loss metrics will yield a certain overall information loss in case the node was added to that cluster - the candidate with minimal information loss is then added to the cluster. This process is repeated until the cluster reaches a certain constraint (e.g. size :=k -factor) upon which another random node is chosen to constitute the next cluster. This procedure is repeated until all nodes have been assigned; if a cluster of size $<k$ should remain, its member nodes are dispersed accordingly.

Since the algorithm does not take all possible node combinations into account, but simply chooses an arbitrary node and compares all the candidates in a loop, the algorithm runs in quadratic time w.r.t. the input size in number of nodes. This worked well within milliseconds for a problem size of a few hundred nodes, but took up to 60 mins. on the whole adult dataset.

In implementing and demonstrating this algorithm, the authors intended to recreate the original paper's experiment. However, as no suitable real-world graph structure was available to the authors at the time of this writing and any artificially generated network would result in dubious results for the classification tasks applied, we decided to leave out the structural component of the algorithm and focus only on the generalization information loss for this paper, leaving the entire approach to future research initiatives.

3.3 Process

To examine the impact of perturbation and anonymization of datasets on the quality of a classification result, we designed the following processing pipeline:

1. Taking the original (preprocessed) dataset as input, we transformed its attributes to boolean values, so instead of *native-country* $- >$ *United-States* we considered *United-States* $- >$ *yes/no*.
2. We then ran 4 different classifiers on it and computed precision, recall as well as F1 score. The four classifiers used were *gradient boosting, random forest, logistic regression* and *linear SVC*.
3. From the obtained results we extracted the 3 attribute values most contributing to a "positive" (>50k) result as well as the top 3 attribute values indicating a "negative" (<=50k) prediction as depicted in Fig. 7
4. For each of these 6 attribute values, we subsequently deleted a specific percentage of data rows containing that value from the original dataset, resulting in 30 reduced datasets. The 5 percentages used were 0.2, 0.4, 0.6, 0.8 as well as 1.0.
5. To each of those datasets we re-applied the four chosen classifiers successively and recorded the respective impact on the quality of the classification result. The results can be seen in Figs. 9 and 10.
6. In order to measure the effects of k-anonymization on classifier performance, we used the SaNGreeA's GIL component described in the following section to generate datasets with a k-factor of $k = 3$, $k = 7$, $k = 11$, $k = 15$ as well as $k = 19$. Furthermore, we used each of these settings with 3 different weight vectors: (1) equal weights for all attributes, (2) age information preferred ($\omega(age) = 0.88$, $\omega(other\_attributes) = 0.01$) and (3) race information preferred ($\omega(race) = 0.88$, $\omega(other\_attributes) = 0.01$). We then re-executed all classifiers on the resulting 15 datasets and recorded the respective results, which can be seen in Fig. 8.

4   Results and Discussion

We expected a steady decline in the quality of classification results over all three scenarios: (1) anonymization of datasets, (2) perturbation by selectively deleting attribute values of positive significance w.r.t the result, (3) perturbation by selectively deleting attribute values of negative significance w.r.t the result.

The actual results satisfied our expectations only in the first two cases, with the shape of the actual outcomes being a little bit surprising. As can be seen in Fig. 8, the F1 score of all algorithms applied declines more drastically at the

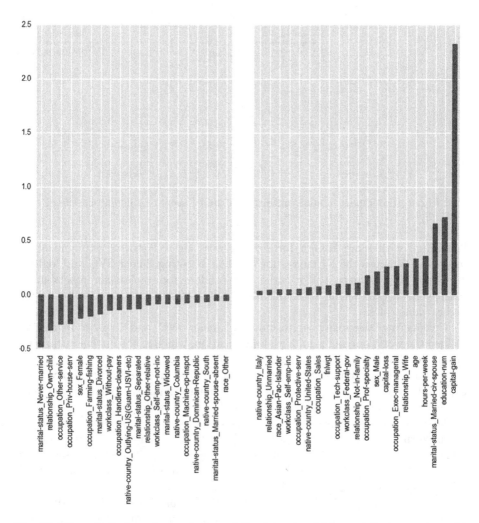

Fig. 7. The attribute values of the adult dataset which contribute most positively/negatively to the classification result. The columns to the right strongly indicate a yearly income of above 50 k, whereas the columns to the outer left indicate a yearly income of below 50 k. The least significant columns in the middle part were cut out.

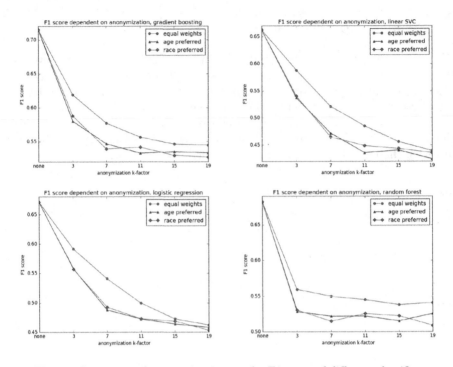

Fig. 8. The impact of anonymization on the F1 score of different classifiers

beginning, with more benign further losses as the k-factor of anonymization increases. Whereas the F1 curves for gradient boosting, linear SVC and logistic regression approximate a $1/x$ curve, the random forest classifier reacts more sensitively to even slight anonymization, but seems to stay more robust with higher values of k.

Considering the exact performance, Linear SVC and logistic regression yielded the worst outcomes under anonymization, which is not further surprising given their lower scores on the original input data to begin with.

As far as the second case is concerned (Fig. 9), our experiments showed the expected drop in algorithm performance, although the impact shows a different behavior: In the case of deleting rows with capital gain values of >2000 US-Dollars, the decline seems to be linear, whereas for the other two attribute values the performance seems to collapse with higher rates of erasure. Moreover, this behavior is more or less the same for all applied algorithms. This seems to point to the fact that especially significant attribute values can uphold a good performance even in low quantities.

The only real surprise occurred with applying our classifiers to the datasets perturbed by deleting percentages of attribute values indicating a low yearly income (Fig. 10). As with scenario 2 we expected to see a progressive decline in performance - but with all classifiers the results either stayed approximately the same or even improved in some cases (please consider the extremely narrow scale

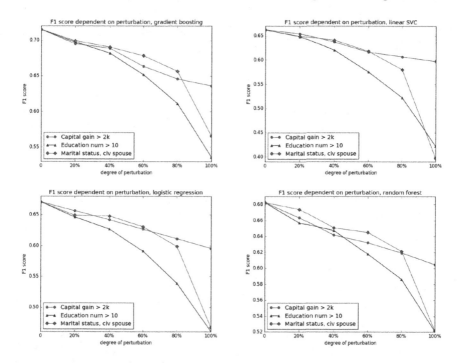

Fig. 9. The impact of perturbation (selectively deleting quantiles of rows containing one of the TOP 3 positively contributing attributes) on the F1 score of different classifiers

in the respective plots). As the classification score is dependent on (in-)correctly classifying both positive and negative outcomes, this seems rather surprising and will require further investigation.

5   Open Problems Future Challenges

- **Explain the unexpected behavior** for the datasets perturbed by selectively deleting rows containing the TOP 3 negatively contributing attribute values.
- **Find a natural dataset** which already contains a graph structure emerged in the real-world rather than a graph generator. We assume that for many modern applications the experiments conducted in this work would be highly relevant to social network analysis and anonymization, and we are planning to conduct such a research effort in a sequel to this investigation.
- **Consider the structural information loss** on a suitable real-world graph and re-apply our methodology to that data-structure. Once realistic results have been obtained, the effects of the same algorithm on artificially generated graphs might be examined, offering another perspective on the information content/structure introduced into datasets by different types of such generators.

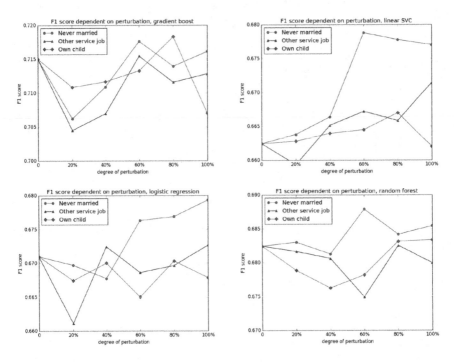

Fig. 10. The impact of perturbation (selectively deleting quantiles of rows containing one of the TOP 3 negatively contributing attributes) on the F1 score of different classifiers

- **Analyze the exact influence** different kinds of information loss due to anonymization/perturbation have on the different algorithms. In this work, we have only chosen a series of classifiers to demonstrate our approach. However, other classes of machine learning algorithms might yield interesting results as well, and we are motivated to conduct such future research ourselves.
- **Interactive machine learning.** We have, amongst other settings, experimented with different weight vectors in our approach regarding anonymization. However, such parameters do not easily lend themselves to be produced by an algorithm, since minimizing an artificial metric of information loss does not produce safe datasets in itself. Moreover, data utility is highly dependent on the specific area of application; therefore choosing parameters with regard to the particular demographic and cultural clinical environment is best done by a human agent. The problem of (k-)anonymization thus represents a natural application domain for interactive Machine Learning (iML) with a human-in-the-loop [7,8,10]. The authors will strive to design and implement such experiments in the future.

6   Conclusion

This paper examined the question of how different ways of perturbing or anonymizing knowledge bases would influence the results of machine learning algorithms applied to those datasets. We have seen that newly introduced regulations (inside the European Union) as well as data privacy concerns of database owners naturally lead to the challenge of minimizing the cost/efficiency impact of those requirements not only on the technical, but also the machine learning infrastructure of affected businesses and organizations. Consequently, we conducted a series of experiments to simulate the decline in the F1 score of several classification algorithms on an established dataset. Our results show that selective deletion of valuable data items is less destructive than general anonymization, so that complying with regulations concerning the "right to be forgotten" is still preferable to taking preemptive steps to de-identify personal information in databases. Our results are highly selective however and should be corroborated by applying a wider spectrum of algorithms to larger, more diverse datasets.

References

1. Aggarwal, C.C.: On k-anonymity and the curse of dimensionality. In: Proceedings of the 31st International Conference on Very Large Data Bases VLDB, pp. 901–909 (2005)
2. Aggarwal, G., Feder, T., Kenthapadi, K., Motwani, R., Panigrahy, R., Thomas, D., Zhu, A.: Approximation algorithms for k-anonymity. J. Priv. Technol. (JOPT) (2005)
3. Campan, A., Truta, T.M.: Data and structural k-anonymity in social networks. In: Bonchi, F., Ferrari, E., Jiang, W., Malin, B. (eds.) PinKDD 2008. LNCS, vol. 5456, pp. 33–54. Springer, Heidelberg (2009)
4. Chester, S., Kapron, B., Ramesh, G., Srivastava, G., Thomo, A., Venkatesh, S.: k-anonymization of social networks by vertex addition. ADBIS **2**(789), 107–116 (2011)
5. Ciriani, V., Capitani, D., di Vimercati, S., Foresti, S., Samarati, P.: κ-anonymity. In: Yu, T., Jajodia, S. (eds.) Secure Data Management in Decentralized Systems. Advances in Information Security, vol. 33, pp. 323–353. Springer, US (2007)
6. Duchi, J.C., Jordan, M.I., Wainwright, M.J.: Privacy aware learning. J. ACM (JACM) **61**(6), 38 (2014)
7. Holzinger, A., Plass, M., Holzinger, K., Crisan, G.C., Pintea, C.M., Paladem, V.: Towards interactive machine learning (iml): applying ant colony algorithms to solve the traveling salesman problem with the human-in-the-loop approach. In: Buccafurri, F., Holzinger, A., Kieseberg, P., Tjoa, A.M., Weippl, E. (eds.) CD-ARES 2016, LNCS, vol. 9817, pp. X-XY. Springer, Heidelberg (2016)
8. Holzinger, A.: Interactive machine learning for health informatics: when do we need the human-in-the-loop? Brain Inform. (BRIN) **3**(2), 119–131 (2016)
9. Kapron, B., Srivastava, G., Venkatesh, S.: Social network anonymization via edge addition. In: 2011 International Conference on Advances in Social Networks Analysis and Mining (ASONAM), pp. 155–162. IEEE (2011)
10. Kieseberg, P., Malle, B., Frühwirt, P., Weippl, E., Holzinger, A.: A tamper-proof audit and control system for the doctor in the loop. Brain Inform. 1–11 (2016)

11. Li, N., Li, T., Venkatasubramanian, S.: t-closeness: privacy beyond k-anonymity and l-diversity. In: IEEE 23rd International Conference on Data Engineering, ICDE 2007, pp. 106–115. IEEE (2007)
12. Machanavajjhala, A., Kifer, D., Gehrke, J., Venkitasubramaniam, M.: l-diversity: privacy beyond k-anonymity. ACM Trans. Knowl. Discovery Data (TKDD) 1(1), 1–52 (2007)
13. Nergiz, M.E., Clifton, C.: Delta-presence without complete world knowledge. IEEE Trans. Knowl. Data Eng. 22(6), 868–883 (2010)
14. Samarati, P.: Protecting respondents identities in microdata release. IEEE Trans. Knowl. Data Eng. 13(6), 1010–1027 (2001)
15. Sweeney, L.: Achieving k-anonymity privacy protection using generalization and suppression. Int. J. Uncertainty Fuzziness Knowl. Based Syst. 10(5), 571–588 (2002)
16. Sweeney, L.: k-anonymity: a model for protecting privacy. Int. J. Uncertainty Fuzziness Knowl. Based Syst. 10(05), 557–570 (2002)
17. Zheng, W.-S., Gong, S., Xiang, T.: Reidentification by relative distance comparison. IEEE Trans. Pattern Anal. Mach. Intell. 35(3), 653–668 (2013)
18. Zhou, B., Pei, J., Luk, W.: A brief survey on anonymization techniques for privacy preserving publishing of social network data. ACM Sigkdd Explor. Newslett. 10(2), 12–22 (2008)

Author Index

Printed in the United States
By Bookmasters